Health Informatics

This series is directed to healthcare professionals leading the transformation of healthcare by using information and knowledge. For over 20 years, Health Informatics has offered a broad range of titles: some address specific professions such as nursing, medicine, and health administration; others cover special areas of practice such as trauma and radiology; still other books in the series focus on interdisciplinary issues, such as the computer based patient record, electronic health records, and networked healthcare systems. Editors and authors, eminent experts in their fields, offer their accounts of innovations in health informatics. Increasingly, these accounts go beyond hardware and software to address the role of information in influencing the transformation of healthcare delivery systems around the world. The series also increasingly focuses on the users of the information and systems: the organizational, behavioral, and societal changes that accompany the diffusion of information technology in health services environments.

Developments in healthcare delivery are constant; in recent years, bioinformatics has emerged as a new field in health informatics to support emerging and ongoing developments in molecular biology. At the same time, further evolution of the field of health informatics is reflected in the introduction of concepts at the macro or health systems delivery level with major national initiatives related to electronic health records (EHR), data standards, and public health informatics.

These changes will continue to shape health services in the twenty-first century. By making full and creative use of the technology to tame data and to transform information, Health Informatics will foster the development and use of new knowledge in healthcare.

More information about this series at http://www.springer.com/series/1114

Eta S. Berner
Editor

Informatics Education in Healthcare

Lessons Learned

Second Edition

 Springer

Editor
Eta S. Berner
University of Alabama at Birmingham
Birmingham, AL
USA

ISSN 1431-1917   ISSN 2197-3741   (electronic)
Health Informatics
ISBN 978-3-030-53815-6   ISBN 978-3-030-53813-2   (eBook)
https://doi.org/10.1007/978-3-030-53813-2

This Springer imprint is published by the registered company Springer Nature Switzerland AG
The registered company address is: Gewerbestrasse 11, 6330 Cham, Switzerland

To our students, from whom we have learned much

Preface

Twenty-five years ago almost the only individuals involved in healthcare who had even heard the term "informatics" were those who identified themselves as medical or nursing informaticians. Today, we have a variety of subfields of informatics including not just medical and nursing informatics, but informatics applied to other health professions (such as dental or pharmacy informatics), as well as health informatics, biomedical informatics, bioinformatics, and public health informatics, among others. In addition, there has been growth of a spectrum of informatics education programs, from new undergraduate majors to medical subspecialty fellowship programs. There are even informatics summer programs for high school students.

This book addresses the broad range of informatics education programs available today. My own background in health professions education over 45 years ago at the beginning of my career and in online informatics education in my work today has provided me with a tacit understanding of the breadth of content, pedagogical techniques, strategies, and approaches to informatics education in a wide variety of areas. As a leader of UAB's Center for Health Informatics for Patient Safety/Quality and the UAB Curriculum Development Center that was part of ONC's health IT workforce development program, I have seen the rapidly growing interest in the development of new informatics education programs and the growth of informatics as a profession.

The aim of this book is to make the tacit knowledge explicit and to share some of the lessons learned by a group of very experienced informatics educators. The contributors to this volume are internationally recognized informatics educators, and this short preface cannot do justice to their expertise. However, to give the reader a snapshot of their knowledge and experience, the following is a description of the contributors' expertise as related to the particular chapters that they wrote.

Dr. Jacqueline Moss, who coauthored the overview chapter with me, is an experienced nursing informatics educator, who has been integrally involved in informatics education at the national level and throughout her institution in other areas in addition to nursing informatics.

The authors of the chapters describing different training programs in the USA have direct experience with the programs they describe. *Dr. Valerie Florance* is Associate Director of Extramural Programs at the National Library of Medicine (NLM) at the US National Institutes of Health (NIH). Dr. Florance has been responsible for oversight of the many NLM-funded informatics training programs. She describes the NLM programs in Chap. 2 and the NIH Data Science training activities in Chap. 10. In addition to Dr. Moss, *Drs. Marisa Wilson and Beth Elias* are coauthors of the chapter on nursing informatics (Chap. 3). Dr. Wilson and Dr. Elias have taught nursing informatics in a variety of institutions and are involved with national efforts in nursing informatics education. *Amanda Dorsey, Meg Bruck, and Sue Feldman* bring the perspective of health informatics students, instructors, and program directors to Chap. 4. Ms. Dorsey and Ms. Bruck were both students in the University of Alabama at Birmingham (UAB) MSHI program and have gone on to become broad-based informatics educators. Ms. Dorsey led the transition of the MSHI program to an online format, and she and Ms. Bruck developed a variety of courses in health informatics as part of the ONC workforce development program. Dr. Feldman is currently program director of the UAB MSHI program. She also brings experience as a member of the Health Informatics Accreditation Council (HIAC) of the Commission on Accreditation for Health Informatics and Health Information Management Education (CAHIIM). In addition to her contributions to Chap. 4, she is the lead author of Chap. 17 on accreditation of HI programs and is a contributor to Chap. 6 on undergraduate informatics education. *Dr. Saif Khairat* is the lead author on Chap. 6. He is chair of AMIA's Education Committee and has conducted an extensive review of the growing number of undergraduate informatics programs.

The growth of programs to educate specialists in bioinformatics has also been developing rapidly. While some of these programs have been more focused on computational biology, many of them have focused on translational bioinformatics and are often incorporated within broader informatics training programs. The authors of Chap. 5 focus on translational bioinformatics and bring multi-institutional expertise in education in translational bioinformatics. *Dr. Susan Fenton* oversees the informatics education programs at the School of Biomedical Informatics (SBMI) at UT Houston. *Dr. Assaf Gottlieb*, also at SBMI, is actively involved in its Center for Precision Medicine. *Dr. Meredith Zozus* has led bioinformatics education at Duke, the University of Arkansas, and the University of Texas at San Antonio.

The contributors of the chapters on informatics education programs for other health professionals bring a similar breadth of experience as those for the dedicated informatics programs. *Dominic Covvey* is internationally recognized for leading the development of competency descriptions for multiple roles including informatics researchers, applied informaticians, and clinician users of informatics applications. *Margaret Schulte* was the leader of the HIMSTA project described in Chap. 8 and also has years of experience as a leader of HIMSS' education activities and in her work with the Commission on Accreditation of Healthcare Management Education (CAHME). *Drs. Peter Embi and Philip Payne* are widely recognized as major leaders in the USA in the area of clinical research informatics (CRI). Dr. Embi led the first AMIA CRI conference and also developed an AMIA 10 × 10 course in this area. Both authors have published seminal articles in this domain.

The chapters on informatics education outside the USA have been expanded significantly in this edition. In the first edition, we had a single chapter on three different regions: Latin America, Sub-Saharan Africa, and the Asia Pacific region. In this edition, we have separate chapters for each region with the informatics education activities in additional countries within regions described. All of the chapter authors on worldwide informatics education are experienced educators within their own country and around the world.

Dr. John Holmes and *Jeffrey Williamson* were instrumental in working with AMIA's Global Health Informatics Partnership that was involved with disseminating informatics educational materials to countries around the world. *Dr. Paula Proctor* and her colleagues (*Drs. Ursula Hubner, Elizabeth Cummings, Jen Bichel-Findlay, Michelle Honey, and Karen Day*) who authored Chap. 12 represent nursing informatics from multiple continents. The authors of Chap. 13, on informatics education in Latin America (*Drs. Paula Otero, Mariela Leikam, Zulma Gonzalez, Heimar de Fatima Marin, Ignacio Pérez Araveña, and Saadia Zawadzki*), are leaders within their countries and have also engaged with each other in collaborative informatics activities across countries in Latin America. *Ngai Tseung Cheung, Juanita Fernando, Oomen John, Alvin Marcelo, Iris Thiele Isip-Tan, Cheng Ooi Low, Daniel Li, and Vajira HW Dissanayake* developed highly regarded informatics education programs in a variety of countries in the Asia Pacific region. Finally, *Drs. Caroline Perrin, Cheick-Oumar Bagayoko, and Antoine Geissbuhler* have years of collaboration with colleagues in Sub-Saharan Africa.

This edition also has two new sections that contain updates of some of the chapters in the previous edition as well as additional chapters. The section on assessment of individuals and programs contains the chapter on the clinical informatics subspecialty certification (Chap. 16), which was updated and expanded. *Drs. Reed Gardner* and *Charles Safran* were leaders of the task forces that led to the approval of the clinical informatics subspecialty, and lead chapter author *Dr. Christoph Lehmann* has led the Clinical Informatics Examination Committee now that it has been established. *Dr. Howard Silverman* runs a Clinical Informatics Fellowship Program and has been a leader nationally of the Clinical Informatics training directors. *Dr. Cynthia Gadd* was the leader of the team that did the initial work to establish an advanced health informatics certification examination for those who are not eligible for the medical subspecialty exam. A new chapter (Chap. 17) in this section includes discussion of CAHIIM's informatics education program accreditation. It was written by *Dr. Sue Feldman* (described above), *Dr. Suzanne Austin Boren, Linde Tesch*, and *Dr. Annette Valenta*, all of whom have been directly involved with CAHIIM's accreditation activities. Dr. Boren leads the Health Informatics Program at the University of Missouri and has also led CAHIIM's Health Informatics Accreditation Council. Ms. Tesch is Senior Education Officer at CAHIIM, and Dr. Valenta was chair of the AMIA Accreditation Committee that developed the foundational domains used by CAHIIM in their accreditation process. Dr. Valenta is also an author of Chap. 19 bringing her extensive experience in teaching online informatics programs. She was program director of the online health informatics masters' program and developed the AMIA 10 × 10 program at the University of Illinois at Chicago (UIC).

The last section on online informatics education contains updates and expansions of three chapters in the previous edition. The authors of Chap. 19 have taken the insights gained by years of experience in online education and articulated them in a series of strategies that will be useful for others, especially those who have struggled with the issues that are raised. In addition to Dr. Valenta's and my own expertise in online informatics education, the other authors bring additional expertise and experience. *Ms. Lorrinda Khan* has years of online learning experience, both as an instructor and as an instructional design expert. *Dr. Michael Dieter* was program director for the online master of health informatics program at UIC.

The other chapters in this section (Chaps. 18 and 20) are written by *Dr. William Hersh*. Dr. Hersh is internationally recognized as an informatics educator. He is the leader of OHSU's informatics education activities which include not only the NLM-funded informatics training program, but he also led the university-based training program funded by ONC as part of the ONC workforce development program. He was a leader in other ONC-funded workforce programs including the Curriculum Development Centers program and the National Training and Dissemination Center. In addition to his work with the ONC workforce programs, Dr. Hersh was the impetus behind the AMIA 10 × 10 program and was director of the first 10 × 10 program. He was also a contributor to the NIH BD2K program of online educational materials.

In addition to the outstanding contributions of the chapter authors, I want to express my appreciation for the support of Grant Weston, Anand Shanmugam, and the Springer editorial team.

Birmingham, AL   Eta S. Berner

Contents

Contributors

Ignacio Pérez Aravena Department of Biomedical Informatics, DUOC UC Institute, Las Condes, Chile

Cheick-Oumar Bagayoko, MD, PhD Centre d'Innovation et Santé Digitale (Digi-Santé-Mali), Bamako, Mali

Centre d'Expertise et de Recherche en Télémédecine et E-santé (CERTES), Bamako, Mali

Eta S. Berner, EdD, FACMI, FHIMSS, FIAHSI Department of Health Services Administration, School of Health Professions, University of Alabama at Birmingham, Birmingham, AL, USA

Department of Medical Education, School of Medicine, University of Alabama at Birmingham, Birmingham, AL, USA

Jen Bichel-Findlay, HScD, MN, MPH, RN, FACN, CHIA Australasian Institute of Digital Health Nursing and Midwifery Community of Practice, Sydney, NSW, Australia

Suzanne Austin Boren, MHA, PhD University of Missouri, Columbia, MO, USA

Meg N. Bruck, MSHI Department of Health Services Administration, University of Alabama at Birmingham, Birmingham, AL, USA

Ngai Tseung Cheung, MBBS, BSc (Med), MSc, DIC Head of Information Technology and Health Informatics/CMIO, Hong Kong Hospital Authority, Hong Kong, Hong Kong

H. Dominic J. Covvey, BA, MSc, FACMI (Retired) Faculty of Science, University of Waterloo, Waterloo, ON, Canada

Elizabeth Cummings, RN, BA, BIS (Hons), PhD, FAIDH School of Health Sciences, University of Tasmania and Deputy Chair, Nursing Informatics, Sydney, NSW, Australia

Karen Day, RN, RM, MA, PhD, FACHI Faculty of Medical and Health Sciences, The University of Auckland, Auckland, New Zealand

Michael G. Dieter, PhD, MLIS, MBA Department of Biomedical and Health Information Sciences, University of Illinois at Chicago, Chicago, IL, USA

Vajira H. W. Dissanayake, MBBS, PhD, FNASSL Specialty Board in Biomedical Informatics, Postgraduate Institute of Medicine, University of Colombo, Colombo, Sri Lanka

Amanda D. Dorsey, MSHI, FHIMSS Department of Health Services Administration, University of Alabama at Birmingham, Birmingham, AL, USA

Beth L. Elias, PhD, MS, FHIMSS University of Scranton, Scranton, PA, USA

Peter J. Embi, MD, MS, FACMI Regenstrief Institute and Indiana University, Indianapolis, IN, USA

Sue S. Feldman, RN, MEd, PhD Department of Health Services Administration, University of Alabama at Birmingham, Birmingham, AL, USA

Susan H. Fenton, PhD, RHIA, FAHIMA PI, Gulf Coast Regional Extension Center, UTHealth School of Biomedical Informatics, Houston, TX, USA

Juanita Fernando, PhD, FACHI MERQ, Public Health and Preventive Medicine, Medicine, Nursing and Health Sciences, Monash University, Clayton, VIC, Australia

Valerie Florance, PhD, FACMI National Library of Medicine, NIH, DHHS, Bethesda, MD, USA

Extramural Programs, National Library of Medicine, National Institutes of Health, Department of Health and Human Services, Bethesda, MD, USA

Cynthia Gadd, PhD, MBA, MS, FACMI Department of Biomedical Informatics, Vanderbilt University, Nashville, TN, USA

Reed M. Gardner, PhD, FACMI, FIAHSI Department of Biomedical Informatics, University of Utah, Salt Lake City, UT, USA

Antoine Geissbuhler, MD, FACMI, FIAHSI HI5lab, Department of Radiology and Medical Informatics, Geneva University, Geneva, Switzerland

Division of eHealth and Telemedicine, Geneva University Hospitals, Geneva, Switzerland

Zulma Gonzalez, RN Department of Health Informatics, Hospital Italiano de Buenos Aires, Buenos Aires, Argentina

Assaf Gottlieb, PhD Center for Precision Health, UTHealth School of Biomedical Informatics (SBMI), Houston, TX, USA

William Hersh, MD, FACMI, FACP, FIAHSI Department of Medical Informatics and Clinical Epidemiology, Oregon Health and Science University, Portland, OR, USA

John H. Holmes, PhD, FACE, FACMI, FIAHSI Department of Biostatistics, Epidemiology, and Informatics, University of Pennsylvania Perelman School of Medicine, Philadelphia, PA, USA

Michelle Honey, RN, BA, MPhil, PhD, FIMIA-NI Faculty of Medical and Health Sciences, The University of Auckland, Auckland, New Zealand

Ursula Hübner, PhD, FIAHSI University of Applied Sciences Osnabrück, Osnabrück, Germany

Iris Thiele Isip-Tan, MD, MSc Medical Informatics Unit, College of Medicine, University of the Philippines, Manila, Philippines

Oommen John, MBBS, MD, MBA The George Institute for Global Health, New Delhi, India

University of New South Wales, Sydney, NSW, Australia

Asia Pacific Association for Medical Informatics, New Delhi, India

Saif Khairat, PhD, MPH Carolina Health Informatics Program, University of North Carolina at Chapel Hill, Chapel Hill, NC, USA

School of Nursing, University of North Carolina at Chapel Hill, Chapel Hill, NC, USA

Lorrinda Khan, MFA University of Maryland University College, University of Maryland Global Campus, Adelphi, MD, USA

Christoph U. Lehmann, MD, FACMI, FAAP, FIAHSI Departments of Pediatrics, Population & Data Sciences, and Bioinformatics; Clinical Informatics Center, UT Southwestern, 5323 Harry Hines Blvd, Dallas, TX, USA

Mariela Leikam Department of Health Informatics, Hospital Italiano de Buenos Aires, Buenos Aires, Argentina

Daniel Li, MD, MBI Integrated Health Information Systems, Singapore, Singapore

Cheng Ooi Low, MBBS, MRCP Singapore Health Services, Singapore, Singapore

Alvin Marcelo, MD, FIAHSI Professor of Surgery and Health Informatics, University of the Philippines, Manila, Philippines

Heimar de Fatima Marin, RN, MS, PhD, FACMI, FIAHSI Department of Nursing Informatics, Federal University of São Paulo (UNIFESP), São Paulo, Brazil

Jacqueline A. Moss, PhD, RN, FAAN Department of Family, Community, and Health Systems, School of Nursing, University of Alabama at Birmingham, Birmingham, AL, USA

University of Alabama at Birmingham, Birmingham, AL, USA

Paula Otero, MD, MSc, FIAHSI Department of Health Informatics, Hospital Italiano de Buenos Aires, Buenos Aires, Argentina

Philip R. O. Payne, PhD, FACMI Washington University in St. Louis, St. Louis, MO, USA

Caroline Perrin, PhD HI5lab, Department of Radiology and Medical Informatics, Geneva University, Geneva, Switzerland

Division of eHealth and Telemedicine, Geneva University Hospitals, Geneva, Switzerland

Paula Procter, RN, MSc, SFHEA, FBCS, CITP Sheffield Hallam University, Sheffield, UK

Charles Safran, MD, MS, FACMI, FIAHSI Division of Clinical Informatics, Department of Medicine, Beth Israel Deaconess Medical Center and Harvard Medical School, Boston, MA, USA

Margaret Schulte, DBA, FACHE, CPHIMS Commission on Accreditation of Healthcare Management Education, Philadelphia, PA, USA

Howard D. Silverman, MD Department of Biomedical Informatics, The University of Arizona College of Medicine – Phoenix, Phoenix, AZ, USA

Linde H. Tesch, MS Commission on Accreditation for Health Informatics and Information Management, Chicago, IL, USA

Annette L. Valenta, DrPH, FACMI Department of Biomedical and Health Information Sciences, University of Illinois at Chicago, Chicago, IL, USA

Jeffrey J. Williamson, MEd Department of Education, AMIA, Bethesda, MD, USA

Marisa L. Wilson, DNSc, RN-BC, FAMIA, FIAHSI, FAAN University of Alabama at Birmingham, Birmingham, AL, USA

Saadia Zawadzki Department of Medical Technology, School of Medicine, Universidad de la República (UdelaR), Montevideo, Uruguay

Meredith Nahm Zozus, PhD UT Health Sciences Center San Antonio, San Antonio, TX, USA

Acronyms and Abbreviations

AACN	American Association of Colleges of Nursing
AAMSI	American Association for Medical Systems and Informatics
ABMS	American Board of Medical Specialties
ABP	American Board of Pathology
ABPM	American Board of Preventive Medicine
ACGME	Accreditation Council for Graduate Medical Education
ACMI	American College of Medical Informatics
AHI	Applied Health Informatics
AHIMA	American Health Information Management Association
AMIA	American Medical Informatics Association
ANA	American Nurses Association
ANCC	American Nurses Credentialing Center
APAMI	Asia-Pacific Association for Medical Informatics
ARRA	American Recovery and Reinvestment Act
ASL	Asynchronous learning
AUPHA	Association of University Programs in Health Administration
BIOTEC	National Center for Genetic Engineering and Biotechnology (Thailand)
BISTI	Biomedical Information Science and Technology Initiative
BSN	Bachelor of Science in Nursing
CAHIIME	Commission on Accreditation for Health Informatics and Information Management Education
CAHIMS	Certified Associate in Health Information and Management Systems
CAHME	Commission on Accreditation of Healthcare Management Education
CBMI	Regenstrief Institute Center for Biomedical Informatics
CCNE	Commission on Collegiate Nursing Education
CDC	Curriculum Development Center
CE	Continuing education
CEO	Chief executive officer

CERTES	Center for Research Expertise in Telemedicine and eHealth (Centre d'Expertise et de Recherche en Télémédecine et E-santé)
CHCF	California Health Care Foundation
CHI	Center for Health Informatics (Singapore)
CHIRAD	Centre for Health Informatics Research and Development (South Africa)
CIN	Computers, Informatics, Nursing (Journal)
CIO	Chief information officer
CMIO	Chief medical information officer
CMS	Centers for Medicare & Medicaid Services
CMS	Clinical Management System (Hong Kong)
COSTAR	Computer Stored Ambulatory Record
CPHIMS	Certified Professional in Health Information and Management Systems
CPOE	Computerized physician (or provider) order entry
CRI	Clinical Research Informatics
CTRI	Clinical and Translational Research Informatics
CTSA	Clinical and Translational Science Awards
DHHS	Department of Health and Human Services (USA)
DNP	Doctor of Nursing Practice
EBM	Evidence-based medicine
EBP	Evidence-based practice
EDUCTRA	Education and Training in Health Informatics
EFMI	European Federation for Medical Informatics
EHR	Electronic health record
EMR	Electronic medical record
EMRAM	Electronic Medical Record Adoption Model (HIMSS)
ENRICH	Enhancing Research Informatics Capacity for Health Information in Colombia
EU	European Union
EXPASY	Expert Protein Analysis System
FEMI	Federación Médica del Interior (Uruguay)
FOA	Funding Opportunity Announcement
G2HI	Gateway to Health Informatics (Singapore)
GBS	Graduate Biomedical Sciences
GHIP	Global Health Informatics Partnership
GMDS	German Medical Informatics Association
GNU	Refers to a free software license
GPRS	General Packet Radio Service
GWAS	Genome-wide association studies
HELINA	Health Informatics in Africa
HELP	Health Evaluation through Logical Processing
HIBA	Hospital Italiano of Buenos Aires
HIBBS	Health Informatics Building Blocks

HIM	Health information management
HIMSS	Healthcare Information and Management Systems Society
HIMSTA	Health Information Management Systems Technology and Analysis
HIPAA	Health Insurance Portability and Accountability Act
HIT	Health Information Technology
HITECH	Health Information Technology for Economic and Clinical Health
HITPRO™	Health Information Technology Competency Exams
HSP	Hybrid Skills Development Program (Singapore)
ICT	Information and communications technologies
IDA	Infocomm Development Authority (Singapore)
IMIA	International Medical Informatics Association
INFOMED	Telematic Network for Health (Cuba)
INS	Informatics nursing specialist
IOM	Institute of Medicine
IR	Information retrieval
IS	Information systems
ISD	Information Services Department
ISfTeH	International Society for Telemedicine and eHealth
IT	Information technology
ITU	International Telecommunication Union
JAMA	Journal of the American Medical Association
JAMIA	Journal of the American Medical Informatics Association
KHI	Kigali Health Institute
LDS	Latter-Day Saints
LMS	Learning Management System
MIT	Massachusetts Institute of Technology
MLAA	Medical Library Assistance Act
MOC	Maintenance of Certification
MOOC	Massive Open Online Course
MRI	Magnetic resonance imaging
MRS	Medical Record System (OpenMRS)
MSHIM	Master of Science in Health Information Management
MSN	Master of Science in Nursing
MU	Meaningful use
MUMPS	Massachusetts General Hospital Utility Multi-Programming System
NCBI	National Center for Biotechnology Information
NCHS	National Center for Health Statistics
NCSBN	National Council of State Boards of Nursing
NEHR	National Electronic Health Record (Singapore)
NHIP	National Healthcare Information Project (Taiwan)
NIH	National Institutes of Health
NIHI	National Institutes of Health Informatics (Canada)

NLM	National Library of Medicine
NRSA	National Research Service Award
NTDC	National Training and Dissemination Center
NUR	National University of Rwanda
NUS	National University of Singapore
OER	Open Educational Resources (OER Africa)
OHSU	Oregon Health & Science University
ONC	Office of the National Coordinator (for Health Information Technology)
PAHO	Pan American Health Organization
PDB	Protein Data Bank
PHR	Personal health record
proTICS	Professionalization Program in Information Technology & Communication in Health
PURE-HIT	Professional University Resources and Education for Health Information Technology
QUIPU	Andean Global Health Informatics Research and Training Center
RAFT	Reseau en Afrique Francophone pour la Télémédecine (Research in Africa for Telemedicine)
RCR	Responsible Conduct of Research
RDHI	Research and Development Health Informatics
REACH-Informatics	Regional East African Center for Health Informatics
REC	Regional Extension Center
REHCE	Regional e-Health Center of Excellence (Kigali)
REIMICOM	Malian Medical Information and Communication Network
RHIT	Registered Health Information Technician
RN-BC	Registered Nurse – Board Certified
SCAMC	Symposium on Computer Applications in Medical Care
SWOT	Strengths, Weaknesses, Opportunities, Threats (Analysis)
TBI	Translational bioinformatics
TIGER	Technology Informatics Guiding Education Reform
TMI	Thai Medical Informatics Association
TMT	Taiwan Electronic Medical Record Template
UAB	University of Alabama at Birmingham
UBT	University-based Training
UCSF	University of California—San Francisco
UIC	University of Illinois at Chicago
UP-HI	University Partnership for Health Informatics (University of Minnesota)
VistA	Veterans Health Information Systems and Technology Architecture
WEB	Workshop on Education in Bioinformatics
WHO	World Health Organization

Part I
Introduction to Lessons Learned

Chapter 1
Introduction and Overview

Eta S. Berner and Jacqueline A. Moss

In the last 25 years, there has been a proliferation in the number and types of informatics education programs. Interest in health and biomedical informatics education has increased dramatically in response to the increase in use of healthcare information technology (HIT) in both clinical and research settings. Accompanying the growth in these programs is the concurrent interest in the development of informatics certification processes and program accreditation standards. Some of the impetus for informatics education in the U.S. comes from the growing use of HIT in clinical settings as a result of the HITECH Act [1], a part of the American Recovery and Reinvestment Act, which tied adoption of Health IT to incentives from the Centers for Medicare and Medicaid Services (CMS). In research settings, drivers for the increased use of health IT include the growing interest in personalized and precision medicine, the growth of the bioinformatics field, and the emphasis on biomedical informatics to support research as a part of the Clinical and Translational Science Awards (CTSA). Internationally, as technology infrastructures have grown, there is increasing use of HIT and the concomitant need for education not only for informatics professionals, but for the clinicians and others who use these systems.

While there have been many definitions of informatics in the literature over the years [2–7], it is more productive to examine the scope of the field, rather than a specific definition, when we talk about education in informatics in healthcare. The

E. S. Berner (✉)
Department of Health Services Administration, School of Health Professions, University of Alabama at Birmingham, Birmingham, AL, USA

Department of Medical Education, School of Medicine, University of Alabama at Birmingham, Birmingham, AL, USA
e-mail: eberner@uab.edu

J. A. Moss
Department of Family, Community, and Health Systems, School of Nursing, University of Alabama at Birmingham, Birmingham, AL, USA
e-mail: mossja@uab.edus

© Springer Nature Switzerland AG 2020
E. S. Berner (ed.), *Informatics Education in Healthcare*, Health Informatics,
https://doi.org/10.1007/978-3-030-53813-2_1

following description of the scope of the field was developed by the first author (ESB) over 20 years ago, with recent adaptation. This definition was developed as a result of conversations with students, to help clarify their understanding of the purpose and scope of their informatics education.

> Informatics involves developing and utilizing a broad range of **information technology** to facilitate the collection, management, exchange, analysis, use (and re-use) and storage of **patient (including clinical and genomic), fiscal, and administrative information** to support and improve (1) the **quality** of patient care and health outcomes, (2) **secure access** to information, (3) professional and organizational **efficiency**, and (4) the **decision making** capabilities of health professionals, administrators and others within the healthcare organization.

The highlighted areas above indicate that information technology supports the field, but the focus of informatics is on the **information**, rather than the technology per se. This book describes the major initiatives in informatics education internationally. It includes educational initiatives to produce informatics researchers, applied informatics practitioners, and informatics education programs for other healthcare practitioners as well. The focus is on the lessons learned from the variety of health and biomedical informatics programs, some of which are fairly young, while others have been established for decades. Although we will describe a variety of types of programs for different audiences, some common themes run through these programs.

Interdisciplinary Basis

The practice of informatics, and therefore the education necessary for this practice, draws on knowledge from a wide variety of disciplines. Informatics practice, and the research of phenomena central to this practice, involves knowledge that informs the optimal design of information systems for the optimization of data collection, delivery, and analysis, as well as usefulness and usability for end-users. All of the relevant knowledge and skills related to aspects of organizational science, information science, human factors, computer science, and cognitive science must also be nested within the associated healthcare context. This context may be primarily driven by end users, such as in consumer health informatics, nursing informatics or pharmacy informatics, or public health informatics.

Informatics education programs, regardless of their healthcare focus, include content from other related supporting disciplines and apply this content to either the design of research for the generation of knowledge in informatics or the application of this knowledge to the practice environment. Each professional domain applies this interdisciplinary content in relation to their healthcare focus; however all informatics specialties are based on the same or very similar theoretical underpinnings. Several of the chapters in this book explicitly describe curricular content in some detail and the interdisciplinary nature of the content is obvious. In addition, as the chapters in the section on Assessment of Individuals and Programs in

Informatics illustrate, the standards for certification of individuals and accreditation of programs implicitly or explicitly include these supportive interdisciplinary underpinnings.

Informatics Competencies

Another consistent theme echoed by multiple contributors to this edition, is the assertion that all healthcare professionals require basic competencies in the use of information technology to work in today's technology rich environment. A competency is "an expected level of performance that integrates knowledge, skills, abilities, and judgment" [8]. First, all healthcare professionals need to acquire basic computer and information science competencies to be able to interact, not only with electronic medical records, but also with a variety of patient information and communication technologies that are increasingly a part of every aspect of healthcare. Second, every healthcare professional needs to be information literate. Finding, evaluating, and synthesizing the best evidence helps ensure that patients receive the highest level of care available from their providers. Those managing the organization and delivery of this care require current and accurate information to effectively and efficiently manage care access and organizational resources. Finally, all healthcare professionals require basic competencies related to the management and analysis of data. Development of data management competencies enables individuals and organizations to understand the need for ensuring the privacy and confidentiality of data, standardized data collection, and patient and organizational outcomes analysis. Chapters 3, 7, 8, 16 and 17 in particular list competencies that reflect these emphases and provide references that include the recommended competencies in more detail.

Standards for Certification and Accreditation

As the field of informatics education has matured there has been increased interest in certification of individuals' competencies and accreditation of informatics education and training programs that produced these individuals. Different organizations are often involved in certification of individuals than are involved in the accreditation of the programs preparing these students. The International Medical Informatics Association has focused on informatics education program accreditation on a worldwide basis [9]. In this book we include other examples of accreditation efforts. For instance, as described in Chap. 8, the Commission on Accreditation of Healthcare Management Education (CAHME) is responsible for accrediting programs in healthcare management. Within their accreditation guidelines are the information management competencies that are expected to be taught by educational programs. None of these accreditation programs oversees a certification program for individuals. On the other hand, there are certification programs for individuals that are not specifically tied to program accreditation. The HITPRO examination that was initially designed for students graduating from the ONC-funded workforce program (see Chap. 20) did not require specific educational preparation for the credential. The CPHIMS credential, administered by the Health Information and Management Systems Society (HIMSS), that is designed to certify healthcare IT managers like those described in Chap. 4, also does not prescribe specific educational preparation. The American Nurses Credentialing Center (ANCC) in association with the American Nurses Association offers a credential for nurse informatics specialists (Chap. 3), but a different organization, the American Association of Colleges of Nursing (AACN), is involved in accrediting nursing education programs. However, graduating from an accredited informatics program is currently not required for eligibility for the certification examination.

On the other hand, the clinical informatics subspecialty examination for physicians described in Chap. 16 is closely tied to preparation in an accredited training program, especially after the initial years of the examination. Although the Informatics Fellowship program accreditation is done by the Accreditation Council for Graduate Medical Education (ACGME), there is close collaboration between the organizations that certify individuals and accredit programs.

The Commission on Accreditation for Health Informatics and Information Management Education (CAHIIM) [10], which began as a Health Information Management (HIM) accrediting body, has now added health informatics to its name and mission and some informatics programs are starting to seek accreditation from them, as described in Chap. 17. There is a new Health Informatics Certification Commission that is in the process of determining eligibility criteria for granting certification (see Chap. 16).

As informatics education programs proliferate and more individuals are trained, we can expect to see that both individual certification and informatics education accreditation will become more important. For this reason, we have devoted a specific section of this book to the issues of accreditation and certification.

Adaptation to Current and Future Needs

One of the challenges of developing informatics education programs in today's world is that the world keeps changing and the change is in the direction of requiring more and more varied informatics competencies, even if one is not an "informatician" and especially if one is. 'Big data' and 'data science' have become buzzwords [11], but being able to use those data that, with the help of electronic health records, we are now able to collect, will require some traditional and some new informatics competencies. Chapters 10 and 20 discuss new educational programs in data science. Similarly, the focus on Meaningful Use in the U.S. [12] has led to more interest in informatics-trained professionals. New developments in genomic research have spurred the development of programs in bioinformatics education (Chap. 5), as well as programs for translational scientists [13] that integrate both clinical and bioinformatics (Chaps. 5 and 9). Existing programs for health professionals have also seen the need to incorporate informatics into the basic educational preparation of clinicians (Chaps. 3, 7 and 12) and other health professionals (Chap. 8). Chapter 4 focuses directly on the need to adapt curricula to a changing external environment, but virtually all of the chapters recognize that informatics competencies will change and evolve as the environment in which they apply changes.

Online Education

One of the major changes that has been occurring in education generally is a trend toward more and more education being delivered online via distance learning technology. Several informatics programs described in this book are either primarily or entirely delivered online. Examples of online curriculum content, strategies for creating online content, and feasible methods of content delivery are included in these chapters, but there is now an entire section (Chaps. 18, 19 and 20) that focuses specifically on online educational programs. Chapter 19, in particular, is focused specifically on the different assumptions and expectations of students and teachers in online education as compared to face-to-face programs. While the focus of this book is on informatics education, and not distance learning per se, there is a great deal of information for those who want to start a distance-accessible informatics education program.

Arrangement and Focus of Book

This book is arranged in five major sections with additional introductory and concluding chapters. This overview is the introductory chapter. The last chapter, Chap. 21, synthesizes and integrates the key points from the other chapters for a comprehensive view of the lessons learned from the variety of informatics education programs described.

The other major sections include chapters on:

1. Training Informatics Specialists in the U.S. (Chaps. 2, 3, 4, 5 and 6)
2. Informatics Education for Other Health Professionals (Chaps. 7, 8, 9 and 10)
3. Informatics Education Worldwide (Chaps. 11, 12, 13, 14 and 15)
4. Assessment of Individuals and Programs in Informatics (Chaps. 16 and 17)
5. Use of Distance Learning for Informatics Education (Chaps. 18, 19 and 20)

The section on training informatics specialists in the U.S. includes chapters on the National Library of Medicine (NLM) training programs (Chap. 2), as well as programs to train IT managers and other IT and informatics workforce professionals (Chap. 4). Chapter 3 on Nursing Informatics focuses on both educating nurse informaticians as well as integrating informatics into general nursing curricula. In addition to programs that train applied informatics in clinical settings, this section also includes chapters on training specialists in bioinformatics (Chap. 5) as well as undergraduate informatics majors (Chap. 6).

The other chapters that involve integrating informatics education into other educational programs are covered in the next section, Informatics Education for Other Health Professionals. These professionals include physicians (Chap. 7), health administrators (Chap. 8), and clinical and translational researchers (Chap. 9). Chapter 10, the last chapter in this section, focuses on informatics and data science training for students in basic science training programs.

The third major section of this book includes chapters on informatics education in non-U.S. settings. This section is significantly expanded from the previous edition. Chapter 11 includes a description of the efforts and challenges of translating some of the U.S. programs into educational programs in other countries. Conversely, Chaps. 13, 14 and 15 provide the perspectives of the recipients of some of those programs, as well as a description of informatics education programs developed in the local settings. The focus of these chapters is on the many countries with limited resources for healthcare in general, and for informatics education in particular. While Chaps. 13, 14 and 15 focus primarily on medical and health informatics, Chap. 12 describes nursing education in a variety of countries outside the U.S.

Although competencies are described throughout many of the chapters, the section on assessment of programs and individuals describes the activities of certification programs for medical subspecialists and others (Chap. 16) and accreditation of informatics programs (Chap. 17).

Within the section on distance learning, Chap. 18 describes the AMIA 10 × 10 programs which have been used for continuing education not just in the U.S., but in other countries as well. Chapters 19 and 20 address some of the challenges of online education. Chapter 19 focuses on the various assumptions that both students and teachers bring to online education and describes strategies for managing these assumptions. Chapter 20 discusses the benefits and challenges involved in using freely available online educational materials. Each chapter of the book ends with lessons learned and/or key take-away points.

While the lessons learned provide 'words of wisdom' from internationally recognized informaticians and educators, the references in this book provide a comprehensive compilation of the scholarly literature on the history and current status of informatics education in the U.S. and globally. Both the lessons and the references will be useful for informatics educators who are embarking on developing the new informatics education programs that are sorely needed as we navigate the expanding digital healthcare age.

References

1. Blumenthal D. Launching HITECH. N Engl J Med. 2010;362(5):382–5. https://doi.org/10.1056/NEJMp0912825.
2. Greenes RA, Shortliffe EH. Medical informatics. An emerging academic discipline and institutional priority. JAMA. 1990;263(8):1114–20.

3. Friedman CP, Altman RB, Kohane IS, McCormick KA, Miller PL, Ozbolt JG, Shortliffe EH, Stormo GD, Szczepaniak MC, Tuck D, Williamson J. Training the next generation of informaticians: the impact of "BISTI" and bioinformatics—a report from the American College of Medical Informatics. J Am Med Inform Assoc. 2004;11(3):167–72. https://doi.org/10.1197/jamia.M1520.
4. Stead WW, Searle JR, Fessler HE, Smith JW, Shortliffe EH. Biomedical informatics: changing what physicians need to know and how they learn. Acad Med. 2011;86(4):429–34. https://doi.org/10.1097/ACM.0b013e3181f41e8c.
5. Kulikowski CA, Shortliffe EH, Currie LM, Elkin PL, Hunter LE, Johnson TR, Kalet IJ, Lenert LA, Musen MA, Ozbolt JG, Smith JW, Tarczy-Hornoch PZ, Williamson JJ. AMIA board white paper: definition of biomedical informatics and specification of core competencies for graduate education in the discipline. J Am Med Inform Assoc. 2012;19(6):931–8. https://doi.org/10.1136/amiajnl-2012-001053.
6. Bernstam EV, Hersh WR, Johnson SB, Chute CG, Nguyen H, Sim I, Nahm M, Weiner MG, Miller P, DiLaura RP, Overcash M, Lehmann HP, Eichmann D, Athey BD, Scheuermann RH, Anderson N, Starren J, Harris PA, Smith JW, Barbour E, Silverstein JC, Krusch DA, Nagarajan R, Becich MJ. Synergies and distinctions between computational disciplines in biomedical research: perspective from the Clinical and Translational Science Award programs. Acad Med. 2009;84(7):964–70. https://doi.org/10.1097/ACM.0b013e3181a8144d.
7. Valenta AL, Berner ES, Boren SA, Deckard GJ, Eldredge C, et al. AMIA Board White Paper: AMIA 2017 core competencies for applied health informatics education at the master's degree level. J Am Med Inform Assoc. 2018;25(12):1657–68. https://doi.org/10.1093/jamia/ocy132.
8. American Nurses Association. Competency model. https://www.nursingworld.org/~4a0a2e/globalassets/docs/ce/177626-ana-leadership-booklet-new-final.pdf. Accessed 8 May 2020.
9. Mantas J, Hasman A, Shortliffe EH. Assessment of the IMIA educational accreditation process. Stud Health Technol Inform. 2013;192:702–6.
10. Commission on Accreditation for Health Informatics and Information Management Education. Welcome to CAHIIM. 2013. http://cahiim.org/. Accessed 8 April 2020.
11. Davenport TH, Patil DJ. Data scientist: the sexiest job of the 21st century. Harv Bus Rev. 2012;90(10):70–6, 128.
12. Blumenthal D, Tavenner M. The "meaningful use" regulation for electronic health records. N Engl J Med. 2010;363(6):501–4. https://doi.org/10.1056/NEJMp1006114.
13. U.S. Department of Health and Human Services [HHS]. National Institutes of Health. National Center for Advancing Translational Science. CTSA Clinical & Translation Science Awards Program. https://ncats.nih.gov/ctsa. Accessed 8 May 2020.

Part II
Training Informatics Specialists in the US

Chapter 2
Training for Research Careers in Biomedical Informatics and Data Science Supported by the National Library of Medicine

Valerie Florance

In a previous volume, the history of NLM in university-based training for biomedical informatics was discussed in detail [1]. In this chapter, the focus is on current research training initiatives sponsored by the National Library of Medicine, both extramural and intramural, for informaticians and librarians.

Extramural Training for Research Careers in Biomedical Informatics and Data Science

Until July 1, 2017, NLM's University-based training for research careers in biomedical informatics and data science was guided by applications received in 2011. The solicitation for NLM's university based training programs issued in 2011 offered 5 years of funding for predoctoral and postdoctoral training in one or more of the following areas:

- Health care/clinical informatics (HC): Applications of informatics principles and methods to direct patient care, such as advanced clinical decision support systems and multimedia electronic health records, to the provision of informational support to health care consumers. Special tracks might be offered for nursing informatics, dental informatics, imaging informatics, or other appropriate clinical themes.
- Translational bioinformatics (TB): Applications of informatics principles and methods to support 'bench to bedside to practice' translational research, such as genome-phenome relationships, pharmacogenomics, or personalized medicine.

V. Florance (✉)
Extramural Programs, National Library of Medicine, National Institutes of Health, Department of Health and Human Services, Bethesda, MD, USA
e-mail: florancev@mail.nlm.nih.gov

© Springer Nature Switzerland AG 2020
E. S. Berner (ed.), *Informatics Education in Healthcare*, Health Informatics,
https://doi.org/10.1007/978-3-030-53813-2_2

Special tracks might be offered in health effects of environmental factors, genome-wide association studies (GWAS), or other similar areas.
- Clinical research informatics (CR): Applications of informatics principles and methods to support basic clinical trials and comparative effectiveness research. Special tracks might be offered in areas such as biostatistics, in-silico trials, merging and mining large disparate data sets that mix images, text and data.
- Public health informatics (PH): Applications of informatics principles and methods to build integrated resources for health services research, for decision support in public health agencies, to support regional or global health research, or syndromic surveillance. Special tracks might be offered in areas such as health literacy, information design for consumers, health effects of climate change [2].

Regarding the nature of the training, the solicitation expressed the expectation that supported training would include these features:

- A core curriculum that includes required coursework in informatics concepts and principles, quantitative methods, and techniques of computer science/engineering or other information fields.
- Practicum experience in the application domain (e.g. courses in the public health system for public health informatics trainees)
- Elective options providing opportunity for advanced training in fields basic to informatics
- Trainee research experience, with emphasis on the process by which students are assisted in selecting research projects

Applicants are also encouraged to describe experiences that seek to integrate informatics methods and the application domain, including details about how these experiences will be structured. For all courses listed as part of the program that are not under the direct control of the principal investigator's home academic unit (e.g. his/her home department), applicants must document through appropriate letters that their trainees will have routine access to these courses.

The application must specify a core curriculum addressing informatics concepts and methods that supports the entire program, spanning all application domains that are addressed. While the proposed core curriculum may include variations that customize it to specific domains, the preponderance of courses and other educational elements comprising the core must apply to all application domains [2].

Fourteen programs were supported from the 2011 solicitation, 12 of which were renewals of existing programs, with 5-year awards for programs beginning July 1, 2012.

Data Science

Fifteen days prior to the start of these 14 programs, the Data and Informatics Working Group of the Advisory Committee of the Director at NIH issued its report recommending increased, NIH-wide emphasis on the infrastructure, workforce and investment needed "to enable researchers to easily find, access, analyze, and curate research data" [3]. This report also led to the launch at NIH of the Big Data to Knowledge (BD2K) program [4]. The Training committee of BD2K saw a need for the type of interdisciplinary training NLM had provided for decades in its University-based training programs. The structure of NLM's informatics training programs served as the model for the first BD2K Big Data Science T32 training program, whose funding solicitation contained this description of the requirements: "Big Data Science is interdisciplinary and includes three major scientific areas: (1) computer science or informatics; (2) statistics and mathematics; and (3) biomedical sciences. It is anticipated that the training program will have a sufficient number of mentors in all three areas, including biomedical sciences researchers, and will utilize the idea of multiple mentorship. Participating training faculty should include investigators who develop new technologies and practical tools, who generate and utilize Big Data, and who have a variety of biomedical expertise, from clinical to basic sciences, and with multiple disease specialties. The primary PD(s)/PI(s) must ensure that the appropriate faculty work collaboratively and in a sustained manner across scientific disciplines and organizational lines to jointly mentor trainees" [5].

The NIH Strategic Plan for Data Science, issued in 2018, defines data science as "the interdisciplinary field of inquiry in which quantitative and analytical approaches, processes, and systems are developed and used to extract knowledge and insights from increasingly large and/or complex sets of data" [6]. NLM had long considered data science to be a component of informatics, but had not used that phrasing in earlier competitions for its University-based training programs. In 2016, NLM's solicitation for new five-year awards for university-based informatics training offered support for Institutional Training Grants for Research Training in Biomedical Informatics and Data Science. Instead of treating data science as a separate training area, data science examples were incorporated into the familiar list of desired training areas outlined above.

For example, in the Health care/clinical informatics (HC) area, special track examples were expanded to include precision medicine and clinical data science. In the Translational bioinformatics (TB) area, example special tracks included mining large scale genome-phenome datasets, intelligent tools for curation, visualization and analysis of biomedical big data. The clinical research informatics (CR) area mentioned biostatistics, merging and mining large disparate data sets that mix images, text and data, and the Public health informatics (PH) area mentioned syndromic surveillance and data visualization for population health.

In addition, within NLM's training program, the National Institute of Environmental Health Sciences offered support for training in environmental exposure informatics, defined as "research focusing on the effects of environmental exposures … to discover how the environment affects people in order to promote healthier lives through research that advances our understanding of environmental exposures and their population, clinical, mechanistic and phenotypic consequences" [7].

As a result of this solicitation, 16 5-year training grant awards were issued, to begin July 1, 2017, of which 3 were new programs; 6 of the awardees offer trainee slots in exposure informatics.

In 2017, supplemental funds were offered by NLM to the 16 programs to support curriculum development or faculty enrichment activities related to biomedical data science that would be shared with other training programs. Fourteen of 16 programs requested and received this support. In several cases, several programs worked together to develop data sets or hands-on exercises that would benefit all trainees. Examples of shared curriculum resources include the following:

Github sharable data science curriculum resources from NLM university-based training programs are available at https://github.com/biomedicalinformatics/DataScience

- Rice University—a semester course for Data Science
- Yale University—Introduction to B cell repertoire analysis and PySeqLab for supervised learning in structured prediction
- Pittsburgh—6 tutorials including causal inference, microbiome analysis, image segmentation, and social media

Additional sharable data science curriculum resources are available at other sites, including

- Columbia—tools for OHDSI are available at https://github.com/OHDSI/
- Buffalo—iLab These topic aligned sets of Jupyter notebooks, which collectively constitute a data science lab course, are available at https://halsted.compbio.buffalo.edu/iLab
- OHSU—a variety of curriculum materials on informatics and data science including data literacy, a python bootcamp, an NHANES data scavenger hunt and others, some for undergraduates, at https://github.com/laderast/laderast.github.io
- Harvard—brought together representatives of the 15 other NLM training programs, along with selected outsiders, to develop a core curriculum for biomedical data sciences. A series of webinars was followed by an in-person workshop held in February 2018. Participants at the workshop made recommendations in the areas of quantitative and computational methodology; quantitative and computational foundations; data skills; biomedical skills; and professional skills. Notes from those sessions, a workshop report and links to relevant resources are available online [8].

In 2018, supplemental funds were again offered to NLM's 16 University-based programs for efforts to (1) share curriculum materials with other NIH-funded training programs at their university, (2) to share or co-develop biomedical data-science curricula with in partnership with minority serving educational institutions (MSIs) or library schools, (3) to provide summer training experiences to high school and undergraduates students. Fifteen programs participated in this round of enrichment.

Reproducibility of Published Research

Another NIH area of interest during this period that affected NLM's university-based training for research careers is reproducibility of published research. Initial focus at NIH addressed laboratory-based preclinical research and NIH issued guidance for the information that must be considered during review of research applications. More complete guidance addressing rigor and transparency and providing training resources is offered on the NIH Grants and Funding site, which states "Scientific rigor is the strict application of the scientific method to ensure unbiased and well-controlled experimental design, methodology, analysis, interpretation and reporting of results" [9]. However, with the recognition that basic biomedical research increasingly involves quantitative and computational methods, NLM's training programs and others have expanded the required 'responsible conduct of research' instruction they offer to include factors about the use and manipulation of data.

A review of the progress reports from grantees, includes the following examples of topics covered in Responsible Conduct of Research in Biomedical Informatics and Data Science training offered at NLM university-based training programs [10]:

- University of Buffalo: Bioethics course, mock IRB evaluation sessions, case studies. Topics: virtue ethics, ethics of care pragmatism; precision medicine and ethics—confidentiality, privacy, social justice and health disparities
- Colorado: Computation-focused bioethics course including data safeguarding and privacy, core ethical principles of research, collaboration and the ethical challenges it poses, responsible authorship, ownership of intellectual property, and the impact of biotechnology and massive computing power. Lecture, role playing, active debates. This course also collaborates with the Colorado Clinical and Translational Science Institute. Ethics topics are folded into other courses.
- Columbia: Topics include the following: (1) research misconduct; (2) "every day" ethical issues faced by biomedical scientists; (3) the use of laboratory animals in scientific research; (4) human research participants and scientific research; (5) authorship practices in scientific publications; (6) conflicts of interest arising from scientists acting as policy consultants and experts; (7) data sharing and data secrecy; (8) mentoring; (9) research with stem cells, and (10) the role of scientists in society. In addition, G6002 Research Methodology in Biomedical Informatics incorporates competencies that include being able to formulate hypotheses, design suitable experiments, and carry them out with sensitivity to ethical standards. As part of that course, students are required to learn appropriate research protocols by submitting a practice IRB proposal.
- Stanford: The course covers Ethical, Social, and Legal implications; how to approach ethical dilemmas that commonly arise in biomedical research, including issues in the practice of research such as in publication and interpretation of data, and issues raised with academic/industry ties. It also covers contemporary debates at the interface of biomedical science and society regarding research on stem cells, bioweapons, genetic testing, human subjects, and vertebrate animals.

Quarterly topics have included discussions of CRISPr to edit the human germ-line, clinical data sharing and "research parasitism", and whether using crowd-sourcing requires IRB approval.

- Wisconsin: The course "Responsible Conduct of Research for Data Scientists" uses case studies and discussion. For development of an "Omic" or software medical device, discussions will revolve around fairness and bias as well as expectations of the FDA for documentation and quality control. Another course topic focuses on issues arising from microbiome data. In this context, students discuss issues pertaining to what research is human subjects research, the role of data analysis and coordinating centers, project management, intellectual property, publication embargos, and authorship. In addition, data privacy laws and norms in European countries and others will be compared to those of the US. For microbiome data that contains human DNA contaminants, what are the ethics involved in releasing these data publicly?

Between October 2016 and April 2018, as part of NLM's strategic planning, NLM's Director and Associate Director for Extramural Programs visited 13 NLM-funded institutional training programs. The visits were a means of assessing local characteristics of the programs and hearing about benefits and challenges 'on the ground' and strategies being used to incorporate data science into the curriculum. Meetings were held with trainees, program administrators and faculty at each location, using agendas and participant lists developed by the program director at the host site. Though all NLM university-based training is meant to prepare pre- and post-doctoral fellows for research careers in biomedical informatics and data science, the programs differ in aspects of structure, topical emphasis, academic placement within their organizations, interdepartmental collaboration and the ways they engage and support trainees. A report summarizing findings of the 13 visits identified areas to consider and explore relating to alternate support models, career transition support, and the need for expanded training opportunities in this area [11]. These recommendations serve as the basis for future initiatives that support the NLM Strategic-Plan [12].

Research Training in Biomedical Informatics and Bioinformatics Offered at NLM

In addition to supporting extramural training in university settings, NLM supports several training initiatives at its home base in Bethesda, Maryland. Programs described below are offered by NLM at the NLM location.

Lister Hill National Center for Biomedical Communications (LHNCBC) Biomedical Informatics Training Program. This program provides "biomedical informatics and clinical informatics training and research opportunities for individuals at various stages in their careers" [13]. The program brings interns and fellows from the US and abroad to NLM. Seven different training initiatives are offered, ranging from summer electives for medical school residents to postdoctoral research fellowships that can last up to 3 years. There is also a Visiting Scientist program. Training topics at NHNCBC include lexical systems, indexing, image processing, consumer question answering, data de-identification, and an array of topics related to storage and use of clinical data [14].

National Center for Biotechnology Information (NCBI) Computational Biology Branch (CBB). This program is part of the NIH Intramural Research Program. Postdoctoral fellows and students receive research training as part of one of ten research groups in this center. "The expertise of CBB group is concentrated in sequence analysis, protein structure/function analysis, chemical informatics, and genome analysis. Research interests further cover a wide range of topics in computational biology and information science. These include, but are not limited to, database searching algorithms, sequence signal identification, mathematical models of evolution, statistical methods in virology, dynamic behavior of chemical reaction systems, statistical text-retrieval algorithms, protein structure and function prediction, comparative genomics, taxonomic trees, population genetics, and systems biology. Many of the basic research projects conducted by CBB investigators serve to enhance and strengthen NCBI's suite of publicly available databases and software application tools" [15].

Specialized Training for Research Librarians

For more than 40 years, NLM has supported training for health sciences librarians through programs such as the NLM Associate Fellowship program, which offers a one-year postgraduate residency at NLM to prepare new librarians for future leadership roles in health sciences libraries and health services research. More than 200 librarians have participated in this program [16].

In 2000, the Annals of Internal Medicine published an editorial describing an evolving role for health sciences librarians as members of research and care members in health settings. Defined as 'in context information specialists', the idea for informationists grew from early programs in clinical libraries, in which librarians joined the rounding teams [17]. Three years later, NLM launched a fellowship grant program for informationist training. The fellowship identified four priority areas for this training: Clinical—to work in health care delivery, clinical research, or clinical trials; Biomedical research—to work in biomedical research, research administration, or the curation of scientific data; Public health—to work in public health administration at the national, regional or local level; Consumer health—to work within organizations or with the general public on consumer health information issues [18].

During the life of the Informationist Fellowship grant programs, eight fellowships were supported with seven focused in public health or clinical care settings and one centered in curation of scientific data. In 2012, following publication of the report of the ACD Work Group on Informatics and Data referenced earlier, NLM took a different approach, with focus on research-based informationists. In this funding program, scientists with active research project grants from participating NIH Institutes and Centers could apply for a grant supplement funded by NLM to bring an informationist onto the research team [19]. To date, more than 50 librarians have been supported through this program, which contributed to the rise of interest in 'research data management' as a focus in academic libraries. In 2013, the Journal of eScience Librarianship issued a special issue entitled "The Role of the Informationist or Embedded Librarian in the Scientific Research Process", with articles published by informationists supported by this supplement program [20]. In 2016, a second article assessed the program by interviewing researchers and librarians about their experience with the program [21].

In April 2019, NLM brought together practicing librarians and faculty from library schools and information schools at a 1.5 day workshop "Developing the Librarian Data Science and Open Science Workforce" [22]. After surveying the landscape, the attendees identified core skills beyond those primarily focused on the traditional library that would be required for open science and data science librarians. These skills include data skills, computational skills, subject matter and research skills, interpersonal skills and commitment to lifelong learning [22, p. 4]. In considering next steps for action, the report notes the need for expanded training content beyond research data management to an array of data-related topics and noted the growing importance of experiential learning in this area. The report also provides a list of existing courses [22, pp. 24–27]. Worthy of note, in 2019, Simmons College announced a post-masters inter-professional informationist certificate program whose development was supported by the Institute on Museums and Library Services and seven academic health sciences libraries [23]. Several people involved in the new program at Simmons attended this workshop.

Data Science Training for All Staff at NLM

For its own staff, NLM developed a 'datascience@NLM' training initiative. Each staff member, regardless of academic background, was asked to complete a data science readiness survey to assess their current strengths in an array of data science areas and indicate what areas they hoped to learn or enhance. The areas were Advanced Mathematics, Computer Science, Data Mining and Integration, Data Visualization, Machine Learning, Operations Research, Programming and Scripting, Research Design and Statistical Modeling [24].

Staff rated their current abilities in these areas as comprehension, basic, foundational, full performance, and expert. Eight skill development profiles (DS support, DS facilitation, Data Life Cycle Management, Data visualization and information design, Systems and data operations, Intermediate data science and Advanced data science) were framed and presented to staff in the survey; each respondent could choose a 'persona' to which they aspired. Each respondent received in return an

'Individualized Training Plan', a diagrammatic view of the 'gaps' and a comprehensive Data Science Course Catalog for self paced or formal courses available online.

A Data Science Fundamentals Course was offered to all NLM staff in June 2019 [25]. A pilot summer program offered a 3-month in-depth boot camp for 25 members of the staff. At an August 2019 data science open house, coordinated by NLM's Library Operations Division, more than 70 staff developed posters relating themes of data science to their work. Supervisors are working with staff to incorporate their data science training plans into performance evaluations. A case study of the Datascience@NLM initiative that includes graphics and examples of staff engagement activities is available on request from the Data Science Training Team at NLMDataScience@nih.gov [26].

In summary, looking broadly at NLM's training initiatives described here, it is clear that, together, increased sophistication and capabilities in the computational infrastructure and growth in size and scope of digital data sets pose a continuing challenge to educators in informatics. In addition to accommodating different learning styles, informatics and data science education for health must make room for (1) a growing contingent of trainees whose career goals may direct them initially to industry rather than to academic settings, (2) academic researchers who need to update their skills, account for advanced data management requirements and develop long-term interdisciplinary collaborations; (3) skilled staff whose technological skills must grow and change constantly; (4) undergraduate students who want coursework or graduate degrees in data science techniques. In some settings, instructors find it more efficient to separate undergraduate and graduate trainees. Some institutions fail to take advantage of their health sciences libraries in ways that could help them address (2) and (3) above. Consideration must also be given at academic centers to industry partnerships that could meet the needs of both parties to train and retain talented informaticians and data scientists.

References

1. Florance V. Training for informatics research careers: history of extramural informatics training at the National Library of Medicine. In: Berner ES, editor. Informatics education in healthcare: lessons learned. London: Springer-Verlag; 2014. p. 27–42. https://doi.org/10.1007/978-1-4471-4078-8.
2. NLM Institutional Training Grants for Research Training in Biomedical Informatics (T15). Bethesda, MD: National Library of Medicine. Funding opportunity announcement issued February 2011. https://grants.nih.gov/grants/guide/rfa-files/RFA-LM-11-001.html
3. National Institutes of Health Data and Informatics Working Group, Draft Report to the Advisory Committee to the Director. Bethesda, MD: National Institutes of Health. June 15, 2012, p 5. https://acd.od.nih.gov/documents/reports/DataandInformaticsWorkingGroupReport.pdf
4. National Institutes of Health Common Fund. Common Fund Programs. Big Data to Knowledge. Bethesda, MD: National Institutes of Health. https://commonfund.nih.gov/bd2k
5. Predoctoral Training in Big Data Science (T32). Grant funding opportunity announcement. https://grants.nih.gov/grants/guide/rfa-files/RFA-HG-14-004.html

6. NIH Strategic Plan for Data Science. 39 pages. Released 2014. Bethesda, MD: National Institutes of Health, p 29. https://datascience.nih.gov/sites/default/files/NIH_Strategic_Plan_for_Data_Science_Final_508.pdf

7. NLM Institutional Training Grants for Research Training in Biomedical Informatics and Data Science (T15). Grant funding opportunity announcement issued February 2016. https://grants.nih.gov/grants/guide/rfa-files/RFA-LM-16-001.html

8. Biomedical Data Science Curriculum Initiative, February 2018 Workshop. Boston: Harvard Medical School Blavatnik Institute, Biomedical Informatics. https://dbmi.hms.harvard.edu/education/biomedical-data-science-curriculum-initiative/february-2018-workshop

9. Enhancing Reproducibility Through Rigor and Transparency. Bethesda, MD: National Institutes of Health. https://grants.nih.gov/policy/reproducibility/index.htm

10. National Library of Medicine. University-based Training Programs. https://www.nlm.nih.gov/ep/GrantTrainInstitute.html

11. Florance V. NLM's university-based training for research careers in biomedical informatics and data science: observations and recommendations. Unpublished 9-page report. Bethesda, MD: National Library of Medicine Division of Extramural Programs, 2018.

12. A Platform for Biomedical Discovery and Data-Powered Health. National Library of Medicine Strategic Plan, 2017–2027. Bethesda, MD: National Library of Medicine, December 2017. https://www.nlm.nih.gov/pubs/plan/lrp17/NLM_StrategicReport2017_2027.html.

13. National Library of Medicine Lister Hill Center for Biomedical Communications. Biomedical Informatics Training Program. Bethesda, MD: National Library of Medicine. https://lhncbc.nlm.nih.gov/biomedical-informatics-training-program.

14. National Library of Medicine. Lister Hill Center Biomedical Informatics Training Program, preceptor list. Bethesda, MD: National Library of Medicine. https://lhncbc.nlm.nih.gov/biomedical-informatics-training-program-preceptors.

15. National Library of Medicine, National Center for Biotechnology Information, NCBI Computational Biology Branch. Bethesda, MD. https://www.ncbi.nlm.nih.gov/research/.

16. National Library of Medicine. History of the NLM Associate Fellowship Program. https://www.nlm.nih.gov/about/training/associate/history.html

17. Davidoff F, Florance V. The informationist: a new health profession? Ann Intern Med. 2000;132(12):996–8. https://doi.org/10.7326/0003-4819-132-12-200006200-00012.

18. NLM Individual Fellowship for Informationist Training. (F37) Grant funding opportunity announcement issued October 2003; https://grants.nih.gov/grants/guide/pa-files/PAR-04-013.html.

19. NLM Administrative Supplements for Informationist Services in NIH-funded Research Projects, funding opportunity announcement. Bethesda, MD: National Library of Medicine. https://www.nlm.nih.gov/ep/InfoSplmnts.html.

20. Informationist Careers for Librarians—A Brief History of NLM's Involvement. Florance, V. Journal of eScience Librarianship. https://escholarship.umassmed.edu/jeslib/vol2/iss1/2/

21. Assessing the National Library of Medicine's Informationist Awards. Deardorff, A.; Florance, V; VanBiervliet, A. Journal of eScience Librarianship. https://escholarship.umassmed.edu/jeslib/vol5/iss1/8/

22. Federer L, Clarke S, Zaringhalam M, Huerta M. Developing the Librarian Workforce for Data Science and Open Science. Bethesda, MD: Office of Strategic Initiatives, National Library of Medicine, no date. Unpublished 27 – page report.

23. Simmons University. Inter-Professional Informationist Certificate. https://www.simmons.edu/graduate/academic-programs/graduate-and-certificate-programs/inter-professional-informationist

24. Building Data Science Expertise at NLM. The NLM Director's Blog, April 2019. Bethesda, National Library of Medicine. https://nlmdirector.nlm.nih.gov/2019/04/09/building-data-science-expertise-at-nlm/.

25. DataScience@NLM Data Science Basics course. https://videocast.nih.gov/Summary.asp?Live=31941&bhcp=1

26. National Library of Medicine. Case Study: Building a Workforce for Data-Driven Research and Health. Unpublished report. Bethesda, MD: National Library of Medicine, 2019.

Chapter 3
Education in Nursing Informatics

Marisa L. Wilson, Beth L. Elias, and Jacqueline A. Moss

Introduction

The efficient use of information and communication technology and informatics processes is a key competency of all care providers including nurses. This chapter will review the importance of informatics to nursing, the current mandate for nursing informatics education among all practicing nurses and informatics nurse specialists, the issues with foundational knowledge among nursing educators, and the resources available to improve the informatics education and professional development of all clinical care providers including nurses. The goal of this chapter is to create the recognition that this topic is of great import to all nurses and nurse leadership; however, there is a significant gap in competency which needs to be remedied since it impacts the optimal use of technology and data at the point of care. This chapter focuses on informatics in US nursing education. Chapter 12 addresses nursing informatics education in other countries.

M. L. Wilson (✉) · J. A. Moss
University of Alabama at Birmingham, Birmingham, AL, USA
e-mail: mwilsoa@uab.edu; mossja@uab.edu

B. L. Elias
University of Scranton, Scranton, PA, USA
e-mail: beth.elias@scranton.edu

© Springer Nature Switzerland AG 2020
E. S. Berner (ed.), *Informatics Education in Healthcare*, Health Informatics,
https://doi.org/10.1007/978-3-030-53813-2_3

The Importance of Informatics to the Past, Present and Future of Nursing

The art and science of nursing has long required the use of data to create information and knowledge from which to make informed clinical decisions and to create care systems that are efficient and effective for patients, families, consumers, communities, populations, and professional care partners. This is not new. Florence Nightingale, in 1863 stated:

> In attempting to arrive at the truth, I have applied everywhere for information, but in scarcely an instance have I been able to obtain hospital records fit for any purposes of comparison. If they could be obtained, they would enable us to decide many other questions besides the one alluded to. They would show subscribers how their money was being spent, what amount of good was really being done with it, or whether the money was not doing mischief rather than good; they would tell us the exact sanitary state of every hospital and of every ward in it, where to seek for causes of insalubrity and their nature; and, if wisely used, these improved statistics would tell us more of the relative value of particular operations and modes of treatment than we have any means of ascertaining at present. They would enable us, besides, to ascertain the influence of the hospital with its numerous diseased inmates, its overcrowded and possibly ill-ventilated wards, its bad site, bad drainage, impure water, and want of cleanliness—or the reverse of all these—upon the general course of operations and diseases passing through its wards; and the truth thus ascertained would enable us to save life and suffering, and to improve the treatment and management of the sick and maimed poor [1, p. 176].

Using information to determine appropriate care has been key to the nursing profession from its inception. Florence Nightingale (1820–1910), who is credited with propelling the practice of nursing into a profession, used data to provide information on the effect of nursing care on morbidity and mortality rates among soldiers during the Crimean War and later went on to use the data to improve hospital care for all patients [2]. She made these strides, of course, through manual extraction and manipulation of data.

Nurses continue to follow Nightingale's lead as knowledge workers with their focus on clinical decision-making guided by data incorporating technology into the process. Peter Drucker in 1959 defined a knowledge worker as a high level worker who applies theoretical and analytical knowledge, acquired through formal training, to develop services [3]. This process supports the high-level of problem solving that is required in nurses' work. For nursing, the problem solving that goes into knowledge work is highly complex because it must be individualized to each particular patient and circumstance. Information and communication technology can provide the data and information needed to help support the individualized knowledge work required and to ensure that patients, families, communities and populations are provided safe care and improved outcomes.

As computers became available in the 1960s, pioneering nurses began to explore ways that computing power could be used to successfully drive care on the clinical side of healthcare. Harriet Helen Werley, PhD, RN, FAAN, FACMI became the first "nurse informatician" even before there was an official name for this specialty. In the late 1950s, Dr. Werley was officially designated as the first nurse researcher at

Walter Reed Army Institute of Research. In this role, Werley participated in conferences initiated by IBM to identify data processing needs for healthcare and explored the potential uses for computer applications by clinicians [4]. In the 1970s, as the field of clinical informatics began to grow, Dr. Werley looked for opportunities to use information technology to reuse clinical data for research and management [5].

Today, in a technology rich environment, registered nurses hold over 3.1 million jobs, exceeding the number of physicians by approximately five to one [6]. Over 60% of nurses work in hospitals; however many are providing care to patients in ambulatory settings, nursing and residential care, the government, and educational services all of which use information and communication technologies and which should use informatics processes to move data to information to knowledge [7]. Nurses' work is as diverse and complex as the patients they serve. Nurses function as part of an interprofessional team and in this role, it is important to consider that nurses often serve as the information hub of the healthcare team in acute, home, and long-term settings. They collect vast amounts of data from patients, family members, other members of the healthcare team, and physiological monitoring and treatment devices such as cardiac monitors and insulin pumps. They then document these data, either on paper or electronically, and disseminate it to others either through the patient record, with communication technologies, or face-to-face.

Regardless of setting, the National Academy of Medicine, in *The Future of Nursing 2020–2030*, mandates that all nurses are to practice to the full extent of their education and training, assume leadership positions, improve data collection, create a culture of health, reduce health disparities, and improve the health and wellbeing of the US population in the twenty-first century all of which rests on a foundation of competent use of information and communication technologies and informatics processes [8].

For nurses to successfully function in their role today, they must be competent in the use of the technology and informatics processes whether they are basic practitioners, advanced practitioners, or faculty in nursing. Moreover, as technology becomes more sophisticated and ubiquitous within all settings, the role of the informatics nurse specialist, those nurses who are prepared to support nursing practice through the application of nursing science, computer science, and information science to improve the health of populations, communities, families and individuals through information management and communication technologies must evolve [9]. This educational content is as dynamic as information technology itself today and will only continue to change and grow as information technology, the profession of nursing, and the healthcare environment evolves.

Health Information Technology Use

The growth in health information technology, specifically Electronic Health Records (EHR) in acute care hospitals has been rapid between 2008 and 2015. In 2008, 9.4% of non-Federal acute care hospitals had adopted a non certified EHR to use to carry out care [10]. By 2015, 96.9% of non-Federal acute care hospitals were using a certified EHR to manage care which was a ninefold increase over 2008 [10]. Much of this increase in use can be attributed, in part, to the Institute of Medicine's (IOM) Quality Chasm series of reports in which the IOM raised serious concerns about patient outcomes and safety [11–13]. In these reports the use of information technology is discussed as a means to improve patient safety while increasing efficiency. The IOM linked heath information technology and practice applications with the expectation of improved data collection and data quality which would allow for evidence-based practice, decision support and reduced waste. Healthcare organizations are also expected to use the health information technology to conduct routine data analysis to improve patient care and outcomes, and to ensure regulatory compliance and reporting. Healthcare organizations and providers are also now being evaluated on quality measures that are tied to the use of information technology by both regulatory agencies and payors [14]. As we attempt to quantify measures around patient outcomes and safety, the higher level of data quality that can be achieved through the effective use of HIT is essential. Nurses are at the core of many of these activities.

In addition to regulatory agencies and payors, patients are also evaluating their healthcare providers. Patients increasingly expect their providers to communicate using information and communication technologies such as email, messaging services like twitter and through web browser-based patient portals. Patients and health consumers are expecting connected health through social media, wearables, remote monitoring, biometrics, and shared data [15]. In the competition for healthcare dollars, the need to focus on consumer centered and participatory medicine to attract patients is going to push organizations towards on-demand, connected, and data driven patient engagement in order to succeed [15]. Professional groups such as the Healthcare Information and Management Systems Society (HIMSS) [16], The College of Healthcare Information Management Executives (CHIME) [17], and U.S. News & World Report [18] are adding to this pressure by publishing the results of surveys and rankings of healthcare organizations that focus on health information technology completely or in part.

With the financial support provided in the American Recovery and Reinvestment Act, we have seen the number of health information technology tools to provide information support at the point of care increase [19]. Now, the future of healthcare will rely on all providers entering into partnerships with patients and consumers to form a team with technology making the connections possible, with technology assisting patients and providers to make informed decisions, and with technology as a tool to build trust [20].

It is clear that nurses will be information and communication technology users in their professional practice, making their education regarding the use of these technologies even more important. At the bedside, devices that nurses have traditionally used in their work, such as patient monitors, intravenous pumps, and even hospital beds are being redesigned to integrate with data and communication systems to both collect and provide data at the point of care, in the home and in the community to improve patient safety. Increasingly, these technologies are being designed to be

worn by patients in the outpatient setting both to collect data and to provide therapeutic interventions such as insulin pumps, implantable defibrillation devices, and
remote monitoring devices. As more of us age-in-place, in the future the number
and sophistication of these devices will continue to grow. Nurses interact constantly
with these integrated information systems, inputting and accessing data. In a study
of nurses' information exchange in an intensive care unit, interaction with electronic sources was the second most frequent mode of information exchange exceeding all human interaction except information exchange with another nurse in the
unit [21].

In all practice settings, nurses play an important role in the selection, customization, and implementation of HIT. They are essential members of inter-professional
committees that work to customize interfaces, integrate workflow, train users, and
develop policies and procedures related to the successful implementation and use of
health information technology. Because of their role as care coordinators, nurses are
in a position to help decrease resistance and smooth the transition to new technologies and systems for other healthcare providers by providing just-in-time assistance
at the point of care [22]. Adequately preparing nurses to knowledgably function in
these roles will help ensure that these technologies are successfully implemented
and applied to the practice setting.

Educational Mandate

According to the American Nurses Association, a competency is "an expected level
of performance that integrates knowledge, skills, abilities, and judgment" [23,
p. 12]. This definition clearly emphasizes the need to apply didactic content to
achieve successful and effective performance in actual practice.

The effort to define nursing informatics competencies began in the 1970s to
explicate the needed computer competencies for practice at the basic and advanced
levels. The earliest competency recommendations tended to focus on the development of basic computer skills such as keyboarding, operating the basic applications,
and file management [24, 25]. Over the years, it became apparent that nurses also
needed to learn skills related to information literacy and information management
to implement and evaluate patient response to evidence-based practice (EBP) interventions [26]. Over the last 10 years, defining informatics competencies for nurses
across levels of practice and roles has been the subject of research studies. These
studies have primarily employed survey design to collect data on needed competencies from those in nursing education, informatics, and practice. Over the last two
decades, informatics competencies have been identified for all levels of nursing
education [27], for various interprofessional and international care providers [28],
and for executive nursing leaders [29].

Many organizations have called for the inclusion of nursing informatics content
into nursing curriculum across all levels of nursing education and some have worked
to provide guidance to educators on what competencies nurses need to practice

safely in an increasingly technological environment. These organizations include: the National League for Nursing [30], Quality and Safety Education for Nurses (QSEN) [31], Technology Informatics Guiding Educational Reform (TIGER) competency collaborative [28], and the American Association of Colleges of Nursing [32].

The primary organization responsible for guiding the development of nursing curriculum at all levels is the American Association of Colleges of Nursing (AACN). The AACN is a consortium of over 800 schools of nursing and works to define and guide the provision of quality nursing education. To support a consistent and effective curriculum, the AACN leads consensus-based efforts to define competencies that are expected for both the pre-licensure and graduate level nurses. This effort has resulted in the publication of the AACN Essentials Series. The AACN Essentials provides frameworks to guide curriculum development in undergraduate nursing education, master's education, and in the preparation of nurses earning a doctorate of nursing practice (DNP) degree [33–35]. Each of these Essentials documents includes specific guidance for the informatics competencies to be included at each level of education. The Essentials documents clearly indicate that informatics education is a required and integral component of nursing professional practice that must be woven throughout nursing education.

To ensure that the AACN Essentials documents are put into practice is the work of the Commission on Collegiate Nursing Education (CCNE) [36]. Working in partnership with the AACN, and using the Essentials documents as a guide, the Commission on Collegiate Nursing Education (CCNE) is responsible for reviewing nursing educational programs for accreditation. The CCNE is recognized by the United States Secretary of Education and works through a program of voluntary participation by Schools of Nursing. Certified Schools of Nursing programs for pre-licensure and graduate levels agree to undergo regular review and thorough evaluation by the CCNE to ensure the highest level of quality and ongoing improvement. The CCNE pays particular attention to the bridging that must take place between the competencies learned at different levels of nursing education, with each level of competency building on the next throughout all levels of educational preparation. Poorly defined or ineffective competencies therefore will not allow for the continued building of informatics or other skills that are required as nurses continue their education or as they move out into practice.

While the AACN can be said to be the main guiding body when it comes to BSN education, the National Council for State Boards of Nursing (NCSBN) is making its own contribution. The NCSBN is a consortium of United States' Boards of Nursing and other national Boards of Nursing and is responsible for development of the National Council Licensure Examination for Registered Nurses (NCLEX-RN). State boards of nursing require passing the NCLEX-RN for the licensure of nurses for practice. The NCLEX-RN examination includes questions related to competencies in informatics outlined in the AACN BSN Essentials documents.

To further support BSN students as they complete their undergraduate education and move into practice, the NCSBN has developed *Transition to Practice*, a standardized transition to practice model with supporting tools [37]. As part of this effort, six learning modules were developed, training module 5 is about informatics. This module includes computer and information literacy competencies clearly identifying them as critical to a successful transition from the educational environment to practice.

Nursing Education

Because most Bachelors of Science in Nursing (BSN), Masters of Science in Nursing (MSN), and Doctorate of Nursing Practice (DNP) programs in the United States undergo accreditation from the AACN and use the AACN Essentials documents as a framework for curriculum design, the informatics competencies reflected in these documents are integrated into these programs. At all levels of nursing educational preparation, the informatics competencies outlined in the Essentials documents and tested for by state boards of nursing for licensure and certification are related to three areas: computer competency, information literacy, and information management.

Despite informatics competencies being explicated in the AACN Essentials documents, the NLN, QSEN, and TIGER, a gap in informatics competency in practicing nurses and nursing leaders exists [38–41]. There have been many reasons posited as to the sources of this gap. First, faculty informatics competency is weak as the average age of a nursing faculty member is 57.2 for an assistant professor, 51.2 for an associate professor, 62.4 for a professor, which means they were mostly likely educated prior to the infusion of the competencies into programs [42]. Second, the structure of the previous Essentials as written made it difficult for non-Informatics-knowledgeable faculty to comprehend what was being asked for in terms of a student outcome. Third, the pace of technological and organizational changes within health care and the complexity of the interactions between nurses, technology, and data in shifting locations was not well represented in the existing Essentials so a rewrite of all Essentials for all levels of nurses is underway.

In the next section, a description of the re-envisioned Essentials will be presented. A word of caution, as of the writing of this chapter, these re-envisioned Essentials are still undergoing public comment [43]. The re-envisioned essentials are based on the competency development work of the HIMSS TIGER initiative, which incorporates a synthesis of previous informatics competencies for practicing clinicians [43].

The AACN Re-Envisioned Essentials: Domain 8—Informatics

In the re-envisioning of the AACN Essentials, there is a new model of academic nursing. This new model contains two levels of nursing practice: Level 1 (Entry to Practice) and Level 2 (Advanced Practice). Level 2 includes all nurses being educated at the Masters and Doctor of Nursing Practice levels [43]. Both levels contain ten Domains or spheres of knowledge. The Domains are:

1. Knowledge for Nursing Practice
2. Person Centered Care
3. Population Health
4. Scholarship for Nursing Practice
5. Quality and Safety
6. Interprofessional Partnerships
7. Systems Based Care
8. Informatics and Healthcare Technologies
9. Professionalism
10. Personal, Professional and Leadership Development [43]

All of the domains are meant to work together. For example, the need for nurses to lead informatics implementations would be in Domains 8 and 10. Domain 8, Informatics and Healthcare Technologies will focus specifically on the use of informatics practices with information and communication technologies to manage and improve the delivery of safe, high-quality, and efficient health care services in accordance with best practices and following professional and regulatory standards. Within Domain 8, there are five competency expectations and within each level (entry to practice and advanced), there are specific subcompetencies appropriate for that level which are singular in focus, actionable, and measureable. The five competencies found in both levels encompass the following concepts:

1. Evaluate the various information and communication technology tools used in the care of patients, communities, and populations.
2. Demonstrate appropriate use of information and communication technology to gather data, create information, generate knowledge and develop wisdom.
3. Describe how patient care and clinical interactions are supported by information and communication technology and informatics processes.
4. Examine how information and communication technology supports chronicling of care and communication between providers, patients, and systems in micro, meso, and macro systems.
5. Use information and communication technologies in accordance with legal, professional and regulatory standards and workplace policies in the delivery of care.

The very specific nature of the subcompetencies will drive the education. The subcompetencies encompass such concepts as:

1. Understanding the full complement of information and communication technologies in use in patient, consumer, and population care and best practices for their use.
2. Effectively using of communication technology to support team care.
3. Identifying and evaluating the data to information to knowledge process.
4. Applying data models and standardized terminology to individual and population based care.

5. Promoting information literacy in self and others.
6. Analyzing of the role of the nurse in the information life cycle
7. Understanding the concepts of interoperability, information exchange, and integration.
8. Assessing risk and benefit to the use of technology.

Educating Nurses for Basic Practice

The AACN Re-Envisioned Essentials for the entry to practice students outlines the competencies that are requisite components of a BSN or Entry MSN curriculum. With these re-envisioned Essentials, a BSN prepared nurse is expected to find and understand evidence-based practice guidelines and to be able to integrate them with their critical thinking skills to evaluate their patients' status. They must also be able to document this status in a variety of information systems and to communicate in a clear and timely manner with other healthcare providers using a variety of voice and information system tools to coordinate patient care. Additionally, nurses must be able to use increasingly complex and informatics-enabled point-of-care devices to monitor their patients as part of their daily work. These nurses are expected to understand the life cycle of the data they enter and how to use that data to generate information. Nurses at this level are to understand how to best care for and educate their patients, consumers, and populations using appropriate technology, internet based resources, and social media tools. They are to use clinical decision support tools along with critical thinking and clinical reasoning.

Entry to practice nursing students can do this within the regular classroom setting. However, clinical simulation has proven to be an effective method to provide experiential learning regarding technology use for the entry-to-practice student. The use of simulated electronic health records to document and retrieve both simulated and actual patient data has become very popular in schools of nursing, particularly in areas where the use of the actual hospital electronic health record is prohibited. Using a simulated record in a simulated patient experience with high-fidelity mannequins and patient care technology such as smart pumps, medication bar code scanners, and medication dispensing machines can provide the student with experience using these technologies in a real-world situation prior to encountering them in the practice setting. Below are some examples of potential simulations that focus on informatics competencies.

Example 1: Students who are immersed in simulation featuring a 'patient' who is experiencing chest pain, will need to skillfully interact with multiple technologies to care for this 'patient'. Initially, the student will be expected to assess the simulated patient and collect pertinent history and physiological information. This will involve the proper use of bedside medical devices routinely in use to provide continuous monitoring of blood pressure, pulse, temperature, and heart rhythm while simultaneously communicating and documenting these data into the electronic record. The student will then need to access past medical data in the electronic record, synthesize these data with current data being collected and communicate these findings to physicians and other healthcare providers. Increasingly, in the clinical setting, this is being accomplished not just through the use of the electronic record or telephone, but through the use of intrusive interruptive technologies such voice-over-Internet devices, communication tools and text messaging through smart phones. After the student has communicated patient findings to other providers, the student begins to provide care to the simulated patient, including administration of medication and drawing blood for laboratory analysis.

Example 2: Medication administration involves the use of multiple types of information and communication technologies that can be integrated into the student simulation. To administer medication to their simulated patient, the student must:

- Access and check the medication order in the electronic record
- Access and read information regarding administration of the medication, including: preparation of the medication, route and administration technique (i.e. intravenous push, drip, etc.), contraindications, drug-drug interactions, side effects
- Access and check any laboratory or physiological data that may be associated with administration of the drug (i.e. potassium level and blood pressure when administering Lasix)
- Access and check any other patient data that could impact administration, such as drug allergies, drug-drug interactions, or other patient contraindications (i.e. recent subdural hematoma and anticoagulants)
- Scan the simulated patient's armband and the drug bar-code
- Program the drug into a smart-pump intravenous administration device
- Monitor bedside device technology for the simulated patient's response to the drug administration.

While completing the patient simulation the student is required to document findings, medication administration, implemented therapies and interventions, monitor and react to laboratory and physiological data, all while interacting with patients, family members and other members of the healthcare team to coordinate the provision of care and to provide accurate information accurately and professionally. Familiarizing the student with these technologies through simulation can help decrease the chance for error when the students encounter these devices in actual practice and can increase their confidence in the clinical setting.

While the actual technologies can be very expensive for schools of nursing to purchase, a recent study has shown that there is little difference in the student's experience when interacting with an actual or simulated device. In a study comparing student performance and experience when taught to use intravenous smart-pumps using an actual pump and a simulated pump interface displayed on a tablet computer, researchers found little difference between the two devices [44]. Thus, not only may simulations provide a "safe" environment for student learning potentially risky procedures, but they also may be less expensive and of equal quality to real-life practice.

As schools prepare to educate entry to practice nursing students and as they implement clinical simulation activities in the curriculum, it is important to consider the incorporation of health information technology into the scenarios both in the classroom and in the simulation environment. While teaching the entry to practice nursing student the activities within assessment, diagnosis, intervention, treatment and evaluation, as well as team interaction, faculty should consider the inclusion of information technology within the experience as important as the process steps for the primary activities [45, 46]. This can be done successfully in simulation.

Educating Nurses for Advanced Practice

Advanced practice nurses are educated at both the MSN and DNP level of education. The MSN advanced practice nurse is prepared to deliver high-level complex care to individuals and groups. Those advanced practice nurses prepared at the DNP level are prepared not only to provide individual and group level care, but to develop, implement, and evaluate system-level interventions that influence the quality of care provided to patient populations.

The AACN Re-Envisioned Essentials document provides guidance on what specific computer and informatics skills and knowledge advanced practice nurses require at each level [43]. At Level 2, Domain 8 emphasizes minimally five broad areas of knowledge and skills that must be acquired: the use of a wide variety technology to deliver and enhance care, the use of communication technology to integrate and coordinate care, data management and analysis to improve care outcomes, accessing and using health information for evidence-based care and health education, and facilitation and use of a variety of information and communication technology tools following ethical and regulatory guidance [43]. At Level 2, a high degree of information literacy and information technology competence is required to support the role of the advanced practice nurse. As noted in the re-envisioned Essentials, advanced practice nurses at the Masters and DNP level must not only understand how to use information technology tools for patient care as a BSN would, they must also be able to evaluate what information technologies are optimal for their practice and the practice of others to enhance care outcomes [43]. In addition, nurses at this level must be prepared to use information technologies for the evaluation and analysis of patient data to improve patient outcomes, as well as for the education of other healthcare professionals and patients. The role of the advanced practice nurse expands beyond direct patient care to include practice guidance, policy promotion and design of education. The information technology competencies developed in the Level 1 Essentials lay a foundation to support these goals.

For both the MSN and DNP level 2, the educational emphasis and experiences should be on acquiring the skills and knowledge to successfully apply the requisite competencies to practice. Too many educational programs confine their informatics content to an overview course on the use of informatics in healthcare without giving students the tools they need to competently work with technology in practice. Types of educational strategies that may be employed at the advanced practice level are: the use and evaluation of online literature sources; the use of simulated and actual electronic health records; the modeling and design of databases; the use of software programs for data management and statistical analysis; and project design, management, and evaluation.

As an example of a way to address the relevant informatics knowledge and skills, assignments can be designed that teach students the basic elements of database models and design. The purpose of these assignments is to enable the advanced practice nurse to work with database and information system engineers, in the design of systems that collect and manage standardized patient data. The assignments also teach the student about the effect of different database models on their ability to analyze and track patient outcomes or how to use the data for developing evidence-based patient care protocols.

Advanced practice nurses, on graduation, are frequently involved with the evaluation and selection of bedside and system-wide technology solutions. An example of a skill-based project at the DNP program level that we have used is the development of an informatics-based Request for Proposal (RFP). The Informatics RFP is a standard business process that identifies a need, assesses the need, defines technical and functional criteria for an informatics tool to address the need, defines evaluation criteria for potential solutions, and quantifies organizational resources required. In healthcare organizations RFPs are considered formal legal documents and are sent to potential vendors as the initiation of vendor selection and an informatics implementation process. The assignment is team-based and requires that students clearly and effectively communicate and work together to develop the RFP, as they will be expected to do in their practice.

By going through the RFP process, students gain working knowledge of the processes used to identify needs and to systematically approach the process of technology evaluation and selection. In addition, because the RFP is a formal business process, students are able to see the technology in the comprehensive context of the organization at the systems level. As with the database assignments, the RFP assignment can be challenging for students who may not immediately be comfortable thinking from an organizational perspective and who may not be familiar with the concept of an informatics application lifecycle. Strategies to mitigate these challenges are similar to those used for the database assignment. Faculty being present as a guide, teacher and consulting team member provides students with access to a subject matter expert, as they would have in the real world. This approach can also help support healthy team building and interactions by clearly, regularly voicing team goals and modeling positive team behavior.

Educating Informatics Nurse Specialists

As the use of technology in nursing care grew, so did the realization that nurses were needed who had specialized training to design, implement, and integrate these technologies into nursing practice. Although nurses have been working in this endeavor for over 50 years, the American Nurses Association (ANA) recognized Nursing

Informatics as a nursing specialty in 1992. While Nursing Informatics has a great deal in common with the broader specialty of health informatics, the focus on data, information, knowledge, and wisdom in Nursing Informatics education is from the nursing perspective and relates to phenomena of interest for nursing [23].

The first specialty master's degree in Nursing Informatics was offered by the University of Maryland in 1989, followed by the first doctoral program in Nursing Informatics in 1992. Since this time the number and types of informatics specialty training programs in nursing has grown with the need for these nurses in practice and research. These programs offer a variety of educational options, including master's degrees, post-master's certificates, and doctoral degrees. Nurses prepared at the master's level in nursing informatics assume the title of Informatics Nursing Specialists (INS) [23]. Those holding a baccalaureate or master's in nursing with either extensive practice experience or informatics education can obtain board certification in nursing informatics, and the credential of Informatics Nursing–Board Certified (RN-BC), from the American Nurses Credentialing Center (ANCC) (https://www.nursingworld.org/our-certifications/informatics-nurse/).

The American Nurses Association [23] Nursing Informatics Scope and Standards of Practice provides: the attributes and definition of the specialty of nursing informatics, a guide for educators and those practicing nursing informatics, a reference for employers and regulatory agencies to define nursing informatics practice competencies and role responsibilities, and a source for information for others interacting with the profession legally and financially:

> Nursing informatics (NI) is a specialty that integrates nursing science, computer science and information science to manage and communicate data, information, knowledge, and wisdom in nursing practice. NI supports consumers, patients, nurses, and other providers in their decision-making in all roles and settings. This support is accomplished through the use of information structure, information processes, and information technology [23, p. 1].

The first publication of the scope and standards document was published in 1994; the current version is the fourth iteration of this guide.

The Nursing Informatics Scope and Standards of Practice describes the role of the Informatics Nurse Specialist within the context of the metastructures (Data, Information, Knowledge, Wisdom) [23, pp. 3–7] and the concepts and tools from information science and computer science (information technology, information structures, information management, and information communication) [23]. The Informatics Nurse Specialist functions in one or more of 13 functional roles including: (1) Administration, leadership and management; (2) Systems Analysis and Design; (3) Compliance and integrity management; (4) Consultation; (5) Coordination, facilitation, and integration; (6) Development of systems, products, and resources; (7) Educational and professional development; (8) Genetics and genomics; (9) Information management/operational architecture; (10) Policy development and advocacy; (11) Quality and performance improvement; (12) Research and evaluation; and (13) Safety, security, and environmental health [23, p. 19]. These functional units provide the framework for the development of educational programs in nursing informatics.

The MSN Informatics Nurse Specialist (INS) programs throughout the country generally have course work in three major areas: organizational and financial management, systems analysis and design, and project management although many have added in quality and safety, data science, and evaluation. The organizational and financial management training provides the INS with an understanding of informatics from the business and enterprise perspective. This perspective gives them the skill set to ensure a good fit between the needs and constraints of the organization and information technology solutions. The systems analysis and design training prepares the INS with an in-depth understanding of all phases of the information technology lifecycle, from initial needs assessment through long-term use to final phase out. By including training in project management, the INS is given skills that enable them to successfully plan, execute and complete an informatics implementation or management project.

It is important to note that at this writing the American Nurses Association Scope and Standards of Nursing Informatics Practice is undergoing a major revision to meet the expectations of the stakeholders and communities of interest. New informatics models are being considered. New concepts and tools from the information and computer sciences are under consideration for inclusion. These include: user experience, usability, clinical decision support and expert system development, big data, analytics, artificial intelligence, machine learning, natural language processing, and deep learning.

In addition, core courses specific to nursing MSN programs (i.e. evidence-based practice), and nursing informatics (i.e. nursing documentation and standardized terminologies) are included in their programs of study. Not all, but some, MSN INS programs also require a clinical component, where students are required to work in the practice setting with a preceptor who is working in the area of information systems analysis, customization/design, and implementation. It will be important for all engaged in the education of the Informatics Nurse Specialist to be aware of these changing expectations of the graduate of the programs.

Moreover, programs educating the masters level Informatics Nurse Specialist should incorporate the foundational domains proposed by the American Medical Informatics Association (AMIA) [47]:

1. Health
2. Information Science and Technology
3. Social and Behavioral Science
4. Health Information Science and Technology
5. Human Factors and Socio-technical Systems
6. Social and Behavioral Aspects of Health
7. Social, Behavioral and Information Science and Technology Applied to Health
8. Professionalism
9. Interprofessional Collaborative Practice
10. Leadership

There is much overlap between the AMIA Foundational Domains and the ANA Scope and Standards of Nursing Informatics Practice that is undergoing revision. It is incumbent upon the director of a Masters in Nursing Informatics program to be aware of both sets of competency expectations (AMIA and ANA) and to use the re-envisioned AACN Essentials at Level 1 as the foundation upon which to build a program to meet the need of today's informatician and to afford the graduate the opportunity to sit for either the ANCC RN-BC (https://www.nursingworld.org/our-certifications/informatics-nurse) or the AMIA AHIC (https://www.amia.org/ahic) when it becomes available.

Informatics Nurse Specialists will play a key role in the healthcare team as agents of, and guides through, HIT change. Whether it is in the clinical setting, as an implementation consultant or in working for an HIT vendor these advanced practice nurses will help bridge the gap between the world of the healthcare practitioner and the information technologist. They will work to ensure that the voice of nursing is represented in all aspects of HIT from initial design to longitudinal evaluation in the clinical setting. As professional nurses they will also continue the tradition of patient advocacy, helping HIT developers and vendors remember those who are at the center of patient care.

Preparing Faculty

Faculty Teaching All Nurses

Despite the long history of informatics as an expected competency of nurses at all levels of practice, there still remains a gap [48]. Some schools of nursing have had moderate success in implementing nursing informatics content into curricula across all levels of practice; however, many have struggled to achieve this goal. Incorporating informatics content, either as a stand-alone course or woven into other courses, will become more critical as the Re-Envisioned AACN Essentials are released, as these will impact accreditation through CCNE with significantly clearer and measurable informatics competency expectations for all nurses. Nonetheless, the major barrier to integrating informatics competencies into nursing school curriculum is the lack of adequately prepared faculty to teach informatics content [48, 49]. The average age of doctorally-prepared nursing faculty is 53.5 years [42]. Very few nursing faculty were educated at a time when informatics content and competencies were included in the nursing curriculum. In addition, very few nursing faculty have any informatics background or education and few nurses prepared in informatics pursue an academic role [48, 49]. This leaves fewer faculty who have an understanding of key areas required to train students in informatics across programs, such as the conceptual basis of informatics, informatics implementation and evaluation and emerging healthcare technologies. As a result, many new nurses are entering a professional environment rich in informatics without adequate preparation in using it effectively and efficiently [50]. This lack of preparation can negatively impact nurses' patients as well as their own professional evaluations. Calls from the American Nursing Association, HIMSS TIGER and the American

Association of Colleges of Nursing to address this lack of preparation have largely been ineffective due to the lack of a mandate on how to integrate informatics content. The new AACN Essentials will present a need for deep and ongoing faculty development to improve the level of understanding of non-informatics focused faculty who will teach this content in revised courses in new programs of study.

Resources such as those available from the HIMSS TIGER Virtual Learning Environment (https://www.himss.org/what-we-do-Initiatives-tiger/virtual-learning-environment), AMIA's 10x10 program (https://www.amia.org/amia10x10), the Nursing Knowledge and Big Data Science Initiative (http://www.nursingbigdata. org), and the Summer Institute in Nursing Informatics (https://www.nursing.umaryland.edu/academics/pe/events/sini/) can provide online and in-person professional development experiences for faculty who are tasked with bringing informatics into a nursing curriculum. The key is for these faculty members to recognize the breadth and depth of what they may not know.

Faculty Teaching the Graduate Informatics Nurse Specialist

In contrast to faculty teaching the general entry to practice or advanced nurse general informatics content, the faculty teaching the Informatics Nurse Specialist at the masters or higher level must be able to fully support the advanced informatics content as described in the ANA Scope and Standards and/or in the AMIA Foundational Domains [23, 47]. This means that program leadership must have a minimum of a doctoral degree in the field and his or her responsibilities must be clearly documented. All faculty teaching in these programs must demonstrate competence in the subject matter, be an effective teacher, and must maintain scholarly productivity in the domain of informatics. Program directors who would want their students to be eligible for either certification, the ANCC RN-BC in Informatics or the AMIA AHIC, may need to consider having the informatics program at the masters level be accredited by the Commission on Accreditation for Health Informatics and Information Management Education (CAHIIM) (https://www.cahiim.org).

Online Nursing Informatics Education

Many healthcare educational programs now include courses or parts of courses that are taught online. Online courses are particularly useful in graduate education where many students have work and family responsibilities that preclude them from attending face-to-face courses that are taught in a synchronous format [51]. Online courses also allow nurses to further their education geographically distant from their homes at institutions with faculty knowledgeable in informatics, and without removing them from the patient populations that are so in need of their expertise. Three major challenges are associated with teaching nursing and other healthcare informatics content in a distant accessible format: development of faculty and technical resources to support online course development and delivery, developing experiential learning activities that can be delivered in an online format, and engaging students in meaningful team-based learning [52, 53]. Part VI of this book discusses other challenges in online informatics education.

The use of online and blended courses in nursing education has a long history and most schools of nursing have courses that are delivered via distance and many have entire programs that are in an online or blended format [54, 55]. This is in part due to the US Health Resources and Services Administration's (HRSA) funding of distant accessible nursing programs to educate advanced practice nurses for populations in disadvantaged and rural areas. The intent of these programs is to increase the quality and access to healthcare in these populations. Online courses can be completed without removing nurses from the populations whom they serve. These programs may also relieve the concerns that might arise with moving to take traditional live programs that students may not return to these high need areas. Over the years, these grants have helped develop high quality, sustainable programs with a depth of faculty expertise in online delivery not often seen in other professional education disciplines.

The success of these programs has hinged on having adequate instructional technology resources. The necessity to devote adequate time and resources to a systematic faculty development program in online educational pedagogy cannot be overstated. Faculty are often apprehensive about teaching online initially, particularly if they have little experience using other educational technologies. Staff trained in instructional technology can smooth the way by preparing initial course shell structures, providing formal and just-in-time training, and providing individually-tailored support. Faculty need to be free to do what they do best; provide the best learning experience possible for their students.

Teaching students via distance can be a challenge in informatics courses where the acquisition of skills individually and working with a team are course objectives. Many software tutorials to develop database and other skills can be found online that can be accessed without charge to the student. In addition, instructors can develop step-by-step instructional modules through the use of learning object development software such as Adobe Captivate (http://www.adobe.com/products/captivate.edu.html). Developing effective student project teams online is a little more difficult. There are tools within online learning software that can support the formation of effective teams when combined with team building activities. For instance, using semi-structured team-building wiki teams can personalize the group space within the course, craft a mission statement, define team rules and roles, discuss previous team experiences and talk about what they wish to accomplish as a team participant. Adding a virtual classroom to the team's tools, with the ability to jointly edit documents and share desktops gives the students the ability to work together in a shared real-time virtual space.

Finally, communication both between faculty and students and between students is crucial to a successful online course. Communication modes include: email, discussion boards, blogs, wikis, synchronous webinars, discussion rooms, telephone, texting and face-to-face. Expert faculty use most of these communication modes in the same course, matching the communication mode selection with both the type of communication and the preferred mode of student communication. It may be even more important in an online course than in a face-to-face course that faculty are excellent communicators and respond to students quickly and clearly. As in any class, being responsive to students and their needs communicates to students that you care as an instructor and that their learning and success is important to you.

Summary

Healthcare Information Technology is dynamic and rapidly changing. Nurses will be challenged to adapt and engage with what can be described as a moving target. The importance of educating nurses not only in the use of information and communication technology but in becoming life-long informatics learners cannot be overstated. Patient care, quality measures and job satisfaction will all depend to a significant degree on the ability of the nursing workforce not only to grow with technology but to play a role in guiding that growth.

From the clinical practice-based competencies of the Bachelor's prepared professional nurse, the systems and information technology-based competencies of the INS, the leadership and population health-based competencies of the Doctorate of Nursing Practice and knowledge creation-based competencies of the Doctor of Philosophy in Nursing, understanding informatics is essential to all aspects of becoming and practicing as a nurse, teaching as a nursing school faculty member and in conducting nursing research. Nursing is a practice profession and at each level of nursing education, educational emphasis in informatics should be on equipping nurses to apply informatics competencies in practice to enhance the care and health of individuals. As informatics educators at all levels we face an exciting future rich with potential to advance the practice of nursing with the help of informatics and information technology.

Key Take-Away Points
- Technological competency, information literacy, and information management are key competencies for successful nursing practice. These are the basic competencies needed by both faculty and students to practice in all environments today.
- International and interprofessional research work points to a significant gap in competency in the use of informatics and information technology in the care setting.
- Courses that only provide an overview of informatics as a field are not sufficient to meet this need. Courses directed at successfully incorporating informatics and information and communication technologies must align these skills and best practices to care provision and best communication processes and operational workflows.

- Faculty professional development in order to teach informatics is mandatory and the existing informatics speciality organizations should coordinate to provide this development. Faculty who have not been formally trained in the specialization of informatics must avail themselves of professional development activities and administration must support this.
- Faculty teaching in nursing informatics graduate specialization programs should be knowledgeable and experienced informaticians with the academic background to cover necessary content. These faculty members should be aware of the competency expectations of the graduates of these programs and the CAHIIM accreditation requirements. Faculty teaching content within the specialization should also maintain up to date knowledge through engagement with professional organizations.
- Students are more easily able to transfer content to the clinical setting when the educational experience most closely mirrors what they will encounter in practice; simulation is an effective strategy to achieving fidelity for optimum transference.
- Instructional designers to support faculty in developing and delivering distance-accessible courses enhance course quality and the educational experience for both faculty and students.
- Successful online instructors maintain near-constant contact with their students through multiple modes of communication. Well-designed courses engage students through varied and interactive content.

References

1. Nightingale F. Notes on hospitals, 3rd ed. Longman, Green, Longman, Roberts, and Green, London, 1863. Available from: https://archive.org/details/notesonhospital01nighgoog/page/n7/mode/2up. Accessed 9 April 2020.
2. Selanders E. Florence nightingale. Encyclopedia Britannica Online: Academic Edition. http://www.britannica.com/EBchecked/topic/415020/Florence-Nightingale. Accessed 20 Jan 2020.
3. Drucker P. The landmarks of tomorrow. New York, NY: Harper Collins; 1959.
4. Werley HH, Lang NM. Preface. In: Werley HH, Lang NM, editors. Identification of the nursing minimum data set. New York: Springer; 1987. p. xvii.
5. Ozbolt J. Harriet Helen Werley, PhD, RN, FAAN FACMI Lieutenant Colonel, U.S. Army (Ret). J Am Med Inform Assoc. 2003;10(2):224–5.
6. Smilet RA, Lauer P, Berg JG, Shireman E, Reneau KA, Alexander M. The 2017 National nursing workforce survey. J Nurs Regul. 2018;9(Suppl 3):S1–S54.
7. Bureau of Labor Statistics, U.S. Department of Labor, Occupational Outlook Handbook, Registered Nurses. https://www.bls.gov/ooh/healthcare/registered-nurses.htm. Accessed 22 January 2020.
8. National Academy of Medicine. The future of nursing 2020–2030: Health and Medicine Division. https://campaignforaction.org/new-future-of-nursing-study-to-look-to-2030-watch-opening-session/. Accessed 30 Dec 2019.
9. Peltonen LM, Nibber R, Lewis A, Block L, Pruinelli L, Topaz M, Perezmitre EL, Ronquillo C. Emerging professionals' observations of opportunities and challenges in nursing informatics. Nurs Leadersh. 2019;32(2):8–18.

10. The Office of the National Coordinator for Health Information Technology [ONC]. Adoption of Electronic Health Record Systems among U.S. Non-Federal Acute Care Hospitals: 2008–2015. ONC Data Brief No. 35. https://www.healthit.gov/sites/default/files/briefs/2015_hospital_adoption_db_v17.pdf. Accessed 30 Jan 2020.
11. Committee on Quality of Health Care in America IoM. Crossing the quality chasm: a new health system for the 21st century. Washington, DC: Institute of Medicine; 2001.
12. Committee on Identifying Priority Areas for Quality Improvement IoM. Priority areas for national action: transforming health care quality. Washington, DC: Institute of Medicine; 2003.
13. Committee on Identifying and Preventing Medication Errors IoM. Preventing medication errors: quality chasm series. Washington, DC: National Academies Press; 2007.
14. CMS.gov. Centers for Medicare & Medicaid Services. Clinical Quality Measures. U. S. Department of Health and Human Services. https://www.cms.gov/Regulations-and-Guidance/Legislation/EHRIncentivePrograms/ClinicalQualityMeasures. Accessed 20 Jan 2020.
15. American Hospital Association. Digital transformation anywhere care: a vital sign of where the health care field is heading. https://www.aha.org/system/files/media/file/2019/09/MarketInsights_DigitalTransformation.pdf. Accessed 30 Dec 2019.
16. HIMSS. Analytics maturity models for optimized care. https://www.himssanalytics.org. Accessed 30 Dec 2019.
17. Becker's Health IT and CIO Report. CHIME releases list of "most wired" hospitals: here are the top 10. http://Beckershospitalreview.com. Accessed 30 Dec 2019.
18. U.S., News and World Report. Most connected hospitals 2015–16 results. https://health.usnews.com/health-news/best-hospitals/articles/2015/10/15/most-connected-hospitals-2015-16-results. Accessed 30 Dec 2019.
19. 111th U.S. Congress 2009. American recovery and reinvestment act of 2009. vol 123 STAT. 179. U. S. Congressional Record.
20. Snowden A. Health information and management systems society (HIMSS). Four areas of digital health that are driving the future of healthcare. https://www.himss.org/resources/four-areas-digital-health-are-driving-future-healthcare. Accessed 22 Jan 2020.
21. Moss J, Elias B. Information networks in intensive care: a network analysis of information exchange patterns. AMIA Annu Symp Proc. 2010;2010:522–6.
22. Jones S, Moss J. Computerized provider order entry: strategies for successful implementation. J Nurs Adm. 2006;36(3):136–9.
23. American Nurses Association. Nursing: scope and standards of practice. 3rd ed. Silver Spring: American Nurses Association; 2014.
24. Armstrong ML. Computer competence for nurse educators. Image J Nurs Sch. 1986;18(4):155–60.
25. Bryson DM. The computer-literate nurse. Comput Nurs. 1991;9(3):100–7.
26. Grobe SJ. Nursing informatics competencies for nurse educators and researchers. NLN Publ. 1988;14–2234:25–40.
27. Staggers N, Gassert CA, Curran C. Informatics competencies for nurses at four levels of practice. J Nurs Educ. 2001;40(7):303–16.
28. HIMSS. The TIGER Initiative (Technology Informatics Guiding Education Reform). https://www.himss.org/nursing-informatics-competencies. Accessed 20 Jan 2020.
29. American Organization for Nursing Leadership. Nursing informatics for the executive leader. https://www.aonl.org/nursing-informatics-executive-leader. Accessed 30 Dec 2019.
30. National League for Nursing (NLN). Informatics. http://www.nln.org/professional-development-programs/teaching-resources/toolkits/informatics-teaching/informatics. Accessed 30 Dec 2019.
31. Quality and Safety Education for Nurses (QSEN). Competencies. https://qsen.org/competencies/. Accessed 20 Jan 2020.
32. American Association of Colleges of Nursing. American Association of Colleges of Nursing Website. https://www.aacnnursing.org. Accessed 30 Dec 2019.
33. American Association of Colleges of Nursing. The essentials of baccalaureate education for professional nursing practice. Washington, DC: American Association of Colleges of Nursing; 2008.

34. American Association of Colleges of Nursing. The essentials of master's education in nursing. Washington, DC: American Association of Colleges of Nursing; 2011.
35. American Association of Colleges of Nursing. The essentials of doctoral education for advanced nursing practice. Washington, DC: American Association of Colleges of Nursing; 2006.
36. American Association of Colleges of Nursing. Commission on collegiate nursing education—CCNE accreditation. https://www.aacnnursing.org/CCNE. Accessed 30 Dec 2019.
37. National Council of State Boards of Nursing. Transition to practice. https://ww2.learningext.com/newnurses.htm. Accessed 20 Jan 2020.
38. Pordeli L. Informatics competency-based assessment: evaluations and determination of competency gaps among practicing nurse informaticists; 2018. https://www.himss.org/library/informatics-competency-based-assessment-evaluations-and-determination-nursing-informatics-competency. Accessed 20 Jan 2019.
39. Collins S, Yen P-Y, Phillips A, Kennedy M. Nursing informatics competency assessment for the nurse leader: the Delphi study. J Nurs Adm. 2017;47(4):212–8. https://doi.org/10.1097/NNA.0000000000000467.
40. Hubner U, Shaw T, Thye J, Egbert N, de Fatima Marin H, et al. Technology informatics guiding education reform—TIGER. Methods Inf Med. 2018;57(Open 1):e30–42. https://doi.org/10.3414/ME17-01-0155.
41. Hubner, U., Thye, J. Shaw, T., Elias, B., Egbert, N et al. (2019). Towards the TIGER International Framework for Recommendations for Core Competencies in Health Informatics 2.0: Extending the Scope and the Roles. MedInfo 2019: Health and Wellbeing-Networks for All. L. Ohmo-Machado and B. Seroussi (Eds.).
42. American Association of Colleges of Nursing. Nursing faculty shortage. https://www.aacnnursing.org/news-information/fact-sheets/nursing-faculty-shortage. Accessed 20 Jan 2019.
43. American Association of Colleges of Nursing. Essentials task force. https://www.aacnnursing.org/About-AACN/AACN-Governance/Committees-and-Task-Forces/Essentials. Accessed 20 Jan 2020.
44. Elias BL, Moss JA, Dillavou M, Shih A, Azuero A. Evaluation of nursing student perspectives of a simulated smart pump. Clin Simul Nurs. 2013;9(12):e599-e606.
45. Shaw RJ. Telepresence robots for pediatric clinical simulations: feasibility and acceptability. Pediatr Nurs. 2018;44(1):39–43.
46. Ammenwerth E, Hackl WO. Topics for continuous education in nursing informatics: results of a survey among 280 Austrian nurses. Stud Health Technol Inform. 2019;260:162–9.
47. Valenta AL, Berner ES, Boren SA, Deckard GJ, Eldredge C, et al. AMIA Board White Paper: AMIA 2017 core competencies for applied health informatics education at the master's degree level. J Am Med Inform Assoc. 2018;25(12):1657–68. https://doi.org/10.1093/jamia/ocy132.
48. Risling T. Educating the nurses of 2025: technology trends of the next decade. Nurse Educ Pract. 2017;22:89–92. https://doi.org/10.1016/j.nepr.2016.12.007.
49. Bove LA. Integration of informatics content in baccalaureate and graduate nursing education: an updated status report. Nurse Educ. 2019; https://doi.org/10.1097/NNE.0000000000000734.
50. Honey M, Procter P. The shifting sands of nursing informatics education: from content to connectivity. Stud Health Technol Inform. 2017;232:31–40.
51. Cipher DJ, Shrestha S, Mancini ME. Demographic and academic factors associated with enrollment in online MSN programs. J Nurs Educ. 2017;56(11):670–4.
52. Skiba DJ. Students, technology, and teaching: findings from the 2016 ECAR report. Nurs Educ Perspect. 2017;38(1):51–2.
53. Gazza EA. The experience of teaching online in nursing education. J Nurs Educ. 2017;56(6):343–9.
54. Mackavey C, Cron S. Innovative strategies: increased engagement and synthesis in online advanced practice nursing education. Nurse Educ Today. 2019;76:85–8.
55. Chilton J, He Z, Fountain R, Alfred D. A process for teaching research methods in a virtual environment. J Prof Nurs. 2019;35(2):101–4.

Chapter 4
Applied Informatics for Health IT Managers

Amanda D. Dorsey, Meg N. Bruck, and Sue S. Feldman

Even as our society sees more traditional experiences becoming digital, informatics as a discipline, and certainly informatics education, are still misunderstood. The discipline of health informatics itself is evolving from traditional subject matter areas like nursing, medicine, information retrieval, and computer programming toward consumer driven healthcare and augmented intelligence. The career paths of graduates of these programs, likewise, have changed accordingly, and a "one size fits all" approach to delivering formal academic programs in health informatics is nearly an impossibility.

Assumptions about the competencies, or the knowledge, skills, and abilities, of health informatics graduates still vary widely, although alignment of professional organizations with accrediting bodies is bringing these competencies into better focus (see Chaps. 16 and 17 for a description of Health Informatics certification and accreditation). Even as we move to an accreditation model that allows comparison of programs across specifically defined categories, management of our stakeholders' (i.e. future or prospective employers, hospitals, vendors, etc.) expectations are still somewhat challenging. This variability has also allowed for a degree of flexibility in areas such as curriculum development, professional development, and relationship building with external partners. The health informatics program at the University of Alabama at Birmingham (UAB), an early exemplar of an applied health informatics program with a focus on educating health IT managers and developing leaders, has been able to address the maturation of health informatics and the requisite skills needed in the health IT industry. In this chapter, we examine some of the key external influences that have guided the growing importance of managing information technology in healthcare and the continuing need for

A. D. Dorsey (✉) · M. N. Bruck · S. S. Feldman
Department of Health Services Administration, University of Alabama at Birmingham, Birmingham, AL, USA
e-mail: adorsey@uab.edu; mbruck@uab.edu; sfeldman@uab.edu

© Springer Nature Switzerland AG 2020
E. S. Berner (ed.), *Informatics Education in Healthcare*, Health Informatics,
https://doi.org/10.1007/978-3-030-53813-2_4

individuals with a background in health informatics to oversee the use of those systems. We conclude with some key lessons learned along the way.

A Brief History Lesson

A series of legislative actions over the past 50 years has led to the need for informatics as a discipline. A growing concern was who would manage all of that data and information? Who had access to it? What could be done with it? As health informatics has matured, we also need to consider who will implement the systems being built to collect and analyze the data. These are legitimate concerns that are often overlooked by administrators who want the data collected, analyzed, and visualized to drive operational decisions. This is complicated by the plethora of "micro-system" implementations. Micro-systems are systems within systems, such as clinical decision support within the electronic health record.

The 70s and 80s saw an expansion of technology beyond the mainframe billing systems, and the benefits of computing power were no longer limited to those working behind the scenes and with very specialized computer science training. To meet the demands of the increase from federal and state reporting agencies about care provision, some of the clinical disciplines such as laboratory, radiology and pharmacy began to see the use of automated systems. In terms of operations, billing systems were among the first to be implemented at the administrative layer. Large amounts of data were beginning to be readily available to members of the clinical and administrative communities within hospital settings. Many questions remained relative to the future about how to manage the data these systems were producing, and the level of knowledge, skills, and attitudes needed by those in leadership positions responsible for the clinical and administrative systems.

Formation of a Graduate Program in Health Informatics

During the 1980s, the National Library of Medicine (NLM) began awarding grants to U.S. educational institutions for the purposes of funding graduate education and research in many areas of healthcare and biomedical informatics. The NLM program allowed these institutions to recruit trainees, who would then go on to study and conduct research centered on healthcare, computers, and information and communications technology.

With the advent of many new technologies in healthcare settings and increasing demands to show productivity and efficiencies, many hospitals sought to expand responsibilities for their IT beyond the duties of a data processing manager and, therefore, hired a Chief Information Officer (CIO). While the CIO's job was more strategic in nature, the healthcare industry did not have individuals with formal training in this area. Data Processing Managers typically had a strong command of the technical environment, but lacked depth in understanding the business of health-care, the analysis and design of systems, and an understanding of the information needs of the administrative and clinical communities they served. The need for this type of individual, and its lack in most healthcare settings, was one of the driving forces in the development of a graduate program that would train individuals to fulfill the skill set required of healthcare CIOs [1].

Original UAB Health Informatics Curriculum

The courses based on the CIO roles and functions included a set of core founda-tional courses that all students took. These courses took were almost 70 credit hours, making it one of the longer programs of its type at the time. Geared toward training generalists, the curriculum was designed to graduate individuals versed in a wide variety of topics ranging from clinical documentation to data communica-tions to database management and systems analysis and design. Because the pro-gram also had an emphasis on addressing of the skills needed by future CIOs and technology leaders, courses in understanding the business of healthcare, such as financial management, organizational behavior, and management science were also required.

During the early 2000s, the curriculum underwent extensive revision. In addition to revising the curriculum, the program was reduced to 45 credit hours over 2 years, thereby allowing the program to be competitive with the number of health informat-ics master's degrees and concentrations beginning to emerge across universities in the U.S.

Until 2014, three options for completing the MSHI degree were offered. The first option was a thesis-based research option where students could conduct origi-nal research under the supervision of an Informatics faculty member. This option was primarily intended for students who planned to pursue a doctoral degree after their master's degree. The second option was a non-thesis research project which was designed for the student to gain insight into the techniques of informatics-specific problem solving. They used these insights to prepare a written report and a presentation on the findings to faculty members, fellow students, and their project mentor(s). The third option was an administrative internship which provided an immersion experience by which students could gain more informatics-specific experience.

Lessons Learned

By basing the curriculum on the skill set of the role we were training for and by using empirical data to help define that skill set, our students were able to function well in the newly emerging role of managing the enterprise IT systems.

Core Track Model

In 2014, the MSHI program moved to a core/track model that consisted of a first year of core informatics courses (core), and the second year specialty courses (track) [2]. The tracks consisted of tracks in user experience, data analytics and health information management. Three primary factors compelled this move. The first was that the previous curriculum focused mostly on training generalists who could help healthcare organizations transition from paper-based medical records to electronic health records (EHRs). But with the implementation of the Health Information Technology for Economic and Clinical Health (HITECH) Act in 2009 [3], EHR adoptions soared and demand for the generalists we had been training began to wane. The second reason compelling the curriculum change was the need for individuals who could help organizations optimize their newly installed EHRs and facilitate a better user experience for the clinicians who were now required to use them. Finally, we saw that the introduction of EHRs would increase the volume and velocity at which organizations would be producing data. We anticipated the organizational need for analysts and data visualization experts as a driver of better patient care and strategic decision making.

During this shift in the curriculum, we also eliminated the administrative internship and thesis option for degree completion because so many of our students were working full time already and most were not interested in advanced degrees. At this same time, the non-thesis research project, or capstone, became the culminating project required to fulfill the requirements of the MSHI degree. The capstone course was a 6-credit hour, one semester course that required students to complete a rigorous health informatics-focused project. The capstone project was designed to allow students to apply the knowledge, skills, and attitudes acquired during the core and the track coursework toward focused investigation of informatics-based problems in real-world settings and for application of problem-solving methodologies for development and execution of solutions. Capstone projects were managed academically by the program director with student accountability to the industry partner, serving as the external project advisor/mentor, who was the ultimate stakeholder and recipient of the student's project deliverable. This created a steady stream of applied projects that provided value to all stakeholders.

Lessons Learned

Revising the curriculum to the core-track model allowed us to remain responsive to the new demands in the marketplace by adding new tracks.

Expansion of Capstone Project

Within a few years we noticed that our students were embarking on increasingly complex capstone projects, industry partners were starting to approach us about project needs, project advisors/mentors were thinking more rigorously about project ideas, and our enrollment had increased. This confluence of events created the need to revisit our capstone requirement. The literature supports both spreading the capstone over multiple semesters and multiple faculty as a means to provide a more enriching learning experience for the student as well as a method to increase the breadth and depth of the capstone learning experience [4–6]. We decided to spread the capstone over three semesters (in the last year of the program), and students were advised by a variety of health informatics faculty. This created a Capstone course that consisted of three-courses spread across three semesters.

The first semester of the capstone course, one credit hour in the fall semester of the second year, covers the fundamentals of study design, including literature reviews, data collection methods, and stakeholder communication, with the final deliverable being a project outline of the student's project idea. This course is followed in the spring semester by another one credit hour course. This second course increases the student's focus and hones the project. Students learn about aligning multiple project elements to a timeline. Deliverables in this course include the submission of an application to the UAB Institutional Review Board (IRB) and a well-defined project proposal. This project proposal becomes the "project contract" for the third course in the sequence. The third course, three credit hours in the final semester of the second year, focuses on project execution. During this period, students are responsible for managing all project elements and presenting their project findings to the faculty, subject matter experts, and project stakeholders. Students also turn in a written paper. Because all projects receive IRB approval, we have found that this oftentimes leads to publications and poster presentations at major informatics conferences. Since 2017, several students have had their capstone projects published in leading peer reviewed publications. Completing a rigorous project that is of interest to an external party (project advisor/mentor) is advantageous and has resulted in employment opportunities for our students.

Lessons Learned

1. *Sequencing a capstone over multiple semesters and multiple faculty advisors facilitates increased rigor and at the same time decompressed the timeline for the student, making it less stressful to complete.*
2. *The interaction with the industry partner in a real-world setting has given students visibility within their own or another organization.*
3. *The capstone projects have served as a pipeline for presentation, publications, and employment opportunities for our students.*

Changing Student Body and Healthcare Environment

The original MSHI program was designed to attract individuals with varying backgrounds of professional and academic training. Because of the strategic needs of the CIO, those with management experience were preferred, since they could more easily move into a senior leadership position upon graduation. The first students entered the program in spring of 1991 and had work experience that varied from 5 to 15 years across a variety of positions. As health informatics has matured, so too have our recruiting and enrollment approaches. This has resulted in a significantly more diverse student body in terms of knowledge base, education focus, and age. Likewise, we have expanded recruitment to include disciplines such as industrial engineering, not typically thought to be the background for a health informatics student. We also started an undergraduate healthcare management to MSHI fast track program (similar to a 4+1 program). In this program, students begin the MSHI program while still taking undergraduate coursework. This has populated our program with undergraduate students with a healthcare management focus. Having students in our department's health informatics track that is part of our health administration PhD has added yet another dimension of student background and experience to the MSHI classroom.

With this increase in diversity, the classroom of today better mirrors diversity seen in the real-world environment of a health informatician: entry level person, clinician with no health IT background, technical person with no healthcare background, manager who is doing health informatics work, student body and healthcare environment without the formal educational foundation, and administrators. While the scope of this diversity is not for every program, we have found that group projects better simulate real life, leadership courses lead to multi-layered discussions with organic mentoring, and capstone projects are rigorous and can be built upon across lifecycle stages.

This diversity, however, is not without its challenges. While teaching and cohort management may be more efficient with a homogenous group, it is important to define what kind of graduate the program wants to produce. Our perspective was to respond to industry demands and provide students with the real-world environment within the safety net of school. With increased enrollment, the decision to move to a shared academic advising model across all informatics faculty, including the program director, led to a more focused experience for students. We also repositioned some course content to provide a broader foundation of healthcare and technical systems. These changes have allowed us to go from a class of primarily clinicians and administrative students with the average age of 45 years, to a class of about 25% fast track entry level, 25% clinicians, 25% students with IT knowledge, and 25% mid-late careerist administrators, with an average age for the class of 30 years.

Lessons Learned

1. *The changing educational landscape combined with the needs of students and demands of the field should promote a continual reassessment of coursework and requirements to better align with market demands.*
2. *Identifying the type of graduates that the program wants to produce helps to drive enrollment, curriculum, and diversity*

3. *Diversity in enrollment helps to simulate real-world diversity. This creates an environment to grow and learn from others and apply leadership knowledge and skills.*

Changing Learning Environment

By the mid 2000s it became clear that much of the flexibility offered by the program came at a cost. Students often lacked continuity with one another during their matriculation, which is an important element in the long-term success/satisfaction with graduate programs. Students often commented about the lack of unity among their fellow students, who they would see in class for a few semesters, but then might not see again for another year. If the program desired graduate students who would be invested in their education beyond graduation, it needed to provide a more cohesive delivery format and give the students more of a sense of community and belonging. To align students' expectations and reduce the administrative time spent managing matriculation plans of individual students, the decision was made to decrease some of the curricular flexibility and move to a cohort model, admitting students as a "class" only in the fall semester. Since implementing the cohort model, faculty and administrators have seen an increase in camaraderie, networking and sense of identity among the students. Again, responding to the market, this time the educational market, we made the decision to move to an online learning environment. More and more of the emerging programs were online and prospective students were inquiring about the ability to learn online.

The shift to an online learning environment was appropriately met with some skepticism from graduates from the traditional face-to-face model and faculty, as well. Common questions that were asked include "How would the students get to know one another if they never saw each other?" and "How could group work happen if everyone was not in the same place?" Additionally, faculty would need to become adept at communicating with students by different means (i.e. phone, email, conferencing tools). Contributing to the overall success of the switch from face-to-face to online learning was the fact the faculty embraced online learning environments and communication methods. Faculty were well supported at the university level by two important organizations, (1) The Center for Teaching and Learning (CTL) which provides faculty with support programs that encourage effective and innovative techniques in the online teaching environment, and, (2) the UAB Division of eLearning and Professional Studies, which supports faculty through instructional design and media production services as well as academic technology tools and training. At the school level, faculty teaching in online programs are supported by an Instructional Support Services team that provides design and support services. In terms of students getting to know each other and facilitating group work, we have two required in-person residential visits per year. During these visits, there are times when students are together for social and course activities. The university also provides ample support of conferencing tools such as GoToMeeting, Zoom, etc.

Students have reacted favorably to the shift to online learning because it allows them to maintain their current employment while obtaining their degree. Faculty frequently discuss lessons learned from group projects within their courses, and pay careful attention to the composition of the online groups so that they are diverse in terms of age, skill, temperament, experience, and background. Most recently, as part of its academic quality improvement process, the university has gone beyond the idea that students must simply *work* in teams, to emphasizing that students should be trained in how to *work effectively* in teams. With the combination of groupwork and interactions at residential visits, students have become very familiar with one another and have formed close and lasting friendships beyond graduation.

Lessons Learned

1. *The shift to a predominantly online learning environment was successful because of dedicated faculty and institutional support systems that promoted online learning.*
2. *Addressing students' concerns about being able to be with their classmates was an important consideration in the decision to have on campus residential visits.*

Managing the Challenges of the Future: Shifts in Informatics Foci, Regulation/Legislation, and Emerging Technologies

The health informatics leader of the future will need to be considerably more knowledgable than the leader of the past. This is primarily due to the breadth and depth of the health informatics discipline and its influence on healthcare.

Broadening of Health Informatics Foci

Health informatics is no longer a singularly focused discipline. Rather, it requires consideration of multiple foci: complementary disciplines, competency in education, and consumer-contributed data.

Complementary Disciplines Health informatics includes multiple sub-domains such as consumer health informatics, public health informatics, and many more, which can lead to confusion for prospective students, as well as our own industry. While all these sub-domains could fall under the larger domain of health informatics, some students confuse health informatics with bioinformatics, which has very different educational needs and skill sets. According to the US National Library of Medicine, health informatics is "the interdisciplinary study of the design, development, adoption, and application of IT-based innovations in healthcare services delivery, management, and planning" [7]. Bioinformatics is defined as, "the collection, classification, storage, and analysis of biochemical and biological information using computers especially as applied to molecular genetics and genomics" [8]. It is important for educational programs to be clear on the domain(s) and foci of their programs, to prevent misplaced expectations on the part of students.

Health Informatics Competencies The American Medical Informatics Association (AMIA) has developed a set of foundational domains for knowledge, skills, and attitudes, as applied to health informatics very broadly. CAHIIM, as the accrediting body for health informatics, has developed a set of accreditation standards that align with the foundational domains. There are 10 foundational domains within which some level of program-specific competencies are built in: (1) health, (2) information science and technology, (3) social and behavioral science, (4) health information science and technology, (5) human factors and socio-technical systems, (6) social and behavioral aspects of health, (7) social, behavioral, and information science and technology applied to health, (8) professionalism, (9) interprofessional collaborative practice, and (10) leadership [9]. These foundational domains and health informatics program accreditation are discussed in Chap. 17.

The future of health informatics education will need to conform to AMIA's foundational domains while maintaining program identity. For example, faculty in our program went through a series of exercises to identify the knowledge, skills, and attitudes with which our students will graduate. Next, we took a deep dive into our current curriculum to identify areas that could be collapsed to make room for new content. The knowledge, skills, and attitudes that were identified that we were not covering were able to take the space opened by the collapsed curriculum.

Consumer-Contributed Data We may be on the edge of a tipping point in healthcare where the majority of those caring for themselves or others are digital natives. Furthermore, a subset of those digital natives are comfortable advocating for their own healthcare. Mobile technology with health-related applications greatly contribute to the ease of use, the accuracy, and the volume of consumer contributed data. Additionally, mobile technology has put the Internet at everyone's fingertips. The issue of trust around consumer contributed data still remains, and as such, clinicians are reluctant to have these data automatically consumed by the electronic health record. However, as telemedicine matures, there may be some increased tolerance for consumer contributed data. Health informatics programs will need to consider the knowledge, skills, and attitudes our students need in order to design, develop, and implement solutions that foster increased accuracy of consumer contributed data so that these data are useful as consumers advocate for themselves in the healthcare environment.

The Regulation/Legislation Landscape

Since the beginning of the twentieth century, the health IT regulation/legislation landscape has been in a constant state of flux and it can be a challenge to keep the curriculum current. For instance, although the Health Insurance Portability and Accountability Act (HIPAA) [10] was enacted in 1996, the initial standards for privacy and security of protected health information were not finalized until 2003. During this time, there was a great deal of confusion about the exact requirements of the law and when the standard would take effect as there were numerous extensions and waivers and exemptions. When the HITECH Act, part of the American Recovery and Reinvestment Act (ARRA), passed in 2009 [3], this changed how HIPAA was imagined and revisions were needed to account for the electronic environment. As consumers of healthcare become more knowlegable and become better advocates for their health-related rights, HIPAA will continue to change. Since privacy and security are a key part of the health informatics curriculum, these changes continue to be incorporated into the curriculum in a dynamic manner to accommodate the regulation/legislation landscape and ensure that our students are graduating with knowledge that is current and relevant.

The HITECH Act had many far reaching impacts on health informatics education beyond HIPAA. Our existing program's curriculum has prepared many successful individuals throughout its history. However, we now face near constant change in the knowledge, skills, and attitudes for health IT professionals. HITECH, in part, has shaped how we define Health Informatics. Furthermore, health IT has proliferated across healthcare systems as support for accomplishing the quadruple aim: reduced costs, better healthcare outcomes, improved patient experience, and improved clinican experience [11]. As such, health informatics education needs to prepare a workforce equipped to support these technologies, ensure usability, visualize data, and translate to policy and decision makers.

Emerging Technologies

Health informatics educational programs need to consider emerging technologies across the healthcare continuum and across multiple user groups, such as clinicians, allied health professionals, administrators and consumers.

Whle there are technologies that are aimed at the users, there are also technologies aimed at the technology. Augmented intelligence (AI) is a good example of technology for technology. AI is defined as "the use of computerized algorithms that approximate, and in many cases, supercede human computing capability and capacity" [12]. AI is a broad category that includes processes such as machine learning, natural language processing, and robots. Health informatics education needs to consider application programming interfaces (APIs) and implementation and use in the clinical environment.

Health informatics educators need to consider how new technologies should be embedded in the curriculum—and then how to mature the content as the technology matures. One example of this might be collaborations between technology firms, such as Google, and large health systems.

As mentioned earlier, our curriculum has undergone the second major redevelopment in 5 years. This redevelopment is taking advantage of the maturity of health informatics as a discipline to include education around nacent and emerging technologies.

Role of Professional Organizations

Professional organizations will play an important role in shaping health informatics education and health informaticists of the future. Currently, there are two primary organizations with which health informaticists identify: American Medical Informatics Association (AMIA) and Health Information and Management Systems Society (HIMSS). With privacy, security, and data governance having roots in health information management (HIM) (i.e. medical record administration), there is crossover of HIM professionals into health informatics and vice versa. This crossover can also be seen as it relates to billing information systems and the need to use those data to drive outcomes. HIM professionals identify primarily with American Health Information Management Association (AHIMA). As mentioned, the crossover suggests that these are primary affiliations and not exclusive.

From a program perspective, graduating from an accredited program serves to elevate the education of the health informatics leader. The Commission on Accreditation for Health Informatics and Information Management Education (CAHIIM) is the accrediting body for both health informatics and health information management education programs. AMIA and AHIMA both recognized the growing need for a well-educated work force to lead digital health forward. As such, both professional organizations partner with CAHIIM.

Membership and visibility within professional organizations have merit for students. Understanding the role of professional organizations in education and career development and advancement is important for students and for faculty. In terms of students, our program encourages and supports student involvement in all professional programs. For example, at the first residential visit, all incoming students are provided with HIMSS student memberships. We also support student participation in various extracurriculuar activities sponsored by these professional organizations. Such student-led activities include case competitions, design challenges, code competitions, volunteering at national, state, and regional meetings, etc. We have found that these student-led extracurricular activities provide a layer of real-world education that is difficult to achieve from a book or within a course. These activities also help develop team comraderie and leadership in a way that is different from the classroom. While there is an outcome (1st place, 2nd place, etc.), there is no grade. We have found that this places a different value on the relationships.

In terms of faculty, many of our faculty are consistenly on the rosters of national, state, and regional professional and accreditation organizations. This participation has always been encouraged by department and school leadership. As such, our faculty are frequently in a position to lead and learn from other programs across the nation.

Lessons Learned

1. *Student involvement in professional organizations provides opportunities far exceeding what can be learned in a course.*
2. *Professional organizations are useful for students for leading and learning from others.*

Summary

The educational path that has been forged for future informatics managers has been an interesting and rewarding one. Informaticians, once a voice in the wilderness for promotion of information and communication technologies to improve healthcare outcomes, have begun to see support from professional associations, academia, and more recently, even from public citizens. The joining of these voices has mostly been harmonious, and the traction that has been gained has led to an increasingly higher focus on the necessity of formal informatics education and training. But the present rate of change in both our technical and political realms will ultimately determine our future. Issues such as the fate of the Affordable Care Act payment reform [13], the ability to finally reach true interoperability and to keep up with the unprecedented era of "big data" need to be very carefully considered and integrated into the curriculum. Effective management of technology has the capacity to significantly affect healthcare organizations' business objectives, and the rate of change we are experiencing now will only increase. The ability to impart and balance the enduring curricular components that are the foundation of many programs with the rapid rate of change in the health IT industry will present many new challenges to program directors. With the "digital natives" now integrated into our classrooms, we must shift from our traditional means of delivering education to thinking about reaching students in ways that we have not done before. There is no shortage of management challenges facing us, and our future as program directors, faculty, advisors and mentors remains tenable for the foreseeable future.

Key Take-Away Points

- The changing nature of healthcare and the role of health IT along with significant changes in accreditation models will necessitate ongoing curriculum review and modification to address the emerging needs.
- Health IT practitioner input to academic programs is valuable when students are being trained for health IT roles.
- It is mutually beneficial for health informatics educators to maintain involvement with health informatics professional associations. The associations can provide guidance on curriculum content and networking opportunities for both faculty and students. Health informatics educators' can provide input into professional informatics associations' educational activities.

References

1. Johns ML. The development of a graduate program in health information management. Methods Inf Med. 1994;33(3):278–81.
2. Blumenthal D. Launching HITECH. N Engl J Med. 2010 Feb 4;362(5):382–5.
3. Dorsey AD, Clements K, Garrie RL, Houser SH, Berner ES. Bridging the gap: a collaborative approach to health information management and informatics education. Appl Clin Inform. 2016;6:211–23.
4. Howe S. Where are we now? Statistics on capstone courses nationwide. Adv Eng Educ. 2010;2(1):1–27.
5. Brianna L, Lexis L, Schuijers J, Samiric T, McDonald S. Using capstones to develop research skills and graduate capabilities: a case study from physiology. J Univ Teach Learn Pract. 2012;9(3):6.
6. Dutson AJ, Todd RH, Magleby SP, Sorensen CD. A review of literature on teaching engineering design through project-oriented capstone courses. J Eng Educ. 1997;86(1):17–28.
7. National Institutes of Health: The National Library of Medicine. https://www.nih.gov/about-nih/what-we-do/nih-almanac/national-library-medicine-nlm. Accessed 12 Jan 2020.
8. Merriam Webster Dictionary. Bioinformatics. https://www.merriam-webster.com/dictionary/bioinformatics Accessed 13 Mar 2020.
9. Valenta AL, et al. AMIA Board White Paper: AMIA 2017 core competencies for applied health informatics education at the master's degree level. J Am Med Inf Assoc. 2018;25(12):1657–68.
10. U.S. Department of Health and Human Services [HHS]. Health Information Privacy. http://www.hhs.gov/ocr/privacy/. Accessed 2 Apr 2020.
11. Bodenheimer T, Sinsky C. From triple to quadruple aim: care of the patient requires care of the provider. Ann Fam Med. 2014;12(6):573–6.
12. Davenport T, Kalakota R. The potential for artificial intelligence in healthcare. Future Healthcare J. 2019;6(2):94–8.
13. Patient Protection and Affordable Care Act, 42 U.S.C. § 18001; 2010.

Chapter 5
Translational Bioinformatics Curricula in Graduate Biomedical Informatics Programs

Susan H. Fenton, Assaf Gottlieb, and Meredith Nahm Zozus

Background

Bioinformatics is defined by Merriam-Webster as "the collection, classification, storage, and analysis of biochemical and biological information using computers especially as applied to molecular genetics and genomics" [1]. In 2006, the American Medical Informatics Association (AMIA) defined translational bioinformatics as "the development of storage, analytic, and interpretive methods to optimize the transformation of increasingly voluminous biomedical data, and genomic data, into proactive, predictive, preventive, and participatory health" [2]. There is some vagueness, however, in the distinction and similarity between computational biology and bioinformatics. The definitions have evolved over time, and now some regard bioinformatics as the tools and pipelines, e.g., defining bioinformatics as the "creation of tools (algorithms, databases) that solve problems" where the goal is building useful tools that work on biological data, and classify the pursuit as engineering [3]. In comparison, computational biology has been defined as "the study of biology using computational techniques" where the goal is generating new knowledge about

S. H. Fenton
PI, Gulf Coast Regional Extension Center, UTHealth School of Biomedical Informatics, Houston, TX, USA
e-mail: Susan.H.Fenton@uth.tmc.edu

A. Gottlieb
Center for Precision Health, UTHealth School of Biomedical Informatics (SBMI), Houston, TX, USA
e-mail: Assaf.Gottlieb@uth.tmc.edu

M. N. Zozus (✉)
Clinical Research Informatics, UT Health Science Center San Antonio, San Antonio, TX, USA
e-mail: zozus@uthscsa.edu

© Springer Nature Switzerland AG 2020
E. S. Berner (ed.), *Informatics Education in Healthcare*, Health Informatics,
https://doi.org/10.1007/978-3-030-53813-2_5

biology and living systems [3]. Today however, most research at the molecular and cellular level is reliant in some way on extensive computation.

The need to train individuals for large-scale computation using molecular and cellular-level data has outpaced the supply of skilled individuals and has been pressing since the turn of the century [4]. More recent estimates project further expansion of the TBI workforce to meet these needs [5]. The initial needs saw the rise of approximately 50 masters' programs offering either an MS track or master's degree in bioinformatics in the United States [4]. Bioinformatics and specialized Translational Bioinformatics PhD programs followed.

Federal funding for bioinformatics and translational bioinformatics training has been critical in building capacity to train the next generation of life sciences researchers with computational skills and bioinformatics researchers alike. However, the number of people trained to make use of already available resources and funding, to build the infrastructure, to ask these novel questions, and to answer them is small [6]. The National Science Foundation (NSF) was an important factor in subsidizing the cost and influencing the direction of bioinformatics and computational biology PhD programs in the United States. In 1998, the National Human Genome Research Institute (NHGRI), a component of the National Institutes of Health (NIH) offered support for "predoctoral, postdoctoral and short-term training in genomic analysis and interpretation" [4]. They were joined by the National Institute of General Medical Sciences (NIGMS) focusing on PhD training in bioinformatics and computational biology and the NSF, through its Integrative Graduate Education and Research Training (IGERT) program, supporting cross-disciplinary predoctoral training in bioinformatics. In 2001, in the second cycle of training grant support for pre- and postdoctoral training in medical informatics, The National Library of Medicine (NLM) acknowledged that, "…there will be high demand for specialists capable of applying informatics to biomedical research". As such, NLM emphasized the need for (1) informatics training targeted at biomedical research, and the need for (2) exposure to the informatics of biomedical research in the core training for informaticians [7]. The NLM University-based Biomedical Informatics Training program solicitations since have included a focus area of Translational Bioinformatics, i.e., bioinformatics targeted at improvements in human health. Each of these federal funding programs played a significant role in building capability in universities across the country for educating the second generation of bioinformatics professionals and researchers for the 'post-genomic' era of biomedicine. Chapter 2 describes these training programs in more detail.

Challenges in Bioinformatics Training

Although Friedman and colleagues have emphasized that the interaction between the computational and biomedical sciences, "is the essence of informatics" [8], the concerted command of such disparate disciplines presents significant challenges to preparing individuals with similar facility in each discipline. Significant challenges in broader Bioinformatics education, and specifically in Translational Bioinformatics education, have been articulated in the literature.

One such challenge is that education in Bioinformatics is needed across a continuum of life sciences trainees spanning undergraduate, graduate and post-graduate levels [9–15]. Further, training programs are needed for life sciences researchers as well as those training for research careers focused on development of new methods in Bioinformatics [16, 17]. In addition, due to the speed of bio-technological advances, post graduate skills building and continuing education are needed for life sciences and Bioinformaticists alike. While the need has arguably fluctuated over time [18] there is today continuing demand for bioinformatics education across levels and disciplines [19–21]. Some promote training at all levels—formal and informal [22]. Others have integrated bioinformatics experiences in undergraduate basic science education [23]. Still others have focused training efforts on users of bioinformatics services [24] including, for example, advanced courses on the analysis of microarray and high-throughput sequencing (HTS) data for bench scientists [25]. International collaborative efforts such as the Global Organisation for Bioinformatics Learning, Education and Training, (GOBLET) have developed rigorous training for those in the life sciences [26] and continuing education workshops in bioinformatics [27]. Still others have focused on pre- and postdoctoral training and associated short-term offerings for those developing new bioinformatics methods [4, 8, 28]. Translational Bioinformatics programs may have the opportunity to support, or to share coursework or other curricular experiences with programs focused on different types of trainees. These opportunities for interaction across different types of trainees can enrich training for all.

At the same time, the scientific breadth of even translational bioinformatics can be quite large spanning informatics methods from genes to metabolites [4]. Comprehensive coverage across trainee levels and the reach of genes in biological systems—from genes to metabolites—increases faculty demands. Specialization of faculty and programs of research force strategic decisions that often lead to a focus on one or more areas of biomedical science, e.g., genomics, microbiome, proteomics or structural biology [4]. Specialization increases the effort required for student recruiting and preadmission counseling to assure the appropriate match of student interest and faculty expertise. Given the two-dimensional span across trainee level and genetic reach, lack of faculty has persisted as a key challenge in Bioinformatics education [4, 28, 29].

Differences in knowledge, skills and culture exist between computational and biological disciplines [28, 29]. Curriculum will need to address the science and the culture of the disparate fields, and at the same time, immerse students in both the theory and the experimental aspects of bioinformatics research [4]. For example, seminar speakers from both biological backgrounds as well as computer and information science, and journal clubs should include content from each discipline along with the scientific approach.

Bimodal student backgrounds also present a challenge. The two main groups of students are those with (1) a biological science background and (2) an engineering or computer science background. Some students may have experience in both domains, but are significantly stronger in one [8, 28]. The curriculum will need to support students in acquiring core competency in both the biological and computer and information sciences as well as the theory and the experimental aspects of bioinformatics research and do so within a reasonable timeframe. The scale-up of biomedical research has additionally ushered in an era of high-throughput, big data, and the need for high performance computing and visual analytics [29]. Curriculum development is challenged by the need to balance emphasis on diverse topics across biomedicine and information and computer science with the need for mastery of one or more areas and to do so within a reasonable degree completion time-frame [8].

Existence of career opportunities in Translational Bioinformatics in academic and industry sectors presents multiple challenges to programs. Career exploration and planning toward exposure to the career paths, rewards and challenges in both industry and academic settings becomes necessary within curricula [4] as does opportunity to consider the differences between service or operational positions versus a career as a research scientist. Further, the bioinformatics workforce shortage and lucrative industry opportunities may tempt students to nonacademic positions prior to completing doctoral programs [4].

Finally, bioinformatics research approaches and methods require additional consideration. Today's expectations for open science, sharing and reuse of research resources and data have ushered in an era of comprehensive and detailed documentation, data standardization [29] and metadata. Students need exposure to the data and resource sharing mechanisms, expected data standards, and research reproducibility and replication in general. Today, Bioinformatics program curricula continue to be influenced by these challenges.

Factors in Deciding to Offer Translational Bioinformatics Education

With the addition of translational bioinformatics to informatics domains and activities, multiple biomedical informatics educational programs added translational bioinformatics to their offerings. Today, fourteen of the sixteen NLM T15 programs offer training in Translational Bioinformatics [30].

Incorporating translational bioinformatics education into a biomedical informatics program is a strategic decision to be considered carefully. The most important consideration is whether translational bioinformatics fits with the mission and vision of the current biomedical informatics program. There are important questions to be asked, each of which may have a different prioritization depending on the program.

The needs of the market for biomedical informatics training programs is important, especially for master's prepared graduates. Master's graduates will not be able to scientifically lead translational bioinformatics initiatives, so it is vital to ensure that graduates can find desirable jobs in a reasonable time frame. The market assessment involves convening employers and other interested stakeholders to assess their needs. This is necessary to determine whether the demand for translational bioinformatics graduates is sufficient to support a translational bioinformatics training program. Academic health systems, therapeutic development companies, biotechnology companies and biotechnology software vendors are all possible employers at the masters and doctoral levels. If the program will be offered online, it may be necessary for a program to expand the market assessment beyond the local geographic region.

An assessment of local and regional competition for translational bioinformatics training programs should be conducted by those considering addition of a new program concurrently with the market assessment. In addition to an assessment of any nearby biomedical informatics programs, this may include examining related programs within the university or at other universities. For example, graduate programs in biomedical sciences may already have significant bioinformatics training options, translational or otherwise. If the translational bioinformatics program is to be at the doctoral level, any local master's bioinformatics or similar program will also be direct competition.

The availability of a pipeline of students for the program is important for program success. Estimates of student numbers, as well as sources, must be realistic. The students who are usually interested in translational bioinformatics tend to have a different background from other biomedical informatics students. Bioinformatics students largely possess significant previous training in biology or microbiology or similar fields. However, biomedical informatics students may come from computer science or engineering, health professions fields, or a wide variety of backgrounds that may include non-STEM fields such as business or management, clearly very different from biology. Recruitment efforts will need to encompass new areas and activities to meet enrollment targets. And programs will need to become facile with helping students with such varied backgrounds reach an acceptable competency level in both the biological and computational sciences prior to advanced coursework.

Another consideration is whether the institution already has faculty or access to faculty with the appropriate qualifications in other departments to provide the translational bioinformatics training program. If these faculty are not immediately available, faculty positions may need to be added. Often the approval process for additional faculty positions can be difficult and time-consuming. The interest areas of the faculty should also be a consideration. If for example, all of the faculty are from one lab and focus on one area, for example, Genome Wide Association Studies, (GWAS), it may be difficult to rigorously cover proteomics, protein structural modeling or metabolomics. Such a predominant focus would necessitate declaring the specialty of the program and counseling students on the research opportunities available as well as those that would not be possible in the program. In particular, some trainees rely on temporary academic research positions such as graduate research assistants. This means that not only does the expertise of the faculty need to cover the program courses, but also provide research opportunities for the trainees.

Finally, incorporating a new domain such as translational bioinformatics is likely to result in changes to the structure of the biomedical informatics program. For example, entrance requirements may include biochemistry or molecular biology and may substantially differ for those pursuing the Translational Bioinformatics track. Residency may be necessary to accommodate coursework and research with wet lab components, which would impact primarily online programs. Addition of the track also impacts demands on core courses or necessitates addition of other curricular experiences to best prepare students for upper level Translational Bioinformatics courses or research. Adding Translational Bioinformatics as a new emphasis area may necessitate the addition of a new division or other changes to the programmatic or departmental structure, such as integration with clinical or basic science coursework.

Biomedical informatics continues to evolve and the educational programs must also evolve. A change, such as the addition of translational bioinformatics is a significant undertaking and requires thoughtful planning.

Curriculum

With the 1999 Biomedical Information Science Technology Initiative (BISTI) report on biomedical computing [31], the subsequent American College of Medical Informatics (ACMI) study [8] and the 2001 Workshop on Education in Bioinformatics (WEB) [22] there was a concerted effort to identify and promote strong bioinformatics and Translational Bioinformatics curricula. Altman [28], Zatz [4], Friedman [8], and Ranganathan [22] made early reports of desired features of Bioinformatics programs. These reports suggested establishing structures that promote interdisciplinary collaboration between biologists, computer scientists, those trained as bioinformaticists and others from a broad range of departments [4].

Multiple reports described coursework to level-set and integrate students from disparate backgrounds and to build core competency in biomedical science, computer science, statistics and bioinformatics [4, 8]. The ACMI report [8] further emphasized the need for curricular flexibility to support "individualized gap filling" as well as interest pursuit. The same report specifically advocated that the strongest programs are those that integrated basic information and computing sciences with an appropriate biomedical domain, i.e., where coursework or other curricular experiences explicitly related the basic information or computing sciences to problems in biomedicine [8]. The fraction of the total training experience that explicitly combines basic computational and biomedical topics (rather than covering the material in separate discipline-specific courses and leaving the competency to apply computational methods to cellular and molecular-scale informatics problems to learners to "put two and two together") was offered as an evaluative metric of training programs [8].

Exposure to the scientific methods and culture of both biology and computational disciplines was similarly emphasized in multiple reports [4, 28, 29]. Today, we see inclusion of student participation in, and presentation at, journal clubs, local seminars and attendance at national meetings to expose the students to current bioinformatics research problems and methods for approaching them. Earlier papers emphasized that "bioinformatics students may need more than one advisor for optimal training", asserting that the, "interdisciplinary nature of the field is often manifested in research projects that are jointly administered by biologists and computer scientists" [28]. We continue to see this in our programs. Further emphasizing the need for biomedical domain mentorship, multiple reports advocated research experiences with direct immersion in research and development toward important biomedical problems [4, 8].

The training experiences need to be sufficiently broad biomedically and computationally to avoid producing graduates that are narrowly defined by specific scientific problems such that they are not capable of generalizing from their knowledge and experience to new problems with novel and unanticipated features [8]. This is critical for developing the next generation in a discipline in which the science moves quickly. Further, because the field evolves rapidly, curricula will need to impart competency in self learning [22]. The ACMI study [8] posited that training programs emphasizing multiple application domains across biomedicine offer superior training environments to those that emphasize one application domain exclusively [8].

Effective PhD and post-doctoral training programs are situated in healthy ecosystems of ongoing faculty-directed research in which trainees are directly involved [8]. In addition, exposure to and career advising including academic and nonacademic career options should be available [4]. Curricular experiences that expose trainees to the differences between operational and lead researcher orientations should also be included.

For trainees seeking academic careers, teaching opportunities and instruction in pedagogy are important in order to train future faculty who can educate the next generation of bioinformaticists [4]. Training in ethics relevant to bioinformatics research and practice [4] and today, training in responsible conduct of research is required of those in federally supported training positions [32].

Altman [28], Friedman [8], and Welch [17] have all articulated topics to be covered in Bioinformatics programs. Multiple others, e.g., Dubay et al. [29] describe curricular aspects of particular programs. Unfortunately, curricular information needed to facilitate comprehensive characterization of programs is often not available online. Like Welch et al. [17] we attempted an inventory of topics covered and courses offered by programs based on publicly available information on program web sites. In doing so, we found differences in how specific topics are partitioned among courses and varying specificity of information on the content of specific courses. This variability would have severely limited the accuracy and thus, utility of such an approach. Welch et al. similarly concluded that self-reporting of program features by cognizant program officials would be the best mechanism to produce a survey that is comprehensive, inclusive, and accurate [17].

In 2012, Welch et al. reported results from the Curriculum Task Force of the International Society for Computational Biology (ISCB) survey of Bioinformatics core facility directors [33]. The 2012 ISCB survey was conducted to gather input regarding the skill set needed by bioinformaticians and found that widespread disparities across programs in what was taught, how it was taught, and the intended target audiences. The survey was followed in 2014, with further work including an analysis of career opportunities and existing curricula toward a definition of curricular guidelines for training bioinformaticians [17]. From their work, a set of Bioinformatics competencies was developed for three levels of trainees, (1) Bioinformatics users—defined as those "who access data resources to perform job duties in specific application domains," (2) Bioinformatics scientists—defined as "biologists who employ computational methods in order to advance the scientific understanding of living systems", and (3) Bioinformatics engineers—defined as those who "create the novel computational methods needed by bioinformatics users and scientists" [17]. The work was further developed through competency workshops at ISCB and GOBLET meetings and resulted in the refined set of 16 ISCB Core Competencies for Bioinformatics listed below [16].

A. General biology
B. Depth in at least one area of biology (e.g., evolutionary biology, genetics, molecular biology, biochemistry, anatomy, physiology).
C. Biological data generation technologies.
D. Details of the scientific discovery process and of the role of bioinformatics in it.
E. Statistical research methods in the context of molecular biology, genomics, medical, and population genetics research.
F. Bioinformatics tools and their usage.
G. The ability of a computer-based system, process, algorithm, component, or program to meet desired needs in scientific environments/problem.
H. Computing requirements appropriate to solve a given scientific problem (e.g., system, process, algorithm, component or program; define algorithmic time and space complexities and hardware resources required to solve a problem).
 I. GUI/Web-based computing skills appropriate to the discipline (e.g., effectively use bioinformatics and analysis tools through web).
J. Command line and scripting-based computing skills appropriate to the discipline.
K. Construction of software systems of varying complexity based on design and development principles.
L. Local and global impact of bioinformatics and genomics on individuals, organizations, and society.
M. Professional, ethical, legal, security, and social issues, and responsibilities of bioinformatics and genomic data in the workplace.
N. Effective communication of bioinformatics and genomics problem/issue/topics with a range of audiences, including, but not limited to, other bioinformatics professionals.
O. Effective teamwork to accomplish a common scientific goal.
P. Engage in continuing professional development in bioinformatics.

The competencies are applied to ten personas such as a physician, a life sciences researcher or a Bioinformatics software engineer to illustrate the goals of each type of learner and to connect those to relevant curricular experiences. To support this, the competencies are leveled for each role at the appropriate level on the revised Bloom's Taxonomy [34].

Altman recommended the following entrance requirements: undergraduate exposure to the natural sciences (physics, chemistry, biology) in addition to quantitative technical disciplines (computer programming, applied mathematics, basic statistics) [28]. In the program at the University of Arkansas for Medical Sciences (UAMS), strong incumbents lacking in one but not both areas have been conditionally accepted with the requirement that coursework to fill the gap be completed by the end of the first semester in the program. It has been suggested, that addition of basic bioinformatics at the undergraduate level, especially for life science majors and optionally for physical and computer science majors would develop the multidisciplinary skills required for bioinformatics [22].

Magana et al. [35] in a review of the bioinformatics education literature, identified a need to clearly define the curriculum and the content that should be taught together with appropriate pedagogical approaches and evaluation and assessment mechanisms. They reported that evaluations were often based on final course grades and student self-assessments, perceptions of the materials, confidence in attaining specific learning outcomes, and attitudes toward the learning experience. As such, they recommended that evaluations go beyond these and move toward assessing learning outcomes and rigorous research in bioinformatics education. They found little evidence of documented curricular alignment of learning objectives and their assessment reported in the bioinformatics educational literature and concluded that there was a need for better identification of learning outcomes and better integration of assessment and pedagogical methods [35].

Insights from Bioinformatics Programs

When erecting a bioinformatics program, it is worthwhile to learn from experience of existing programs. We share here insights from two programs: The University of Texas Health Science Center's School of Biomedical Informatics (SBMI) and Department of Biomedical Informatics, Biomedical Informatics graduate program in the University of Arkansas for Medical Sciences (UAMS). While two programs are not representative of the entire range of programs available across the US, they may provide important insights. The SBMI Translational Bioinformatics track undertook curriculum development in Spring, 2017 and enrolled its first students in Fall of 2018. The UAMS Translational Bioinformatics Track initiated curriculum development in 2015 and enrolled the first cohort in the fall of 2016.

The first challenge that faculty from SBMI faced in initiating their bioinformatics program was deciding on the initial offerings. As no input from prospective students was available at the time, faculty had to form a curriculum based on available offerings from other programs and from the core competencies of the existing faculty. One insight from that process is that whatever the initial offering is, be prepared to evolve the program based on early experience and evaluation as well as the demand for the elective courses and inputs from "early adopter" students. The curriculum committee at UAMS initially faced the challenge by conducting an environmental scan of existing Translational Bioinformatics programs. However, for the aforementioned reasons, primarily lack of sufficiently detailed and publicly available information on program web pages, the initial environmental scan was only of superficial value. To develop the core courses, intended to be taken by students in all Biomedical Informatics tracks, the curriculum committee iteratively enumerated topics needed by all Masters' and Doctoral students. Each topic was leveled for each track according to the highest level needed for the track using the following categories.

0—No knowledge of the topic is required for the track
1—Awareness: general highest-level knowledge about a topic including definitions, composition, typology and relationships to other relevant topics
2—Conceptual knowledge: theory, concepts and principles of the topic; how and why something works with no expectation of applying the concepts or tools to accomplish a task
3—Procedural knowledge: How to apply methods or tools to accomplish a task, i.e., application of a tool or analysis technique to analyze data
4—Engineering knowledge: Application of theory, methods and tools to recognize a problem and to design, build and implement a solution for it. In professional informatics, this is referred to as Tower of Achievement (TOA)
5—Scientific knowledge: Application of the aforementioned knowledge and research training to identify knowledge gaps in a discipline and design, conduct and report research that generates the needed knowledge.

The least common level was taken as the cognitive level at which the topic would be covered in the core courses. This created an explicit boundary for each track where the pre-requisite core left off and the track-specific courses needed to start for good curricular scaffolding. After the initial core course was taught, the core topics were re-arranged into an expanded 15 hour core comprised of three, 3-credit hour courses titled: (1) Biomedicine for Informaticists, (2) Information Modelling—From Data to Knowledge, and (3) Computational Methods for Informaticists, and three 2-credit hour survey courses including Sequences & Biologic Information, Clinical Information and Public Health Information.

A second challenge involved raising awareness about the new offered program. This was done through internal advertisements to students enrolled in other biomedical informatics programs as well advertisements to prospective students in other sources of media. However, a good source for incoming students in the SBMI program was the introductory course to bioinformatics, where students were exposed to the topics and faculty from higher level courses through faculty lectures in the introductory course. This led to the third challenge, which involved maintaining a constant stream of students through the program. The UAMS Translational Bioinformatics Track recruits students at career and graduate fairs at primarily universities in Arkansas, regional Bioinformatics meetings such as the Mid-South

Computational Biology & Bioinformatics (MCBIOS) meeting, and the web pages of Translational Bioinformatics track Faculty. Part of the insight from the SBMI and UAMS programs was the recognition of the need for constant monitoring of the number of enrolled students in each course, learning to prune or shift to every other year courses that garnered less interest.

A challenge to any program, and a bioinformatics program in particular, is the evaluation of whether graduating students have acquired the needed skill sets to advance their academic or industry careers. SBMI has only begun to conduct the initial evaluation of the graduates pursuing academic paths, but, as a result, initiated a process to reevaluate the program aims. The UAMS program has created an initial evaluation plan, but as of this writing was only in its third year.

Trends for the Future Program Design

Bioinformatics is still a constantly evolving field and correspondingly, bioinformatics programs should continuously evolve to meet the changing needs and trends in the field. As a global trend, it is anticipated that Bioinformaticians will need to be very versatile and have understanding that extends into clinical domain knowledge and software design. These are several trends in bioinformatics programs that we see emerging and which could impact the curriculum of bioinformatics programs in the near future.

1. **Partnering to provide Bioinformatics Literacy and Basic Quantitative Training for Students in Basic Biomedical Science Graduate Programs.** One trend that is already happening is the initiation of programs that serve multiple types of researchers, coming from diverse disciplines such as schools of medicine and biology departments. This trend has persisted, is visible in the literature and will require Bioinformatics programs to accommodate different levels of knowledge and skills and correspondingly fit the courses to these different populations. Partnering with other disciplines will benefit both those disciplines by exposing them to the new technologies and research opportunities. This partnership will also benefit the Bioinformatics community, exposing them to existing research questions that can potentially be solved using bioinformatics approaches. Finally, enhancing the literacy of physicians in the understanding and interpretation of genomics and other 'omics data should be integrated into the core medical curriculum [36].

2. **Translation of Bioinformatics Findings into the Clinical Setting**. While many existing bioinformatics programs tend to stand on their own with little overlap with other fields of biomedical informatics, in order to prepare students for a bioinformatics-oriented career, an integration with clinical aspects of biomedicine becomes indispensable. As genetic information and its interpretation is moving from the bench to the bedside and revolutionizing healthcare, bioinformaticians will need to understand the clinical aspects in order to keep

pace with the changes. The following are examples of such integration. The first example is the translation of results from the bench to the bedside. Traversing the gap from bench to bedside requires the intent to impact assessment of disease risk, prevention and treatment, often involving putting high throughput data such as genotype and transcriptional data into clinical use. The road between useful results in the lab, and implementation in a health system is often long and full of hazards. Bioinformaticians who have also been trained in other aspects of Biomedical Informatics, in particular those in health systems, could serve as mediators of such a process.

The second example follows the insertion of interfaces such as the Health Level Seven (HL7) Fast Healthcare Interoperability Resources (FHIR) framework into electronic health records systems. This interface enables integration of genetic data into the health records and enables clinicians to get both the genetic and the clinical view of the patient in one system. This insertion of genetic knowledge into clinical systems involves significant gaps. These gaps include limited literacy and training for clinicians in interpreting results and difficulties in translation of these results into clinical actions. Also, in this scenario, bioinformaticians could play a key role in serving as a bridge between the clinicians and the genetic information, but this would involve better understanding of the clinical aspects that a stand-alone bioinformatics program may not provide.

3. **Increase in Use of Data from Genes and Gene Products in Clinical Studies**. As the amount and breadth of gene information increases, so does the need to validate computational findings in clinical studies such as clinical trials. Although today there may be limited use of genetic information in clinical trials, we expect this to change in the coming years. A recent study of clinical data management competencies and practice settings [37] documented the growing diversity of studies for which data were managed and the types of data managed and those anticipated in the future. Data about genes and gene products ranked highly. Knowledge about clinical study design and conduct needs to be incorporated into bioinformatics programs in order to provide skilled personnel to support the increasing number of studies collecting and using genetic information and for those individuals to be considered invaluable parts of such trials by pharmaceutical companies and by the emerging artificial intelligence start-ups that target the pharmaceuticals market.

4. **Consumer Needs for Interpretation of Direct-to-Consumer Genetic Testing Results.** Direct-to-consumer (DTC) genetic testing has been accelerating in the past decade following sharp decreases in test costs, with many companies entering the market. While initial tests focused on detecting relatives and providing ancestral origins of the customers, these DTC companies have recognized that health information is a highly sought-out added value that consumers seek. However, regulatory considerations restrict the interpretation of the genetic results to a few well-established cases. We anticipate that the demand to connect genetics and phenotyping will nevertheless increase, with the spawning of specialized companies already underway. Tenenbaum suggests that translational bioinformatics programs should consider three potential effects of these devel-

opments in the curriculum: (1) the emphasis on the clinical aspects of new findings, i.e. how established is the evidence and are there actions that a consumer can take once becoming aware of the results; (2) whether there should be the addition of ethics components that will enable evaluation of the potential risks in revealing incidental genetic findings to consumers, especially when the evidence is inconclusive or there are no actions that the consumer can take with regard to a new finding; and (3) whether there needs to be more emphasis on privacy, focused on the specific privacy issues associated with genetics, revealing details that are not specific only to the consumer but also their relatives or even their racial or ethnic group [38].

5. **Increase in Automation and Available Tools**. An evolving trend in Bioinformatics is the increase in automation and available tools for individuals that have limited-to-no training in bioinformatics. This is a natural step in the development and dissemination of technology but will require bioinformaticians to leave the traditional command line interfaces in favor of more approachable graphic tools that can accommodate researchers with more basic computational skills. They will need to master the steps that are part of traditional software development, including software and interface tool design, deployment of the tool and support its users. Human interface designs and visualization techniques should be added to the programs in order to prepare bioinformaticians for this likely eventuality.

This commendable step comes with a caveat, however. While these tools often provide push-button results, without clear understanding of the underlying computational methodology, the results may be biased or lead to wrong interpretations. Researchers and students need to have good understanding of how the algorithms upon which the tool was built work, the limitation and case scenarios where the tool is expected to perform well, and the expected effects of tuning each parameter of the program. In practicality, this will not only require the bioinformatician to design good tools, but also provide adequate tutorials and usage examples in order to educate the user about the limitations and the different use cases relevant to the tool. In terms of programs, this would include teaching students about instructional design, proper documentation and clarity in writing.

Key Lessons Learned

1. Translational bioinformatics is a broad field. Twenty years after the initial programs were started, schools seeking to implement these programs still face challenges.
2. The decision to implement a translational bioinformatics program must be carefully considered from many perspectives including but not limited to organizational structure, faculty, and student recruitment.

3. There is no one single translational bioinformatics curriculum and no accreditation exists for these programs, although core competencies have been recommended by the International Society for Computational Biology (ICSB).
4. Translational bioinformatics programs are constantly evolving.

References

1. Merriam-Webster.com "Bioinformatics." Dictionary, Merriam-Webster, https://www.merriam-webster.com/dictionary/bioinformatics. Accessed 15 Mar 2020.
2. Americal Medical Informatics Association (AMIA), Informatics areas: translational bioinformatics. https://www.amia.org/applications-informatics/translational-bioinformatics. Accessed 15 Mar 2020.
3. Altman RB, Bioinformatics & Computational Biology = same? https://rbaltman.wordpress.com/2009/02/18/bioinformatics-computational-biology-same-no/. Accessed 8 Mar 2020.
4. Zatz MM. Bioinformatics training in the USA. Brief Bioinform. 2002;3(4):353–60.
5. Overby CL, Tarczy-Hornoch P. Personalized medicine: challenges and opportunities for translational bioinformatics. Per Med. 2013;10(5):453–62. https://doi.org/10.2217/pme.13.30.
6. Butte AJ. Translational bioinformatics: coming of age. J Am Med Inform Assoc. 2008;15(6):709–14.
7. National Institutes of Health, National Library of Medicine, Institutional training grants for informatics research, RFA-LM-01-001. Release Date: March 29, 2001. https://grants.nih.gov/grants/guide/rfa-files/RFA-LM-01-001.html. Accessed 16 May 2020.
8. Friedman CP, Altman RB, Kohane IS, McCormick KA, Miller PL, Ozbolt JG, Shortliffe EH, Stormo GD, Szczepaniak MC, Tuck D, Williamson J, American College of Medical Informatics. Training the next generation of informaticians: the impact of "BISTI" and bioinformatics—a report from the American College of Medical Informatics. J Am Med Inform Assoc. 2004;11(3):167–72.
9. Williams JJ, Teal TK. A vision for collaborative training infrastructure for bioinformatics. Ann N Y Acad Sci. 2017;1387(1):54–60.
10. Brazas MD, Blackford S, Attwood TK. Training: Plug gap in essential bioinformatics skills. Nature. 2017;544(7649):161.
11. Clay MR, Fisher KE. Bioinformatics education in pathology training: current scope and future direction. Cancer Inform. 2017;16 https://doi.org/10.1177/1176935117703389.
12. Emery LR, Morgan SL. The application of project-based learning in bioinformatics training. PLoS Comput Biol. 2017;13(8):e1005620.
13. Smith DR. Bringing bioinformatics to the scientific masses: as the demand for high-level bioinformatics is growing, training students in the field becomes ever important. EMBO Rep. 2018;19(6):e46262.
14. Wilson Sayres MA, Hauser C, Sierk M, Robic S, Rosenwald AG, Smith TM, Triplett EW, Williams JJ, Dinsdale E, Morgan WR, Burnette JM 3rd, Donovan SS, Drew JC, SCR E, Fowlks ER, Galindo-Gonzalez S, Goodman AL, Grandgenett NF, Goller CC, Jungck JR, Newman JD, Pearson W, Ryder EF, Tosado-Acevedo R, Tapprich W, Tobin TC, Toro-Martínez A, Welch LR, Wright R, Barone L, Ebenbach D, McWilliams M, Olney KC, Pauley MA. Bioinformatics core competencies for undergraduate life sciences education. PLoS One. 2018;13(6):e0196878.
15. Attwood TK, Blackford S, Brazas MD, Davies A, Schneider MV. A global perspective on evolving bioinformatics and data science training needs. Brief Bioinform. 2019;20(2):398–404.
16. Mulder N, Schwartz R, Brazas MD, Brooksbank C, Gaeta B, Morgan SL, Pauley MA, Rosenwald A, Rustici G, Sierk M, Warnow T, Welch L. The development and application of

bioinformatics core competencies to improve bioinformatics training and education. PLoS Comput Biol. 2018;14(2):e1005772.

17. Welch L, Lewitter F, Schwartz R, Brooksbank C, Radivojac P, Gaeta B, Schneider MV. Bioinformatics curriculum guidelines: toward a definition of core competencies. PLoS Comput Biol. 2014;10(3):e1003496.

18. Gollery M. An assessment of the current state of bioinformatics education. Bioinformation. 2006;1(7):247.

19. Tractenberg RE, Lindvall JM, Attwood TK, Via A. The Mastery Rubric for bioinformatics: a tool to support design and evaluation of career-spanning education and training. PLoS One. 2019;14(11):e0225256.

20. Williams JJ, Drew JC, Galindo-Gonzalez S, Robic S, Dinsdale E, Morgan WR, Triplett EW, Burnette JM, Donovan SS, Fowlks ER, Goodman AL, Grandgenett NF, Goller CC, Hauser C, Jungck JR, Newman JD, Pearson WR, Ryder EF, Sierk M, Smith TM, Tosado-Acevedo R, Tapprich W, Tobin TC, Toro-Martínez A, Welch LR, Wilson MA, Ebenbach D, McWilliams M, Rosenwald AG, Pauley MA. Barriers to integration of bioinformatics into undergraduate life sciences education: a national study of US life sciences faculty uncover significant barriers to integrating bioinformatics into undergraduate instruction. PLoS One. 2019;14(11):e0224288.

21. McGrath A, Champ K, Shang CA, van Dam E, Brooksbank C, Morgan SL. From trainees to trainers to instructors: sustainably building a national capacity in bioinformatics training. PLoS Comput Biol. 2019;15(6):e1006923.

22. Ranganathan S. Bioinformatics education—perspectives and challenges. PLoS Comput Biol. 2005;1(6):e52.

23. Furge LL, Stevens-Truss R, Moore DB, Langeland JA. Vertical and horizontal integration of bioinformatics education: a modular, interdisciplinary approach. Biochem Mol Biol Educ. 2009;37(1):26–36.

24. Schneider MV, Watson J, Attwood T, Rother K, Budd A, McDowall J, Via A, Fernandes P, Nyronen T, Blicher T, Jones P, Blatter MC, De Las RJ, Judge DP, van der Gool W, Brooksbank C. Bioinformatics training: a review of challenges, actions and support requirements. Brief Bioinform. 2010;11(6):544–51.

25. Carvalho BS, Rustici G. The challenges of delivering bioinformatics training in the analysis of high-throughput data. Brief Bioinform. 2013;14(5):538–47.

26. Attwood TK, Bongcam-Rudloff E, Brazas ME, Corpas M, Gaudet P, Lewitter F, Mulder N, Palagi PM, Schneider MV, van Gelder CW, GOBLET Consortium. GOBLET: the global organisation for bioinformatics learning, education and training. PLoS Comput Biol. 2015;11(4):e1004143.

27. Brazas MD, Ouellette BF. Continuing education workshops in bioinformatics positively impact research and careers. PLoS Comput Biol. 2016;12(6):e1004916.

28. Altman RB. A curriculum for bioinformatics: the time is ripe. Bioinformatics. 1998;14(7):549–50.

29. Dubay C, Brundege JM, Hersh W, Spackman K. Delivering bioinformatics training: bridging the gaps between computer science and biomedicine. Proc AMIA Symp. 2002;2002:220–4.

30. National Institutes of Health, National Library of Medicine (NIH-NLM), Areas of emphasis for NLM's University-based Biomedical Informatics and Data Science Training Programs. https://www.nlm.nih.gov/ep/GrantTrainInstitute.html. Accessed 15 Jan 2020.

31. National Institutes of Health, National Library of Medicine (NIH-NLM), National Library of Medicine programs and services 2000. Publication no. 80-256. National Library of Medicine, Bethesda MD.

32. National Institutes of Health, NOT-OD-10-019, Update on the Requirement for Instruction in the Responsible Conduct of Research, November 24, 2009. https://grants.nih.gov/grants/guide/notice-files/not-od-10-019.html. Accessed 3 Mar 2020.

33. Welch LR, Schwartz R, Lewitter F. A report of the Curriculum Task Force of the ISCB Education Committee. PLOS Comput Biol. 2012;8:e1002570.
34. Anderson LW, Krathwohl DR, editors. A taxonomy for learning, teaching, and assessing: a revision of Bloom's taxonomy of educational objectives. Boston, MA: Allyn & Bacon; 2001.
35. Magana AJ, Taleyarkhan M, Alvarado DR, Kane M, Springer J, Clase K. A survey of scholarly literature describing the field of bioinformatics education and bioinformatics educational research. CBE Life Sci Educ. 2014;13(4):607–23.
36. Yan B, Ban KHK, Tan TW. Integrating translational bioinformatics into the medical curriculum. Int J Med Educ. 2014;5:132–4.
37. Zozus MN, Lazarov A, Smith LR, Breen TE, Krikorian SL, Zbyszewski PS, Knoll SK, Jendrasek DA, Perrin DC, Zambas DN, Williams TB, Pieper CF. Analysis of professional competencies for the clinical research data management profession: implications for training and professional certification. J Am Med Inform Assoc. 2017;24(4):737–45.
38. Tenenbaum J. Translational bioinformatics: past, present and future. Genomics Proteomics Bioinformatics. 2016;14(1):31–41.

Chapter 6
Undergraduate Health Informatics Education

Saif Khairat and Sue S. Feldman

Introduction

Health Informatics Education continues to expand to encompass almost all clinical specialties and Information Technology (IT) domains. The focus on health informatics education has primarily been within graduate studies such as Masters, PhD, or the new Sub-Specialty in Clinical Informatics. Due to the variety in post-graduate education, graduate students and/or returning professionals have various informatics training opportunities. Additionally, new emerging initiatives have focused on introducing health informatics to high school students [1]. However, Health informatics education at the undergraduate level is not as well established. Despite graduate-level initiatives such as the Health Information Technology Scholars (TIGER) initiative, the Office of the National Coordinator for Health Information Technology (ONC) Workforce Development program, and others, there is still a need to provide inter-professional education at the undergraduate level [2–5]. As the field of informatics continues to grow and healthcare becomes more complex and data driven, there is a growing need to introduce fundamental health informatics concepts to undergraduate students to enhance their knowledge base and stimulate their interest and possible pursuit of a career in health informatics.

There is a critical need to develop interprofessional undergraduate Health Informatics (HI) programs that address fundamental informatics concepts and core competency knowledge, skills, and attitudes. Building a broad-based undergraduate

S. Khairat (✉)
Carolina Health Informatics Program, University of North Carolina at Chapel Hill, Chapel Hill, NC, USA

School of Nursing, University of North Carolina at Chapel Hill, Chapel Hill, NC, USA
e-mail: Saif@unc.edu

S. S. Feldman
University of Alabama at Birmingham, Birmingham, AL, USA
e-mail: sfeldman@uab.edu

© Springer Nature Switzerland AG 2020
E. S. Berner (ed.), *Informatics Education in Healthcare*, Health Informatics,
https://doi.org/10.1007/978-3-030-53813-2_6

health informatics program would include core undergraduate informatics competencies allowing various graduate health informatics education pathways. Such education pathways include continuing in health informatics or one of the many sub-specialties such as nursing informatics (as a registered nurse), bioinformatics, etc.

As is the case with many undergraduate programs, providing an opportunity for undergraduate students to major in health informatics provides a structured learning environment that can create an awareness of the discipline as well as facilitate the transition to the kind of cognition needed for graduate work.

Need for Undergraduate Health Informatics Education

The need for undergraduate health informatics education is apparent. Many high schools have education and career pathways introducing students to the alignment of college education and associated careers. Accredited graduate health informatics programs are increasing at rapid rates (https://www.cahiim.org/programs/program-directory). The gap that we have identified is the lack of widespread offerings of undergraduate health informatics programs. Having such widespread undergraduate health informatics program offerings would not only support graduate health informatics programs, but also would support other graduate programs that are starting to realize the importance of including health informatics content in their programs (examples include health administration, physical therapy, occupational therapy, quality and safety, etc.).

Undergraduate health informatics education creates a much-needed bridge between high school and graduate school. Furthermore, description of health informatics majors would provide high school guidance counselors with a basis from which to inform themselves about the benefits of health informatics as a viable profession and career path for their high school students.

As we begin to think about the ecosystem of health informatics education and its reach from high school through graduate school, the need for undergraduate health informatics education comes into focus. In order to better understand the need for undergraduate health informatics programs, it is essential to understand the current state of undergraduate health informatics education—what it is, what it is not, and what it can become.

Current State of Undergraduate Health Informatics

Several U.S. and international institutions have developed an undergraduate major in health informatics. However, some programs rely heavily on previously developed health information management curricula with a combination of both health informatics and health information management (HIM) without a clear focus on either one. While this provides a broad base of awareness for the student, it risks not providing the knowledge that is needed to be successful in rigorous graduate health informatics programs. Furthermore, it perpetuates a confusion between health information management and health informatics.

As we think about advocating for competencies for undergraduate health informatics programs, it is critical to provide increased specificity around the differences between HIM and HI. HIM is "the profession specifically devoted to health record science and classification/terminology, continues to play an integral role in ensuring the proper secondary use of patient data" [6]. Health informatics (HI) can be defined as "the acquisition, storage, and use of information in a specific setting or domain" [7]. The differences between HIM and HI exist in the scope of HI that includes patient-centered tools, provider-facing tools, and provider-patient interactions. Therefore, it is important to realize that constructing an HI curriculum should be different from an HIM curriculum. HI focuses on individuals, whether patients or providers, as well as Health Information Technology (HIT), while HIM has a distinct and important focus on standards such as taxonomies and ontologies to ensure high-quality data exchange between HIT systems.

We did a scan of current global undergraduate health informatics offerings. This initial scan, shown in Table 6.1, speaks to the inconsistency across curricula and credits for a traditionally defined undergraduate major in health informatics. Traditional undergraduate education is 120 credits with 60 of those credits occurring in the chosen major field of study [8].

Table 6.1 Undergraduate programs in health informatics (as of June 5, 2020)

University	School	Degree	Time	Health Informatics major credits
University of Waterloo, Ontario, CAN	Public Health and Health Systems	Health Informatics	6–8 courses	Not found online
York University, Toronto, CAN	School of Health Policy and Management	Cross-Disciplinary Certificate In HI in addition to undergrad course	Not found online	30 credits
Dalhousie, Nova Scotia, CAN	School of Computer Science	Bachelor of Informatics	4 years	Not found online
Athabasca University , Alberta, CAN	Faculty of Health Disciplines	Nursing Informatics	Not found online	3
University of Victoria, Victoria, CAN	School of Health Information Science	B. Sci in Health Information Science	4 years	Not found online
Conestoga College, Ontario, CAN	School of Health and Life Sciences	Bachelor of Applied HI	4 years	Not found online
Penn State World campus Online, PA	RN-BS program	Undergraduate certificate in Nursing Informatics	Not found online	9 credits

(continued)

Table 6.1 (continued)

University	School	Degree	Time	Health Informatics major credits
University of Tasmania, Australia	College of Health & Medicine	Bachelor of eHealth	2–5 years	Not found online
University of Leeds, England	Yorkshire Centre of Health Informatics	Undergraduate medical degree	4 years	Not found online
University of Heidelberg, Germany	Not found online	Bachelor in medical informatics	4 years	Not found online
eHCF School of Medical Informatics, India	Not found online	e-health care foundation medical informatics certificate	3 months	Not found online
University of South Alabama, AL	Information Systems and Technology	BS in Health Informatics	4 years	40
Georgia State University, GA	College of Nursing and Health Professions and College of Business	Bachelor of Interdisciplinary Studies in health informatics	4 years	60
Georgia State University, GA	Computer Science and Health Administration	Bachelor of Business Administration::CIS	4 years	21
King University, GA	Not found online	BS Health Informatics	4 years	48
University of Iowa, IA	Computer Science	BA Informatics	4 years	46
University of Coastal Georgia, GA	Not found online	BS Health Informatics	4 years	Not found online
University of Central Florida	Community Innovation and Education	BS in Health Informatics and Information Management	4 years	Not found online
Northern Kentucky University	Not found online	BS Health Informatics	4 years	22

An important corollary to understanding the current state of undergraduate programs in health informatics is program accreditation. In the US, the Commission on Accreditation for Health Informatics and Information Management Education (CAHIIM) accredits **undergraduate health information management (HIM)** programs and **graduate health informatics (HI)** programs.

Acceleration of accreditation for graduate programs in health informatics has been driven by a maturing HI field and the collaboration of the American Medical Informatics Association (AMIA) and CAHIIM to establish educational foundational domains and associated accreditation standards, respectively. This need for the establishment of educational focus and accreditation standards also exists in undergraduate health informatics programs. One solution would be adoption of the AMIA Foundational Domains, development of competencies, and alignment with CAHIIM accreditation standards.

Foundational Domains for Undergraduate Health Informatics Education

Foundational domains for graduate health informatics education are well established. As such, it makes sense to adapt the same foundational domains as the basis for undergraduate health informatics education. It is important to note that in final development there likely will not be a linear translation in the foundational domains, but rather an adaptation of the foundational domains. This is primarily because the foundational domains were developed for graduate students—those coming with a general education background, whereas for undergraduate students, they would be in the process of getting a general education background. As a start, we propose beginning with the foundational domains set by AMIA for graduate health informatics education [9], with a plan to adapt them for undergraduate health informatics education. The current foundational domains are:

- F1-Health,
- F2-Information Science and Technology,
- F3-Social and Behavioral Science,
- F4-Health Information Science and Technology,
- F5-Human Factors and Socio-technical Systems,
- F6-Social and Behavioral Aspects of Health,
- F7-Social, Behavioral, and Information Science and Technology Applied to Health,
- F8-Professionalism,
- F9-Interpersonal Collaborative Practice, and
- F10-Leadership.

Detailed descriptions of the foundational domains can be found in the 2017 AMIA Board White Paper on core competencies [9]. More information about the genesis of the foundational domains can be found in Chap. 17.

Within each foundational domain are competencies. The competencies for graduate health informatics education set the stage for identifying similar competencies for undergraduate health informatics education. We propose that the competencies for undergraduate health informatics education could provide awareness of the general knowledge upon which graduate health informatics education can build. Ideally, this progression of education would better prepare students for the rigor and independence of a graduate health informatics program. This rigor and independence can be realized in the Miller's Levels as adapted for Health Informatics.

Miller's Pyramid as Adapted for Health Informatics

Miller's Pyramid, originally developed for clinical graduate education [10], was adapted for graduate health informatics education. This adaptation was accomplished as a means to provide CAHIIM with a way to assess knowledge, skills, and attitudes for accreditation standards. Chapter 17 explains Miller's Pyramid in more detail, but briefly Miller's Pyramid is a framework for graduate medical education student assessment in the clinical environment [10]. Miller defined four levels of assessment from assessment of basic knowledge to performance in practice. Because of the ability to align knowledge, skills, and attitudes with traditional uses of Miller's pyramid, in January 2017, CAHIIM adapted Miller's Pyramid for use in graduate health informatics education.

Whereas the graduate level pyramid covers all four levels of Miller's Pyramid as adapted for health informatics (KNOW, KNOWS HOW, SHOWS, DOES), we suggest that the undergraduate level of Miller's Pyramid should build on previous work [11], and that it be further adapted for undergraduate health informatics to include two additional layers (HEARD OF and KNOWS ABOUT) and would overlap with the graduate level by including KNOWS and KNOWS HOW. Figure 6.1 illustrates

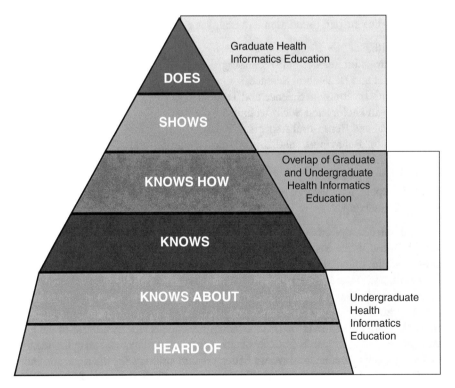

Fig. 6.1 Miller's Pyramid as adapted for health informatics (adapted with permission from Cheeks [11])

each level as well as the overlap of graduate and undergraduate health informatics education.

HEARD OF and KNOWS ABOUT can be thought of as the underpinnings to higher levels of knowledge, skills and attitudes for creating an awareness that is often the precursor to cognition. For example, as students progress from being introduced to/aware of a concept (HEARD OF) to knowing *about* the concept (KNOWS ABOUT), they increase in professional authenticity and progress by integrating critical thinking with previously learned knowledge (KNOWS) and advance toward demonstrating that they know how to use the knowledge (KNOWS HOW).

The HEARD OF, KNOWS ABOUT, and KNOWS all align with the AMIA Foundational Domains F1, F2, and F3 as they represent foundational *knowledge* [9], or as in the case of HEARD OF and KNOWS ABOUT, *awareness*. The KNOWS HOW level best aligns with AMIA Foundational Domains F4-F10 that include knowledge, skills, and attitudes [9] and prepares the undergraduate student for performance at the SHOWS HOW and DOES level in graduate health informatics education.

To incorporate knowledge, skills, and attitudes into the framework presented above, we recommend following the work initiated by CAHIIM's Health Informatics Accreditation Council (HIAC), drawing on work done by Mehay and Burns [12]. To draw on this work, we propose that the undergraduate portion of the Miller's Pyramid as adapted for health informatics develops awareness at the first two layers (HEARD OF and KNOWS ABOUT) and then progresses to cognition (KNOWS and KNOWS HOW) to prepare the student for the higher behavioral levels of the pyramid (SHOWS and DOES) that are accomplished in graduate level health informatics education (see Chap. 17 for more detail on the behavior levels).

Recognizing that programs may have different foci, each undergraduate health informatics program decides to what degree each competency is assessed within the four levels of the Miller's Pyramid as adapted for health informatics (HEARD OF, KNOWS ABOUT, KNOWS, AND KNOWS HOW).

Concepts of Undergraduate Health Informatics Education

As the field of HI expands to cover undergraduate education, educators and administrators need to think about the core competencies required in order to prepare the future workforce. While much work has been done toward establishing graduate level health informatics competencies across various disciplines, [3, 5, 9, 13–16] little has been done to establish core competencies for undergraduate health informatics education. A precursor to developing those core competencies is to develop concepts around which an undergraduate health informatics curriculum could be built. Using the graduate level health informatics foundational domains developed by Valenta et al. [9], we suggest curricular concepts for undergraduate health informatics education that begin to align with core competencies at the appropriate Miller's Level for undergraduate education (see Fig. 6.1).

- Concept # 1: Define Health Informatics: This concept would define the scope of the field to educate students about the role of a health informatics professional within healthcare.
- Concept #2: Comparative Health Systems: This concept covers healthcare delivery, policy, and reimbursement systems across North America. The objective of teaching this concept is to help students understand the context in which they will practice. Educators outside the US would include similar information about their country's health system.
- Concept #3: Tools of Health Informatics: This concept includes tools commonly used in healthcare to assist with data capture, acquisition, and visualization and students should become familiar with them.
- Concept #4: Health Informatics Methods: This includes methods of analysis and usability assessment that can assist with implementation and adoption of health informatics applications. Like the tools, students need to be aware of some of the common methods.
- Concept #5: Standards: Students need familiarity with terminologies and structures, their importance and how they are applied in practice.
- Concept #6: Ethical/legal, Privacy, Security: Health ethics and privacy and security laws occupy a crucial place in the practice of health informatics and students need to be aware of these laws.
- Concept #7: Application and Analysis: Awareness of the application and analysis of real-world data captured by health information systems. The objective is to introduce to students how health informatics tools can be used to generate new knowledge and evidence-based practice.
- Concept #8: Telehealth: Telehealth is one of the new and growing technologies that students need to be aware of and students need to be introduced to these new developments, including definitions and payment mechanisms.
- Concept #9: Global Health Informatics: Application of health informatics in world health situations. Students need to be aware of how informatics is applied in a variety of countries.
- Concept #10: Public and Population Health Informatics: This concept addresses the use of health informatics to impact public and population health. It is important for students to be aware of informatics applications beyond the acute care setting.
- Concept #11: Mobile health technologies: Understanding user experience relative to remote monitoring and chronic disease self-management is of growing importance and students should be familiar with these applications.
- Concept #12: Consumer health informatics: Consumer needs and expectations around the use of health informatics will impact information seeking and care. Students need to understand the needs and how these needs influence the design and use of informatics applications for healthcare consumers.

- Concept #13: Human Factors: Usability of technology and principles of human factors are important for the design and use of health informatics applications and students need to understand how these principles can improve interface design and interaction.
- Concept #14: Personalized Medicine: The objective of this concept is to introduce students to ways of bridging health informatics and bioinformatics toward improved health outcomes.
- Concept #15: Digital Health Literacy: Students need to understand the impact of digital health literacy on healthcare delivery.
- Concept #16: The future of health Informatics: Students need to understand the role of health informatics across the healthcare system and across different professions.
- Concept #17: Careers in health Informatics: The objective is to provide students with an awareness of different career paths for prospective health informatics professionals.

The Future of Undergraduate Programs in Health Informatics

Graduate programs in health informatics started as a vehicle for educating and training information technology and healthcare professionals who were tasked with health informatics jobs, but without the depth and breadth of knowledge they needed [5, 17]. The maturation of graduate programs in health informatics has created a top down push for earlier preparation in health informatics. Consistent with the development of graduate programs in health informatics, undergraduate programs are emerging throughout North America and beyond. In this chapter, we described the AMIA Foundational Domains and 17 concepts within those domains. The next steps are to align the concepts with appropriate competencies for undergraduate education and then align the programs with CAHIIM program accreditation standards. Doing so creates a solid pathway from undergraduate to graduate health informatics education and may well serve to increase the rigor of both academic levels and elevate health informatics professionals.

Key Take Away Points

- There is growing recognition of the need for health informatics programs in undergraduate education.
- Undergraduate education programs should be designed to align with the foundational domains, competencies and assessment approaches of graduate health informatics programs.

- Undergraduate programs can be designed to provide awareness and basic knowledge that can prepare students for the more advanced performance expectations in graduate programs in health informatics.
- There are key concepts that can form the focus for undergraduate health informatics education.

References

1. Unertl KM, Finnell JT, Sarkar IN. Developing new pathways into the biomedical informatics field: the AMIA High School Scholars Program. J Am Med Inf Assoc. 2016;23(4):819–23.
2. Shaw T, Sensmeier J, Anderson C. The evolution of the TIGER initiative. Comput Inform Nurs. 2017;35(6):278–80.
3. Mohan V, et al. Design and evaluation of the ONC health information technology curriculum. J Am Med Inform Assoc. 2014;21(3):509–16.
4. Connors HB, et al. Health information technology scholars program: from implementation to outcomes. Nurs Educ Perspect. 2017;38(1):3–8.
5. Feldman SS, Hersh W. Evaluating the AMIA-OHSU 10x10 program to train healthcare professionals in medical informatics. AMIA Annu Symp Proc. 2008;2008:182–6.
6. Fenton SH, et al. Health information management: changing with time. Yearb Med Inform. 2017;26(1):72–7.
7. Hersh W. A stimulus to define informatics and health information technology. BMC Med Inform Decis Making. 2009;9:24.
8. Attewell P, Monaghan D. How many credits should an undergraduate take? Res Higher Educ. 2016;57(6):682–713.
9. Valenta AL, et al. AMIA Board White Paper: AMIA 2017 core competencies for applied health informatics education at the master's degree level. J Am Med Inform Assoc. 2018;25(12):1657–68.
10. Miller GE. The assessment of clinical skills/competence/performance. Acad Med. 1990;65(9):S63–7.
11. Cheeks B. The Miller pyramid and prism. [cited 2020 January 4]. https://www.gp-training.net/training/educational_theory/adult_learning/miller.htm
12. Mehay R, Burns R. Miller's pyramid of clinical competence adapted by R. Mehay and R. Burns. In: Mehay R, editor. The essential handbook for GP training and education. London: Radcliffe Publishing; 2009. p. 414.
13. Schleyer RH, Burch CK, Schoessler MT. Defining and integrating informatics competencies into a Hospital Nursing Department. Comput Inform Nurs. 2011;29(3):167.
14. Westra BL, Delaney CW. Informatics competencies for nursing and healthcare leaders. AMIA Annu Symp Proc. 2008;2008:804–8.
15. Skiba DJ. Informatics competencies for nurses revisited. Nurs Educ Perspect. 2016;37(6):365–7.
16. Khairat S, et al. A review of biomedical and health informatics education: a workforce training framework. J Hosp Admin. 2016;5(5):10.
17. Dorsey A, et al. Bridging the gap. Appl Clin Inform. 2015;6(02):211–23.

Part III
Informatics Education
for Other Health Professionals

Chapter 7
Educating the Informatics-Enabled Physician

H. Dominic J. Covvey

Over the last several decades, the potential positive impact of information and communications systems has become increasingly obvious. This presents a challenge to all physicians to become capable of at least using these systems or, potentially, of being involved in deploying them.

The discipline of Health Informatics, also referred to as Biomedical Informatics, Medical Informatics, or Clinical Informatics, has emerged from the realization of the significance of information-related challenges in health care and the realization of the potential of information systems to address these challenges. These realizations have, in turn, led to an understanding of the need to define systems-related competencies (knowledge, skills, experience, attitudes and values) and to imbue a wide variety of professionals, especially physicians, with the concepts of this discipline.

The discipline of Health Informatics (HI) is expressed in three major career paths or channels. The first channel is the realm of scientists and theoreticians who conceptualize both significant health information-related challenges and the new tools and methodologies to address these challenges. Some have called this channel Research and Development Health Informatics (RDHI). The National Library of Medicine (NLM) training programs described in Chap. 2 focus on this channel. The second channel is a more prevalent and practical one related to the selection, deployment, use and evaluation of the tools and methods developed by the RDHI scholars. This channel has been described as Applied Health Informatics or e-Health (electronic Health). Those who work in this channel elect to become directly involved in implementing information and communications systems in healthcare environments. Typically, they are members of the team of professionals that serves an institution, often in an Information Services Department (ISD) or in a liaison capacity between other departments and the ISD. The third channel is the one in which most

H. D. J. Covvey (✉)
Faculty of Science, University of Waterloo, Waterloo, ON, Canada
e-mail: dcovvey@uwaterloo.ca

© Springer Nature Switzerland AG 2020
E. S. Berner (ed.), *Informatics Education in Healthcare*, Health Informatics,
https://doi.org/10.1007/978-3-030-53813-2_7

clinicians have found or, inevitably, will find themselves. What is involved here affects every physician and challenges him or her to become sufficiently knowledgeable about systems and appropriately skilled in their use. With appropriate competencies, the physician will be able to function at the level of productivity that has become necessary for efficient and effective healthcare. We have called this channel Clinician Health Informatics and the individual, the Informatics-Enabled Physician.

Defining Competencies

We have undertaken a number of efforts to define the competencies required in each of these three channels. Our fundamental work is available in the document 'Pointing the Way: Competencies and Curricula in Health Informatics' [1]. This project was carried out over two years by approximately 100 Canadian and American representatives of various stakeholder groups, including educators, clinicians (predominantly physicians and nurses), healthcare industry professionals (from hospitals, clinics and private product and services companies), leading health informaticians and students [2]. Our process engaged three teams, of about 20 individuals each, selected from the participants, with the remainder acting as reviewers and providing periodic feedback.

Each of the three teams addressed one of the channels previously cited: Research and Development Health Informatics, Applied Health Informatics or Clinician Health Informatics. Each team began with a straw version of the competencies developed by the author and proceeded to refine it. Early on, we decided to use a Work Breakdown Structure approach to deriving competencies. First, we defined a set of potential roles that someone in any of the three channels could potentially fill. We termed these 'Macro-Roles' and recognized that more than one could be filled simultaneously. Next, we defined the 'Challenges' that an individual would face in each of these roles. Examining each challenge, we determined what the individual needed to do to address each challenge—these we called 'Micro-Roles' or 'Task-Level Competencies'. For each of these micro-roles we then defined the knowledge, skills and experience that an individual would need to acquire in order to carry them out. Our penultimate step was to create a set of 'Competency Categories' that subsumed these detailed competencies. These competency categories are shown in Table 7.1.

The final step in this process was to identify the importance of each challenge to individuals in each of the macro-roles. This enabled us to give role-specific guidance regarding the importance each competency category has to each role.

The result of this work listed hundreds of detailed competencies. On advice from a colleague (personal communication, Dr. Francis Lau), we created a website that brought all this material together and made it more interesting to read. Furthermore, this website provides a way that an individual can both understand the competencies and interact with them to determine his or her self-assessed capabilities relative to

Table 7.1 Clinician health informatics competencies

1. Personal competencies
2. Learning, critical and evaluative thinking, and reading competencies
3. Teaching and supervision competencies
4. Research and concept/methodology development competencies
5. Justification case building (quantitative + qualitative) and evaluation competencies
6. Re-engineering and designing of work and IM processes, (including management of change)
7. Group work competencies: collaboration, team/project leadership, building, management, and participation
8. Technology selection, evaluation, and management competencies
9. General planning, administration, and management competencies
10. Communication, presentation, and publication competencies
11. General computing competencies
12. Health computing competencies
13. General health system-related competencies
14. Information and data collection, architecting, analysis, and management, and distribution competencies

any of the macro-roles. The system also can assist the individual in locating material to upgrade his or her competencies. This system is freely available online [3]. Several articles are also available on this work and its results [4].

Our more recent effort reviewed the Clinician Health Informatics competencies together with recent literature, and determined a set of competencies we perceive all physicians need to have regardless of specialty or professional role. These are outlined in the material that follows.

Choices and Challenges

Although it may not be possible at the start of a medical career to choose decisively in which channel one wishes to function, experience indicates that, eventually, a choice will be made. Without question, the physician-in-training must enter the third channel, and become informatics-enabled. This means that the individual will acquire knowledge about a variety of technologies, about what these technologies can do for healthcare, and about how to make productive use of them. In addition, a number of skills need to be acquired, such as the ability to use programs that support healthcare processes and the ability to interact with a variety of systems. Ideally, these competencies would be acquired in medical school.

Of course, an individual at some point in his or her career may elect to participate more directly in the deployment and implementation of systems. This is important, as the involvement of physicians and other clinicians in the deployment of systems is essential. However, a great deal more knowledge and additional skill must be acquired in order to participate adequately at this more involved level. These more broad and, sometimes, in-depth competencies can be acquired through a Health

Table 7.2 Career paths and requirements

Career channel	Competencies	Minimum credentialing
Research & development HI	Broad discipline of RDHI with depth specialization	Graduate degree in HI
Applied HI/e-Health	Broad discipline of applied HI	Undergraduate/college degree, diploma or other certification in AHI
Informatics-enabled physician	Broad, shallow knowledge and skills in HI	Medical school-based or continuing education in HI

Informatics education program, either degree-based or continuing education. Some certification exam programs provide review courses as well [5, 6]. There is also the possible, but challenging, path of self-directed learning complemented by mentorship. Suffice it to say that, for this channel, some degree of formal continuing education will be crucial.

Perhaps the most challenging path is to elect to become a certified or otherwise credentialed Health Informatician, a professional fully competent in Health Informatics and capable of teaching and doing research. Generally speaking, this will require a minimum of a graduate degree and significant experience in actual healthcare situations. In this case, the physician is electing a new or parallel career, the latter expressing both a commitment to medicine itself and to the discipline of Health Informatics (see Chap. 16 for a description of the clinical informatics medical subspecialty certification program). These three choices are summarized in Table 7.2.

The Informatics-Enabled Physician

There are many tasks performed by clinicians that can be optimized by informatics tools and methods. It is useful to examine the basic tasks that physicians perform that are amenable to support:

- *Recordkeeping*: the entry, organization, quality assurance, retrieval and visualization of patient care information.
- *Information Retrieval*: identifying sources of, searching for, retrieving, organizing and visualizing information from the literature or from sets of patient records, for example, for public health purposes.
- *Clinical Decision Making*: making decisions related to diagnosis or intervention.
- *Workflow*: the organization, regularization and optimization of processes for patient care, administration, management, teaching and research.
- *Planning*: defining and maintaining a focused course of action towards objectives.
- *Imaging and Image Management*: acquiring, storing, organizing and indexing, processing, visualizing and communicating medical images (e.g., in Diagnostic Radiology, Pathology).

- *Ordering and Results Reporting*: requesting various health services, for example clinical chemistry or medications, and obtaining results.
- *Collaboration*: interacting with other members of the care team or with colleagues and students in teaching and research.
- *Procurement*: defining the requirements for and participating in, the acquisition of new tools for health care. These may include clinical technologies, such as an MRI machine, or computing technologies such as an electronic medical record system for the provider's office.
- *Communication*: providing information to or obtaining information from, one's colleagues, patients or service organizations.
- *Analysis and Visualization*: processing data and information and presenting results in a comprehensible form. This information may relate to patient care, teaching, administration or research.
- *Learning and Teaching*: acquiring or disseminating new knowledge and skills and/or remaining current.
- *Business Operations Management*: performing nonclinical tasks to manage and operate a project, department, a practice or an organization.
- *Assessment and Evaluation*: reviewing results of interventions or experiments.
- *Research*: seeking new knowledge through investigations (e.g., clinical trials, case reviews or laboratory experiments).

There are many more possibilities, but the list above indicates common tasks, amenable to technological support, which are performed by physicians. It is reasonable to assert that, in today's and tomorrow's world, it will be essential for physicians to be able to use supportive technologies in order to make processes, in which they are engaged, or for which they have responsibility, more efficient and more effective.

Required Competencies

If these key tasks are to be performed optimally, physicians require a set of competencies (Note that this is not an exhaustive list):

1. **Understanding the technologies that can be applied to clinical practice, administration, teaching and research, as well the cofactors that make this technology effective and the concepts that surround these.** We define cofactors as management of change, adoption support, work process re-engineering, end user education and training, human resources and organizational restructuring and supportive communication. This understanding has sometimes been called 'Computer Literacy', but a better descriptor might be 'Computer, Applications and Process Literacy'. The technologies include both local and central information systems (including Internet-based systems), the software that they run, and the communications technology that connects them. Topics also include tools: for personal productivity support (e.g., word processing,

presentation, spreadsheet, database and the like); for searching, for accessing and integrating medical data, information and knowledge, including -omic, public health and research information; for managing and operating organizations, departments and practices; for clinical data management including images, signals and other data types; for decision support; for care performance evaluation and comparison; for information sharing with colleagues and patients; for accessing evidence; for teaching and research; for operations/ workflow improvement and other crucial tasks.

2. **Understanding the value and impacts of systems**. This includes understanding the evidence of the potential qualitative and quantitative effectiveness and efficiency effects of systems, what has worked, critical success factors, and common challenges to the realization of positive impacts.

3. **Understanding the nature of data**, **information and knowledge**. It is necessary to understand the kinds and sources of data and metadata (data describing data), information and knowledge, how they can be retrieved, how they can be organized and processed, how results can be visualized, and how they can be stored for long-term availability.

4. **Comprehending the nature of how decisions are made and the technological mechanisms for assisting humans in making decisions**. This will also include an understanding of the capabilities and limitations of systems that support decision-making, how information to support decisions is represented and stored and how systems provide decision support, as well as an understanding of human cognition and memory and their limitations. Often this will require an understaning of Artificial Intelligence and Machine Learning technologies.

5. **Understanding the nature and capabilities of electronic records systems**. An understanding of how data is captured, how it is organized and indexed, how it is stored, how it is retrieved and how it is presented and used is central to being an Informatics-Enabled Physician. Typically, one will need to learn about the different types of record systems, the structure of their data storage, vocabularies and data standards, how physicians interact with systems, how systems can interact with each other and how we can assure that the meaning of stored information is consistently communicated (via data standards). Because records systems so totally affect practice, topics such as how legislation influences their creation and use (for example, privacy laws) and how they are affected by ethics, security, etc. are important. This includes the risks and untoward effects associated with such systems.

6. **Understanding the nature of healthcare workflow and how humans and systems interact in a complex and busy environment**. At least a basic understanding of what workflow and workflow reengineering are about and how to improve workflows is very important. Topics include graphic and other representations of workflow, how to detect and correct workflow bottlenecks, methods for measuring processes, the documentation of context and the integration of data flow, and methods of modifying and restructuring roles.

7. **Seeing how systems can better connect individuals to form teams and support team activities**. This includes the support of the care team's work, as well as mechanisms to communicate better with patients, particularly in long-term care settings. The capabilities of technologies to enable the distributed participation of the members of the care team are important knowledge, as is knowledge related to the creation of efficient inter-person workflows.

8. **Understanding the implementation and use of systems**. Virtually every clinician will be challenged to participate in the acquisition and implementation of systems and be a resource in assuring their adoption. This will require knowledge of the nature of procurement and its processes, particularly new approaches to procurement, as well as of the stages of the system lifecycle from conceptualization, through acquisition installation, implementation, testing, use and evaluation. Related to this area, knowledge of the impacts of systems is fundamental. These include impacts on users and the organization and will address the untoward impacts as well is the positive ones. This is crucial so that failures can be minimized or avoided. Additional topics include basic introductions to: key system types (e.g., for the office, clinic, home), the systems development process (particularly 'Agile' approaches), the challenges of software engineering, the capabilities and limitations of systems, system and information usability, and the diffusion of innovations and system adoption.

9. **Understanding the economics of systems and how to evaluate their impacts**. It will be important to understand how the use of information systems, such as EHRs, can affect reimbursement for care. It will also be important to understand concepts related to budgeting for systems, how to measure value, how to assess advisability regarding development and implementation and how to assess the qualitative and quantitative impacts of systems.

10. **Understanding how systems can support learning**. This involves an understanding of how we learn and how systems can support learning processes. Knowledge is needed of techniques that can be used to enhance learning and to make educational systems a part of virtually all of one's activities, from self-learning, to providing patients with learning tools.

11. **Appreciating the context into which systems are introduced**. This includes the importance of understanding organizational culture, fiscal constraints, human resources limitations, organizational and operational challenges, the status of existing systems and users' perceptions of them, previous success and failures, and regulatory and legal issues.

12. **Being aware of key contextual topics**: These include: basic clinical epidemiology; privacy, confidentiality and security; technical and data standards; techniques for managing formal meetings and discussions and achieving consensus; policy development and promulgation; project management, project prioritization and project termination; staff education and training; and the availability and experience with key systems.

Becoming an Informatics-Enabled Physician

Optimally, the competencies identified here would be acquired during basic medical training. Some schools have interpreted this as requiring specific courses in Health Informatics. Many schools have found that the already crowded curriculum cannot admit yet another course or courses. In fact, it may make more sense for the material to be integrated into existing courses.

The author participated in a Canada Health Infoway [7] Academic/Learning Advisory Group from 2007 to 2009 that surveyed medical school and pharmacy programs in Canada to determine the level of Electronic Health Record (EHR)-related education included in the curricula of Canadian universities. The taskforce found that there was virtually no informatics in the curricula at that time. Among the findings of this group were that the importance of the EHR was not really recognized and accepted, that there was no room in the curriculum for things like the EHR and IT training, that there was a dearth of faculty qualified to teach these subjects, and that there was little research related to them. In 2011 the author provided an educational session to the Association of Faculties of Medicine in Canada and it appeared that little progress had been made to that time. Similar results were found by McGowan and colleagues in a survey done with U.S. medical schools [8]. For those deeply involved in Health Informatics, the failure of medical schools to recognize the need for informatics competencies in their graduates and to implement adequate informatics education and training is frustrating. One conclusion from this work is that medical school faculty require a significant upgrading of informatics awareness and informatics competencies, or the problem will persist. One answer is to pursue the development of 'Informatics-Enabled Physician' continuing education programs.

A more distributed approach—that could be termed 'informatics-embedding'—could be implemented by educating faculty regarding how to introduce the concepts cited here into their syllabi. For example, in teaching anatomy, online systems that provide a virtual cadaver or virtual organs that can be virtually dissected could be used. In Physiology, computer models of cells, organs or body systems, permitting the interactive alteration of parameters, could help the student achieve a deeper understanding of physiological function. In fact, the informatics-embedding approach may be superior and could result in not only medical students but also medical faculty becoming more knowledgeable.

At the present time, we are beset by the reality that little of the material above is formally included in medical curricula, a fact that must be corrected as soon as possible. For those whose training did not incorporate informatics, the solution is either to engage in continuing education programs or in self-directed learning. Two of the most comprehensive continuing education programs in Health Informatics are the American Medical Informatics Association's (AMIA's) 10 × 10 program [9] (see also Chap. 18) in the United States or the National Institutes of Health Informatics' Applied Health Informatics Bootcamp in Canada [10].

Of course, self-directed learning is always a possibility, and many resources exist online or can be audited at various schools. Probably the most important amendment to strictly self-directed approaches is to proceed with a mentor, and these are available through the same organizations mentioned above.

The e-Health Team

It is useful to outline briefly the nature and composition of the e-Health team so that the potential for physician involvement is clear. The e-Health Team is the agency in an institution for the realization of the potential of health information technology. The e-Health Team comprises a number of different types of expertise.

Ideally, one or a few individuals fully competent in Health Informatics provide leadership for the e-Health Team. Other members of the team include those who focus on Health Information Technology (HIT)-individuals who are technology-focused and deeply knowledgeable in matters like procurement, implementation, management and use of systems. The charge of this latter group is to bring systems into operation and assure their use.

Health Information Management (HIM) professionals also provide a significant contribution to the team. Their background in information management and information retrieval makes them important members of the e-Health Team.

There will also be members with either special technology expertise, for example, in system software or networking, or with competencies in areas such as project management or evaluation. Of course, the e-Health Team may engage other types of expertise, such as finance, quality assurance, and workflow professionals, as well as educators and trainers, etc. Perhaps most crucially, though, the e-Health Team needs to include representatives of the disciplines impacted by a system, for example clinicians, technologists and managers.

All members of the e-Health Team must have the knowledge of the healthcare environment, its operations and functions, as well as the technologies and methodologies being implemented. Even the purely technical contributors to the e-Health team need the same types of knowledge required by the Informatics-Enabled Physician. This places a burden on institutions to ensure that all members of their e-Health team are competent in the broad spectrum of informatics at least at a basic level. In other words, the entire team must be informatics-enabled.

Attitudes: A Sometimes Weak Competency

It is incumbent on Health Informatics programs to regularly assess what we produce. What happens if we ask those who employ our graduates: "How are we doing?" It is likely that the response is generally a positive one, perhaps moderated with a bit of constructive criticism. But sometimes we might not get the answer we wanted.

Crucial competencies that are often not well-assessed, are the attitudinal competencies. Often, when we enumerate competencies, we stop at knowledge (what we need to know), skills (what we must be able to do) and experience (the applying of our knowledge and skills). However, there are two other components of competency: attitudes and values.

How Can We Identify the Attitudes We Expect of Health Informaticians?

The Oxford Advanced Learner's Dictionary defines 'attitude' (in the sense of an emotion) as: the way that you think and feel about somebody or something, or the way that one behaves towards somebody or a thing [11]. Thus, attitudes are expressed towards someone or something.

In an article published in Health Care Information Management & Communications Canada [12] we asked ourselves the question: "What are the attitudes an informatician should be expected to exhibit in regard to various stakeholders?"

We defined the following 'stakeholders' to which informaticians expose their attitudes:

- Self and Family.
- Other People they Impact, e.g., applies to all types of people, or specifically to employer, clients (including patients), staff/colleagues, students.
- Their Work/Teaching/Research.
- Others' Work/Teaching/Research (including students, mentees, staff, superiors, authors whose work they review).
- Organizations and Their People, e.g., the healthcare process/system, healthcare providers, professional associations.
- The Discipline of Health Informatics, e.g., the advancement of the knowledge base of HI itself; teaching, lecturing, speaking and mentoring.
- One's Own Code of Ethical Behavior.
- The Law, Regulation and Standards of Morality, e.g., related to fraud, plagiarism, crimes of various types and abusive behavior.

The article describes some suggestions for attitudinal aspects that could begin to form a framework for assessment. The article also describes ways that attitudinal competencies could be taught. Some suggestions include case-based instruction where students could respond to data and discuss the cases. Another suggestion involves engaging the students in role-playing with video critiques, which give them a chance to see and reflect on their own behavior.

A colleague made a number of suggestions on how we should teach attitudes in our HI (personal communication).

One way is to present students with cases that illustrate attitudes or the need for them. One could present some inconsistent (numbers with incorrect statistics about those numbers) or unfounded (e.g., you must drink 8 glasses of water each day) information used to drive a decision, and then elicit student reactions that depend on attitudes like appropriate skepticism, for example. One could then discuss how one can maintain an appropriately skeptical and evidence-based mindset.

Another way is through role-playing. A student could take the role of a salesperson and another of a client, where one or the other manipulates a situation. This could be observed by a class and then critiqued. The article emphasizes the need for carefully designed scenarios to stimulate student thinking [12]. Whatever method is used, it must be interactive and carefully scripted so that the issues require some thinking in order to dissect them out and address them.

Beyond the Informatics-Enabled Physician

Those who elect to delve more deeply and become more directly involved in the informatics domain will, generally, participate in a formal education program. Undergraduate programs leading to a bachelor's degree and graduate programs leading to Masters or PhD degrees in Health Informatics are available and there are, in the US, an increasing number of clinical informatics fellowship programs (see Chap. 16).

It is important to consider the type of career one desires, to obtain advice from an independent source and to select carefully the program one will enter. Different schools have different approaches, and certain programs may not be fully adequate. It would be wise to consider programs that have been created and evaluated by the National Library of Medicine in the United States (see also Chap. 2). Information on advanced programs is available at the AMIA website [13] and at the NIHI website [14]. Proceeding to advanced training can position a person to have an extremely interesting and stimulating career strongly valued by organizations one has the opportunity to serve. Such a career combines the best of clinical practice with one of the most dynamic fields imaginable.

Summary and Conclusions

It should be clear that medical schools have not responded adequately to the emergence of enabling information and communication technologies. Today's and tomorrow's world will expect that physicians are able to not only cope with information and communications systems but also be able to function more productively than has been the case classically. Physicians will be expected to be competent users of information technology, will be expected to consider information systems as an asset for performance management and productivity improvement and will be expected to formulate future practice based on a technological infrastructure.

It should be emphasized, though, that we still need research into required competencies so that the body of competency knowledge is brought and kept up-to-date. Credible individuals taking on this task could be essential to the diffusion of Health Informatics knowledge into medical practice. These competencies will need to include attitudes as well as knowledge and skills.

Given the challenges of the dynamic field of health care, it will be essential that physicians-in-training acquire an adequate knowledge of systems and their capabilities, learn basic skills to introduce and support efficient use of these systems, and understand in depth how these systems can be integrated into the way they think and they practice.

Ideally, medical schools will respond by incorporating material and experiences that imbue trainees with key knowledge and skills so they can satisfy the expectations of the world they enter. It is arguable as to the best way to incorporate informatics into the medical curriculum. However, it is not arguable as to the importance of doing this.

We are all fortunate that, with time, it has become possible to define generic informatics knowledge and skills, rather than having to train individuals on specific systems. We are now at a point whereby general principles, consensus knowledge and common skills will afford the medical school graduate the basics to function in today's digital economy. Given this, and given the work of leaders who have articulated and continue to refine curricular content, it is quite possible to define the Health Informatics content that must be melded into all medical curricula and that can be done reasonably painlessly. It does take effort and negotiation, and faculty will have a learning challenge, but undertaking this effort and addressing this challenge will ensure that we have the complement of physicians capable of functioning in the modern world.

Key Take-Away Points

- Many faculty in medical schools are minimally aware of what Health Informatics and e-Health can deliver to the process of health care. It is essential that Health Informatics be 'marketed' more effectively and that faculty awareness of Health Informatics be greatly enhanced.
- Medical school curriculum developers must become knowledgeable about the work that has been done to define the informatics competencies required of clinicians in each of the three channels. There is still work to be done, however, on what might, based on evidence, be called an 'absolutely must acquire' set of competencies.

- Medical schools must embrace, and learn from, a sufficient cadre of highly competent informatics educators if the goal is to imbue clinicians with the needed competencies.
- A productive way of creating informatics-enabled professionals is to educate and train medical school faculty in Health Informatics and have them integrate Health Informatics knowledge and skills into existing courses.
- Continuing education programs, preferably available via distance learning, are needed to create and maintain an up-to-date complement of informatics-enabled clinicians.

References

1. Covvey HD, Zitner D, Bernstein R. Pointing the way: competencies and curricula in health informatics. 2001. http://www.nihi.ca/nihi/ir/Pointing%20the%20Way%20MASTER%20 Document%20Version%201%20Final.pdf . Accessed 30 March 2020.
2. Covvey HD, Zitner D, Bernstein R, MacNeill JE. The development of model curricula for health informatics. Stud Health Technol Inform. 2001;84(Pt 2):1009–13.
3. National Institutes of Health Informatics (NIHI). Applied health informatics learning and assessment site. 2012. http://www.nihi.ca/hi/index.php. Accessed 30 March 2020.
4. MacNeill JE, Covvey HD. The development of a model curriculum for applied health informatics. Proceedings AMIA annual symposium; 2000. p. 527–31.
5. Healthcare Information and Management Systems Society (HIMSS) Certified Professional in Healthcare Information & Management Systems (CPHIMS). http://www.himss.org/health-it-certification/cphims?navItemNumber=13647. Accessed 30 March 2020.
6. American Medical Informatics Association (AMIA). Clinical Informatics Board Review Course. https://www.amia.org/clinical-informatics-board-review-course. Accessed 16 April 2020.
7. Canada Health Infoway. Canada Health Infoway – Inforoute Sante du Canada. 2012. https://www.infoway-inforoute.ca/. Accessed 30 March 2020.
8. McGowan JJ, Passiment M, Hoffman HM. Educating medical students as competent users of health information technologies: the MSOP data. Stud Health Technol Inform. 2007;129(Pt 2):1414–8.
9. American Medical Informatics Association (AMIA). AMIA 10 × 10 courses training health care professionals to serve as informatics leaders. 2013. http://www.amia.org/education/10x10-courses. Accessed 30 March 2020.
10. National Institutes of Health Informatics (NIHI). Health informatics bootcamp. 2013. http://www.nihi.ca/index.php?MenuItemID=21. Accessed 30 March 2020.
11. Oxford Learning Dictionaries. https://www.oxfordlearnersdictionaries.com/us/. Accessed 16 April 2020.
12. Covvey HD. You've Got an Attitude, Dude, Health Care Information Management & Communications Canada, 3rd Quarter, 2011, pp. 68–9.
13. American Informatics Association (AMIA). Academic informatics programs. 2020. http://www.amia.org/education/programs-and-courses. Accessed 30 March 2020.
14. Covvey HD, Fenton SL. Survey of health informatics programs and health information management programs in Canada, 2010–2011. http://www.nihi.ca/nihi/ir/HI-HIM%20Program%20 Survey%202010-2011.pdf. Accessed 30 March 2020.

Chapter 8
Informatics Education for Health Administrators

Margaret Schulte

Who Is the "Healthcare Administrator?"

The healthcare administrator is the professional responsible for the overall strategic and business leadership and management of the healthcare provider organization. This person may have been professionally grounded in a clinical profession, a business-orientation, or a public health background. As the healthcare leader at a middle or senior level, the individual is responsible for the many measures of organizational performance that reflect the fulfillment of the mission and strategic direction of the organization. The administrator, whether in senior or middle management, requires not only skill and experience in management, but also accurate information and sound data and analytics for decision-making. It is this latter, that mandates that graduates of higher education programs in healthcare management be prepared with competencies in information and data management among the many other competencies that they will develop.

The discussion that follows speaks to the educational needs of the student who aspires to an organizational leadership and management role, whether that role is in the management of a primarily clinical function, or of a provider enterprise that is geographically dispersed with many types of related functions such as those of payor, medical device supplier, educator (e.g. nursing school), research or other function. Other chapters of this book address the educational requirements of specific professions within the healthcare enterprise (physicians, nurses, data management, etc.) for whom many similar leadership competencies are required. In this chapter, the focus is on the education of those who aspire to career advancement in healthcare management.

M. Schulte (✉)
Commission on Accreditation of Healthcare Management Education, Philadelphia, PA, USA

© Springer Nature Switzerland AG 2020　　　　　　　　　　　　　　　　　101
E. S. Berner (ed.), *Informatics Education in Healthcare*, Health Informatics,
https://doi.org/10.1007/978-3-030-53813-2_8

Introduction

Healthcare executives and managers at all levels and roles in the provider organization require and interact with clinical and organizational information, data and information systems on a daily basis. Information systems are essential to all aspects of the healthcare organization including patient safety, efficiency, clinical quality performance improvement, administrative, financial and strategic management, population health management and patient engagement. Yet, historically, healthcare systems and practitioners were slow to adopt enterprise information systems and, importantly, to adopt information systems that are integrated with one another for the sharing of clinical data and information, for analysis and process improvement, and for accurate billing and revenue enhancement. More recently, in the last approximate 10 to 15 years, hospitals, health systems and medical practitioners in the US have rapidly moved up the information technology adoption curve with the implementation of the electronic health record (EHR). The federal Meaningful Use Program, which was enacted in 2009 under the American Recovery and Reinvestment Act (ARRA) offered financial incentives to hospitals and providers to adopt the electronic health record (EHR). This measure spurred the provider sector to adopt information technology at a dynamic pace. In 2017, the Office of the National Coordinator for Health Information Technology (ONC) estimated that 86% of office-based physicians had adopted an EHR and 96% of all non-federal acute care hospitals possessed certified health IT systems [1].

As information technology has proliferated in healthcare, provider organization leadership teams have seen their roles intensify in implementation and use of information systems and ultimately in analytics and the use of the data that those systems provide for quality and process improvement, and for strategic decision-making. Health Information Technology (Health IT) is a core part of the infrastructure that the provider organization needs to remain a viable entity. From the outset, it is the leadership team who must provide guidance, determination and commitment to organizational change, as well as to overcoming resistance (sometimes overwhelming resistance) to adoption and change and to making the ongoing financial investment that an IT implementation demands.

With the EHR in place, the opportunities for advancements in medical science and in health system management have increased exponentially. Graduates of healthcare management programs need to be prepared to address the problems that arise with Health IT as well as to maximize the opportunities that the current and new technologies represent. For example:

- Maintenance of the privacy and security of patient information requires constant vigilance in light of sophisticated hacking technologies and the monetized value of patient data [2].
- Artificial intelligence has moved rapidly into the clinical world and requires new skills of staff and management in clinical and administrative settings [3].

- Connected health devices and digital therapeutics that provide new tools and insight to manage patient behavior, deliver health care and improve outcomes have come onto the horizon [4].
- Blockchain and other emerging technologies offer ever new possibilities for the healthcare enterprise [5].

The scale of the health sector and its impact on the economy and society is enormous. The combination of providers and care organizations alone represent a $3.5 trillion impact on the national economy of the US, which accounts for 17.9% of the gross domestic product (GDP) [6]. The financial impact is even higher in the global context in which many of our provider and other care delivery organizations work.

In this complex arena, healthcare delivery in the US is made more complicated in that it is very fragmented, and that fragmentation is mirrored in information technology systems. This lack of integration of information systems between and among all providers of care continues to loom as a problem for improvements in population health status and in reducing cost and access to care. Large and geographically dispersed provider organizations share patient information electronically within their own "walls", but for too many the sharing generally stops at the perimeters of those organizations. This is a complex problem, and one that is constantly "on the plate" of the healthcare executive.

In short, when health administration graduates move from academia into lower and middle-management roles in provider organizations or when they move upward on the management career ladder, they need to be prepared to be competently involved in IT and analytical decision-making, in implementation teams and in information/data management and security. They need to be prepared to understand the role of top management and to support the strategies within which IT acquisition, implementation and application decisions are made. Equally importantly, they need to embrace new technologies and to understand the potential that the data access and analytics make possible for innovation and performance improvement.

It is incumbent upon academia to ensure that students in healthcare management are prepared for the changing needs of their future employer organizations and for their management roles as related to information systems and data. Graduates of healthcare management programs will be in the pool of talent that will drive the future performance of the health sector and the information and insight that information systems can and will provide are a critical foundation to their success.

Health IT Education in Healthcare Management Programs

Programs for graduate and undergraduate education for health administration have generally mirrored the development curve that IT implementation and adoption have followed in health care. It is only in the last decade or more that higher education programs in healthcare management have committed on a widespread scale to development and delivery of a curriculum to prepare students for their future responsibilities in integrating the demands and promises of IT into their daily professional work.

Over a relatively short period, higher education programs in healthcare management at both the undergraduate and graduate levels have offered ever more expansive curricula content in healthcare IT. This has progressed from an early approach in which content was included in existing courses to achieve discipline-specific competencies e.g. finance, operations, quality improvement, to full courses on the subject area. Even more recently, some programs have developed degrees and/or concentrations in healthcare IT.

Undergraduate and Masters' Level Curricula Offering Healthcare IT

Up until about 10 years ago, IT course offerings were hampered by the lack of qualified faculty and accessible content in most programs across the country. This gap in healthcare management education was recognized by the Commission on Accreditation of Health Management Education (CAHME) and by the Association of University Programs in Health Administration (AUPHA). CAHME is the accrediting body for graduate programs in healthcare management and AUPHA is a "global network of colleges, universities, faculty, individuals, and organizations dedicated to the improvement of healthcare delivery through excellence in healthcare management and education" [7]. In a collaborative arrangement, CAHME and AUPHA joined forces to develop a plan to address the gap and to support healthcare management education programs in their health IT curriculum offerings. The plan was funded with a three-year grant from the Health Information and Management Systems Society (HIMSS) for the development of a health IT and information management curriculum that would be made available to graduate and undergraduate healthcare management programs throughout the country at no cost to them.

The project, which was titled the Health Information Management Systems and Technology Analysis (HIMSTA) project, resulted in a full course offering of a syllabus with competency objectives, audio-slide lectures, readings and references, suggested discussion questions, assessment questions and student project ideas. The curriculum was developed based on the competency objectives presented in Table 8.1 below. It was released to academia through the AUPHA in 2012. A learning module was created and produced for each competency objective. The "course" was made available to programs throughout the country for use in its entirety or of any of the 14 modules of which it was comprised.

With the introduction of the HIMSTA 'course' in 2013, programs received a state-of-the-art competency model, course syllabus and references on which they could build their course offerings. Health IT management courses were increasingly developed and offered by healthcare management programs during the time of the development of the HIMSTA project and following it until they became, as they are today, ubiquitous in these programs.

Table 8.1 HIMSTA curriculum competency objectives [8]

---

1. Information Management

Understand the major features of the information revolution; the role of knowledge workers; the differences between data, information and knowledge; data analysis and reporting; and major trends in IT; particularly as they relate to Health IT.

2. Strategy & Planning

Develop and align information systems strategy and plan with the organizational strategy and plan to support the achievement of organizational goals.

3. Assessment, System Selection and Implementation

Understand the purpose, use, and key functions of various administrative and clinical information systems and the factors that may influence adoption.

Design and plan for the selection and acquisition of a new or upgraded healthcare information system.

Appreciate the necessary resources, processes and support needed to effectively manage the implementation of healthcare information systems projects.

Demonstrate ability to apply project management principles, tools, and techniques to health information technology implementation.

4. Management of Information Systems and Resources

Manage information systems assets and functions to reach organizational goals.

Promote and manage the change that is necessary to reach the organization's information systems goals.

5. Assessing emerging technologies

Explore innovative uses of existing and emerging technologies to optimize healthcare delivery and improve efficiency.

6. Assessment of the Value of IT

Establish measurable goals and objectives, and assess the extent to which a health information technology implementation achieved those goals and objectives

7. Knowledge Domain: Security and Privacy

Demonstrate knowledge of legal and ethical issues and principles for protecting patient privacy and the security of health data.

Assess and implement policies related to the security of systems to protect data integrity, validity, and privacy.

8. Knowledge domain: Systems and Standards

Understand the role of standards and protocols in health information technology, the principal systems of protocols applicable to Health IT and the policies and development bodies responsible for Health IT standards

Assess the core elements of information systems and their networks in order to effectively manage both the systems and data assets.

Health IT courses that are offered today focus on competencies similar to those defined in the HIMSTA project, many with the addition of focus areas that address current issues in Health IT such as enhanced security, population health, artificial intelligence, etc.

Addition of Concentrations and Degree Programs

Some schools have taken the offering of management curricula in health IT further in response to market demand for more and more professionals with in-depth competence to pursue careers in managing what is today the immense infrastructure of enterprise IT systems including those in healthcare provider organizations, payers, public health, research and other related organizations. While the need for clinicians with specialized training in health IT systems has grown, the corollary need for non-clinician managers has also increased. In response, some schools and departments have expanded their programmatic curricula to offer degrees (Bachelors, Masters and PhD levels) and/or concentrations in specialized areas of health IT. These programs are typically offered to clinician and non-clinician students.

For example, the University of Alabama at Birmingham (UAB) offers a Graduate Program in Health Informatics (see Chap. 4). The UAB program describes Health Informatics as:

> a rapidly emerging discipline that connects people, technology, and data to better improve healthcare outcomes. Health Informatics professionals work with the processes and tools used to implement, maintain, and evaluate health informatics systems and applications. The Health Informaticist is a cross-cutting leader who drives analytics and usability [9].

This graduate program at UAB is also offered in a dual degree program for the students who want to combine it with a Master of Science in Health Administration.

> The MSHA/MSHI dual degree program allows students to get a deeper study of health informatics, an increasingly essential part of healthcare administration, with a strong healthcare leadership degree. Both degree programs are offered from the Department of Health Services Administration in the School of Health Professions [10].

In another example, the University of Central Florida's Department of Health Management and Informatics offers Bachelor's and Masters' degrees in Health Administration and a Bachelor of Science in Health Informatics and Information Management and a Master of Science in Health Care Informatics. The Master of Science in Health Care Informatics is designed for the student whose goal is to serve as a professional analyst in any of a number of roles or as a "project manager, EMR consultant, Chief Information Officer (CIO), or Senior Vice President" [11].

George Washington University offers a Master of Science in Management of Health Informatics and Analytics in their School of Public Health. It is offered alongside the Master of Public Health (MPH), Master of Health Administration (MHA) and Master of Business Administration (MBA). The program identifies career paths of Medical Information Officer, Chief Information Officer, Nurse Administrator, and Health Informatics Director for students completing this degree which reflects the common interests among physicians, nurses, administration and information services in the disciplines that are designed to support and serve in the middle and top management of the enterprise. These disciplines are reflected in the competency goals for the program:

- Effectively oversee organizational change
- Manage strategic and technological initiatives
- Apply healthcare law and policy knowledge
- Improve both business and clinical outcomes
- Implement and maintain ethical decision-making practices
- Integrate concepts of health informatics into areas of clinical care or research
- Solve real-world issue(s) related to healthcare [12].

Sources for Curricular Content

There are several sources that can be used to identify potential health IT content for the education of healthcare managers. One source is the accreditation bodies for healthcare management educational programs. Other sources to identify updates in the field and address challenges are professional membership organizations that represent professionals with direct responsibility in healthcare IT management such as ACHE, HIMSS, CHIME and APHA. These organizations, with descriptions from their websites, are described below.

- American College of Healthcare Executives (ACHE)
      For over 85 years, the American College of Healthcare Executives (ACHE) has focused on one mission—advancing leaders and the field of healthcare management excellence. (ACHE is) the professional home to more than 48,000 healthcare executives who are committed to integrity, lifelong learning, leadership and diversity and inclusion [13].
- The Healthcare Information and Management Systems Society (HIMSS)
      HIMSS is a global, cause-based, not-for-profit organization focused on better health through information and technology. HIMSS leads efforts to optimize health engagements and care outcomes using information and technology [14].
- The College of Healthcare Information Management Executives (CHIME)
      CHIME is an executive organization dedicated to serving chief information officers (CIOs), chief medical information officers (CMIOs), chief nursing information officers (CNIOs) and other senior healthcare IT leaders. (CHIME has) more than 2800 members in 51 countries and over 150 healthcare IT business partners and professional services firms [15].
- The American Public Health Association (APHA)

The Health Informatics Information Technology Section of APHA improves the public's health and promotes prevention and early intervention by advancing the use of innovative and effective information technology and informatics applications. Our mission is to improve the public's health and promote prevention and early intervention by advancing the use of innovative and effective information technology and informatics applications [16].

Accreditation and Certification Bodies

Higher education in health IT education is guided in part by specialized accrediting bodies. These bodies include:

The Commission on Accreditation of Healthcare Management Education (CAHME), which is the accrediting body for graduate programs in healthcare management. CAHME's mission is "to serve the public interest by advancing the quality of healthcare management education globally [17]. It accomplishes its mission by:

- Setting measurable criteria for excellent healthcare management education
- Supporting, assisting and advising programs which seek to meet or exceed the criteria and continuously improve
- Accrediting graduate programs that meet or exceed the criteria
- Making this information easily available to interested constituencies" [17].

CAHME accreditation standards do not specify course content for accredited programs. Instead, their standards call for evidence of leadership competencies that will enable the graduate to lead change and impact and influence their organizations in the mission-focused strategic directions that are supported by information systems. They have many examples of different types of IT curricular content in accredited graduate healthcare management programs.

According to the AUPHA website, the Association of University Programs in Health Administration

> is a global network of colleges, universities, faculty, individuals and organizations dedicated to the improvement of health and healthcare delivery through excellence in healthcare management and policy education. Its mission is to foster excellence and drive innovation in health management and policy education, and promote the value of university-based management education for leadership roles in the health sector. …AUPHA's membership includes the premier baccalaureate, master's and doctoral degree programs in health administration education in the United States, Canada, and around the world. Its faculty and individual members represent more than 400 colleges and universities [7].

At the undergraduate level, AUPHA certifies healthcare management programs. In the most recent criteria, AUPHA, under Criterion 23, requires that the "program will provide adequate coverage of all content in a list of 18 content areas." Among these is information systems management and assessment. This is detailed in the "Guidelines for Undergraduate Certification Criteria, 2017." The Curriculum and Teaching Criteria titled "Information Systems Management and Assessment", requires curriculum content which

Explores the critical role information technologies and systems play in healthcare organizations. The focus is often on the underlying technologies including hardware, applications, the Internet, and E-Health; planning and project management and the future of information technology in healthcare management [18].

These certification requirements have been an incentive for Undergraduate Programs to enhance their curricula to include information management and information technology competencies and content.

The Commission on Accreditation for Health Informatics and Information Management Education (CAHIIM) accredits programs in healthcare informatics. Established in 2006, CAHIIM attained recognition from the Council for Higher Education Accreditation (CHEA) in 2013 to reflect the expanded scope needed to meet the demands of a dynamic and growing market for professionals from clinical and management disciplines with advanced competencies in informatics [19] (CAHIIM is discussed in Chaps. 16 and 17).

Informatics Education for Health Administrators: The Future

The literature regarding the relationship between health IT curricula and healthcare management success outcomes is sparse, dated, and more anecdotal than quantitative. However, in June of 2012, the Institute of Medicine (IOM) published a Discussion Paper titled "A CEO Checklist for High-Value Health Care" that had been prepared by 11 highly respected management and clinical leaders in healthcare. This paper was designed to "inform and stimulate discussion" [20] not to serve as a guideline or research paper. In this paper, the authors drafted 10 items that they defined as key to the creation of a high-value healthcare system. Several of these items refer directly to health IT and/or indirectly to the core infrastructure that IT brings to the institution that is focused on creating high-value. Those checklist items related to the use of Health IT call for leadership and organizational commitment to:

- Infrastructure fundamentals:

  - IT best practices—automated, reliable information to and from the point of care
  - Evidence protocols—effective, efficient, and consistent care

- Care delivery protocols

  - Integrated care—right care, right setting, right providers, right teamwork

- Reliability and feedback

  - Embedded safeguards—supports and prompts to reduce injury and infection
  - Internal transparency—visible progress in performance, outcomes, and costs [20]

The items in the checklist are meant to be integrated into the culture of the organization and to serve as core items to transform that organization into a high value enterprise delivering improved quality and reduced costs for patients, payers, and the community. They are the factors that are internal to the organization and that the executive leadership can manage as compared to external forces that cannot be controlled by an organization's leadership, but must be anticipated, assessed and appropriately prepared for. Of the ten (10) items on the checklist, fully half of them are directly related to the implementation and management of IT systems. They emphasize the reasons why it is critical that graduates of masters and undergraduate programs in health administration understand, and gain competency in, the essentials of implementation and management of health IT systems. Next to the physical structures of the hospital or health system, the information system is one of the major investments that the organization will make. Beyond this, it is also the one major investment that will be transformational for the organization. Each of the items in the last four (4) bullet points in the CEO checklist rely on an IT infrastructure that supports the generation of meaningful data to, for example, guide the design and implementation of integrated care, and to support internal transparency and sharing of data and information.

More recently, ACHE devoted its Spring 2018 issue of Frontiers of Health Services Management to "Harnessing technology innovation to improve patient care." In opening the discussion on this topic, Editor Trudy Land asks "How do organizations develop and use new technology, and how do they measure the value of their investments? What innovative business models will drive the development or adoption of new technology" [21]? Ms. Land goes on to note the many ways in which technology is evolving to better involve and communicate with patients and coordinate care, to improve quality and safety, and to succeed in the value-based reimbursement system in which hospitals, health systems and providers of care function.

In short, the case is strong for the education of the next generation of healthcare leaders in understanding, analysis, decision-making and application of management principles in health information systems and information management. Graduate and undergraduate programs in health administration have progressed quickly in the last decade to develop and integrate competency goals and content in healthcare IT into their curricula. These curricula provide the educational experience, and foster the development of essential health IT competencies, that students need to move successfully into leadership and management roles after graduation. Currently, most healthcare management programs across the country include health information management, informatics and/or information systems content in their curricula. Some courses focus on informatics, others on information management, and others on information technology. Another approach is to teach health IT in an array of disciplines and courses such as finance, quality improvement, and project management. Each of these latter lends itself to a narrow exposure to health IT and, not necessarily, to information and technology management. For example, when IT content is taught in a finance course, the content tends to focus on financial systems; when taught in a quality improvement course, the focus tends to be on data and measurement. While each of these is important to the student, a more comprehensive coverage of health IT and information management serves to better prepare the student for management roles in provider organizations.

Summary

Over the coming years, healthcare IT will continue to grow and demand funding dollars, but, more importantly, it will provide the data and information that healthcare providers need to improve care delivery processes, develop the kinds of quality improvement programs that will advance patient safety and ensure that better results are delivered for the dollars spent, and improve financial performance. It will impact the way in which medicine is practiced, the ways in which medical teams work together, and the role of the patient in his/her own care. It will provide the information that is essential to drive improved quality, greater efficiency and better access to care. In short, it will support the much-needed transformation of healthcare delivery in the U.S.

However, IT is only one "cog in the wheel" of this transformation. It is the element that delivers essential data to make the transformation possible when managers and leaders have the competence to make strategic decisions regarding IT deployment, bring a sustainable vision and commitment to the process and make effective long and short term decisions that overcome barriers and require the use of the technology. Educational programs in health administration are the foundation on which that knowledge and those competencies are developed and through which the incoming generation of leaders are prepared for leadership roles. It is important that faculty have the tools they need to teach the essentials of health information management and systems in order to prepare students for that role. The library of materials for this purpose is growing daily, and the HIMSTA curriculum can provide the framework and a host of teaching tools to use those materials in a meaningful and effective curriculum.

Key Take-Away Points

- Health information systems infrastructure is key to the successful transformation of healthcare delivery and to the strategies that health IT leaders pursue to achieve this transformation.
- Health IT and information management comprise an important competency for graduates of healthcare administration programs.
- Health IT curricula and teaching resources are available to undergraduate and graduate programs in health administration.

References

1. Office of the National Coordinator for Health Information Technology (June 17, 2019) Quick Stats. https://dashboard.healthit.gov/quickstats/quickstats.php. Accessed September 20, 2019.
2. Yaraghi N. Hackers, phishers, and disappearing thumb drives: Lessons learned from major health care data breaches. Center for Technology Innovation at Brookings. May 2016. https://www.brookings.edu/wp-content/uploads/2016/07/Patient-Privacy504v3.pdf.   Accessed January 24, 2020.
3. Bresnick J. Top 12 artificial intelligence innovations disrupting healthcare by 2020. April 11, 2019. https://healthitanalytics.com/news/top-12-artificial-intelligence-innovations-disrupting-healthcare-by-2020. Accessed January 24, 2020.

4. Deloitte. Digital therapeutics: improving patient outcomes through convergence. 2019. https://www2.deloitte.com/content/dam/Deloitte/us/Documents/life-sciences-health-care/us-lshc-digital-therapeutics.pdf. Accessed January 24, 2020.
5. Krawiec RJ, Housman D, White M, Filipova M, et al. Blockchain: Opportunities for Health Care. Deloitte. Aug 2016. https://www2.deloitte.com/content/dam/Deloitte/us/Documents/public-sector/us-blockchain-opportunities-for-health-care.pdf. Accessed January 24, 2020.
6. Centers for Medicare and Medicaid Services. National Health Expenditure Data: Historical. 2019. https://www.cms.gov/Research-Statistics-Data-and-Systems/Statistics-Trends-and-Reports/NationalHealthExpendData/NationalHealthAccountsHistorical.html. Accessed September 20, 2019.
7. Association of University Programs in Health Administration. Vision, Mission, Values. 2016. https://www.aupha.org/about/visionmissionvalues. Accessed November 1, 2019.
8. Association of University Programs in Health Administration. HIMSTA Curriculum. 2012. https://network.aupha.org/himstacurriculum. Accessed November 1, 2019.
9. University of Alabama at Birmingham, Department of Health Services Administration, Health Informatics. 2019. https://www.uab.edu/shp/hsa/graduate/mshi. Accessed September 29, 2019.
10. University of Alabama at Birmingham, Department of Health Services Administration, Health Informatics. 2019. https://www.uab.edu/shp/hsa/graduate/residential-msha/dual-degrees-certificates. Accessed September 29, 2019.
11. University of Central Florida, Department of Health Management and Informatics. 2019. https://ccie.ucf.edu/hmi/programs/hci/faqs/. Accessed October 20, 2019.
12. George Washington University, Online Master of Science (M.S.) in Management Health Informatics and Analytics. 2019. https://publichealthonline.gwu.edu/health-informatics/. Accessed September 29, 2019.
13. American College of Healthcare Executives. 2019. https://www.ache.org/about-ache. Accessed October 24, 2019.
14. HIMSS Frequently Asked Questions. 2019. https://www.himss.org/himss-faqs. Accessed October 24, 2019.
15. College of Healthcare Information Management Executives. 2019. https://chimecentral.org/about/history-mission/. Accessed October 24, 2019.
16. American Public Health Association. Health Informatics Information Technology. 2019. https://apha.org/apha-communities/member-sections/health-informatics-information-technology. Accessed November 3, 2019.
17. CAHME Mission Statement. 2018. https://cahme.org/healthcare-management-education-accreditation/why-cahme/. Accessed August 15, 2019.
18. AUPHA Criteria for AUPHA Undergraduate Certification. 2017. https://higherlogicdownload.s3.amazonaws.com/AUPHA/5c0a0c07-a7f7-413e-ad73-9b7133ca4c38/UploadedImages/Certification/Guidelines_for_Undergraduate_Certification_rev_2017.pdf. Accessed August 14, 2019.
19. CAHIIM History. 2019. https://www.cahiim.org/about-us/history. Accessed August 14, 2019.
20. Cosgrove D. A CEO checklist for high-value health care. 2012. www.iom.edu/Global/Perspectives/2012/CEOChecklist.asp
21. Land T. Powering up with technology to deliver transformative care and lower costs. Front Health Serv Manag. Spring 2018;34:3. p. 1–2 https://journals.lww.com/frontiersonline/Fulltext/2018/03000/Powering_Up_with_Technology_to_Deliver.1.aspx. Accessed January 20, 2020.

Chapter 9
Clinical and Translational Research Informatics Education and Training

Peter J. Embi and Philip R. O. Payne

Role of Informatics in Clinical and Translational Science

The modern biomedical research domain has experienced a fundamental shift towards integrative clinical and translational research. This shift has been manifested in a number of ways, including the launch of the NIH Roadmap initiative [1–3] that has resulted in the creation of the Clinical and Translational Science Award (CTSA) program [3], as well as the rapid growth of high-throughput bio-molecular technologies and corresponding bio-marker-to-phenotype mapping efforts [4]. A commonly reported thread in a broad variety of reports and commentaries concerned with this evolution focuses on the challenges and requirements related to the collection, management, integration, analysis, and dissemination of large-scale, heterogeneous biomedical data sets [5–8]. However, well-established and broadly adopted theoretical and practical frameworks intended to address these needs are still lacking in the biomedical informatics knowledge base [7, 9–11]. Instead, the development and execution of integrative clinical or translational research is significantly limited by the propagation of "silos" of both data and expertise.

A critical need in overcoming such barriers to the efficient, timely, and impactful conduct of clinical and translational research is the development of a biomedical and informatics workforce educated and trained to make contributions both by leveraging informatics capabilities to accelerate biomedical research and to advance basic and applied science in the field of biomedical informatics itself.

P. J. Embi (✉)
Regenstrief Institute and Indiana University, Indianapolis, IN, USA
e-mail: pembi@regenstrief.org

P. R. O. Payne
Washington University in St. Louis, St. Louis, MO, USA
e-mail: prpayne@wustl.edu

© Springer Nature Switzerland AG 2020
E. S. Berner (ed.), *Informatics Education in Healthcare*, Health Informatics,
https://doi.org/10.1007/978-3-030-53813-2_9

As the conduct of clinical and translational research is an information-intensive task, much work at the intersection of biomedical informatics and biomedical research is needed and has, in fact, been ongoing. Indeed, in recent years, the application of biomedical informatics principles, approaches and tools to the conduct and support of clinical and translational research has evolved. The result is the emergence of two complementary biomedical informatics sub-disciplines that have arisen in response to the unique challenges and opportunities facing research, namely Translational Bioinformatics (TBI) and Clinical Research Informatics (CRI). While definitions vary, we will define these two sub-disciplines as follows:

- **Translational Bioinformatics (TBI)** is the sub-discipline of biomedical informatics concerned with the development of storage, analytic, and interpretive methods to optimize the transformation of increasingly voluminous biomedical data into what has been called P4 medicine (predictive, preventive, personalized and participatory) [4, 12, 13]
- **Clinical Research Informatics (CRI)** is the sub-discipline of biomedical informatics concerned with the development, application, and evaluation of theories, methods and systems to optimize the design and conduct of clinical research and the analysis, interpretation and dissemination of the information generated [5].

Given that these domains of TBI and CRI are both complementary and critical to the conduct of clinical and translational research these two sub-disciplines can collectively be referred to as **Clinical and Translational Research Informatics (CTRI)**, and this overarching sub-domain of biomedical informatics is what we will focus on in this chapter.

As depicted in Fig. 9.1, the combined sub-domain of CTRI overlaps with, and complements, the related, but distinct, informatics sub-domains concerned with aspects of basic and early translational science (e.g. bioinformatics), clinical practice (e.g. clinical informatics), and public and population health (e.g. public health informatics). This range of domains has been referred to as the translational research spectrum with multiple points of translation as shown in Fig. 9.1. As such, it is evident that CTRI spans the T1 and T2 ends of the translational research spectrum.

Challenges and Opportunities of CTRI

Management of Heterogeneous Data Sets

The ability to collect and manage heterogeneous data sets with increasing levels of dimensionality is a significant challenge. The dissemination and adoption of advanced information management platforms that will allow researchers and their staff to focus on fundamental scientific problems rather than practical informatics needs are critical to reducing the burden of managing large multi-dimensional data sets [7, 10, 14, 15]. Central to the ability to realize this opportunity is the imperative

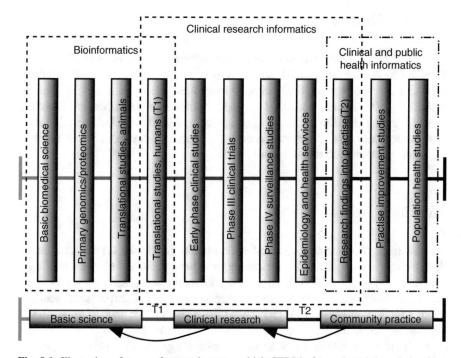

Fig. 9.1 Illustration of types of research across which CTRI is focused, and the relationships between CTRI and the other sub-domains of translational bioinformatics, clinical informatics, and public health informatics. These relationships also parallel the focus areas and methodologies associated with the clinical and translational science paradigm, including the commonly referred to T1 and T2 blocks in translational capacity (where the T1 block is concerned with impediments to the translation of basic science discoveries into clinical studies, and the T2 block with the translation of clinical research findings into community practice) (Reprinted with permission from BMJ, which holds the copyright, from Embi and Payne [5])

that the semantics of such data be well understood and made actionable relative to such operations [16–18].

Appropriate Methods and Tools

The need for knowledge-anchored methods and tools intended to enable the discovery, query, and integration of local distributed data, information, and knowledge resources is critical. This challenge is particularly pressing in multi-disciplinary team-science programs. The challenge is compounded by the fact that knowledge needed to discover, query, and integrate heterogeneous data, and information is often spread over a variety of sources [16]. The utilization of knowledge sources by scientific end-users is significantly hampered due to a lack of easy-to-use tools for knowledge resource discovery and information retrieval. Development of such tools is an opportunity for informatics.

Workflow Facilitation

The provision of systematic and extensible platforms capable of expediting work-flows for knowledge integration and analysis is critical to discovery science para-digms. The challenge in facilitating workflow is exacerbated by the lack of availability of systematic data and knowledge "pipelining" tools that are capable of supporting the definition and reuse of computational workflows incorporating mul-tiple source data sets, contextual knowledge sources, intermediate data analysis steps and products, and output types [19, 20].

Workforce Needs

As illustrated by the challenges and opportunities facing the CTRI sub-domain, there exists "…a major need to educate informaticians, clinical research investiga-tors/staff, and senior leadership concerning the theory and practice of CTRI. Such education was thought to be necessary to ensure appropriate expectation manage-ment; adoption/utilization of CTRI related methods or tools; and the allocation of appropriate resources to accomplish organizational aims" [5].

Such programs enable the creation of a critical pipeline of experts and thought leaders needed to drive CTRI as a discipline, expanding the current state of clinical and translational research informatics education in general.

Indeed, for the reasons stated above and due to significant progress in recent years, CTRI has emerged as a distinct discipline in its own right. Initiatives such as the CTSA program noted above have helped to galvanize the CTRI community and drive important work in CTRI with the goal of advancing clinical and translational science.

Amidst these ongoing efforts and the progress that has recently been made in CTRI both nationally and internationally, it is recognized that the numbers of IT, informatics, and research professionals trained in CTRI is quite small and inade-quate to support the advancements needed if we are to reap the benefits promised by this field.

In order to develop an adequately trained workforce with expertise in the criti-cally important and emerging domain of CTRI, a range of new programs have been under development in recent years. Such programs enable the creation of a critical pipeline of experts and thought leaders needed to drive CTRI as a discipline, expand-ing the current state of clinical and translational research informatics education in general. Those involved recognize that there are multiple levels of education and training needed to expand the research informatics workforce, including a variety of related but distinct programs that will serve audiences needing different levels of training/educational intensity based upon their career goals and job-requirements. These range from short tutorials, to intensive courses, to certificate programs, to formal training culminating in Masters or PhD level education in CTRI.

Table 9.1 Educational program applicability by learner stage/role

	Tutorial	Multi-week course	Certificate program	Master's degree (or PhD)
Student/resident, clinicians, faculty, leadership	X	x		
Investigators, research staff, or informatician liaisons	x	X	x	
Informatician, investigator, or research staff who will use or support research informatics		x	X	x
Informatician with research informatics career focus			x	X

X most applicable, *x* possibly applicable

The different levels of education for learners at varying levels of intensity based upon their stage of training, their role in the research and informatics/IT enterprise, and their career goals guide such program development. A description of the varying types of learners and the related types of training that would likely be relevant/ of interest to such groups of learners is depicted in Table 9.1. As the chart depicts using different size marks, learners in each category on the left may opt for more or less intensive training, but we have indicated with the large "**X**" those offerings we think most appropriate to each type.

To date, such programs are few and far between. However, there are some being delivered at the time of this writing, such as: (1) in-person and online "short courses" in CRI; (2) CRI online training programs; (3) Certificate programs in "Clinical and Translational Research Informatics" via online, distance-learning. A discussion of the curricular content areas will follow, but first we will lay out the different types of education and training opportunities that tend to dominate the current CTRI landscape.

Tutorials and Short Courses

In order to provide a basic understanding of clinical and translational research informatics to a wide audience including students, clinicians, research personnel and even institutional leaders who may not require or be interested in more intensive and lengthy programs of study, some research informatics "short-courses" or tutorials have been developed. Such courses typically consist of a truncated subset of information from a more intensive weeks-long research informatics course, such as the one described below and are delivered both online and in-person.

One such example is a 3-hour tutorial offered at national informatics professional meetings. The goal of such a program is to familiarize the groups listed with the basic concepts, goals, and utility of biomedical informatics approaches as they relate to advancing both the generation of evidence (i.e. through research as well as through common data collection, subject recruitment, and other activities) and the translation of research knowledge into practice.

Driven by the recognition of the importance of education and training focused on research informatics to ensure optimal use of information resources and capabilities across the research enterprise, some have also developed and deployed formal educational programs specifically focused in the CTRI space. One such example was a clinical and translational research informatics online training program developed by Embi and colleagues in collaboration with the American Medical Informatics Association's (AMIA) 10 × 10 initiative [11]. This 10 × 10 program, which was conducted from 2011–2016, provided students with an intensive survey of the field of CTRI delivered mostly via distance-learning, with a concluding face-to-face session that took place at an AMIA national meeting. Using state-of-the-art asynchronous distance education resources and techniques, the program incorporated multiple modes of learning and participant interaction including weekly voice-over-PowerPoint lectures, threaded discussion forums, online knowledge assessments, and a class project that is presented during a concluding face-to-face session. The audience included: (a) investigators interested in learning more about CTRI's relevance to clinical/translational research, (b) informaticians who are interested in strengthening their knowledge of CTRI as a subdomain of biomedical informatics, and (c) other students interested in the domain, such as those from the biotechnology or pharmaceutical industry, government, etc. A typical course schedule/curriculum for the 10 × 10 program is depicted in Table 9.2.

Certificate Programs

Beyond tutorials and short courses, there exists another level of training programs in CTRI that lead to granting of formal university-based certificates and that are often delivered via online/distance-learning offerings. The programs typically draw upon and leverage courses from CTRI tracks of Masters or PhD level curricula, though some are stand-alone. Typical certificate programs include a five-course series consisting of core courses and tracks with the ability for partial customization to suit learners (Fig. 9.2). Courses include such titles as: Introduction to Biomedical Informatics; Clinical and Translational Research Informatics; Decision Analysis and Cost Effectiveness Analysis; and Quality Improvement and Patient Safety; Introduction to Bioinformatics; Computational Genomics; Data Modeling and Database Design; IS/IT Architecture; JAVA Programming for the Enterprise; and Introduction to Research Methods and Biostatistics.

Sometimes, those who start off with the short-course option, will transition to the certificate to gain further knowledge. Typically, enrollees work with their advisor to determine whether they should pursue a T1 or T2 focused program of coursework, or "Track," based upon their interests, background, and career goals. That is, those who are interested in either a T1 (research informatics as applied toward the T1 end

Table 9.2 Curriculum for clinical research informatics 10 × 10 course

Week	Competencies (at the conclusion of this session students will be able to:)
1. Course overview and general biomedical informatics principles	Discuss the goals of the course
	Discuss basic principles of biomedical and health informatics including health system architectures, evaluation, etc.
	Discuss definitions of biomedical informatics and of the clinical research informatics subdomain of biomedical informatics
	Discuss the major challenges and opportunities facing the CRI domain.
2. Overview of clinical research	Discuss the definitions and types of clinical research and the related areas of translational research
	Discuss basic principles of clinical research including the research process, aspects of study design, data collection and analysis, etc.
3. Informatics applications in clinical research, part 1	Discuss the application of research-specific informatics approaches and tools in clinical research
	Discuss the uses of general informatics systems as applied to clinical research
	Discuss informatics methods and tools applied to research hypothesis development
4. Informatics applications to clinical and translational research, part 2	Discuss informatics methods and tools applied to protocol development
	Discuss informatics methods and tools applied to patient recruitment
	Discuss informatics methods and tools applied to adverse event surveillance and pharamcovigiliance
	Discuss informatics methods and tools applied to dissemination and utilization of research findings
5. Research data collection, management and analysis	Discuss current best practices and principles for data collection, management and reporting
	Discuss methods and tools applied to research data collection
	Discuss methods and tools applied to data analysis and reporting
6. Enterprise systems in CRI	Discuss principles and practice of research database and data warehouse development
	Discuss the key elements and features of clinical trial management and electronic data capture systems
7. Data and knowledge standards in CRI	Discuss the importance of standards, terminologies and models in biomedical informatics
	Discuss ontology and model initiatives in CRI
8. Regulatory and ethical issues in CRI	Discuss key issues in privacy, confidentiality and research oversight relevant to CRI practice
	Discuss key ethical considerations in research informatics
	Discuss key principles and tools for trial registration and results dissemination

(continued)

Table 9.2 (continued)

Week	Competencies (at the conclusion of this session students will be able to:)
9. Translational research informatics, and CRI-BMI overlaps	Discuss the applications of informatics principles of translational science (both T1 and T2)
	Discuss the overlap of clinical research informatics and related domains of clinical informatics, translational bioinformatics, and public health informatics
10. Review major CRI initiatives and future directions	Discuss major national and international initiatives driving the CRI Agenda
	Discuss key CRI directions for the future

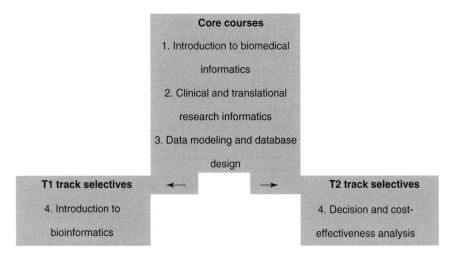

Fig. 9.2 Example curricula for certificate program enrollees, branched into T1 and T2 example tracks

of the translational spectrum) or T2 (research informatics as applied toward the clinical/population health end of the translational spectrum) emphasis, follow a customized "track" focused more so on bioinformatics or clinical informatics respectively, as appropriate. Figure 9.2 demonstrates example curricula for each track students might pursue.

Masters, PhD and Fellowship Programs in CTRI

For those who will focus on CTRI as their primary area of emphasis in a biomedical informatics career, formal training at the masters, doctoral, or fellowship level is appropriate. Training programs have been developed with just such a focus, and provide exploration of exemplary data, information, and knowledge management challenges and opportunities that exist as the intersection of biomedical informatics and both clinical and translational science. Such programs tend to offer a foundation in biomedical informatics, with an emphasis on issues unique to the CTRI subspecialty.

Lessons Learned

When viewed in a holistic manner, the preceding CTRI-focused training landscape and its historical evolution serve to elucidate three important lessons learned, as enumerated below.

Tailoring the Focus of the Curriculum for Different Learner Roles

One key lesson learned by the CTRI community has been that there are a variety of types of individuals who require training and expertise with regards to the domain. For example, some individuals seek training in order to support or enable their ability to serve as CTRI practitioners, wherein they might be responsible for the development, management, and support of various technology platforms and interventions targeting the clinical and translational science domain. Other individuals may seek training in order to inform their pursuit of innovative and novel scientific studies concerned with biomedical informatics theories and methods that may serve to address the clinical and translational research information needs. Finally, individuals in leadership or decision making roles (e.g., policy makers, etc.) may seek training in CTRI in order to inform their analysis and understanding of critical policy, financial, and socio-technical issues with relevance to clinical and translational research that they may need to address.

Each of these types of individuals requires a different type of training, which can be generally differentiated based upon: (1) its breadth (coverage of domain) vs. depth (level of detail); (2) its degree of theoretical vs. application-level orientation; and (3) its focus on different aspects of the research cycle and translational spectrum. For example, clinical and translational researchers who are not primarily CTRI practitioners may need training that has significant depth and application-level orientation with a moderate level of breadth in CTRI, focusing on the particular research areas they will be responsible for in their professional research setting. On the other hand, informaticians who want to specialize as CTRI investigators or researchers may need both a broad and theoretical grounding in the field with a high degree of depth into CTRI areas so as to ensure that they possesses a rigorous, strategic, and methodological understanding of the domain. Finally, policy or decision makers may need a great deal of breadth of understanding of the field, with an equal treatment of theory and applications-level foci, and a low level of depth. All of the aforementioned scenarios illustrate and continue to argue for highly tailored approaches to the design and delivery of CTRI training based on audience type and composition.

Differentiation of Acculturation vs. Training to Determine Type of Instruction

A related lesson that emerged from the ongoing development of CTRI training programs is that it is important to differentiate among the various CTRI roles and how these roles influence the needs of such individuals for either acculturation or training in the field. This differentiation will influence the type of course that is offered. In such a context, acculturation can be thought of as the process of gaining a "survey" level of understanding of the salient issues surrounding a domain, without gaining the theoretical and/or applied skills necessary to pursue practice or research in that area.

In contrast, training is more concerned with the preparation of individuals to actually pursue practice or research in an area. In the CTRI domain, given the diversity of potential stakeholders, there is a corresponding need for both types of education. For example, principal investigators of clinical or translational research programs may need to be acculturated to understand basic concepts and trends in CTRI so that they can efficiently interact with CTRI professionals, but do not necessarily need to gain a deeper level of understanding of underlying theories and methods. In contrast, individuals in the practitioner or investigator roles, as described in the preceding lesson learned, will need a far greater level of understanding regarding the field, necessitating in-depth training. To generalize, acculturation is a type of training need that can likely be achieved via seminars, workshops, and brief tutorials, while training likely requires formal degrees, coursework, or certificate programs, to name a few of many options.

Need for Alignment with Cross-Cutting and/or Foundational Biomedical Informatics Theories and Methods

Finally, as the maturation of CTRI training and education has progressed, it has become increasingly apparent that such efforts need to more carefully and systematically align competencies and curricula with cross-cutting and/or foundational biomedical informatics theories and methods. It is only though such alignment and harmonization that the emergent CTRI community and its members can benefit from historical and empirically evidenced trends in the broader biomedical informatics community (thus realizing the primary advantage of history, namely the ability to learn from it). For example, CTRI investigators and practitioners who seek to explore how EHR platforms can be leveraged to support/enable clinical trial recruitment can and should learn from, and apply, the lessons learned as well as basic theories and methods associated with the clinical informatics community's pursuit of advanced clinical decision support and guideline delivery systems. As such, curricula and education/training programs targeting such CTRI focused individuals need to "interweave" such cross-cutting or foundational knowledge into evolving and CTRI-specific competencies and coursework.

Conclusion

The field of CTRI is advancing rapidly, and there is a great and growing need to educate and train a range of personnel in the theories, methods, resources and regulatory and ethical issues unique to the CTRI domain. As an emergent and rapidly evolving sub-discipline of biomedical informatics, CTRI can extend core theories, methods, and historical lessons from the parent field. Because the CTRI workforce is growing at an accelerated rate, both education and training programs need to continue to develop and be evaluated in a similarly rapid manner. The ongoing efforts such as those illustrated above are beginning to address these educational and training needs to address this important area.

Key Take-Away Points
- CTRI researchers and educators should capitalize on the theories, methods and activities in the broader biomedical informatics domain.
- Multiple training and education scenarios exist to satisfy the need of the CTRI workforce, including formal coursework and degrees, as well as more topical workshops, distance education, and certificate programs.
- The delivery of CTRI education and training can and should be tailored to meet the variable needs, stakeholders, and roles incumbent to the clinical and translational science community, which by necessity also requires the differentiation of training versus acculturation to the field.

References

1. Zerhouni E. Medicine. NIH Roadmap Sci. 2003;302(5642):63–72. https://doi.org/10.1126/science.1091867.
2. Zerhouni EA. Clinical research at a crossroads: the NIH roadmap. J Investig Med. 2006;54(4):171–3.
3. Zerhouni EA. Translational and clinical science–time for a new vision. N Engl J Med. 2005;353(15):1621–3. https://doi.org/10.1056/NEJMsb053723.
4. Butte AJ. Medicine. The ultimate model organism. Science. 2008;320(5874):325–7. https://doi.org/10.1126/science.1158343.
5. Embi PJ, Payne PR. Clinical research informatics: challenges, opportunities and definition for an emerging domain. J Am Med Inform Assoc. 2009;16(3):316–27. https://doi.org/10.1197/jamia.M3005.

6. Chung TK, Kukafka R, Johnson SB. Reengineering clinical research with informatics. J Investig Med. 2006;54(6):327–33.
7. Payne PR, Johnson SB, Starren JB, Tilson HH, Dowdy D. Breaking the translational barriers: the value of integrating biomedical informatics and translational research. J Investig Med. 2005;53(4):192–200.
8. Sung NS, Crowley WF Jr, Genel M, Salber P, Sandy L, Sherwood LM, Johnson SB, Catanese V, Tilson H, Getz K, Larson EL, Scheinberg D, Reece EA, Slavkin H, Dobs A, Grebb J, Martinez RA, Korn A, Rimoin D. Central challenges facing the national clinical research enterprise. JAMA. 2003;289(10):1278–87.
9. Pate C, Chin D, Lutz S, Beard N, Isgur B, Loring J, Carlos RR. Research rewired. Merging care and research information to improve knowledge discovery. PricewaterhouseCoopers Health Research Institute; 2008.
10. Casey K, Elwell K, Friedman J, Gibbons D, Goggin M, Leshan T, Stoddard R, Tate D, Vick P, Vincent J. A broken pipeline: flat funding of the NIH puts a generation of science at risk. National Institutes of Health: Bethesda; 2008.
11. Hersh W, Williamson J. Educating 10,000 informaticians by 2010: the AMIA 10×10 program. Int J Med Inform. 2007;76:377–82.
12. Butte AJ. Translational bioinformatics: coming of age. J Am Med Inform Assoc. 2008;15(6):709–14. https://doi.org/10.1197/jamia.M2824.
13. Butte AJ. Translational bioinformatics applications in genome medicine. Genome Med. 2009;1(6):64. https://doi.org/10.1186/gm64.
14. Maojo V, Garcia-Remesal M, Billhardt H, Alonso-Calvo R, Perez-Rey D, Martin-Sanchez F. Designing new methodologies for integrating biomedical information in clinical trials. Methods Inf Med. 2006;45(2):180–5. https://doi.org/10.1267/meth06020180.
15. Ash JS, Anderson NR, Tarczy-Hornoch P. People and organizational issues in research systems implementation. J Am Med Inform Assoc. 2008;15(3):283–9. https://doi.org/10.1197/jamia.M2582.
16. Payne PR, Mendonca EA, Johnson SB, Starren JB. Conceptual knowledge acquisition in biomedicine: a methodological review. J Biomed Inform. 2007;40(5):582–602. https://doi.org/10.1016/j.jbi.2007.03.005.
17. Richesson RL, Krischer J. Data standards in clinical research: gaps, overlaps, challenges and future directions. J Am Med Inform Assoc. 2007;14(6):687–96. https://doi.org/10.1197/jamia.M2470.
18. Ruttenberg A, Clark T, Bug W, Samwald M, Bodenreider O, Chen H, Doherty D, Forsberg K, Gao Y, Kashyap V, Kinoshita J, Luciano J, Marshall MS, Ogbuji C, Rees J, Stephens S, Wong GT, Wu E, Zaccagnini D, Hongsermeier T, Neumann E, Herman I, Cheung KH. Advancing translational research with the semantic web. BMC Bioinformatics. 2007;(Suppl 3):S2. https://doi.org/10.1186/1471-2105-8-s3-s2.
19. van Bemmel JH, van Mulligen EM, Mons B, van Wijk M, Kors JA, van der Lei J. Databases for knowledge discovery. Examples from biomedicine and health care. Int J Med Inform. 2006;75(3–4):257–67. https://doi.org/10.1016/j.ijmedinf.2005.08.012.
20. Oster S, Langella S, Hastings S, Ervin D, Madduri R, Phillips J, Kurc T, Siebenlist F, Covitz P, Shanbhag K, Foster I, Saltz J. caGrid 1.0: an enterprise grid infrastructure for biomedical research. J Am Med Inform Assoc. 2008;15(2):138–49. https://doi.org/10.1197/jamia.M2522.

Chapter 10
NIH Training and Education for Biomedical Data Science

Valerie Florance

In 2018, the National Academy of Sciences (NAS) published a consensus study report entitled "Envisioning the Data Science Discipline: The Undergraduate Perspective" which identifies three areas of change that define and shape data science education: computing technologies and techniques, employer demand for new skills, and the need for new modes of education [1, p. 1]. Although focused on undergraduate education, the report's recommendations have clear implications for those being trained for research careers in biomedical informatics and data science. The committee's findings focused on developing 'data acumen', which they felt required introduction to key concepts and real-world problems, drawing upon diverse skill sets to frame domain-specific issues and solutions, including mathematical foundations, computational thinking, statistical thinking, data management, data description and curation, data modeling, ethical problem solving, communication and reproducibility. The NAS study also noted the need for new curriculum development approaches to apply teaching methods that best suited data science's interdisciplinary nature [1, pp. 32–33].

Several years earlier, scientists and leaders at the National Institutes of Health (NIH), whose 27 Institutes and Centers support the overarching NIH mission "to seek fundamental knowledge about the nature and behavior of living systems and the application of that knowledge to enhance health, lengthen life, and reduce illness and disability" [2], had seen the wave of change brought to all areas of biomedical research and development by the availability of digital data sets, images and text. These leaders recognized the promise that integrating, linking, visualizing and mining these resources offer to all areas of biomedical research and development. Efforts to address the changes led to two waves of NIH-wide engagement in planning and implementation of goals for data science research and workforce development.

V. Florance (✉)
National Library of Medicine, NIH, DHHS, Bethesda, MD, USA
e-mail: florancev@mail.nlm.nih.gov

E. S. Berner (ed.), *Informatics Education in Healthcare*, Health Informatics,
https://doi.org/10.1007/978-3-030-53813-2_10

In June, 2012, the Working Group on Data and Informatics (DIWG) of the Advisory Committee to the NIH Director issued a report providing recommendations to NIH about steps it needed to take to enhance its existing research and workforce programs. As the report's Executive Summary notes:

> The overall goals of the DIWG's work are at once simple and compelling:
>
> - to advance basic and translational science by facilitating and enhancing the sharing of research-generated data;
> - to promote the development of new analytical methods and software for this emerging data;
> - to increase the workforce in quantitative science toward maximizing the return on the NIH's public investment in biomedical research.
>
> "The DIWG believes that achieving these goals in an era of 'Big Data' requires innovations in technical infrastructure and policy. Thus, its deliberations and recommendations address technology and policy as complementary areas in which NIH initiatives can catalyze research productivity on a national, if not global, scale [3, p. 5]

The DIWG report contained five recommendations, each with a set of sub-recommendations. Notably the final recommendation urged a substantial financial investment by NIH to make the others happen. The recommendations are:

- Promote Data Sharing Through Central and Federated Catalogues;
- Support the Development, Implementation, Evaluation, Maintenance, and Dissemination of Informatics Methods and Applications;
- Build Capacity by Training the Workforce in the Relevant Quantitative Sciences such as Bioinformatics, Biomathematics, Biostatistics, and Clinical Informatics;
- Develop an NIH-Wide "On-Campus" IT Strategic Plan;
- Provide a Serious, Substantial, and Sustained Funding Commitment to Enable Recommendations 1–4 [3, pp. 6–7].

Of particular interest to this chapter is the report's third recommendation on building workforce capacity. This recommendation proposed three different strategies for achieving the goal: quantitative Training (T) and Fellowship (F) awards; enhanced review of quantitative training applications, such as formation of a dedicated study section; and creation of a quantitative component for all future NIH Training and Fellowship awards, which the DIWG felt "would contribute to substantiating a workforce of clinical and biological scientists trained to have some basic proficiency in the understanding and use of quantitative tools in order to fully harness the power of the data they generate" [3, p. 7].

Staff committees at NIH undertook implementation planning for these recommendations which led to the launch of NIH's Big Data to Knowledge (BD2K) initiative in 2013. The BD2K program had four areas of focus emphasizing facilitation of biomedical big data, development of analysis methods and software for big data; enhanced training for biomedical big data and the establishment of centers of excellence for biomedical big data. The program's accomplishments are presented on the NIH Common Fund web site at https://commonfund.nih.gov/bd2k.

In an article published in the Journal of the American Medical Informatics Association (JAMIA) in July 2014, the authors described the early steps that led up to the BD2K launch and its funding strategy for training. They summarized the BD2K training approach as follows: "The second launched BD2K area aimed to enhance the training of methodologists and practitioners in data science. Skills in demand under the data science 'umbrella' include computer science, mathematics and statistics, biomedical informatics, biology and medicine, and others, all incorporated as 'data science.' At the same time, the generation of large amounts of data together with the complex questions being posed, requires interdisciplinary teams to design the studies and perform the subsequent data analyses. The BD2K training initiatives seek to seed the development of investigators in all parts of the research enterprise who are well-trained in data science. Hand-in-hand with training is the need for cultural changes to assure that the contributions of scientists well-trained in data science are appreciated and rewarded, including the provision of appropriate career paths with commensurate incentives and rewards" [4].

A group of NIH staff from several Institutes and Centers was convened to oversee the implementation of the BD2K training goals. Initially, funding announcements were issued and awarded for predoctoral training programs (T32 awards) and for early career awards (K awards). Guidance to applicants in the first funding announcement for Predoctoral Data Science Training defined expectations and design principles that emphasized the need for interdisciplinarity:

- A combination of skills is needed to utilize Big Data, both technical and "soft" skills.
- Technical skills are needed in computer science or informatics, statistics and mathematics, and biomedical science.
- Communication skills are critical to foster collaborations.
- The principles of study design and reproducible research (related to the practices that ensure the reproducibility of analyses of data) should be stressed.
- Big Data scientists must be prepared to be independent researchers, but at the same time, an interdisciplinary, team-science approach is frequently the optimal way to solve Big Data challenges or to use Big Data effectively.
- Individuals and scientists may need additional skills and knowledge to work effectively in interdisciplinary teams.
- Training in the quantitative sciences and experimental design will be increasingly important to researchers and clinicians.
- BD2K training programs should be designed to develop the ability of scientists to work at the intersection of multiple disciplines necessary to utilize Big Data.
- Team mentoring is encouraged.
- Innovative approaches to training are encouraged, in order to take best advantage of the particular talents and expertise available at the institution(s).
- The training environment is critical and should include access to large data sets and ongoing research projects of multiple types.
- Career paths for data scientists that recognize and reward contributions in methodology, computation, or development of tools are important.
- Training individuals to participate across the full spectrum of scientific roles is encouraged, even though the jobs necessary to Big Data Science may not

correspond to traditional scientific, particularly academic, jobs or fit neatly into existing departments.

- Recruitment of talent from diverse scientific backgrounds, such as computer science, engineering, informatics, mathematics, physics, and statistics, to biomedical Big Data Science is important [5].

The Mentored Career Award (K22) in Biomedical Big Data Science for Scientists and Clinicians, another BD2K grant initiative, stated that it was "designed to facilitate the career development of interdisciplinary researchers who will develop technology, methods, and tools to capitalize on the Big Data already being generated by biomedical researchers. Big Data Science is interdisciplinary and involves three major scientific areas: (1) computer science or informatics, (2) statistics and mathematics, and (3) biomedical science. It is anticipated that, by the end of the award period, the awardee will have acquired breadth across all of these areas as well as depth in areas of specialty. Candidates may enter the program from various backgrounds: (1) biologists or clinicians who want to be cross-trained in the quantitative sciences (which includes computer science, statistics, mathematics, informatics, etc.), (2) quantitative scientists who want to be cross-trained in clinical/biological areas or other quantitative areas, and (3) biomedical data scientists who already have some background in areas relevant to Big Data Science but who want to gain further expertise" [6].

On behalf of the NIH BD2K training committee, a Request for Information (RFI) was issued in 2015 to solicit examples of existing training resources that could support training for biomedical big data research and assess availability of resources for teaching and learning biomedical big data science [7]. The RFI Summary report indicated that 16 respondents described more than 200 online resources from 84 institutions and organizations. Most frequently mentioned resources were MOOCs and college courses. The report recommended creation of an educational resource index. These data were used to drive development of additional BD2K funding initiatives relating to curriculum development and hands-on workshops [8]. Based on analysis of the RFI findings, a training coordinating center funding announcement was issued and awarded, to build communication across workforce grant awardees and serve as a home for shared resources across BD2K training and career grant awardees.

A search for "BD2K" in the NIH Reporter shows that between 2014 and 2018, more than 350 awards for more than $1.3 billion were made in that time period. Each listing has an abstract of the project and list of publications or other products. The awards and outputs of the BD2K training initiative are described on the Common Fund web site (https://commonfund.nih.gov/bd2k/highlights). The Common Fund web site for BD2K notes the following accomplishments for the BD2K training initiatives:

- More than 30,000 individuals trained in biomedical data science
- More than 255 biomedical data science resources
- Interactive digital media for analyzing biomedical data sets [9].

Two factors may have limited the longevity of BD2K as a long-term strategy at NIH. First, BD2K was supported by a novel cost-sharing model with initial support by the NIH Common Fund being increasingly replaced by a pool of funds collected from individual Institutes and Centers. Second, contrary to usual NIH practice, all awards in BD2K research and training programs were assigned to just one or a few specific Institutes or Centers regardless of the biomedical focus of the award area. This left awardees without a clear source for grant renewals, and left institute grant program staff managing grant awards unrelated to the mission of their Institute, fracturing the more typical scientific link between grantees and grant award stewards.

Aware that the last BD2K awards would end in 2020, and building on both the 2012 DIWG report and BD2K big data experience to date, in May 2018, NIH developed and issued a Strategic Plan for Data Science at NIH. NIH defines data science as "the interdisciplinary field of inquiry in which quantitative and analytical approaches, processes, and systems are developed and used to extract knowledge and insights from increasingly large and/or complex sets of data." The Strategic Plan, in addition to providing a definition of data science, was designed to guide current and future efforts for supporting improved infrastructure, new directions in discovery, and training strategies that are responsive to the needs of research and use of large and/or complex data sets, whether the data are clinical notes or biomedical images or sequence data from basic biological research [10].

In defining a trans-NIH strategy for data science, NIH included the following: "storing data efficiently and securely; making data usable to as many people as possible (including researchers, institutions, and the public); developing a research workforce poised to capitalize on advances in data science and information technology; and setting policies for productive, efficient, secure, and ethical data use. As articulated therein, the strategic plan commits to ensuring that all data-science activities and products supported by the agency adhere to the FAIR principles, meaning that data be findable, accessible, interoperable, and reusable" [10, p. 6].

The NIH Strategic Plan for Data Science has 5 goal areas:

- **Data Infrastructure,** which includes data storage and security and connecting NIH Data systems;
- **Modernized Data Ecosystem**, encompassing building a data repository ecosystem, supporting storage and sharing of individual data sets and better integration of clinical and observational data into biomedical data science
- **Data Management, Analytics and Tools,** covering support for useful generalizable and accessible tools and workflows, broadened utility of and access to specialized tools, and improved discovery and cataloging resources
- **Workforce Development** to enhance the NIH data science workforce, expand the national research workforce and engage a broader community
- **Stewardship and Sustainability** that includes development of policies for a FAIR data ecosystem and enhanced stewardship of the ecosystem [10, p. 5].

Since the issuance of NIH's strategic plan for data science, hundreds of NIH staff have been engaged in implementation planning to design and launch programs and initiatives. Quarterly reports are provided to Congress, to demonstrate progress on achieving the goals of the strategic plan. The NIH Office of Data Science Strategy (ODSS) coordinates and reports on the implementation efforts [11]. In addition, it provides leadership for new initiatives via seed funding or co-funding support for initiatives that arise from the work of these committees. In the area of biomedical data science training, it also supports data science summer internship and scholar experiences at NIH [12].

Like other Institutes at NIH, the National Library of Medicine (NLM) has a strategic plan that delineates its mission and its contribution to the overall NIH mission. NLM's strategic plan, a Platform for Biomedical Discovery and Data-Powered Health, was issued at the end of 2017 [13]. NLM has long been the NIH leader in training for research careers in biomedical informatics and data science, and as workforce development is one of the three goals in its own strategic plan, NLM staff prepared two special reports in support of the workforce development planning: "Report to the NLM Director on the State of Data Science Workforce Development" and "Core Skills for Biomedical Data Scientists".

The State of Data Science Workforce Development report looks at fellowship and training program data across the 24 NIH Institutes and Centers that offer them [14]. This report also provides a summary of data science training for NIH staff at that time, noting the presence of training teams at several Institutes and centers, including National Cancer Institute, National Institute of Mental Health, and an NIH Special Interest Group in Data Science [14, pp. 39–41]. The authors gathered data on 2016–2017 data science instruction provided by the NIH Center for Information Technology, the Foundation for Advanced Education in the Sciences, NCI, the NIH Library and NIMH and estimated that 264 classes were offered during that period, with attendance (whether in person or webinar) of 6652 federal staff [14, p. 42]. The report's recommendations encourage development of a common, accepted definition of biomedical data science and of its practices within NIH mission interest areas. Other recommendations suggest cross training of data scientists and biomedical scientists and promotion of data science literacy across the NIH workforce.

The second NLM-sponsored report, Core Skills for Biomedical Data Scientists, draws upon three sources: a 2017 Kaggle survey of self-identified data scientists, data science skills taught in BD2K-funded training programs, and 59 data-science related job ads [15]. Analyzing both reported and desired skills across academia, government, industry and nonprofit organizations, the report suggests a minimal set of 5 core skills for biomedical data scientists: (1) General biomedical subject matter knowledge of basic principles of biology, biomedical informatics and basic clinical science; (2) Programming language fluency in R or Python; (3) Methods of predictive analytics, modeling and machine learning; (4)Training in team science and scientific communication; and (5) Implementation of best practices in responsible data stewardship [15, p. 1].

An interesting finding of this report is gap areas between what programs teach and what employers seek. For example, a third of university programs teach regression analysis, but only 8% of job ads mention that as a desirable skill. Other university training emphases that were not a high priority in job ads were: subject matter knowledge, data mining, and probability statistics. On the other hand, employers sought skills in visualization, Python, R and SAS, data management, team science and presentation skills more often that universities taught these topics [15, pp. 8–10].

Data Science Training Within NIH

If new NIH extramural funding initiatives, whether for research or training, are to include data science goals across the 27 Institutes and Centers, the grant program staff who develop them need data science literacy. Many Institutes and Centers have scientific staff, either in their intramural research groups or their extramural grant program or scientific review staff, who received their advanced academic training before the 2012 DIWG report was issued. They have needs similar to extramural scientists for introductory and advanced training in biomedical data science concepts and methods, ethics of data use and team science.

However, to date, data science training for NIH staff has been uneven across the 27 Institutes and Centers. NLM offers access to training materials in advanced data management and data science for its practicing librarians, and provides a link to a BD2K funded video lecture series, Fundamentals of Data Science, with dozens of lectures by experts on such topics as reproducibility, data sharing, open science, issues with clinical data, causal inference, data modeling, machine learning, cloud computing and data pipelines [16].

The State of the Data Science Workforce report referenced earlier provides examples of other Institute-based data science training initiatives within NIH [14, pp. 62–64]. Both NLM and the NIH Clinical Center Library support data science training available to NIH staff and intramural researchers. For example, the training calendar for October at the NIH Clinical Center Library includes sessions on writing custom functions in R, data wrangling in R, Introduction to Data Visualization in R using ggplot. The National Center for Biotechnology Information (NCBI) supports 'code-athons' at NIH and around the country and provides an archive of past code-athons on github (https://ncbi-codeathons.github.io).

In summary, it is fair to say that since 2013, NIH has made a substantial investment in funds and staff time toward the goal of infusing biomedical data science throughout its extramural research and research training initiatives. The BD2K training initiatives provided a robust beginning, but the programs were not coupled to the mission interests of Institutes and Centers. Key to continued success in the training area will be the regular incorporation of data science coursework and skill development requirements into the standard 'parent' funding announcements or Institute-specific offerings for the National Research Service Awards (NRSA) mechanisms for Training (T) [17] and Fellowship (F) [18] support. For example, in September 2019, the National Institute of Diabetes and Digestive and Kidney Diseases (NIDDK) issued a new F31 predoctoral fellowship with this language:

> This training will require mentorship in both bioinformatics and metabolic disease disciplines. In order to advance bioinformatics science and encourage its application to these diseases and disorders, NIDDK invites applications from individuals with novel individual development plans (IDP). The fellowship training plan should focus on interdisciplinary approaches and mentorship among data or computer science and medicine in topics related to diabetes, endocrinology and metabolic diseases [19].

Work is ongoing in the NIH Training Advisory Committee to implement data science requirements in all training initiatives, in support of the NIH Strategic Plan for Data Science. These changes will appear as new Funding opportunity announcements are released. The simplest ways to watch for these changes are listed here, with links to the source sites:

- Subscription to the weekly TOC service https://grants.nih.gov/grants/guide/listserv.htm
- Periodic search in the NIH Reporter for active grants https://projectreporter.nih.gov/reporter.cfm using subject terms related to data science plus selection of the Funding mechanisms, such as T or F awards.

In summary, since 2012, two waves of implementation activities around biomedical data science at NIH have resulted in expansion of opportunities for research training and self-paced curriculum resources at NIH. Several institutes have issued data science research and training initiatives centered in their mission areas. A new Office of Data Science Strategies was established in 2019 to coordinate future activities and provide incentive funds for new initiatives. As new 'parent' funding announcements are issued for the National Research Service Awards (NRSA) fellowships and predoctoral training, language will be added to highlight the need for all basic biomedical research training, whether genetics or molecular biology or any of the other science areas supported by NIH, to provide predoctoral trainees with 'data acumen' of the kind recommended by the National Academy of Sciences [20, p. 28].

References

1. National Academies of Sciences, Engineering, and Medicine. 2018. Envisioning the data science discipline: the undergraduate perspective: interim report. Washington, DC: The National Academies Press. https://doi.org/10.17226/24886
2. National Institutes of Health. Mission and goals. https://www.nih.gov/about-nih/what-we-do/mission-goals
3. National Institutes of Health. Data and Informatics Working Group. Draft Report the Advisory Committee to the Director, June 15. Bethesda. MD: National Institutes of Health; 2012. https://acd.od.nih.gov/documents/reports/DataandInformaticsWorkingGroupReport.pdf

4. Margolis R, Derr L, Dunn M, Huerta M, Larkin J, Sheehan J, Guyer M, Green ED. The National Institutes of Health's Big Data to Knowledge (BD2K) initiative: capitalizing on biomedical big data, J Am Med Inform Assoc. 2014;21(6):957–958. https://doi.org/10.1136/amiajnl-2014-002974.
5. Predoctoral Training in Big Data Science (T32). Grant funding opportunity announcement. https://grants.nih.gov/grants/guide/rfa-files/RFA-HG-14-004.html
6. Department of Health and Human Services. BD2K Mentored Career Development Award in Biomedical Big Data Science for Clinicians and Doctorally Prepared Scientists (K01). https://grants.nih.gov/grants/guide/rfa-files/RFA-ES-16-002.html
7. Request for Information on the NIH Big Data to Knowledge (BD2K) Initiative Resources for Teaching and Learning Biomedical Big Data, RFI NOT-LM-15-001. https://grants.nih.gov/grants/guide/notice-files/NOT-LM-15-001.html
8. National Library of Medicine. RFI NOT-LM-15-001 Summary Report. 2015. Unpublished.
9. National Institutes of Health. Common Fund. Common Fund Programs: BD2K. https://commonfund.nih.gov/bd2k/grants
10. National Institutes of Health. NIH Strategic Plan for Data Science. https://datascience.nih.gov/sites/default/files/NIH_Strategic_Plan_for_Data_Science_Final_508.pdf
11. National Institutes of Health, Office of Data Science Strategy. https://datascience.nih.gov
12. National Institutes of Health. Meet the Graduate Data Science Summer Program Interns. https://datascience.nih.gov/meet-graduate-data-science-summer-program-interns
13. National Library of Medicine. A Platform for Biomedical Discovery and Data-Powered Health. National Library of Medicine Strategic Plan 2017–2027. https://www.nlm.nih.gov/pubs/plan/lrp17/NLM_StrategicReport2017_2027.html
14. Federer L, Zaringhalam, M, Huerta M. Report to the NLM Director. The State of Data Science Workforce Development. January 8, 2018. NLM Data Science Coordinating Unit, Workforce Excellence Team (Bethesda, MD, National Library of Medicine. Unpublished, 59 p.
15. Zaringhalam, M, Federer, L and Huerta, M. Skills for biomedical data scientists. Bethesda, MD, National Library of Medicine. No date, unpublished. 10 pages.
16. University of Southern California. BD2K Guide to Fundamentals of Data Science. https://bigdatau.ini.usc.edu/data-science-seminars
17. Ruth L. Kirschstein National Research Service(NRSA) Institutional Research Training Grant (Parent T32). https://grants.nih.gov/grants/guide/pa-files/pa-18-403.html
18. National Institutes of Health. Individual Fellowships. https://researchtraining.nih.gov/programs/fellowships
19. Bioinformatics Interdisciplinary Predoctoral Fellowship in Diabetes, Endocrinology and Metabolic Diseases. Grant funding opportunity announcement for individual fellowships issued September 29, 2019. https://grants.nih.gov/grants/guide/pa-files/PAR-19-378.html
20. National Academies of Sciences, Engineering, and Medicine. 2018. Envisioning the data science discipline: the undergraduate perspective: interim report. Washington, DC: The National Academies Press. https://doi.org/10.17226/24886.

Part IV
Informatics Education Worldwide

Chapter 11
Translating U.S. Informatics Educational Programs for Non-U.S. Audiences

John H. Holmes and Jeffrey J. Williamson

Informatics is a field with a rich history and is continuously evolving as an academic discipline. The growth of educational materials, such as curricula, course descriptions, syllabi, lecture notes, reading lists, online courses, archived webinars, and other multimedia materials, and textbooks, documents the growth of the field of biomedical and health informatics. In a real sense, these materials provide evidence of a maturing profession dedicated to research and applications of health information sciences. To date, many of these resources stem from educational efforts in the United States. Over the past 25 years, there has been substantial activity in the U.S. that has focused on developing educational programs in biomedical and health informatics. More recently, there has been a rapid development of such programs at academic institutions not usually associated with informatics education. Informatics educational programs in the U.S. exist in a variety of configurations, as described in the previous chapters. There are programs funded by the U.S. government, stand-alone graduate programs, certificate programs, and courses that are sponsored by specialty societies, and even numerous private institutions and universities now deliver informatics education. More recently, health informatics programs are appearing at the undergraduate level. While this growth is exciting to education professionals who direct informatics programs, there is work to do in clarifying and differentiating the coursework that is delivered at all levels of education, particularly as these projects attempt to translate informatics programs for non-U.S. audiences.

J. H. Holmes (✉)
Department of Biostatistics, Epidemiology, and Informatics, University of Pennsylvania
Perelman School of Medicine, Philadelphia, PA, USA
e-mail: jhholmes@pennmedicine.upenn.edu

J. J. Williamson
Department of Education, AMIA, Bethesda, MD, USA
e-mail: jeff@amia.org

© Springer Nature Switzerland AG 2020
E. S. Berner (ed.), *Informatics Education in Healthcare*, Health Informatics,
https://doi.org/10.1007/978-3-030-53813-2_11

In this chapter, we describe the development of educational programs and content in informatics in the U.S. and avenues for translating these artifacts to settings outside the U.S. The remainder of this chapter is organized as follows. We provide a brief survey of the history of the development of informatics education programs prior to discussing issues associated with the translation and dissemination of informatics educational content to settings outside the U.S. We also review some of the methods for dissemination. These are largely information and communication technology (ICT) tools, but they include others as well, such as onsite, in-person courses. We discuss the regional requirements posed by language, culture, infrastructural support, and educational system structure that all impact the success of disseminating educational content. Finally, we discuss avenues for the future translation of educational content, not only from the U.S., but from other countries as well.

Before examining these sections, a few definitions are needed. We have used the term *dissemination* throughout this chapter to mean making available to a wide audience the educational programs and components or materials that have been developed in or by U.S.-based educational programs. Second, although this chapter refers to *translation*, we will use that term in its truest sense: to *carry across*. We do not intend it to be limited to translation from English to another language, although that is certainly an important consideration. However, it must also include the adaptation of educational materials to locations and cultures outside the U.S., and this includes much more than language. Thus, the difference between the two terms is that dissemination refers to the broader activity of making educational materials available, without consideration of the constraints imposed by cultural or infrastructural requirements of non-U.S. users. Thus, translation is dissemination that considers these constraints, such that the materials provide the highest utility for the non-U.S. user. Finally, we use the term "educational materials", even though the chapter title uses the term "programs". Program connotes an organizational structure that includes many educational materials, and we certainly consider these. However, there is much to be said for including such entities as single courses, and even stand-alone lectures that exist outside the structure we typically associate with a program.

Background and History: Informatics Training in the United States

There are several key benchmarks in the growth of informatics that are worth mentioning prior to describing the different types of informatics education programs. In the early 1970s, the National Library of Medicine (NLM) funded the initial group of informatics training programs. A few years later in 1976 the Symposium on Computer Applications in Medical Care (SCAMC) was established, providing an outlet for the presentation of scientific research and scholarship. In 1984 the

American College of Medical Informatics (ACMI) was founded. A merger of SCAMC, ACMI, and the American Association for Medical Systems and Informatics (AAMSI) resulted in the creation of the American Medical Informatics Association (AMIA) in 1989. In 1992 the NLM introduced a weeklong seminar at Woods Hole offering the first short course entitled an *Introduction to Medical Informatics* and in 1994 the *Journal of the American Medical Informatics Association* (*JAMIA*) published its first issue. These formative events in the United States served as foundational elements for the academic discipline of informatics providing pathways for international collaboration, knowledge dissemination, and growth, both domestically and abroad.

National Library of Medicine Training Programs

The U.S. National Library of Medicine offers grants and funding to biomedical informatics programs through its Office of Extramural Programs (see also Chap. 2). There are 16 programs that were funded in the latest round of grants in 2017; these programs offer "graduate education and postdoctoral research experiences in a wide range of areas including: healthcare informatics, translational bioinformatics, clinical research informatics, and public health informatics" [1]. Additional programs may offer other tracks of training in specialized areas of informatics, such as dental and imaging informatics. The NLM-funded informatics training programs leverage their grant funding to grow their curriculum and broaden their base of students. The collaboration of the Regenstrief Institute and Indiana University School of Medicine with the Regional East African Center for Health Informatics at Moi University in Eldoret, Kenya is a good example of this approach to international education outreach and training program development. This collaboration is a joint effort supported by the U.S. Agency for International Development (USAID) and Academic Model Providing Access to Healthcare (AMPATH), a partnership with U.S. institutions based at the Moi University School of Medicine. By leveraging the existing informatics program to procure additional funding through the Fogarty International Center of the U.S. National Institutes of Health, the Regenstrief Institute Center for Biomedical Informatics (CBMI) has become a leader in global health informatics. The CBMI has hosted several Kenyan scientists through the years for training in informatics to support the deployment of a medical record system designed for low resource areas that has evolved through the years and is now known as the Open Medical Record System (OpenMRS). As this project has grown throughout Kenya and sub-Saharan Africa, a need for locally trained professionals to support the deployment of OpenMRS stimulated the development of a Bachelor of Science in Informatics program at Moi University [2]. The curriculum that leads to a degree in informatics contains many courses or elements of courses that are commonly found in U.S. based programs.

Stand-Alone Graduate Programs

Stand-alone graduate programs in informatics offer programs leading to a master's or doctoral degree. There are now more stand-alone graduate programs in informatics than any other type. These programs rely on institutional funding, grant support, and most importantly student tuition to sustain their academic programs. Stand-alone graduate programs can be found in such schools as medicine, nursing, public health, and engineering and they may be located in centers or institutes that combine faculty and students from one or more schools in a university setting.

Certificate Programs

Informatics certificate programs are composed of one or more courses where the student may accumulate academic credit but does not earn a degree. A certificate of completion in a designated area such as health informatics is a common outcome for participation in such a program. Certificate programs are commonly offered either as in-person classroom experiences or online, or a combination of both. These programs usually comprise less than half of the contact hours usually required for a master's degree. The target student for these programs is typically an adult learner or working healthcare professional. These include physicians, nurses, pharmacists, chief medical/nursing information officers, health program administrators, and public health personnel who are looking to supplement their existing knowledge. A certificate of completion from a reputable program confers the recognition that the student has attained a certain level of knowledge and acquired a set of skills that are useful for the practice of informatics in his or her chosen profession. However, certificate programs do not ordinarily provide the depth of knowledge or skills that one would need to pursue informatics as a primary occupation.

The 10 × 10 Program

10 × 10 is a training program launched and administered through the American Medical Informatics Association with the goal of training 10,000 clinicians in basic informatics [3–7]. The 10 × 10 program is described in Chap. 18. Shortly after the program was deployed it enjoyed success as a public program with open enrolment, and the need for focused special courses materialized both domestically and internationally.

The 10×10 program is one of the earliest examples of the translation of informatics educational content outside the U.S. The 10×10 partner at Oregon Health and Science University (OHSU), led by William Hersh, MD, began discussions with AMIA about developing a collaboration with an emerging informatics group in South America that included Paula Otero of Argentina and with a group in Southeast

Asia that included K.C. Lun of Singapore. The purpose of the collaboration was to offer a version of the popular OHSU 10×10 distance learning course to the local constituencies in Argentina and Singapore who desired a basic informatics education. The OHSU course in Argentina had trained several hundred individuals over the prior 3 years, so the proposed collaboration merely strengthened an already strong relationship between the two institutions. Then-President and CEO of AMIA Donald Detmer led discussions about advancing the 10×10 brand globally through a partnership with Drs. Lun and Hersh, and Jeffrey Williamson, AMIA Vice-President for Education and Academic Affairs. However, financial constraints prevented applying the domestic 10×10 business model to an OHSU course that would be administered only through that institution. From this reality, it was determined that a more appropriate model would be to engage educational material providers in countries outside the U.S., and the concept of internationally-focused 10×10 emerged. The extension of the 10×10 concept was seen as complementing AMIA's desire to collaborate with international partners to disseminate content from U.S.-based programs. AMIA had initiated several projects to increase informatics capacity in low- and medium-resource countries. One was a conference of international leaders in informatics and informatics education held in Bellagio, Italy [8], the Health Informatics Building Blocks project (funded by the Rockefeller Foundation), and the other was the Gates Foundation-funded Global Health Informatics Partnership Program.

The 10×10 program is a strong and highly visible means of providing basic informatics educational content. The OHSU program has been translated into Spanish by Dr. Otero, and is in use in Latin America (See Chap. 13 for more information on this program).

In addition, 10×10 provides a way for informatics course leaders in countries outside the U.S. to provide content in their region. The criteria for participation in 10×10 include (1) a requirement that the program include recognized international informatics faculty and (2) there must be an endorsement of the proposed course by the local or regional member society of the International Medical Informatics Association. The course proposal should include a program description, course design, rationale for participation, and an overview of course administration, which parallels the requirements for approval of a 10×10 course proposal from a U.S. institution. Students completing the course receive a 10×10 certificate of completion from AMIA. An institution offering a 10×10 course can be located in any country. For example, the OHSU Gateway 10×10 program provides courses in Argentina and Singapore [9].

Continuing Education Programs

There are many continuing education (CE) programs for health professionals who wish to acquire informatics knowledge. Membership associations and specialty societies design educational programs after assessing the CE needs of their constituencies. Conferences, workshops, webinars, symposia, tutorials, journal-clubs, and more recently, case-based learning opportunities (sometimes called "boot-camps") provide exposure to highly focused subject matter over a period of time ranging from an hour to several days. Enrollees are immersed in these activities and find value in not only the content being delivered but also the opportunity to network with others facing health information technology problems. Because informatics is inter-professional, these organizations are often challenged to produce programs that appeal to the scope and breadth of the health professionals in their target audience.

In order for the field of informatics to continue to grow, there must be the recognition that the many educational resources that have been developed, and will continue to be, should be made available to as wide an audience as possible. Whether these resources are distributed under a revenue-based business model or one that is open and supports the free dissemination of educational material is determined by the developer or the provider. There are potential constraints to making available such materials, and these are discussed later in this chapter; however, the assumption here is that sharing of educational resources across the globe is good for the profession, its students, and society at large.

A Growing Consensus of Informatics Educational Requirements

With the burgeoning of educational programs in informatics, there appears to be a growing need for consensus about the academic requirements, organization of faculty, and management of educational and research programs focused on informatics in U.S.as well as non-U.S. universities and colleges. This is evidenced by numerous publications in the informatics literature [10–31]. Scholars and subject matter experts are taking the issues and challenges around core competencies, certification, and accreditation more seriously than ever. This can only benefit those individuals looking to leverage content for healthcare educators and professionals in other parts of the world.

Many informatics education programs collaborate to formulate guidelines and best practices for education and training. These are disseminated nationally and internationally through informatics communities of practice. Communities of practice include entities like the AMIA Academic Forum, a body of educators from academic institutions who are dedicated to serving the needs of post-baccalaureate biomedical and health informatics training programs, baccalaureate degree programs, and programs focused on training future clinical professionals such as physicians and nurses.

Translating and Disseminating Educational Content: Challenges and Opportunities

As noted in the introduction to this chapter, there are many types of items that could be candidates for translation to other audiences outside the U.S. However, one must consider several important constraints that affect the translation of educational content from the U.S. to other countries. These fall into two broad classes—those that affect the U.S. provider and those that affect the non-U.S. consumer. The U.S. provider is typically a university, healthcare system, or a public health agency, and the content creator is an employee of the provider. This is an important distinction in many settings, because of the question of who owns the intellectual property that is the educational content. Even though a faculty member had designed a course and created all of the educational materials for the course, in most cases that course and all artifacts that are associated with it are the property of the university with which the faculty member is associated. This is because the faculty member was working as an employee of the university. The concept of intellectual property ownership is not universally understood across the U.S., however, and a thorough examination of its implications for each type of setting where educational materials might be produced is beyond the scope of this chapter. Intellectual property issues are clearly a first-order concern when disseminating educational materials to users outside the entity, and this is particularly acute when these materials are expected to generate revenue.

Another constraint that one must consider in translating educational content from the U.S. to other countries is sensitivity to the cultural, social, and organizational contexts of the target country. In the U.S., we sometimes take the context for granted, and sometimes to our detriment, but educational materials based on U.S.-centric knowledge and experience do not necessarily translate well to non-U.S. settings. Perhaps the most obvious barrier is language, and this barrier is manifested on at least two levels: the language of common communication, and the language of technology. Communication in English in a non-English speaking country is certainly challenging, and might actually be inappropriate. One would expect that educational materials developed in English but destined for, say, Croatia, would be translated into Croatian, a non-trivial task that requires a native speaker to supervise that endeavor. Second, even when the target audience is English-speaking, complicated, systems-related concepts that we in the U.S. represent with a language of acronyms and abbreviations require considerable decompression and description. Of course, translating these concepts is doubly-difficult when the target language is not English.

A third potential barrier is the difference in organizational structures between the U.S. and other countries. For example, healthcare delivery models in non-U.S. countries are often quite different from the employer-based healthcare insurance model in the U.S. So-called "socialized medicine" as seen in many other countries exerts a different impact on how health information is gathered, maintained, analyzed, and made available to others.

A fourth barrier is the difference in professional roles. For example, in countries like the United Kingdom, the primary care physician ("GP") serves as the gatekeeper for a patient's care and is normally the practitioner who prescribes medications or orders tests and procedures. This organizational structure has implications for translating U.S. educational content to this kind of setting. Users of the electronic health record (EHR) in the U.S. are vastly more diverse, from across a wide range of health professions.

Fifth, regulatory differences that exist between different countries and the U.S. pose potentially difficult barriers for the U.S. educator wishing to disseminate informatics content. For example, privacy and confidentiality regulations in the U.S. are considered by many to be the strongest in the world, but in reality, there are many regions where ministries of health and other governmental bodies have imposed even stricter constraints on the use of identifiable health information. Such regulations need to be observed rigorously on the part of U.S. educators as they develop course material on such topics as network and system security, master patient indexes, and data archiving. As in the U.S., these regulations usually apply to both clinical practice and research. Other regulations such as those applying to data and communication standards may be different than those in the U.S., and curricula should be developed with sensitivity to these as well.

Finally, organizational, administrative, practitioner, and financial capacity can exert substantial effects on the ability to translate informatics educational content from the U.S. to other countries. It does little good to focus a course on an expensive, complicated electronic health record system that could not be implemented in a region due to cost, lack of experienced systems personnel, or even network or electrical power infrastructure. And in a country where there are few practitioners to provide care for a growing population, the priorities of those practitioners are more likely to be focused on providing that care than on embracing a technology that may or may not have any obvious value.

These are typical concerns that affect the viability of any effort to translate U.S.-based and especially U.S.-centric informatics educational content to another country. There are undoubtedly others, such as difficulties in disseminating online content [32] and these are likely to vary on a country-by-country basis. The most important principle to guide the translation of an educational program or course is that the course developer must always be cognizant of the needs of the target audience, and this often involves considerable investment of resources in order to develop educational content that is meaningful and useful to those in the target audience. One way we can effectively translate and disseminate this content is to explore and use methods that take advantage of whatever technological environment is available in the targeted country. Several of these methods are described in the next section.

Methods for Disseminating Educational Content

Onsite, In-Person Dissemination

It is probably true that in most cases, face-to-face instruction, in person, and in real-time, is the ideal method for disseminating any educational content, and informatics content is no exception. Especially in a discipline that relies heavily on demonstration and hands-on experience with software tools, such an educational experience should be considered whenever possible. However, this is not always practical, especially in situations where students are not able to assemble in a single location because of travel constraints. In these cases, online learning environments provide a cost-effective, resource-sparing means for disseminating content to students. These environments can also enhance the educational experience for instructors and learners through feature-rich software that has been developed over the past decade.

Online Learning Environments

Online dissemination of informatics educational content is rapidly becoming the preferred method for training, although it is not without its challenges, for the reasons described above. Learning management systems (LMS), or virtual learning environments, are web-based software tools that provide support for a variety of communication modalities, including discussion boards, email, and real-time interactive communication. Moodle [33] is an example of an open source LMS that is freely available and distributed under the GNU General Public License, and is an attractive option for dissemination to low-resource countries. Blackboard [34] and Canvas [35] are well-known proprietary LMSs that have a worldwide market. In between these systems, there are numerous LMSs that support a wide variety of instructional needs. Most LMSs support both asynchronous and real-time dissemination of educational content.

Asynchronous Methods

Asynchronous methods of disseminating content online support the posting of material such as documents, slide sets, lecture notes, and multimedia. Communication between instructors and learners (or between learners and other learners) occurs not in real time, but by means of posts that are read and replied to at some point after the posts are made. The simplest methods for asynchronous dissemination include discussion boards and email, which support limited content depending on the software environment. One type of asynchronous dissemination method is the archive of previously recorded real-time content, such as webinars and lectures. These materials can be placed on websites for viewing at learners' convenience.

Real-Time Methods

Interaction between participants in an online educational environment ideally occurs in real-time. In this way, learners and instructors provide and receive nearly instantaneous responses to questions and can engage in discussions as if they were communicating face-to-face in a classroom. Webinars provide one means for learners to experience educational content such as lectures and discussions in a real-time online environment. In a webinar session, an instructor can present a lecture using any assistive technologies, such as a live-streaming application or software such as PowerPoint and multimedia that could be used in any lecture setting. Translation from one language to another for live webinars would demand simultaneous translator services, although an archived presentation could be translated after it is created, and it would likely be easier to perform that translation into more than one language. Translating the materials displayed on the screen would pose a more difficult challenge, since this cannot be accomplished easily in real time. In any event, the dissemination of a presentation to multilingual audiences is possible, using multiple versions of the presentation in the target languages.

A more challenging problem involves disseminating webinars in developing countries, where broadband connections may be unavailable or unreliable. Webinars require substantial bandwidth, owing to the use of audio and especially complicated and dense video. For example, a typical webinar will display an instructor's computer screen with a PowerPoint presentation, perhaps with complex graphics, photographs, and movies. This type of presentation will not be viewable if the capacity of the broadband connection is substandard, say less than 5 Mbps.

These challenges aside, the webinar is an excellent medium for disseminating informatics training and educational content. In addition to providing the potential for real-time interaction with the instructor and other attendees—most webinar providers offer a chat facility—a learner could perform exercises online, perhaps using print material supplied in advance, or online problem sets, much like one would experience at the blackboard in a real classroom. Another advantage to the webinar platform is, as noted previously, its ability to be archived. This is important for allowing those who cannot attend a live webinar due to scheduling conflicts, network outages, or illness. Such learners could go to a website, select a webinar from the archive and watch as if it were live. Of course, they would not be able to participate in discussions or other events that occurred during the live webinar, but there could be added some educational activity that could be experienced asynchronously, such as a quiz that would be completed and submitted by the learner, and subsequently graded by the instructor.

Another approach to using the webinar platform is to create content offline and then disseminate it asynchronously, in an archive. This approach is often used where the educational material is produced in a studio or other environment, without the interruptions or benefit of live participation. One disadvantage of this approach is that there is no student discussion to archive, so the presentation might not be as rich as one would experience were the webinar captured live with student participation. This kind of webinar is best when the material is to be presented as a simple lecture or demonstration. It is in common use in a number of informatics training programs, such as some 10×10 sites. Like the archived live webinar, this "studio-produced" webinar can be used for asynchronous interactions with the instructor and other students through such resources as a discussion board on a learning management system.

There are a growing number of webinar software programs such as Zoom, GoToWebinar, or AdobeConnect that support video and audio, and most support real-time remote desktop capture, as well, so that participants can see the host's computer desktop as if it were their own. This feature is important for those who plan to demonstrate software or show slides as part of a lecture. Finally, all of these systems support recording so that a webinar can be archived for future access. Chapter 19 discusses organizational and instructional strategies for distance learning.

Communities of Practice: HIBBs

The goal of a community of practice (CoP) is to establish a forum in which people who work in a particular profession or occupation can share their knowledge and experience. A CoP can exist in physical environments, such as an annual professional meeting, but more recently, there has been increased interest in online CoPs, as evidenced by discussion boards, listservs, and groups. CoPs exist in many professions, and informatics is no exception, with representation in the American Health Information Management Association (AHIMA), the Health Information and Management Systems Society (HIMSS), the Society for Imaging Informatics in Medicine (SIIM), the Australasian Institute of Digital Health, and the American Medical Informatics Association (AMIA), with the last providing an interesting case study.

AMIA was funded by the Rockefeller Foundation to establish a community of practice model for dissemination of informatics training materials throughout the world. The centerpiece of this model was a tool called the Health Informatics Building Blocks (HIBBs), which is a repository of training modules developed by informaticians for those working with or in health information technology and informatics. The purpose of the HIBBS is to provide open-source, shareable, freely accessible (and free) educational materials for the development of skills and knowledge in the creation, management, and use of information. A building block, or module, is intended to be reusable and portable to many different settings; in that regard, they truly are "building blocks" that can be used as components in a larger curriculum or educational program.

The initial modules were focused on informatics practice and education in Africa, and were developed within AMIA in cooperation with the South African Institute for Distance Education (SAIDE) Open Educational Resources (OER) Africa [36]. The HIBBs modules are available without the need for an account or password [37]. They are licensed by the Creative Commons Attribution-Share Alike 3.0 Unported agreement. This provides substantial freedom in terms of use, allowing the modules to be shared, adapted, and usable for commercial applications, such as tuition-bearing courses, as long as the original work is attributed to the original authors and any subsequent distribution must be made under the license.

As of June 2020, the OER Africa HIBBs include eight modules on basic computer skills, introduction to informatics, health information systems, electronic medical record systems, ethics and legal issues, data quality, research data, bioinformatics, and change management. There is also a template that can be used to create game-based quizzes for use in classes. The HIBBs repository continues to grow, and although there is no empirical evidence of how these modules are being used in educational settings, it is clear that contributors are motivated to create and share their knowledge of critically important aspects of informatics.

The Future of Translating Informatics Educational Materials for Non-U.S. Audiences

There is increasing interest in establishing collaborations between the U.S. and non-- U.S. audiences for disseminating informatics educational content. As more countries and regions outside the U.S. develop the capacity for informatics-assisted healthcare and research, practitioners, administrators, and researchers are in need of highly trained informaticians. With its long history of developing curricula and programs for training informatics professionals the U.S. stands at a unique position to disseminate the fruits of its informatics educators' experience and expertise to other countries where the desire to grow informatics capacity is great.

But there are other countries, particularly in Europe, that stand with the U.S. in this endeavor, and this is manifested in the International Partnership for Health Informatics Education [38]. This organization, founded in 1998, is a collaboration of institutions in Germany, The Netherlands, Austria, Taiwan, and the U.S. to "…promote education through international collaboration of graduate and undergraduate training programs in Medical and Health Informatics."

It is equally important to recognize that the growth of the academic discipline of informatics over the past few decades has occurred not only in North America, but also in other parts of the developed world. Informaticians from Europe, southeast Asia, and South America either have developed or are developing robust informatics programs and training capacity that can complement efforts originating from the United States. Many of these programs are well recognized and highly regarded in the world of academic informatics.

In fact, in interacting and exchanging ideas and teaching practices with colleagues on an international level, it is important to recognize that the exchange of knowledge is bilateral. Informatics research and training programs in the United States are not without their own set of challenges. Exposure to successful approaches during the process of translating content can elevate the international conversation as scholars seek an optimal state of informatics program design. Indeed, this can, and should, occur both in more developed parts of the globe and in low resource areas. The best approach is to recognize that the strategies and solutions developed through cross-programmatic discourse and translation return a rich set of experiences through which all collaborators can benefit.

So what does the future bring when it comes to translating informatics content for use by educators in other parts of the world? We know that programs in the United States exist in many different forms and sizes with administrative homes in schools, departments, centers, and academic units within universities. The lack of uniformity in our informatics training eco-system in the United States means that large-scale, systematic, or enterprise level efforts to translate content can be extremely difficult and fraught with barriers. Challenges are further exacerbated by the difficulty of gaining consensus when multiple stakeholder organizations are involved, even when the stakeholders agree there is a true opportunity or local, regional, or national need. But opportunities exist when relationships within informatics faculty, programs, universities, organizations, and even governments can be leveraged.

In conclusion, it is clear that informatics faculty are eager to collaborate based on genuine commitment to developing or elevating the academic discipline to other parts of the world. This is particularly true where an acute need exists and can potentially help elevate the level of expertise for the betterment of healthcare delivery and human health. Furthermore, as described above, the educational technologies that exist for content translation and deployment are favorable to focused interactions with U.S.-based informatics programs. By accessing and building upon the resources described in this chapter, the informatics instructional materials, educational multimedia, learning objects, and published informatics literature all available in the public domain, there is promise for the translation of informatics programs on a global scale.

Key Take-Away Points

- Informatics capacity-building efforts outside the U.S. benefit from strong collaborations with academic institutions and leaders in the targeted region.
- The benefits of collaborations between U.S. and the non-U.S. institutions are mutual—many successful programs outside the U.S. can provide models for large scale informatics education programs.
- Information and communication technologies offer numerous ways to disseminate informatics educational content effectively.
- Language and infrastructure differences can present challenges in translating U.S.-developed programs to other countries.
- Translating informatics educational content to countries and regions outside the U.S. requires sensitivity to organizational, cultural, and social context.

References

1. National Library of Medicine. NLM's University-based Biomedical Informatics and Data Science Research Training Programs. http://www.nlm.nih.gov/ep/GrantTrainInstitute.html. Accessed 3 June 2020.
2. Moi University School of Information Sciences. Bachelor of Science in Informatics. 2020. https://campusnairobi.mu.ac.ke/index.php/information-sciences.html. Accessed 3 June 2020.
3. Safran C. Informatics training for clinicians is more important than hardware and software. Yearb Med Inform. 2009;4:164–5.

4. Feldman S, Hersh W. Evaluating the AMIA-OHSU 10x10 program to train healthcare professionals in medical informatics. AMIA Ann Symp Proc. 2008:182–6.
5. Hersh W. Recent trends in biomedical and health informatics education: implications for practice, research, and policy. AMIA Ann Symp Proc. 2008:1205–6.
6. Feldman SS, Hersh W. Evaluating the AMIA-OHSU 10x10 program to train health care professionals. AMIA Ann Symp Proc. 2007:953.
7. Hersh W, Williamson J. Educating 10,000 informaticians by 2010: the AMIA 10×10 program. Int J Med Inform. 2007;76:377–82.
8. Kay M, Santos J. Report on the World Health Organization Global Observatory for e-Health strategic planning workshop, April 2008. Methods Inf Med. 2008;47(4):381–7.
9. Gateway Consulting Pte Ltd. Gateway to health informatics – a certified course on health informatics by distance learning and classroom tutorials. 2020. http://gatewaypl.com/gw/courses/ehi/. Accessed 3 June 2020.
10. Kulikowski CA, Shortliffe EH, Currie LM, Elkin PL, Hunter LE, Johnson TR, Kalet IJ, Lenert LA, Musen MA, Ozbolt JG, Smith JW, Tarczy-Hornoch PZ, Williamson JJ. AMIA Board white paper: definition of biomedical informatics and specification of core competencies for graduate education in the discipline. J Am Med Inform Assoc. 2012;19(6):931–8. https://doi.org/10.1136/amiajnl-2012-001053.
11. Hebda TL, Calderone TL. Informatics competencies for healthcare professionals: the technology informatics guiding education reform (TIGER) initiative model. Drug Metabol Drug Interact. 2012;27(3):145–9. https://doi.org/10.1515/dmdi-2012-0013.
12. Jette S, Gagnon J, Tribble DS, Mathieu L. Informatics competency in nursing care. Perceptions of future nurses. Perspect Infirm. 2012;9(2):21–3.
13. Roberts J. e-Health informatics workforce challenges for Europe. Stud Health Technol Inform. 2011;170:123–8.
14. Scott P, Briggs J, Wyatt J, Georgiou A. How important is theory in health informatics? A survey of UK academics. Stud Health Technol Inform. 2011;169:223–7.
15. McCullagh P, McAllister G, Hanna P, Finlay D, Comac P. Professional development of health informatics in Northern Ireland. Stud Health Technol Inform. 2011;169:218–22.
16. Grain H, Hovenga E. Health informatics competencies – underpinning e-health. Stud Health Technol Inform. 2011;168:73–81.
17. Hwang JI, Park HA. Factors associated with nurses' informatics competency. Comput Inform Nurs. 2011;29(4):256–62. https://doi.org/10.1097/NCN.0b013e3181fc3d24.
18. Gray K, Sim J. Factors in the development of clinical informatics competence in early career health sciences professionals in Australia: a qualitative study. Adv Health Sci Educ Theory Pract. 2011;16(1):31–46. https://doi.org/10.1007/s10459-010-9238-3.
19. Chang J, Poynton MR, Gassert CA, Staggers N. Nursing informatics competencies required of nurses in Taiwan. Int J Med Inform. 2011;80(5):332–40. https://doi.org/10.1016/j.ijmedinf.2011.01.011.
20. Covvey HD, Fenton SL, Sabaratnam S, Chanda N. Harmonizing the competency cacophony. Stud Health Technol Inform. 2011;164:45–51.
21. Otero P, Gonzalez Bernaldo de Quiros F, Hersh W. Competencies for a well-trained biomedical and health informatics workforce. Methods Inf Med. 2010;49(3):297–8.
22. Hersh W, Margolis A, Quiros F, Otero P. Building a health informatics workforce in developing countries. Health Aff. 2010;29(2):274–7. https://doi.org/10.1377/hlthaff.2009.0883.
23. Lemmetty K, Hayrinen K, Sundgren S. The impacts of informatics competencies and user training on patient information system implementation. Stud Health Technol Inform. 2009;146:646–51.
24. Patel VL, Yoskowitz NA, Arocha JF, Shortliffe EH. Cognitive and learning sciences in biomedical and health instructional design: a review with lessons for biomedical informatics education. J Biomed Inform. 2009;42(1):176–97. https://doi.org/10.1016/j.jbi.2008.12.002.

25. Desjardins KS, Cook SS, Jenkins M, Bakken S. Effect of an informatics for evidence-based practice curriculum on nursing informatics competencies. Int J Med Inform. 2005;74(11–12):1012–20. https://doi.org/10.1016/j.ijmedinf.2005.07.001.
26. Grant RM, Horkin EJ, Melhuish PJ, Norris AC. Different approaches to the tasks of educating and training information systems professionals, within the National Health Service (UK). Int J Med Inform. 1998;50(1–3):171–7.
27. International Medical Informatics Association (IMIA). Working Group 1: Health and Medical Informatics Education. Stud Health Technol Inform. 2004;109:226–43.
28. Mantas J, Ammenwerth E, Demiris G, Hasman A, Haux R, Hersh W, Hovenga E, Lun KC, Marin H, Martin-Sanchez F, Wright G. IMIA Recommendations on Education Task Force. Recommendations of the International Medical Informatics Association (IMIA) on Education in Biomedical and Health Informatics. First Revision. Methods Inf Med. 2010;49(2):105–20.
29. Valenta AL, Berner ES, Boren SA, et al. AMIA Board White Paper: AMIA 2017 core competencies for applied health informatics education at the master's degree level. J Am Med Inform Assoc. 2018;25(12):1657–68. https://doi.org/10.1093/jamia/ocy132.
30. Silverman HD, Steen EB, Carpenito JN, Ondrula CJ, Williamson JJ, Fridsma DB. Domains, tasks, and knowledge for clinical informatics subspecialty practice: results of a practice analysis. J Am Med Inform Assoc. 2019;26(7):586–93. https://doi.org/10.1093/jamia/ocz051.
31. Gadd CS, Steen EB, Caro CM, Greenberg S, Williamson JJ, Fridsma DB. Domains, tasks, and knowledge for health informatics practice: results of a practice analysis. 2020;27(6):845-52. https://doi.org/10.1093/jamia/ocaa018.
32. McPhee W, Nohr C. Globalization and the cultural impact on distance education. Int J Med Inform. 2000;58–59:291–5.
33. Moodle Trust Moodle™. Welcome to the Moodle community. https://moodle.org/. Accessed 3 June 2020.
34. Blackboard Inc. Technology and Solutions Built for Education. 2013. http://www.blackboard.com/. Accessed 3 June 2020.
35. Canvas for Higher Education. https://www.instructure.com/canvas/higher-education. Accessed 3 June 2020.
36. South African Institute for Distance Education OER Africa. Building African Education. http://www.oerafrica.org/. Accessed 3 June 2020.
37. OER Africa Health Informatics Building Blocks (HIBBS). https://www.oerafrica.org/health-informatics-building-blocks-hibbs?page=0%2C0%2C0%2C4. Accessed 3 June 2020.
38. Jaspers MW, Gardner RM, Gatewood LC, Haux R, Evans RS. An international summer school on health informatics: a collaborative effort of the Amsterdam Medical Informatics Program and IPhiE – the International Partnership for Health Informatics Education. Int J Med Inform. 2007;76(7):538–46. https://doi.org/10.1016/j.ijmedinf.2006.02.008.

Chapter 12
Nursing Informatics Education: A Global Perspective

Elizabeth Cummings, Jen Bichel-Findlay, Paula Procter, Ursula Hübner, Michelle Honey, and Karen Day

Introduction

It is incumbent upon nurse educators to prepare the next generation of nurses to participate in person-centered, interprofessional care in an ever transforming health care delivery system. In the digital era, patients, families and caregivers will use mobile apps, wearable technologies, robots, chatbot health assistants supported by artificial intelligence as well as virtual health visits with their health care team [1–3]. Nurses will need to understand the opportunities and challenges that the digital health ecosystem provides for patients and their families [4]. This chapter offers a moment in time and glimpse of nursing informatics education across a number of countries with remarkably similar stories and all with a determination to provide the best informatics education for nurses wherever they work— Professor Diane Skiba, PhD, FACMI, ANEF, FAAN, Chair, International Medical Informatics Association—Nursing Informatics Special Interest Group

E. Cummings
School of Health Sciences, University of Tasmania and Deputy Chair, Nursing Informatics, Sydney, NSW, Australia
e-mail: elizabeth.cummings@utas.edu.au

J. Bichel-Findlay
Australasian Institute of Digital Health Nursing and Midwifery Community of Practice, Sydney, NSW, Australia
e-mail: Jen.Bichel-Findlay@uts.edu.au

P. Procter (✉)
Sheffield Hallam University, Sheffield, UK
e-mail: p.procter@shu.ac.uk

U. Hübner
University of Applied Sciences Osnabrück, Osnabrück, Germany
e-mail: U.Huebner@hs-osnabrueck.de

M. Honey · K. Day
Faculty of Medical and Health Sciences, The University of Auckland, Auckland, New Zealand
e-mail: m.honey@auckland.ac.nz; k.day@auckland.ac.uk

© Springer Nature Switzerland AG 2020
E. S. Berner (ed.), *Informatics Education in Healthcare*, Health Informatics, https://doi.org/10.1007/978-3-030-53813-2_12

This chapter will outline the development of education in nursing informatics in Europe and Australasia to provide a global view to add to the perspective in Chap. 3 on the United States of America perspective.

Nursing is commonly the largest professional group [5] in health care working in home care, primary, secondary and tertiary care across a number of significant roles that impact upon the experience and outcomes of the patient. Nurses have a major role in meeting the needs of those in their care due to the front-line role they embrace [6]. With the advances in digital developments it is crucial that nurses are fully prepared for the digital disruption to their work that will transform this key front-line role so that patients receive optimum care and experience outcomes appropriate to their care. As stated by the European Union, "Technological change does not only create and destroy jobs but it also contributes to transforming the overall structure of employment" [7, p. 72].

At the center of the provision of nursing care is compassion towards the patient, their relatives and friends. Although this 'soft' skill is not always measurable it is complemented through the profession being open to supportive and measurable digital technology which removes administrative and burdensome documentation tasks while at the same time offering support to new ways of working and ready access to resources which can support decision making for patient care.

Nursing education world-wide understands the need to prepare nurses for future work environments and this is demonstrated in the purposive curricular competencies and capabilities considered in the examples given in this chapter. According to the Organization for Economic Cooperation and Development (OECD) "… best characterizes expected future work environments—jobs will require workers to be equipped with diverse skills: cognitive and meta-cognitive skills (e.g. critical thinking, creative thinking, learning to learn and self-regulation); non-cognitive skills (e.g. empathy and collaboration); and digital skills (e.g. using new digital devices)" [8, pp. 32–33]. In addition, proper use of digital tools will necessitate an understanding of the ethics of data, algorithms and practices [9].

Nurses have been promised the technology holy grail before. Nearly a decade ago, the Institute of Medicine identified that health information technologies will fundamentally change how nurses "plan, deliver, document, and review clinical care" [10, p. 104] and that the use of these tools and systems will require nurses at all levels to develop "skills in analysis and synthesis to improve the quality and effectiveness of care" [10, p. 7]. Models of care provision are changing and nurses need to be agile and resilient as they move towards a 'care anywhere' model [11] where it is expected that nurses will work differently, and potentially remotely, across all healthcare provision domains. In the twenty-first century it is impossible to work without technology and thus nursing informatics is not a 'speciality', but rather a feature of being a health professional in the modern age. However, we must recognize that there is a difference between being digitally capable and being credible in terms of informatics. Data in healthcare is becoming the new currency [12] and as such there is a need to expand nurses' knowledge in the protection of data, in data analysis to inform care provision, and in awareness of how to contribute to cybersecurity.

The following exemplars from countries around the world are offered to enlighten and improve understanding of this vast shift in working practices among the nursing community.

Australia

Both nursing and midwifery registration in Australia are achieved by completing an Australian Nursing & Midwifery Accreditation Council (ANMAC) accredited course. Nursing is a 3-year degree, whereby the graduate gains registration through the Australian Health Professionals Registration Agency (AHPRA) and then renews this registration annually through meeting currency of practice criteria.

Changes to nurse education content generally occur due to the need to improve patient quality and safety, in addition to increasing efficiency and effectiveness. The increased use of informatics tools and technology in the healthcare environment could be a major influencer of all these attributes, and nursing is seen as a major user of these tools and technologies. In response to these changes, since 2013, ANMAC has required nursing degree providers to include nursing informatics entry level courses in order to achieve accreditation. The 2012 Registered Nurse Accreditation Standards are currently under review [13].

In relation to integrating health informatics and health technology content into accredited nursing degrees, ANMAC expects beginning nursing practitioners to be sufficiently prepared to use an array of technologies and informatics. More specifically information literacy, policies, guidelines, and procedures related to social media need to be addressed, as well as a sound understanding among academic staff and enough resources in quantity and quality. ANMAC does not prescribe how informatics content is to be integrated into the curricula and the first nursing degree re-accredited under the 2012 Registered Nurse Accreditation Standards has not yet been evaluated. This degree was designed to ensure that nursing informatics would be integrated throughout the degree, and not be viewed as additional or separate from the core content or context [14].

The Australian Nursing & Midwifery Federation (ANMF) released National Informatics Standards for Nurses and Midwives in 2015; however, they have not yet been endorsed by other national nursing and midwifery professional bodies. This standards document emphasized the need for nurses to have informatics education, the fact that integration of informatics skills into nursing practice is central for nurses at all levels and in all settings, and that attainment of these standards by nurses will support them in delivering safer and more integrated care that is based on timely evidence [15]. The Standards comprise three domains—computer literacy, information literacy and information management [15]—based on an earlier study that demonstrated undergraduate nurses were only offered basic computer training, with no content targeting information literacy and information management [16]. As far back as 2008, the ANMF in its earlier form of Australian Nursing Federation identified the need to build workforce capacity in health informatics and the priority to have a national approach to the development of competencies in informatics for nurses [17]. In 2017, Australian College of Nursing, Health Informatics Society of Australia, and Nursing Informatics Australia released a joint Nursing Informatics Position Statement. Statement 1 demonstrates the importance of nursing informatics education stating "Informatics education for nurses is essential: Education in nursing informatics is essential in all undergraduate and postgraduate nursing programs. Moreover, the workplace must provide education in health informatics to all nursing staff not only at induction but as part of continuous learning" [18, p. 2].

Unfortunately, there continues to be limited understanding of nursing informatics among many of the university lecturers. As reported by Cummings et al., research by Gray et al. (2015) found limited knowledge and teaching experience in health informatics across the board for all health professions in Australia, including lecturers, tutors and professional placement supervisors. Expertise in health informatics is not formally required or recognized in the recruitment of university educators in nursing [19].

All healthcare professionals in Australia are required to be lifelong learners and a large proportion of the nursing workforce is enrolled in higher education. In relation to informatics education Australia has had postgraduate health informatics degrees available since the early 2000s. However, no nursing informatics specific postgraduate programs exist in Australia, and the health informatics postgraduate courses continue to decrease in number despite increasing demand. Very few of the programs focus on research; however nurses who progress to a graduate certificate, graduate diploma or a masters course will usually be exposed to some research training.

In 2018 the Australasian College of Health Informatics (ACHI) introduced their Fellowship Training program for those undertaking doctoral education. The specialized program provides continuing development in informatics and includes 12 months of workplace experience. This provides a training-focused pathway for PhD candidates from technical or clinical backgrounds that prepares them for leadership roles in the health informatics workforce.

Another option that nurses can take advantage of to increase their health informatics knowledge is by completing a short course offered by a registered training provider or by enrolling in a Massive Open Online Course (MOOC) that address specific concepts within nursing or health informatics. While most MOOCs have been created in the United States, a few have been developed locally, such as *eHealth: more than just an electronic record* by the University of Sydney. The Australian Digital Health Agency plans to release their National Digital Health Workforce and Education Roadmap in 2020, which will identify the current state of the Australian health workforce, including their digital capability and likely impacts from the deployment of digital technologies. It is hoped that the roadmap will provide clarity in relation to the educational requirements of the health workforce and how they can be supported to realize the benefits of this planned digital transformation. Three organizations—Health Informatics Society of Australia (HISA), Australasian College of Health Informatics (ACHI) and the Health Information Management Association of Australia (HIMAA)—decided in 2014 to address the lack of formal recognition for health informatics skills in Australia by developing a credentialing program for health informatics. The Certified Health Informatician Australasia (CHIA) credential demonstrates that candidates meet the health informatics core competencies to function effectively as a health informatics professional in a wide range of practice settings [20]. The CHIA credential requires renewal every 3 years through accumulation of continuing professional development activities. Designed with a focus on the Australian healthcare system, CHIA certification plays a key role in enhancing the profile of health informaticians. There are currently over 600 active CHIAs, and nearly 10% of those are nurses. In 2020 the Australasian Certified Health Informatics (ACHI) and Health Informatics Society of Australia (HISA) merged to form the Australasian Institute of Digital Health (AIDH), and Nursing Informatics Australia (NIA) is now the AIDH Nursing and Midwifery Community of Practice. Other health informatics activities in Australia are discussed in Chap. 14.

Preparing graduates for future care delivery is challenging in a digitized environment, given that the majority of undergraduate courses take 3 years to complete, yet there are continuous changes in information management and health technologies. Faculty need to keep pace with informatics-related changes and research developments [21] and higher education providers need to provide students with access to digital tools that mirror those used in the clinical environment. Currently no Australian nursing school/faculty has an electronic medical record or a suite of digital nursing informatics tools for students to use in clinical laboratory sessions. Collaborations need to be developed with vendors to increase opportunities for students to be exposed to the major digital tools used in clinical practice, and healthcare organizations need to support undergraduates by permitting them to access hospital systems during clinical practice so that they can become familiar with their use prior to commencing practice in the workplace [22].

As nurses are knowledge workers, their education should also prepare them to act as custodians of health information so that they can assist patients and families to navigate the large and convoluted quantities of available information [23]. It is vital that nurses understand how data is situated within a governance framework and how clinical nurses and nurse managers need to have access to the right information at the right time in the right format so that evidence-based decisions can be made [23]. Workflows need to be established that are aligned to contemporary models of care so that data entered is accurate and consistent across all staff. It is also fundamental that nurses ensure semantic interoperability in a growing sea of personally generated data, and are aware of the new legal, ethical, social and public policy questions in a connected care age [2]. They also need to be shown how to maintain a sense of presence and caring when using digital tools and technologies, so that patients do not view nurses as "treating the technologies" [2].

Europe

Nurses have a very important role to play in informatics in Europe. As Inge Madsen, President of the European Federation of Medical Informatics—Nursing Informatics Working Group (EFMI-NI) has stated: The countries within Europe are at many stages of development in nursing informatics; our strategy within EFMI-NI is to lead a progressive program which is active in supporting nursing informatics across Europe. There is significant awareness that nurses need to play a very active part in the rapid growth of technology in health care or the alternative is for nursing to become invisible. In the words of Clark and Lang (1992) "If we cannot name it, we cannot control it, practice it, teach it, finance it or put into public policy" [24]. Therefore we need nurses to develop their informatics knowledge so that we can share our knowledge across all health areas in order to add the nursing voice and play an active part in improving patient outcomes through education, innovation, research, practice, technology development and the political level.

In this context 'Europe' is defined as those countries within the European Union rather than all countries belonging to the landmass of Europe. Nursing within Europe is overseen by individual country specific regulators under the wider guidelines from the European Union [25]. These guidelines are primarily contained within Directive 2005/36/EC concerning the recognition of professional qualifications [26]. While accepting the individuality of different member states, this directive draws together a framework that allows for inter-country movement and development. The Directive covers the role of nurses at the point of registration rather than associate, apprentice or support worker levels. Initial registered nurse education is mainly undertaken in universities alongside an academic award and generally takes 3 years of study to complete.

In the 2005 directive there is little mention of digital technology at either undergraduate or post graduate level. In more recent times there has been considerable development of national and European nursing informatics competencies. Different countries started to develop nursing informatics competencies that could support the education of nurses but it was not until the Technology Informatics Guiding Education Reform (TIGER) initiative's International Competency Synthesis Project (2019) that there was a 'coming together' of the competencies into one collective space that demonstrated a common core of activities that could be used to move undergraduate and post graduate nursing forward [27]. The common core competencies described fit into five domains:

1. clinical nursing
2. nursing management
3. quality management
4. IT management in nursing
5. coordination of interprofessional care

Research and teaching are horizontal roles that intertwine with the aforementioned five roles. Alike, electronic learning (and research) capacities are therefore regarded as integral parts of these roles. The final domain accepts that no single healthcare professional can fulfil the expectations of, or care for, patients and their reported outcomes. A comprehensive report of this work can be read in the article by Hübner et al. [28]; however, the main drivers for Europe were clear and formed under the heading of health informatics for nurses.

With the advent of greater reliance upon digital technology the emerging debate is around ensuring that nursing is at the innovation and implementation tables for artificial intelligence, nano technologies, robotics and genomics developments across health care.

An ongoing problem with both undergraduate teaching and the preparation of colleagues to lead/support innovation and implementation of digital technologies across health care, but, in particular, within nursing, is the paucity of teachers with the knowledge and skills to lead sessions for students. Hence there is a developing movement toward online material that can be built into the curriculum rather than re-inventing a complex 'wheel' of educational resources. This has been also highlighted by the gap analysis of the European funded EU*US eHealth Work project. Interestingly, this problem had been identified as a global issue by experts worldwide [29].

Within Europe there are postgraduate courses and continuing professional development available, but, for nursing, these tend toward advancing clinical/community practice and do not tend to address informatics within their content. Part of the reason for such a poor infrastructure at the postgraduate level for nursing informatics may be due to the lack of a career structure away from the traditional areas of nursing practice. Although there are nurses in charge of health IT in the large hospitals, as described in Hübner et al. [30], sometimes working within the IT departments and sometimes being affiliated with the nursing director, these positions tend to have no self-contained job identity. A dramatic shortage of clinical nurses in many European countries today counteracts the parallel need for informatics nurses. As in many countries around the globe including the US, job descriptions in Europe were generally not re-evaluated and necessary skills were not re-assessed when new systems were adopted [29]. This suggests the necessity of raising the awareness for health informatics competencies through education that incorporates informatics as part of clinical training.

There is change happening in this respect, but it is a slow process as directly opposed to the over-rapid progress of health digitization. The recognition for a nursing informatics career path is being led by nursing leadership in different European countries, but a recent article from Sweden highlights some of the difficulties experienced by nurses [31]. These difficulties include trying to do caregiving in the midst of chaos when change seems to be happening too fast; feeling a lack of control of their work and lack of organizational support alongside some fear of role removal. These types of concerns have been expressed in many areas of Europe and more widely.

As an example, in Finland, Professor Kaija Saranto (University of Eastern Finland) who leads the first IMIA accredited masters' program in health informatics, suggests that it is not the proficiency of the nurses that is halting further health informatics development. Rather it is the poor functionalities of the information systems that conflict with practice and disturb nurses' work processes. Professor Saranto states "When data cannot be accessed in a timely manner or the same data is stored in multiple systems, severe safety concerns, difficulties in decision-making, deficiencies in information exchange, and frustration in work processes may arise" [32]. Professor Saranto's words echo much of the urgency now experienced across Europe. There needs to be greater engagement among other health care professionals over and above physicians in the advances in digital and genomic technologies that will impact the delivery of care and improve outcomes for those receiving care.

New Zealand

New Zealand (NZ) is a country made up of three main islands situated in the South Pacific Ocean. With a population of under five million people, and a life expectancy of 80.2 years for men and 83.6 years for women. NZ is challenged with how to provide the best care for all its people across their lifespan [33]. Healthcare is free at the point of service and funded through the government via taxation. NZ's Digital Health Strategy reinforces the opportunity health informatics brings to empower the people of NZ "to live well, stay well and get well" [34]. The nursing component of the health workforce is key to achieving this goal.

Undergraduate

The Nursing Council of NZ is the statutory and regulatory body that controls the education and practice of nursing, working to protect the health and safety of the public by providing mechanisms to ensure that Registered Nurses (RNs) are competent and fit to practice [35]. To become an RN, students complete a 3-year degree level program at one of 17 Schools of Nursing with each program including an equal number of hours of theory and clinical practice. There are approximately 53,500 RNs in NZ, and just under 2000 new graduates each year [35]. The challenge is to ensure new graduate nurses are ready to use information and communication technology (ICT) to improve patient outcomes and clinical efficiency.

From the early 1990s, nursing in NZ has considered how to prepare future nurses to work with technology [36–39]. Despite this strong beginning, nursing informatics has not been uniformly and consistently addressed in nursing curricula. While the Nursing Council of New Zealand does not specify any particular competencies for nursing informatics, this issue was addressed with the development of Guidelines for Nursing Informatics Competencies for Undergraduate Nurses in NZ, which align with the Nursing Council competencies for RNs [40, 41]. These Guidelines are based on principles encompassing key knowledge, skills and behaviors for student nurses to attain over the time of their undergraduate education to be ready to begin practice as an RN. The future challenge is to ensure these Guidelines are used by every School of Nursing and further work is continuing to support this through considering how to best support nurse educators nationally.

Most nursing students are now using ICT in their personal lives as well as in their nursing education, so they bring transferable skills to their nursing practice [42]. However, of concern is the nursing informatics skills of existing RNs. The average age of nurses in NZ is 46.3 years, indicating an older workforce, who may not have been well prepared for nursing informatics and using ICT within their practice [35].

Post-graduate/Continuing Professional Development

Postgraduate health informatics programs are available in three NZ universities, the earliest began in 2001 [29]. Nurses who enroll in these programs are usually looking for a change in their careers rather than equipping themselves for an in-depth nursing informatics role. Few roles exist specifically for nurse informaticians, and those that do exist are leadership roles, (e.g. establishing nursing informatics in a private hospital via nurse-related technology implementations), analyst roles (e.g. business analyst, or management), or project management roles, (e.g. digitization of a nursing service). While the number of nurses completing postgraduate health informatics programs is low, nurses completing other programs may take some health informatics courses and return to their workplace with new skills.

The three universities' postgraduate programs have slightly different approaches—information systems management, health informatics leadership, and a computer science focus. Alternatively, some of the concepts of health informatics are also taught within non-informatics programs, e.g., the postgraduate program in business science. Competencies included in the programs relate to the AMIA competencies [43, 44] as interpreted by New Zealand academics [45]. The nursing informatics programs in NZ do not yet have IMIA accreditation. A typical curriculum includes the principles of health informatics, ethics and governance, technology-mediated care (e.g. decision support systems, artificial intelligence, genomics, robotics), care at a distance (e.g. telehealth, mhealth), information systems evaluation and technology assessment, transformative change, quality improvement, leadership, how health systems are organized, and future implications of health informatics.

Continuing professional development in nursing informatics is inconsistent and does not have guidelines. Opportunities for development tend to be self-directed and include (but are not limited to) conference attendance, participating in ICT projects as an extension of a nursing role, accessing on-line material and enrolling in a MOOC (Massive Open Online Course). A call for micro-credentialing has been issued by some members of the health informatics community, which is being explored by various universities.

Informatics in Nursing Practice

New Zealand's digital health landscape is described pictorially with the patient or consumer as the center of several systems in which patient data are collected, stored, transferred or shared across health events [34]. Key to this are some features of the national informatics infrastructure that nurses meet every day in their practice. Firstly, New Zealand has a national health identifier, the National Health Index (NHI), which is allocated at birth and follows the person through their life [46].

Additionally, all health professionals are assigned a unique identifier called the Health Provider Index (HPI) that is held in a central database which identifies not only the health professional, but also the organization and its location [47].

In line with the national vision for digital health that has the patient/consumer as central, has been the increase in the use of patient portals, allowing patients access to their health information [34]. This changes the role of the nurse, increasing the need for partnership with patients for goal setting, biometric monitoring, helping patients to understand health information they access online while encouraging health promotion and wellness. A further example of increased consumer involvement is within a well-child health service called Plunket, which has moved to using a cloud-based EHR application that allows nurses using tablets to access consumers' notes. Families also have access to their children's health information [48].

Future Challenges

Health informatics has its own discourse language [49], filled with jargon that is often impenetrable for the uninitiated. There is no clear definition of the concept 'health informatics' [43, 50, 51] that NZ nurses can identify with and use in everyday practice. A challenge for the future is to place value on nursing informatics education at undergraduate and postgraduate levels, in order to gain consistent use of language and recognition of definitional boundaries.

Now that clinical informatics is mission-critical we are faced with challenges ranging from basic digital literacy to advanced nursing informatics. We can no longer afford to differentiate between 'digital natives' and 'digital immigrants' [52] because all nurses should be digitally literate in order to do their work. However, we have an ageing nursing workforce. Engaging older people in digital citizenship can be challenging unless the purpose is clear [53]. Employers will be required to ensure that their staff, nurses included, are at least digitally literate and at most, capable of contributing to the governance and operationalization of nursing informatics.

Leadership is essential for nursing informatics to be successful. In New Zealand a Clinical Informatics Leadership Network (CiLN) was established in 2018, to enable the clinical informatics voice to be heard [54]. Traditionally 'clinicians' have been consulted in health informatics initiatives. Recently there has been a move for clinicians to become deeply involved in the planning, implementation, and evaluation of initiatives. Nurses are included in CiLN and there is a call for their voice to be less muted to add value to the digitization of health services, since nurses are the largest workforce to be affected, and may be most able to effect transformative change.

Conclusion

As can be seen from the exemplars above nursing has commonalities the world over; nurses are dedicated to meeting the needs of those in their care in any setting and open to change if it has a positive impact upon care outcomes. For many years, nurses have 'fed' the machine and received little in return, however, advances in data management now can provide metrics related to the delivery of care, and expand understanding of the outcomes of care.

Klasko writes, "… our doctors and nurses will coexist (hopefully cooperate) with deep learning, machine cognition entities; we will select and educate humans to be better humans than the robots, not better robots than the robots; and population health, predictive analytics and social determinants will move to the mainstream of medical education and clinical care" [55]. He goes on to say, "And it will not be one technology. We have to stop talking about "telehealth," for example. We don't get up in the morning and say "I think I'm going to telebank!" It's just that banking has moved from 90% being in the bank to 90% happening at home" [55].

Society has embraced technology where it perceives value in the use of technology in daily life; nursing is no different and after some 40 years nursing may well have something to value across the digital developments.

The following statement by Caron Swinscoe, Chief Nurse and Clinical Informatics Professional Lead, NHS Digital captures the main messages of this chapter.

In the UK there are more than 698,000 nurse, midwives and nursing associates on the Nursing and Midwifery Council's register, from over 164 countries, caring for patients and citizens in many different settings.

Nursing is based on a strong foundation of ethics. Nurses learn about social justice and the determinants of health so they can support all people needing care. That care is then given by taking a holistic, or whole-person, view.

Digital health is about more than the technology. Knowledge and information are invaluable for nurses to help them make the right decisions for their patients. Finding, using, recording, managing, and sharing information to support care, and inform and make decisions about patient care, means it is essential for nursing staff to have the skills and capabilities for working and thriving in a digital society.

Nurses and midwives will always need to give hands-on care, but digital technology and data are creating new opportunities for new nursing roles and to change the way we deliver care in almost every setting. Embracing new technology is key to improving patient care and nursing outcomes. It is important that the profession responds positively to these opportunities and that's why nursing informatics competencies and digital capabilities matter.

References

1. Skiba DJ. Augmented intelligence and nursing. Nurs Educ Perspect. 2017;38(2):108–9.
2. Skiba DJ. Nursing informatics education: from automation to connected care. In: Murphy J, et al., editors. Forecasting informatics competencies for nurses in the future of connected health: IMIA and IOS Press; 2017. p. 9–19.
3. Skiba DJ. The invisible health care professional: exploring the tntersection of data, devices and artificial intelligence. Nurs Educ Perspect. 2018;39(4):264–5.
4. Skiba DJ. Consumer electronic show 2018: a focus on digital health tools. Nurs Educ Perspect. 2018;39(3):194–5.
5. NHS Digital. NHS workforce statistics, February 2018. England: NHS Digital, Health and Social Care Information Centre; 2018.
6. Whitby P. Role of front-line nurse leadership in improving care. Nurs Stand. 2018;33(8). https://doi.org/10.7748/ns.2018.e11018.

7. EC (European Commission). The changing nature of work and skills in the digital age. Brussels: Report of the Joint Research Centre, European Union; 2019. https://ec.europa.eu/jrc

8. OECD (Organization for Economic Cooperation and Development). The future of education and skills: education 2030. Paris: OECD Publishing; 2018.

9. Floridi L, Taddeo M. What is data ethics? Philos Trans A Math Phys Eng Sci. 2016;374(2083):20160360. https://doi.org/10.1098/rsta.2016.0360.

10. Institute of Medicine (US). The future of nursing: leading change, advancing health. In: Committee on the Robert Wood Johnson Foundation Initiative on the Future of Nursing at the Institute of Medicine. Washington, DC: National Academies Press; 2011.

11. Deloitte. 2019 Global health care outlook: shaping the future. 2019. https://www2.deloitte.com/global/en/pages/life-sciences-and-healthcare/articles/global-health-care-sector-outlook.html

12. Healthrust. Data as currency. 2018. https://healthtrustpg.com/healthcare-facility-management/data-as-currency/

13. Australian Nursing and Midwifery Accreditation Council. Standards under review. 2019. Available https://www.anmac.org.au/standards-and-review/standards-under-review/registered-nurse-accreditation-standards-review

14. Cummings E, Shin EH, Mather C, Hovenga E. Embedding nursing informatics education into an Australian undergraduate nursing degree. Stud Health Technol Inform. 2016;225:329–33.

15. Australian Nursing and Midwifery Federation (ANMF), Federal Office. National informatics standards for nurses and midwives. Melbourne: ANMF Federal Office; 2015. Available http://anmf.org.au/documents/National_Informatics_Standards_For_Nurses_And_Midwives.pdf

16. Smedley A. The importance of informatics competencies in nursing: an Australian perspective. Comput Inform Nurs. 2005;23(2):106–10.

17. Bichel-Findlay J, Doran C. Nursing and informatics: a transformational synergy. In: Daly J, Speedy S, Jackson D, editors. Contexts in nursing. 4th ed. Sydney: Elsevier; 2014.

18. Australian College of Nursing, Health Informatics Society of Australia, and Nursing Informatics Australia. Nursing informatics position statement. Melbourne: HISA; 2017. Available https://www.hisa.org.au/wp-content/uploads/2017/08/Nursing-Informatics-Position-Statement_06082017.pdf?x30583

19. Cummings E, Wheton S, Mather C. Integrating health informatics into Australian higher education health profession curricula. In: Aviv S, Borycki E, Reis S, editors. Health professionals' education in the age of clinical information systems, mobile computing and social networks. New York: Elsevier; 2017. p. 323–43.

20. Certified Health Informatician Australasia. About CHIA. 2019. Available https://www.health-informaticscertification.com/about/

21. Kinnunen U-M, Rajalahti E, Cummings E, Borycki EM. Curricula challenges and informatics competencies for nurse educators. In: Murphy J, et al., editors. Forecasting informatics competencies for nurses in the future of connected health: IMIA and IOS Press; 2017. p. 41–8.

22. Shin UH, Cummings E, Ford K. A qualitative study of new graduates' readiness to use nursing informatics in acute care settings: clinical nurse educators' perspectives. Contemp Nurse. 2017;54(1):64–76.

23. Honey M, Procter P. The shifting sands of nursing informatics education: from content to connectivity. In: Murphy J, et al., editors. Forecasting informatics competencies for nurses in the future of connected health: IMIA and IOS Press; 2017. p. 31–9.

24. Clark J, Lang N. Nursing's next advance: an internal classification for nursing practice. Int Nurs Rev. 1992;39(4):109–11.

25. Rafferty A-M, Busse R, Zander-Jentsch B, Sermus W, Bruyneel, L. Strengthening health systems through nursing: evidence from 14 European countries. World Health Organization on behalf of the European Observatory on Health Systems and Policies. 2019. Available https://apps.who.int/iris/bitstream/handle/10665/326183/9789289051743-eng.pdf

26. EU (European Union). Directive 2005/36/EC of the European Parliament and of the Council of 7 September 2005 on the recognition of professional qualifications. 2005. https://eur-lex. europa.eu/eli/dir/2005/36/oj
27. Technology Informatics Guiding Education Reform (TIGER) initiative's International Competency Synthesis Project. 2019. Available https://www.himss.org/professional-development/tiger-initiative/tiger-international-informatics-competency-synthesis-project
28. Hübner U, Shaw T, Thye J, Egbert N, Marin H, Chang C, O'Connor S, Day K, Honey M, Blake R, Hovenga E, Skiba D, Ball MJ. Technology informatics guiding education reform – TIGER: an international recommendation framework of core competencies in health informatics for nurses. Methods Inf Med 2018;57(S 01):e30–e42. Available https://www.thieme-connect.com/products/ejournals/html/10.3414/ME17-01-0155#N68064
29. Hübner U, Thye J, Shaw T, Blake R. D2.3 gap analysis of current state and needs for eHealth workforce – survey results. Horizon2020 Project EU*US eHealth_Work. 2018.
30. Hübner U, Esdar M, Hüsers J, Liebe J, Naumann L, Rauch J, Thye J, Weiss JP. IT-Report Gesundheitswesen. Wie reif ist die Gesundheits-IT aus Perspektive der Anwender*innen? Befragung ärztlicher und pflegerischer Krankenhaus-Direktoren*innen in Deutschland, Österreich und der Schweiz. Hochschule Osnabrück, Osnabrück. 2019.
31. Öberg U, Orre CJ, Isaksson U, Schimmer R, Larsson H, Hörnsten Å. Swedish primary healthcare nurses' perceptions of using digital eHealth services in support of patient self-management. Scand J Caring Sci. 2017;32(2):961–70. Available https://onlinelibrary.wiley.com/doi/full/10.1111/scs.12534
32. Saranto K, Kivekäs E, Sjöblom O, Kimmunen U-M, Palojoki S. How to improve interdisciplinary information flow? In: Holopained A, Pirkko K, Komtio E, Reponen J, editors. The 24th Finnish national conference on telemedicine and eHealth. 'Data-Driven Health'. The Finnish Society of Telemedicine and eHealth; 2019. ISBN 978-952-68112-9-1 (pdf).
33. Stats New Zealand. Population. 2019. Retrieved October 5, 2019 from https://www.stats.govt.nz/topics/population
34. New Zealand Ministry of Health. (2018). New Zealand digital health strategy. Retrieved October 15, 2019 from https://www.digital.health.nz/content/digital-health/en/home/digital-strategy.html
35. Nursing Council of New Zealand. Annual Report. 2017. Wellington, New Zealand, Nursing Council of New Zealand.
36. Collins E, Britnell S, Ditzel L, Honey M. Using curriculum mapping to develop undergraduate nursing informatics: a New Zealand study. Int J Innov Res Med Sci. 2017;2(11):1550–6. https://doi.org/10.23958/ijirms/vol02-i11/19.
37. Hausman JP. Guidelines for teaching nursing informatics. Wellington: Ministry of Education; 1989.
38. Honey M, Day K. Preparing nurses in informatics to address the equity divide. In Paper presented at the New Zealand Nursing Informatics Conference, Auckland; 03 November 2016.
39. Honey M, Nursing Informatics New Zealand Inc. Standards for nursing informatics guidelines. Health Informatics J. 1996;2(4):224–7.
40. Nursing Council of New Zealand. Competencies for registered nurses. Wellington: Nursing Council of New Zealand; 2016.
41. Honey M, Collins E, Britnell S. Guidelines: informatics for nurses entering practice. Auckland; 2018. Retrieved from https://doi.org/10.17608/k6.auckland.7273037
42. Honey M. Undergraduate student nurses' use of information and communication technology in their education. Stud Health Technol Inform. 2018;250:37–40. https://doi.org/10.3233/978-1-61499-872-3-37.
43. Kulikowski CA, Shortliffe EH, Currie LM, Elkin PL, Hunter LE, Johnson TR, et al. AMIA Board white paper: definition of biomedical informatics and specification of core competencies for graduate education in the discipline. JAMIA. 2012;19(6):931–8. https://doi.org/10.1136/amiajnl-2012-001053.

44. Valenta AL, Berner ES, Boren SA, Deckard GJ, Eldredge C, Fridsma DB, et al. AMIA Board White Paper: AMIA 2017 core competencies for applied health informatics education at the master's degree level. J Am Med Inform Assoc. 2018;25(12):1657–68.
45. Parry D, Hunter I, Honey M, Holt A, Day K, Kirk R, Cullen R. Priming a health informatics community in a small nation: the New Zealand experience. Paper presented at the medinfo2013 Conducting medical informatics by converging technologies, conveying sciences and connecting people, Copenhagen; 20–23 August 2013.
46. New Zealand Ministry of Health. National Health Index questions and answers. 2018. Retrieved October 10, 2019 from https://www.health.govt.nz/our-work/health-identity/national-health-index/nhi-information-health-consumers/national-health-index-questions-and-answers
47. New Zealand Ministry of Health. Health Provider Index. 2019. Retrieved October 15, 2019 from https://www.health.govt.nz/our-work/health-identity/health-provider-index
48. Plunket. ePHR: Plunket's electronic Health Record (ePHR) in the field. 2019. Retrieved October 17, 2019 from https://www.plunket.org.nz/ephr/
49. November N, Day K. Using undergraduates' digital literacy skills to improve their discipline-specific writing: a dialogue. Int J Scholarsh Teach Learn. 2012;6(2):2.
50. Friedman CP. What informatics is and isn't. JAMIA. 2012;20(2):224–6. https://doi.org/10.1136/amiajnl-2012-001206.
51. Shortliffe EH, Cimino JJ, editors. Biomedical informatics: computer application in health care and biomedicine. 4th ed: Springer; 2014.
52. Prensky M. Digital natives, digital immigrants. On the Horizon. 2001;9(5):1–6.
53. Damodaran L, Olphert C, Sandhu J. Falling off the bandwagon? Exploring the challenges to sustained digital engagement by older people. Gerontology. 2013;60(2):163–73.
54. HiNZ. Clinical Leaders Group (CiLN). 2019. Retrieved 30 October, 2019 from https://www.hinz.org.nz/page/CiLN
55. Klasko SK. (2019) Is there an avatar in the house? Changing the DNA of health care in the age of artificial intelligence. In: Merkur S. et al., Editor. Quarterly of the European obervatory on health systems and policies. vol. 25(3). p. 5–9.

Chapter 13
Informatics Education in Latin America

Paula Otero, Mariela Leikam, Zulma Gonzalez, Heimar de Fatima Marin, Ignacio Pérez Aravena, and Saadia Zawadzki

Introduction

"eHealth" has been defined as the application of information and communications technologies (ICTs) to health, and a means of improving health services access, efficiency and quality [1]. There is a need to have (1) a proper infrastructure in ICT, (2) trained professionals in health informatics, and (3) expanded digital literacy among members of the healthcare team.

In Latin America PAHO (Pan American Health Organization) proposed a Strategy and Plan of Action on eHealth (2012–2017) that aimed to contribute to the sustainable development of its Member States' healthcare systems [2]. The Strategy on eHealth promoted, among other things, the use of electronic medical records, telehealth and telemedicine, mHealth, eLearning, continuing education for health professionals using ICTs, and interoperability and standardization. The plan emphasized that there is a need to improve the quality of education and provide increased

P. Otero (✉) · M. Leikam · Z. Gonzalez
Department of Health Informatics, Hospital Italiano de Buenos Aires,
Buenos Aires, Argentina
e-mail: paula.otero@hospitalitaliano.org.ar; mariela.leikam@hospitalitaliano.org.ar;
zulmaa.gonzalez@hospitalitaliano.org.ar

H. de F. Marin
Department of Nursing Informatics, Federal University of São Paulo (UNIFESP),
São Paulo, Brazil

I. P. Aravena
Department of Biomedical Informatics, DUOC UC Institute, Las Condes, Chile
e-mail: iperez@duoc.cl

S. Zawadzki
Department of Medical Technology, School of Medicine, Universidad de la República
(UdelaR), Montevideo, Uruguay

© Springer Nature Switzerland AG 2020
E. S. Berner (ed.), *Informatics Education in Healthcare*, Health Informatics,
https://doi.org/10.1007/978-3-030-53813-2_13

access to it. There is also a need to define the needed skills for human resources and the infrastructure needed.

Education in health informatics is a lifelong process that must be adapted to provide what the students need to acquire the competencies that are needed in Latin America, to accompany the growth and evolution of the discipline in the region.

In this chapter we will describe the experience of four countries of the region: Argentina, Brazil, Chile and Uruguay, and will provide an overview of the different initiatives that are ongoing in the region.

Argentina: Experience at Hospital Italiano de Buenos Aires

The Hospital Italiano de Buenos Aires (HIBA) is a non-profit University Hospital founded in 1853. It is an academic center of high complexity that covers the entire spectrum of medical care from the outpatient setting to emergencies, acute care, medical and surgical specialties, critical care, home care and hospitalization, rehabilitation and chronic care. It is accredited by the Joint Commission International (JCI) and its Electronic Health Record has been certified by HIMSS as level 7 (EMRAM), being the second hospital in Latin America to reach this stage. It has its own university (IUHIBA) where different careers in health sciences are taught at graduate and postgraduate levels.

In 1998, HIBA decided to develop and implement an in-house hospital information system [3] which currently integrates all clinical and administrative information in a healthcare network, from the capture of the data at the point of care to its analysis and subsequent improvement. As part of the project, in 2001 the Department of Health Informatics (DHI) was created. The Department performs functions such as health data management and technical management of computer systems. It is composed of different areas responsible for carrying out hospital information management: Clinical Informatics, Software Engineering, Business Intelligence and Biostatistics, Norms and Procedures, IT Infrastructure, Research and Technological Innovation, Implementation, Community Health Informatics, and Training and Quality in Information Systems, each with different responsibilities and with a team of nearly 200 professionals.

In parallel, a 4-year educational program was created, consisting of in-service residency training, aimed at training physicians. This program aimed to train clinicians who could become main actors in the development and implementation of eHealth strategies and represent the link between the areas of healthcare and Information Technology.

The Department of Health Informatics at Hospital Italiano de Buenos Aires has developed over the last 15 years a deep redesign of its activities with the aim of achieving harmony between providing high quality of care, while managing costs and the ability to meet the needs of the population. Since a local and face-to-face program was not enough to meet the growing demand for specialty training, it was clear that a broader-reaching educational strategy was needed. In 2006, thanks to an agreement between IUHIBA, Oregon Health & Science University (OHSU) and the American Medical Informatics Association (AMIA), a distance learning training introductory course in Medical Informatics was launched. Its initial version was a regional adaptation of the course developed by OHSU and part of the AMIA 10 x 10 program [4]. The adaptation included, in addition to the language, characteristics of the regional and local health environments of Public Health Informatics. As of 2018 more than 1500 professionals involved in health informatics had taken the course. Together with this course, the DHI launched other courses aimed at satisfying the different training needs, from courses in basic computer tools for professionals, courses in access to biomedical information sources or introduction to HL7.

During 2010, the Argentine Ministry of Education recognized Health Informatics as a specialty and from then on our medical residents were able graduate with a degree of specialists in Medical Informatics after they finished their residency training [5]. This was a great recognition for this growing discipline in Argentina.

In 2012 we decided to expand the training in health informatics for a health-related workforce, understanding that in the context of complex organizations it is necessary to consider the characteristics of each discipline. The residency training program changed its name from Medical Informatics to Health Informatics and began accepting nursing students. Finally, in 2018, it evolved into an interdisciplinary residency so that other health and health-related professionals can now be admitted.

After almost 20 years of training in health informatics, 49 professionals have graduated from our residency training program. Currently they are working in the different areas of the Department of Health Informatics of HIBA and in other institutions, fulfilling roles of physician and nurse informaticians, from Health informatics Specialist, Clinical Informatics Specialist to Chief Medical Informatics Officer. They also participate in eHealth projects in Argentina and other countries; and they coordinate the development, implementation and evaluation of health information systems and work at the local, state or national level in the Ministry of Health as part of the National eHealth plan.

However, our contribution to the training of specialists in Health Informatics convinced us that a local program in Argentina, in face-to-face mode tailored to Argentina's unique needs, would not meet the greater demand for training in the discipline. An opportunity arose to develop postgraduate training in Spanish, which would be attractive to the Latin American region.

In 2017 we launched the Master in Health Informatics (MIS) degree. Our 2-year Master's degree program in Health Informatics is aimed at professionals in the health sciences, engineering and information, who wish to train in this disciplinary field from different perspectives, and who need to develop the necessary skills to address the different challenges of health information systems. As of 2019, the MIS program has over 250 students that are mostly from Argentina, but also from other Latin American countries such as Uruguay, Colombia, Chile, Mexico, Panama, Paraguay, Ecuador and Bolivia. Our main objective is that our graduates are trained to assume positions that require a deep knowledge of information technologies and health organizations, endowed with creative thinking, capable of solving problems and generating new knowledge in multidisciplinary work teams.

The curriculum is organized around four axes: (a) Health Sciences, (b) Computer Sciences, (c) Administration Sciences (d) Information Sciences. It is designed so that students can develop the necessary skills to apply its principles for the organization, analysis, management and use of information in the health system [6]. In addition, we launched in parallel, a group of distance learning courses aimed at specific areas such as: Health Project Management, based on the PMBOK methodology (https://www.pmi.org/pmbok-guide-standards); Creation of Clinical Decision Support Systems; Principles of Interoperability and Standards in Health; Ubiquity and Telemedicine; and, Organizational Aspects and Change Management in Health.

As a result of our initiative of educating healthcare professionals the DHI was appointed as a Collaborating Centre in Knowledge Management for the World Health Organization/Pan American Health Organization (WHO-PAHO), with the purpose of providing support in digital literacy programs and providing training on health information systems and electronic health records. We also offer support for the implementation of the eHealth Strategy among countries of the Americas and for the development, adoption and use of standards for health data and information exchange between and within countries.

As part of our project of providing training materials in health informatics in Spanish a series of E-books were launched during 2018 on different topics related to Health Information Systems. We think that these e-books can be used as guidance in Spanish for those working on the field in the Latin-American region where there is a lack of information in that language. These 17 books are available through Amazon and include different topics such as:

- Ethics, Security and Legislation of Health Information Systems
- Databases and Business Intelligence in Health
- Community Health Informatics
- Translational Computing
- Computer-Assisted Surgery
- Infrastructure of Health Information Systems
- Support Systems for Decision Making
- The Complexity of Medical Thinking and Decision Making
- Information Systems for Health Management
- Evaluating Health Information Systems
- Principles of Interoperability in Health and Standards
- Software Construction
- GPS: Project Management in Healthcare
- Information Systems for Healthcare
- Developing Software in Healthcare
- ReSIStiendo: Change management in health information systems
- ABC of PubMed

This overview of the experience at Hospital Italiano described how our education project evolved and matured from a program that only aimed to train health informatics professionals that were part of a residency training program to a much richer and wider offering that tries to fulfill the needs of the Latin American region.

Brazil: Health Informatics Education—Lessons Learned

Education is a long-life process that never ends. Considering the evolution of health informatics and information and communication technology resources, education and training in their field became an essential part of educational curricula in the healthcare field. Thus, it was as necessary to establish and deploy programs in health informatics as much as consumer and patient education programs.

In Brazil, since the foundation of the Brazilian Health Informatics Society (Sociedade Brasileira de Informática em Saúde—SBIS) [7] in 1986, building capacity is a major objective of the society members connected to educational organizations and universities. Consequently, the founders of the society looked at competencies and other work that had been done to stimulate the organization of programs and content to be taught, mostly in medical and nursing degrees.

In the late 1980s, the first health informatics content programs developed were integrated into four universities in the country: Universidade Federal do Rio Grande do Sul, Universidade Federal de São Paulo (at the time, known as Escola Paulista de Medicina), Universidade de Campinas and Universidade de São Paulo Faculdade de Medicina (FMUSP) e Escola de Enfermagem (EEUSP). Each school or faculty decided the best content that would fit their students' needs for competencies at that time. Leaders of those health informatics programs recognized that information and communication technology was transforming not only health practice, but training and education models as well.

Since 1991, when the Nursing Informatics Group at the Federal University of São Paulo (UNIFESP) was established, the Nursing Informatics discipline is leading efforts in healthcare facilities. Currently, universities across the country and several nursing schools have established the discipline in the nursing curriculum and organized nursing informatics research groups. Currently, the National Council for Research—CNPQ [8] registered 43 research groups in technology and nursing informatics in the country. The number is progressing compared to the last 5 years, but it is obviously not satisfactory, considering the large size of the country and diversity of technical and economic development levels.

With the introduction of computers in the healthcare area, clinicians became primary users, responsible for data input. Consequently, they had to become computer-literate in order to utilize computer technology in an efficient manner. However, formal education programs such as a specific medical or nursing informatics specialization, master or doctoral course were initiated just after the year 2000. Before that, the content of health informatics was inserted as part of other specialty degrees such as cardiology, obstetrics and pathology [9].

Nevertheless, some unique experiences were implemented in the country. As an example, the Universidade of São Paulo—School of Medicine was the first to offer a Medical Informatics Residency that trained physicians who currently have distinguished positions in the community, nationally and internationally [10].

The educational programs in health informatics were initially offered in the country as a specialization degree program at medical and nursing schools. The major objective was training the trainer. Having professional literacy and skills in the field was the first action to stimulate the inclusion of the discipline in the curriculum. The first graduate program in Health Informatics was implemented in 2001 at the Department of Health Informatics in the Universidade Federal de São Paulo—UNIFESP [11]. The program initially offered masters and doctoral level training. However, due to the evaluation performed by the *Coordenação de Aperfeiçoamento de Pessoal de Nível Superior* (*CAPES*), a Foundation of the Ministry of Education that controls the production and quality of graduate programs in the country, the doctoral level was terminated.

Considering the challenges faced by the training and education sector in health informatics, in 1999 a bilateral collaboration was started for training medical informaticians in Brazil. Participation from U.S. and Brazilian faculty began at the proposal phase and continued until the final implementation and redesigning phase. The major objectives were: (1) to train personnel to develop and apply biomedical informatics methods to enhance healthcare delivery; and (2) to promote exchanges of ideas and distribution of access to computer-based tools that enable more effective cross-border research, establishing a base for sustainability of educational programs through international collaborations. The project persisted 15 years and, in the first phase, trained around 1724 professionals. During the second phase (2004–2009), named ITGH—International Training for Global Health program, the training continued to be offered as a certificate program and a doctoral program in bioinformatics. Both programs were planned on the ITGH request for applications [12]. The Certificate program was conducted onsite in person during the three first years. The third phase of the program, the Biomedical Research Informatics for Global Health Training (BRIGHT), was developed to enhance capacity in different settings in Brazil and extend initiatives toward a global partnership. As these programs based in Sao Paulo evolved, it was decided to extend their reach outside the city, to northern areas of Brazil and to Maputo, Mozambique. The major motivation was to organize a program that could train Brazil's and Mozambique's future scientific leaders to be equipped to use tools of genome science, biomedical and health informatics.

Learning from experience through Brazil, the program in Maputo addressed different training needs of applied informatics research and basic informatics research by two distinct programs, which differed in duration and emphasis. The first was a 1-year certificate program to meet immediate human resource needs in applied biomedical and health informatics, (similar in goals to the formal master's program). The aim of the second program was to offer the possibility for Maputo students to apply for a 5-year doctoral program in Brazil [13, 14].

In 2017, the Ministry of Health established the Brazilian eHealth Strategy Resolution No. 19, June 22, whose implementation corresponded to the following mission:

> ...by 2020, eHealth will be incorporated into the Brazilian Unified Health System (SUS) as an essential dimension and will be recognized as a strategy for consistent improvement of health services through the provision and use of comprehensive, accurate and safe information. It is designed to improve the quality of healthcare and processes in the three spheres of government and the private sector, benefiting patients, citizens, professionals, managers, and health organizations [15].

Among the nine strategic actions listed in the document of the e-Health Strategy of Brazil, promoting the training in digital and health informatics with the concurrent creation of professional certification programs is one of the biggest challenges, due to economic and social development issues present in different regions of the country [15].

The goal of the strategic plan is to create the e-Health career, defining positions, functions and salaries. In addition, a major objective is to promote recognition of e-Health as an area of knowledge and research and development by the research agencies. Thus, grants and support will be available on a dedicated basis. Understanding that the success of the strategic plan depends on human literacy and competencies in digital health, the Ministry of Health has encouraged educational and research centers to offer short courses and to provide training for professionals at different levels of care to acquire competencies related to the ICT use.

On December 14, 2017, during the 4th Ordinary Meeting of the Steering Committee for the Unified Health System Institutional Development Program (Proadi-Sus), the Ministry of Health authorized the project called digiSUS: Human Resource Education to Implement the eHealth Strategy in Brazil, providing local courses and distance education programs to enable the implementation of digiSUS [16].

The education and training programs in Brazil continue to develop. It is noted that the number of informatics professionals is not sufficient to the size, geographical differences and needs of the country. As of 2019, several programs are available. They include five courses as part of an undergraduate degree program (baccalaureate), a six-course certificate (specialization degree) and 12 (twelve) courses for masters and doctoral degree programs (http://www.sbis.org.br/formacao-pesquisa-is). However, considering the number of healthcare facilities and the Brazilian population, the quantity is far from ideal to support the success of a national program in digital health.

As an example, nursing informatics is still not completely integrated into the nursing curriculum of several nursing schools. In addition, nursing informatics competencies are also not established at the national level. Nursing schools and educational institutes decide the curriculum content based on local capacities and needs for performance.

Brazil has 6589 hospitals according to DATASUS—the Health Data Department of the Ministry of Health [17]. Considering the number of hospitals with more than

200 beds, the health insurance providers with more than 100,000 members and municipal health departments in the largest cities, it can inferred that Brazil needs at least 1070 health informaticians [18].

Several challenges remain, such as professional accreditation, the research field recognition by the national research councils, different levels for building capacity and financial support, including consistent funding from stakeholders and government bodies.

It is common sense that training and education programs must incorporate resources and adapt their curricula according to the current demands of the health sector. Then, higher education levels are required to maintain the field, the research perspectives and the education of future generations must be considered, and professionals and students must become independent learners prepared to face and solve different problems and situations, assuring the quality of the care delivery.

Chile: Biomedical Informatics Education in Chile

All healthcare services must be delivered by skilled workers and digital services are no exception. The development and training of medical care teams in advanced knowledge and skills for digital health is vital, as it will ensure that all the healthcare systems will continue to function properly and that care is being practiced safely at the highest level of patient-oriented quality.

Generally, digital capabilities are not taught along with traditional medical competencies and when they are, it is often on an insufficient level. Consequently, healthcare professionals are not fully prepared for the realities of the clinical practice where the technological demands are increasingly high.

The need arises for a specialized workforce, with the technical knowledge that is focused on healthcare informatics system implementations. At the same time, clinical professionals with sufficient expertise in digital health also are needed. This new clinical reality puts health professionals on a path of constant education to be able to take on the tasks that this digital health era will bring to all of us.

In the Chilean educational system, schooling is provided by public, private or mixed institutions where the following structure in general terms is followed: primary school that takes 8 years starting at 6 years old, followed by secondary school with 4 years of instruction. Tertiary education is provided at universities (between 5 and 7 years of tuition) leading to a bachelor's degree, colleges (4 years of tuition) with undergraduate programs, and technical schools (2 years of tuition).

One of the first educational institutions to form a human resource specialized in health informatics was DuocUC Institute. DuocUC is a private non-profit college and technical school founded by Católica de Chile University. It was created for the purpose of training a workforce oriented towards a non-university level, and included technical instruction of young people, professional specialization and continuing education programs. The institution has 17 campuses located in Chile's major cities. Both, technical and college programs were developed by its eight schools: Business and Management, Communication, Construction, Design, Telecommunication and Informatics, Engineering, Natural Resources, Health and Tourism. In addition, DuocUC has been accredited for 7 years, which is the maximum level of national accreditation given by the national accreditation commission of Chile.

The program for biomedical informatics technologists (BMIT) is a 4-year program that has today more than 1200 graduates, 92% of whom are employed in a disciplinary area of biomedical informatics. It is a one-of-a-kind program in Chile. The program is open to anyone who has finished high school. Also, students with previous post-secondary studies, students with previous extensive working experience in the field and students who graduated from a technical high school can enter after undergoing a special exam.

BMIT graduates can integrate health skills with Information and communications technology (ICT) procedures to optimize the quality and efficiency of healthcare management. In order to fulfil such objectives, students receive training in health competences with specific training in ICT tools management linked to information processes. Students are particularly trained to work collaboratively. The program follows the didactic concept learning by experiential learning, appropriate for a vocational study. There is a great need for this kind of education in Chile. More information is available at http://www.duoc.cl/carrera/informatica-biomedica

National Center for Health Information Systems: CENS

In 2016, the National Center for Health Information Systems (CENS) was created as part of a strategy for human capital development. CENS is a non-profit corporation formed by Universidad de Chile, Pontificia Universidad Católica de Chile, Universidad de Concepción, Universidad de Valparaíso and Universidad de Talca, with the support of the Production Development Corporation (CORFO). The purpose of the center is to develop strategies and activities that promote a more connected healthcare system, innovate through health information technologies and close the gaps in knowledge, human capital and application of health information systems. Its main work areas are: Interoperability, Innovation, Human Capital, Quality and Consulting.

The Human Capital area of CENS has developed a Model of Reference Competencies in Health Information Systems in order to establish the knowledge, attitudes and key skills that professionals and technicians need to perform competently in the area of Digital Health. More than 20 public and private institutions, associations and academic representatives participated in the elaboration of the model, defining the vision and main challenges for the development of the Digital Health sector. A qualitative approach was used through the analysis of secondary information, questionnaires and technical panels with these participants. In addition, an analysis of competencies in Digital Health, generated by international entities such as: AMIA [19], CHIA [20], and COACH [21], was done in order to complement the Chilean model.

The Model of Reference Competencies is made up of two areas (Health and Technology Transformation), eight domains or performance areas, 32 competencies and more than 100 sub-competencies. Crosswise, ethical and legal aspects are present in all domains. This model conceives of the organization of the learning process as a continuum and facilitates the construction of formative trajectories for individuals. The model is a benchmark for excellence training in the sector, guiding the design of undergraduate and postgraduate training programs and establishing common training standards.

Another relevant project in Human Capital CENS is the creation of Professional and Technical Profiles that the Digital Health sector needs to define training and certification policies. In Chile there are no standards or profiles to guide the hiring process of professionals and technicians with the necessary skills for the advanced development of the industry and health facilities in the field of Digital Health. CENS, along with its partners, are defining four occupational profiles with their corresponding career paths, using a methodology based on a national reference [22] and the Model of Reference Competencies in HIS.

The identification of the technical and professional profiles will allow the establishment of standards associated with a specific function, which will guide professionals in what is expected of them, as well as the employer by providing guidelines for the hiring of personnel. It also allows orienting a relevant training offer according to the needs of this productive sector. At the individual level, it will facilitate the access to jobs in intelligent industries for people who work and are certified in these profiles, with better wage levels related to the experience in the sector, promotion (access to defined training routes) and, therefore, a more stimulating professional development.

CENS Universities

CENS brings together outstanding academics in the field of health informatics from its five member universities. They have experience in areas of interoperability, design and implementation of health information systems, entrepreneurship and innovation in health, among others. Below are described the main CENS universities.

Pontificia Universidad Católica de Chile This pontifical university founded in 1888 has the highest level of national accreditation, with more than 29,703 students in graduate and postgraduate programs. The institution currently includes digital health competencies in graduate programs in nursing, medicine and health sciences graduate schools.

Universidad de Chile As the oldest university of the country, located in Santiago, it has the highest level of accreditation and more than 41,000 students in graduate and postgraduate programs. It offers two elective subjects for undergraduate medical students, two micro credentials one in Standards and Interoperability in Electronic Health (Summer School), and the other in Health Information Systems (Diploma). Finally, it offers a master's degree program in Medical Informatics. The last three programs mentioned are delivered in collaboration with the Heidelberg Center for América Latina.

Universidad de Concepción This university with the highest level of national accreditation, located in the south of the country, has 25,200 students and it offers Biomedical Informatics to create professionals with advanced knowledge in medical equipment, clinical bioengineering, development and medical informatics. In postgraduate studies, it offers a micro credential (diploma) in Telemedicine and Health Information Technology that provides competencies in the fields of Telemedicine, Medical Informatics and the use of Information and Communication Technologies in Health.

Universidad de Talca This accredited university with more than 11,000 graduate and postgraduate students, offers the Biomedical Engineering degree, developing competencies in directing and managing working groups for the implementation of technology. It also offers collaborative clinical simulations for the development of teamwork skills in medical students.

Universidad de Valparaíso   As an accredited university located in one of the main port cities of the country, it has more than 16,000 students, and offers the Biomedical Engineering degree that aims to train professionals who can provide solutions that positively impact the health of people. It also offers a micro credential in Health Information Systems (diploma) that aims to develop the ability to strategically incorporate technologies and manage development projects and implement solutions.

Uruguay: Degree in Medical Records, History and Challenges of the Uruguayan Health Scenario

As background, it is important to describe the current digital context in Uruguay.

In 2005, Uruguay started a process of digital public management with the objective of strengthening the relationship between citizens and the Government [23]. The aim was to reach a complete online State for the citizens to be able to manage the majority of the procedures of the Central Administration online and effectively use their services.

The 2020 Digital Government Plan suggested for this digital transformation "…gathers different objectives and initiatives which are important in order to advance into the digital transformation of the Uruguayan government in a comprehensive way …."

In February 2018, Uruguay entered the 7 Digital Group (D7) which is the most advanced group of States in digital matters, being the only Latin American and Caribbean country that is part of it. Today, Uruguay's information and communication technology (ICT) development positions it first in Latin America.

It is important to highlight that Uruguay has been distinguished for the reduction of the digital gap thanks to the strategic implementation of two National Digital Inclusion Plans. Firstly, Plan Ceibal is a socio-educational program which was created in 2007 [24]. This plan offers a notebook with Wi-Fi connection for each school-age child and to each public-school teacher. Secondly, there is Plan Ibirapitá [25], which was created afterwards, for the inclusion of the elderly. The plan offers a free tablet with a specially designed interface aimed to be intuitive and friendly. These changes have been simultaneously adjusted with tactical and responsible management of change. In this way, access to technologies and their opportunities have been democratized [26].

In the year 2007, Uruguay faced the challenge of the implementation of the National Integrated Health System (SNIS—initials in Spanish) taking advantage of these improvements. It has been possible to build the National Electronic Medical Record (HCEN—initials in Spanish) which constitutes an essential tool in order to offer continuity of care, with opportunity and communication, efficiently and effectively supporting the care processes. In this context, the degree program in Medical Records found itself forced to be transformed and restructured, to be up to date and also to incorporate new skills that could assist the demands of the new scenario which had been set up at a national level.

From the Origins to the Present Day

The Medical Records Degree was developed in 1952 at the University Hospital of the School of Medicine "Dr. Manuel Quíntela" to address the need to train human resources within the hospital field. This training was quickly established as an academic program at the Institute of Medical Technology of the School of Medicine.

Since then, the current University School of Medical Technology has changed its name, as well as the profile of its graduates in accordance with social changes. Likewise, the names of the issued degrees were modified: Medical Document Assistant (1952), Medical Document Technician (1954), Medical Records Technician (1985), Technologist in Medical Records (2006), and Medical Records Degree (2006).

In 2007, according to the needs and demands of the labor market and facing the creation of SNIS, a very important victory was accomplished: the approval of the degree title. This plan was designed to train well-rounded professionals, with the capacity to interact in investigation groups, and who could engage in planning, organization and management of their working area [27]. At the same time, the intermediate degree of Technologist in Medical Records was created to develop specific areas such as data gathering, analysis and processing, as well as document management.

The demand for medical record professionals has increased according to the demands of the changing healthcare needs, the evolution of Information Systems (SIS—initials in Spanish), the advance in Information and Communication Technologies (ICT) and social, educational and health policies within the region provided by the Pan American Health Organization (PAHO) and the World Health Organization (WHO).

In order to have appropriate decision-making and health management at the micro, meso and macro levels, it is necessary to incorporate complete data that is of good quality. The personnel who collect and record the data are fundamental links in the care process. The strategic functions of Medical Records professionals are key factors for successful decision-making.

Among the competencies of the graduates are the following:

- Handle different standards of semantic interoperability, which is fundamental for reaching the HCEN (National Electronic Health Record) implementation, in addition to SNOMED CT.
- Manage the International Disease Classifications and terminological services tool which is implemented by the clinician for the record in the EHR.
- Directly intervene in the development of the information systems as well as in the use, and projection of the same.
- Be able to interpret a situation and provide recommendations related to the development of information systems.
- Analyze large amounts of data using Data Science tools, and therefore, contribute to the clinical management for decision-making.
- Assure the quality of the information through the auditing of medical data.

The training of the professional in Medical Records gives them highly technical knowledge for the coding of the diagnosis resulting in one of the most important activities related to the diagnosis, prevention and treatment of disease. This can directly influence the health economy of a country, where the Ministry of Health (MS, initials in Spanish) uses the information for decision-making and the creation of health programs.

Also, systematic coding controls the quality of the diagnostic codification. The information obtained is valuable for it allows the epidemiological study of the population or individuals and is used as well as by health institutions and the Ministry of Health. The graduate of these programs has the final responsibility for the statistical reports of morbidity/mortality, health production and vital statistics. The Medical Records professionals actively participate in the preparation of the Electronic Live Birth and Death Certificates. They are also part of multi-professional teams for institutional project management and are one of the responsible figures for the management of changes in Health Institutions due to the digital transformation, including the EHR implementation which provides support to the whole process.

These changes in health care are gradually being achieved and correspond to a national project following the Health Objectives of the PAHO/WHO. Professionals with Medical Records training are also part of committees which are related to the process of patient care. Therefore, the professional actively participates in committees of information quality, informatics, clinical history, care ethics, surgical block and patient safety among others. They are also able to assess the health situation and investigate any area of the community interacting with other disciplines because of their analysis capacity.

Within the Technologist competencies we distinguish the following:

- Solid and responsible collection of medical data.
- Monitoring the inclusion of data and overseeing the quality of the data.
- Management of beds and hospital movements (admission, discharge and/or transfer).
- Address legal processes in the institutions such as birth and death.
- Manage customer service, external consultation and emergency admissions as well as diagnostic and treatment services (outpatient services).
- Assume responsibility to record data in the emergency setting to provide assistance for subsequent management of the costs of care.
- Diagnostic codification of pathologies and elaboration of medical statistics.
- Medical Informatics knowledge in order to act and support the health information systems.

In all cases, professionals, technologists or with a degree, carry on duties in all three levels of care and handle sensitive information, acting under bioethical norms with information certainty and confidentiality. They respect the privacy of the user of the health system by protecting the data according to the Bill 18.331 of Personal Data Protection Habeas Data [28], enacted in 2008. They are also guarantors of data protection and information security when handling sensitive data.

Currently, keeping within the context of the second university reform and changes in the labor market, the approval of new study programs is being managed at the School of Medicine [29]. These changes will transform the denomination of the university titles to Degree or Technologist in Management of Medical Information, after 4 years of study or 3 years, respectively.

Many countries have academic programs that are focused on being a potential instrument for the elaboration of Health Policies. They are more focused on the Record and Health Statistics and as these are part of the SIS, they contribute to the creation and development of networks. Uruguay has the privilege of including this specific career in order to keep on facing new challenges with more qualified human resources.

This overview on different experiences on education on health informatics in Latin America describes the diverse e-health settings and training possibilities available and how the training needs have been addressed with local skills.

Acknowledgements We want to thank Maurizio Mattoli, Director of the Center of Biomedical Informatics—Universidad Del Desarrollo, Alejandro Mauro, Director of Biomedical Informatics, Clínica Alemana and Sandra Gutiérrez, Head of Human Capital at Centro Nacional en Sistemas de Informacion en Salud—CENS who helped with the section on Chile. We also want to thank Mildred de Lima, Stephanie Guirin, Rossana Occhiuzzi, Jorge Sandes and Patricia Valle who collaborated on the section on activities in Uruguay.

References

1. Eysenbach G. What is e-health? J Med Internet Res. 2001 Apr;3(2):E20.
2. Strategy and Plan of Action on eHealth - 51st Directing Council of PAHO [Internet]. Pan American Health Organization; 2011 [cited 2020 Mar 16]. Available from https://www.paho.org/hq/dmdocuments/2011/CD51.R5-e.pdf
3. Luna D, Otero P, Gomez A, Martinez M, García Martí S, Schpilberg M, et al. Implementation of an electronic outpatient medical history: "ITALICA Project". In: 6th symposium on health informatics - 32 JAIIO; 2003.
4. Otero P, Luna D, Lopez A, FGB Q, Langlois E, Marchetti M, et al. Implementation of a distance education program in medical informatics in Latin America. In: CBIS 2018 - XVI Brazilian Congress of Informatics in Health.
5. Baum A, Plazzotta F, Canosa D, Borbolla D, Otero P, Luna D. Informatics Specialists: 10 years of experience in a medical residency program in South America. In: INFOLAC 2011 - Latin-American Conference on Health Informatics.
6. Leikam M, Nuñez M, Zimerman L, Gonzalez Z, Baum A, Tattone M, Luna D, Otero P. Master's degree in health informatics: the challenge of continuing training of human resources in Argentina. In: CBIS 2018 - XVI Brazilian Congress of Informatics in Health.
7. História da SBIS [Internet]. SBIS. Sociedade Brasileira de Informática em Saúde. [cited 2019 Oct]. Available from http://www.sbis.org.br/historia-da-sbis
8. National Council for Research - CNPQ [Internet]. [cited 2020 Mar 12]. Available from http://lattes.cnpq.br/web/dgp/home
9. Marin HF, Lorenzi NM. International initiatives in nursing informatics. In: Weaver CA, Delaney CW, Weber P, Carr RL, editors. Nursing and informatics for the 21st century: an international look at practice, education and EHR trends; 2010. p. 45–51.
10. Ferreira DP, Silveira PS, Burattini MN, Wen CL, Massad E, Böhm G. Avaliação dos dez anos de residência de informática clínica da Faculdade de Medicina da Universidade de São Paulo (FMUSP). In: Annals from the IV national forum of health science and technology; 1998. p. 109–10.
11. Universidade Federal de São Paulo – UNIFESP [Internet]. [cited 2020 Mar 12]. Available from https://www.dis.epm.br/historia/informatica-saude
12. Informatics Training For Global Health (ITGH) [Internet]. [cited 2020 Mar 12]. Available from https://grants.nih.gov/grants/guide/rfa-files/RFA-TW-03-008.html
13. Marin HF, Ohno-Machado L. Biomedical informatics: experience in Brazil and Mozambique. In: 24th International Conference of the European Federation for Medical Informatics Quality of Life through Quality of Information (MIE2012 conference) [Internet]. 2012. Available from https://person.hst.aau.dk/ska/mie2012/CD/Interface_MIE2012/MIE_2012_Content/MIE_2012_Content/SCO/273_CD_SC_Oral_ID_375.pdf
14. Ohno-Machado L. Biomedical Research Informatics for Global Health Training (BRIGHT) program [Internet]. [cited 2019 Oct]. Available from http://projectreporter.nih.gov/project_info_description.cfm?aid=8112693&icde=6661263
15. Ministry of Health. Estratégia de e-Saúde para o Brasil [Internet]. 2017 [cited 2019 Oct]. Available from http://portalarquivos.saude.gov.br/images/pdf/2017/julho/12/Estrategia-e-saude-para-o-Brasil.pdf
16. Marin HF, Zinader JPS, Leão BF. Human resource education in health informatics [Internet]. Survey on the use of information and communication technologies in Brazilian healthcare facilities: ICT in health 2017. 2018. Available from https://www.nic.br/media/docs/publicacoes/2/tic_saude_2017_livro_eletronico.pdf
17. DATASUS – Health Data Department of the Ministry of Health - Brazil [Internet]. [cited 2020 Mar 12]. Available from http://tabnet.datasus.gov.br/cgi/tabcgi.exe?cnes/cnv/estabbr.def
18. Leão BF, Moura Jr. LA. Initiatives of the Brazilian Health Informatics Association (SBIS) for Health Informatics in Brazil [Internet]. Survey on the use of information and communication technologies in Brazilian healthcare facilities: ICT in health. 2017 [cited 2019 Oct]. Available from https://www.nic.br/media/docs/publicacoes/2/tic_saude_2016_livro_eletronico.pdf

19. Valenta AL, Berner ES, Boren SA, Deckard GJ, Eldredge C, Fridsma DB, et al. AMIA board white paper: AMIA 2017 core competencies for applied health informatics education at the master's degree level. J Am Med Inform Assoc. 2018 Dec 1;25(12):1657–68.
20. Certified Health Informatician Australasia (CHIA). Health Informatics Competencies Framework. 2013.
21. Health Informatics Professional Core Competencies [Internet]. Canada's Health Informatics Association (COACH). 2012 [cited 2019 Oct]. Available from https://digitalhealthcanada.com
22. Comisión del Sistema Nacional de Certificación de Competencias Laborales [Internet]. Chile valora. [cited 2019 Oct 20]. Available from https://www.chilevalora.cl/competencias-laborales/que-son/
23. Agencia de Gobierno Electrónico y Sociedad de la Información y del Conocimiento [Internet]. Agencia de Gobierno Electrónico y Sociedad de la Información y del Conocimiento. [cited 2019 Oct 20]. Available from https://www.gub.uy/agencia-gobierno-electronico-sociedad-informacion-conocimiento/
24. Plan Ceibal [Internet]. [cited 2019 Oct 20]. Available from https://www.ceibal.edu.uy/es
25. Vigni N. Memoria anual 2017 | Ibirapitá – Uruguay [Internet]. [cited 2019 Oct 20]. Available from https://ibirapita.org.uy/memoria-anual-2017/
26. Uruguay Digital [Internet]. [cited 2019 Oct 20]. Available from https://uruguaydigital.gub.uy/
27. Degree in Medical Record [Internet]. University Institute of Medical Technology. School of Medicine. University of the Republic. [cited 2019 Oct 20]. Available from http://www.regis-trosmedicos.fmed.edu.uy/
28. Ley No 18331 - Protección de Datos Personales [Internet]. [cited 2019 Oct 20]. Available from https://www.impo.com.uy/bases/leyes/18331-2008
29. Study Program, Degree in Medical Records 2006 [Internet]. University Institute of Medical Technology. School of Medicine. University of the Republic. [cited 2019 Oct]. Available from http://www.eutm.fmed.edu.uy/blog%20direcccion/comisiones%20carreras%20eutm/planes2006/Registros%20M%C3%A9dicos.pdf

Chapter 14
Informatics Education
in the Asia-Pacific Region

**Ngai Tseung Cheung, Juanita Fernando, Oommen John, Alvin Marcelo,
Iris Thiele Isip-Tan, Cheng Ooi Low, Daniel Li, and Vajira H. W. Dissanayake**

N. T. Cheung (✉)
Head of Information Technology and Health Informatics/CMIO, Hong Kong Hospital
Authority, Hong Kong, Hong Kong
e-mail: cheungnt@ha.org.hk

J. Fernando
MERQ, Public Health and Preventive Medicine, Medicine, Nursing and Health Sciences,
Monash University, Clayton, VIC, Australia
e-mail: juanita.fernando@monash.edu

O. John
The George Institute for Global Health, New Delhi, India

University of New South Wales, Sydney, NSW, Australia

Asia Pacific Association for Medical Informatics, New Delhi, India

A. Marcelo
Professor of Surgery and Health Informatics, University of the Philippines,
Manila, Philippines
e-mail: admarcelo@up.edu.ph

I. T. Isip-Tan
Medical Informatics Unit, College of Medicine, University of the Philippines,
Manila, Philippines
e-mail: icisiptan@up.edu.ph

C. O. Low
Singapore Health Services, Singapore, Singapore
e-mail: chengooi.low@ihis.com.sg

D. Li
Integrated Health Information Systems, Singapore, Singapore
e-mail: daniel.li@ihis.com.sg

V. H. W. Dissanayake
Specialty Board in Biomedical Informatics, Postgraduate Institute of Medicine,
University of Colombo, Colombo, Sri Lanka
e-mail: vajira@anat.cmb.ac.lk

© Springer Nature Switzerland AG 2020
E. S. Berner (ed.), *Informatics Education in Healthcare*, Health Informatics,
https://doi.org/10.1007/978-3-030-53813-2_14

Introduction

The commonly used term "Asia-Pacific region" actually has no clear definition and depending on context the countries that are included can vary considerably. For this discussion we shall use one common definition of the Asia-Pacific region, that is, the group of countries along the eastern Pacific rim, including most of what is often called East Asia, Southeast Asia and Australasia [1].

This is a highly heterogeneous group of countries that covers a great swath of territory and encompasses a massive population. The group members frequently have little in common other than geography. The region is highly diverse in almost all aspects, including racially, culturally, and economically as well as in religion, governance and healthcare systems. This wide diversity makes it extremely difficult to try to describe succinctly any aspect of this region, and certainly the area of Health Informatics development is no different.

Many of the countries and territories in the region already have a long history of significant Health Informatics development. Australia launched the Personally Controlled Electronic Health Records system in 2012 as a national electronic records sharing system [2]. Hong Kong deployed a single integrated electronic patient record system across the entire public healthcare sector by 2000 [3] and launched the Electronic Health Record Sharing System in 2016 [4].

In Japan more than 62% of major hospitals have an electronic medical record installed [5]. New Zealand is well known for the high rate of EMR adoption, particularly in the primary care sector [6]. South Korea has a very high EMR adoption rate in both the hospital and ambulatory settings [7]. Singapore launched the first phase of the National Electronic Health Record (NEHR) in 2011 to consolidate health records between various sectors of care [8]. In Taiwan there is a high EMR adoption rate in hospitals and clinics [9].

For these more experienced nations, Health Informatics and e-Health development is already firmly on the policy agenda. However all across the region Health Informatics and Health IT are seen as strategic imperatives to enable more effective, efficient delivery of better quality health care to their populations. Of the 15 founders of the Global Digital Health Partnership, seven were countries of the Asia Pacific region [10].

This brief discussion will not attempt to provide a comprehensive review of all the health informatics education programs in the Asia-Pacific region. Instead we will try to illustrate the situation through several country case studies (presented in alphabetical order).

Australia and New Zealand

The rapid investment in digital health across Australia and New Zealand is seeing a growing unmet demand for Health Informatics (HI) professionals with a spectrum of skills from technical competency through to senior leadership roles. The unmet demand is multidisciplinary, from clinical and biomedical sciences to, to translational experts, coders and technologists. Presently, there is no single educational pathway for persons to follow when training for the HI profession (see also Chap. 12 which describes Nursing Informatics education in Australia and New Zealand).

The Ministry of Health in New Zealand is devising an educational framework to detail the curricula to be used for future digital health training and education [11]. Although strategic objectives are documented here, the framework is not designed as a detailed plan. Rather, it consists of aspirational goals, enabling priorities, guidelines and resources designed to evolve over time as the disruptive digital health future emerges [12].

The Australian Digital Health Agency (ADHA) is currently devising a National Digital Health Workforce & Education Roadmap as a foundation of the national Digital Health Strategy to address the unmet demand [13].

The ADHA Roadmap will integrate the plethora of training and educational HI training programs and education to support establishing a pathway that supports the workforce to better adapt to, use and embrace the changes and opportunities created by digital health innovation. Current Australian and New Zealand HI educational and training program catalogues are listed in alphabetical order in Table 14.1, below. This list is neither exhaustive nor, for some programs, quality controlled.

A census of the Australian HI Workforce occurred in 2018 leveraging earlier studies in the same domain. The Census showed the educational and training and workplace experiences of around 1600, self-identified health informaticians.

Table 14.1 Health Informatics Educational Programs in Australia and New Zealand

Resource	Description	URL
+ACHI Directory of HI Education in Australia and New Zealand	PhDs and Postgrad Research Degrees in HI, Post Grad Programs in HI and Undergraduate degrees	https://www.achi.org.au/education-directory/
+ACHI Directory of Short Course Providers	Single subjects for academic credit & not-for credit, vocational training & incorporated training providers	https://www.achi.org.au/education-directory/short-course-providers/
+ACHI Fellowship by Training Program	Prepares individuals from various disciplines for leadership roles in the HI workforce	https://www.achi.org.au/achi-fellowship-program/
Digital Health CRC	Higher Degree by Research Program	https://www.digitalhealthcrc.com/hdr-program/
Digital Health CRC	Webinars	https://www.digitalhealthcrc.com/webinars/
Health Informatics NZ	University Courses for Postgraduate Study	https://www.hinz.org.nz/page/UniversityCourses
Health Informatics NZ	Online Courses; multiformat, no formal qualification	https://www.hinz.org.nz/page/OnlineCourses
The National Health and Medical Research Council	Training, workshops, workforce development and fellowship program	https://digitalhealth.edu.au/training-workforce-development-workshops-fellowships/

+Australasian College of Health Informatics—ACHI (now known as Australasian Institute of Digital Health)

Findings showed 6.8% of participants did not hold a tertiary qualification in HI, with other health informatics credentials drawn from health librarian and librarian qualifications, computer societies and health management and informatics organizations [14]. A follow-up census is planned for New Zealand in 2020 and the Australian census will also be repeated then.

Hong Kong

Hong Kong has taken a somewhat non-traditional approach to Health Informatics education. The Hong Kong Polytechnic University has a Department of Health Technology and Informatics, specializing in Medical Laboratory Science and Medical Imaging, which represents the only dedicated tertiary department teaching Health Informatics related material. Short course Health Informatics education programs have been offered, such as the Postgraduate Diploma in e-Health Informatics taught by the University of Hong Kong School of Professional and Continuing Education, and the "Applied Clinical Informatics" distance learning collaborative venture between the Hong Kong Society for Medical Informatics, the Hong Kong Polytechnic University which was recognized as an i10 × 10 course (the international variation of the AMIA 10 × 10 program which is described in Chap. 18). Health Informatics units are also offered as part of various master's degree programs at the Chinese University of Hong Kong.

The bulk of Health Informatics education in Hong Kong, however, has been provided as in-service training through positions in the Information Technology and Health Informatics Division in the Hospital Authority (HA). The development of the Clinical Management System (CMS) and its deployment to all the public hospitals and associated clinics in Hong Kong from 1995 onwards has offered a unique opportunity to participate in the development and deployment of a territory-wide electronic medical records system. Since the CMS was (and continues to be) entirely developed in-house, team members are exposed to a very wide range of Health Informatics disciplines, from strategic planning to deployment issues, from information architecture to usability, from clinical engagement to technical development. The HA was also appointed the technical agency for the development of the electronic health record sharing system (eHRSS) for the whole of Hong Kong. This system was launched in 2016 and has given informatics practitioners practical experience in development for and deployment to different sectors of the healthcare system.

To sustain these development efforts the HA has invested in internal training and a large body of internal research, only a fraction of which has been published. In recent years much of the training investment has been devoted to health IT innovation including mobility, patient engagement, clinical artificial intelligence and the Smart Hospital. The HA has created the Institute for Health IT to take forward these innovation efforts, including the launch of the HA Data Collaboration Laboratory (HADCL) which gives university researchers the opportunity to study machine learning using the HA data set from nearly 30 years of real world use [15]. In 2019 the first six university-led health data machine learning projects commenced in the HADCL.

In addition to these training opportunities within Hong Kong the HA is actively cultivating international partnerships with other large healthcare providers with advanced health IT implementations. Visits and exchange programs provide an opportunity for exposure to other modes of health IT and expand the horizons of the local health informatics workforce.

This sustained investment in development and research programs has resulted in a large number of experienced workers in the health informatics industry in Hong Kong and it is anticipated that the demand for such a workforce will increase in the future as the scope of health IT inevitably increases and the eHRSS is deployed to all healthcare sectors.

India

The Government of India recently launched the Ayushman Bharat (Scheme for Healthy India), a centrally sponsored National Health Protection Scheme that aims to provide an annual health cover of 7000 USD to 100 million vulnerable poor households. The program covers secondary and tertiary treatment, from public/private hospitals across the country and strengthens the primary health care services though establishment of 150,000 health and wellness centers across the country. The program envisions a robust digital health infrastructure to ensure efficient coordination of care delivery and beneficiary management. A program of this scale requires that trained health informatics professionals are embedded into the policy, planning and implementation of the scheme. Health informatics education both as higher degrees through research as well as certificate courses have been offered by academic and research institutions in India for over two decades. The national health portal that is a central repository of health information resources lists over ten institutions offering health informatics education [16].

The School of Medical Science &Technology (SMST) established at the Indian Institute of Technology Kharagpur offers an interdisciplinary 3 year Masters Program in Medical Science and Technology (MMST) and is the first of its kind in India. Admission to this program is offered to MBBS doctors each year based a country-wide entrance test and is the only comprehensive health technology and informatics training program in India. The school also offers a M.Tech program in Medical Imaging & Informatics and offers PhD programs.

Indira Gandhi National Open University offers a 6 month postgradate certification in medical informatics to graduates in any discipline. It is offered mainly as a remote learning course. The lack of clinical exposure during the training is a main drawback and therefore the employment options for such certification is limited.

The International Institute for Health Management and Research offers a 2 year Masters in health information management. The course offers an internship opportunity for the students in their final year with an onsite project in health informatics in a clinical or health technology company setting.

A survey reported in the 2010 IMIA Yearbook of Medical Informatics suggests that health informatics courses were still in their infancy in India, mostly offered as online (e-learning) or other modes of distance learning. In general, most of the students were graduates in medicine (allopathic, homeopathic, ayurveda), allied sciences (nursing, physiotherapy) and medical administrators or graduates in engineering or library and information sciences. However in the absence of clearly articulated career pathways for health informatics professionals in India, there has been little uptake for the health informatics education programs that are offered in India [17].

A policy roundtable including health policy and medical education experts along with clinical experts, informatics experts and students was undertaken in 2016 at the All India Institute for Medical Sciences. This roundtable focused on health informatics training needs for undergraduate medical and nursing students and identified the following challenges and barriers to health professionals adopting health information technologies in routine practice.

- Non-availability of electronic health records and e-prescribing modules during their training period;
- Lack of Digital Health tools within clinical workflows to improve methods of generating health record and user centered design that allows patients to interact and contribute into their own health records;
- Medical Informatics training needs to be engaging and not a burden on the existing curriculum;
- Newer technologies such as data science, machine learning, artificial intelligence, Internet of medical things, wearable sensors and robotics should be introduced in undergraduate medical schools.
- Lack of competence among faculty in use of health informatics tools.

In response to the emerging opportunities in India in the light of the national digital health blueprint and the scale-up of the Ayushman Bharat, the recently formed Digital Health India Association has proposed a competency based health informatics curriculum. The course aims to provide a broad understanding of health informatics from the vantage point of those who implement, lead, and develop digital health solutions for improving health, healthcare, public health, and biomedical research. This course also includes an implementation project. The proposed competencies have been developed in close partnership with key stakeholders across the public and private healthcare delivery systems in India. With a concerted scale-up of this approach with support from governments' flagship programs such as Ayushman Bharat and national digital health mission, health informatics capacity in India is set to expand. In order to leverage digital health as an enabler for health systems strengthening as outlined in the National Digital Health Blueprint, a future-ready health workforce capacity with health informatics competence would hold the key and a career pathway through accreditation and board certification of the Informatics training under the National Digital Health Mission would be pivotal for its success.

Philippines

As a science, biomedical informatics had been loosely practiced in the Philippines as early as the 1980s. Trainees in tertiary care facilities were using word processors and databases to store patient information. In 1997 the Medical Informatics Unit (MIU) was established at the University of the Philippines (UP) Manila and three faculty received training in medical informatics at the University of Washington, the National Library of Medicine, and the University of Warwick. When they returned in 2001, these pioneer faculty started working on health information systems projects and in 2005 partnered with the College of Arts and Sciences to launch the Master of Science in Health Informatics (MSHI). This degree program had medical informatics and bioinformatics tracks, accepting students with a degree in medicine or other paramedical fields and a baccalaureate degree in biochemistry or computer science respectively. Presently, the MSHI is the only advanced degree granting program for health informatics in the country.

Graduate students have opportunities to immerse in local health facilities and understand issues in health information management at the grassroots level. The students are often engaged in health informatics projects at the Philippine General Hospital and the National Telehealth Center of the UP Manila's National Institutes of Health.

Subsequently, the program has also welcomed nurses, pharmacists, nutritionists, medical technologists and computer scientists. Most of the students are self-funded although faculty from the UP College of Medicine taking the MSHI program are heavily subsidized. Despite being one of the more popular graduate programs in the UP, only a handful have completed their theses to graduate from the program as MSHI graduate students are often recruited by local and regional healthcare startup companies or are employed by non-governmental organizations or the Department of Health (DOH) in ehealth projects.

A revision of the MSHI program has been submitted for approval, renaming it as the MS in Biomedical Informatics and with three tracks: health informatics, bioinformatics and data science for health.

Since 2004, the UP College of Medicine has offered an elective course in medical informatics for second year medical students. The elective has evolved from simple projects and learning objects to orienting students to problems and opportunities in digital health.

The Philippine Commission on Higher Education (CHED) issued a memorandum order in 2016 which enumerated the possible career paths of the graduates of the Doctor of Medicine program, including the role of health information manager. In the minimum curricular content, medical informatics was also included. Hence several medical schools are trying to establish their own medical informatics units. MSHI faculty have been tapped to teach at these units but as expertise in medical informatics is limited, most schools employ computer science faculty (often without medical training) to teach this course.

A similar CHED memorandum order for the implementation of Outcomes-Based Education (OBE) was issued in 2017 for the Bachelor of Science in Nursing program and in 2018 for the Doctor of Dental Medicine program. Three units of nursing informatics and dental informatics respectively, were included in the curriculum.

The DOH shared its draft national ehealth strategy in 2010. In 2013, the DOH and the Department of Science and Technology (DOST) released a joint department memorandum creating the National eHealth Governance Steering Committee and Technical Working Group (TWG). Subsequently, this steering committee approved the Philippine eHealth Strategic Framework 2014–2020. A capacity-building experts group (CBEG) was included in the TWG, jointly helmed by the UP Manila MIU and the CHED.

The CBEG was tasked to review the current milieu for capacity-building in eHealth to provide leadership and governance for eHealth education and training and to provide recommendations for a standard ehealth curriculum for health professions.

In 2011, at a WHO meeting in Vietnam an informal learning network was convened which became the Asia eHealth Information Network or AeHIN. AeHIN now comprises over 1000 individuals who share resources and advocate for improved digital health strategies and implementation, especially in the context of universal health coverage. The network has summed up their work around the Mind the GAPS framework, encouraging capability buiding for digital health Governance, Architecture, Program Management, Standards and Interoperability. AeHIN has thus served as a hub for health informatics education in the region.

The AeHIN has also set up the Community of Interoperability Labs (COIL), a collection of university-based facilities specialising in resolving interoperability challenges using standardized tools and frameworks. The University of the Philippines Manila Medical Informatics Unit is the base of the Philippine Interoperability Lab.

Singapore

The earliest avenues for clinical informatics education were in the United States and United Kingdom. In the US, the American Medical Informatics Association (AMIA) started the 10 × 10 initiative (see Chap. 18). Universities offered courses targeted at two groups of students - IT professionals who wish to understand healthcare and its use of IT, and healthcare professionals who have a keen interest in IT or embarking on IT transformation for their organizations. Singapore has had its own version of AMIA 10 × 10 since 2009, named Gateway to Health Informatics. It was a collaboration between Oregon Health & Science University (OHSU), AMIA and a private local consultancy firm to bring this popular course to Singapore.

One educational path was for professionals to begin with the AMIA 10 × 10 courses, and carry this course credit to an accredited university, for instance

OHSU. Students can then continue with their post-graduate education via distance learning, covering major areas of clinical informatics, healthcare, computer science, organizational behavior and project management.

Besides formal programs, certifications were the other educational route professionals could pursue. The Certified Professional in Healthcare Information and Management Systems (CPHIMS) by HIMSS is one example.

Over the years, local universities caught on to this new emerging trend. The Centre for Health Informatics (CHI) was established jointly in 2012 with the Info-communications Development Authority of Singapore (IDA) and the Department of Information Systems in NUS School of Computing. Partnering with leading health informatics experts from local and foreign institutions, CHI set up training and development programs and seminars to develop health informatics human capital. For undergraduates, topics in clinical informatics are included in degree programs such as the Bachelor of Science, Biomedical Engineering at the Singapore University of Social Sciences. Medical students undergoing clinical attachments at public healthcare institutions (PHIs) are also exposed to the use of Electronic Medical Records (EMRs).

Course fees are often sponsored by healthcare organizations. Generous funding from various government agencies played an instrumental role in the quick pickup of clinical informatics. According to its website (https://www.skillsfuture.sg/tesa) TechSkills Accelerator (TeSA) is "a SkillsFuture initiative driven by Infocomm Media Development Authority (IMDA) in partnership with strategic partners such as Workforce Singapore (WSG) and SkillsFuture Singapore (SSG), and in collaboration with industry partners and hiring employers. It aims to enhance training and placement opportunities for ICT jobs across the economy, by facilitating the reskilling or upskilling of individuals to meet industry needs." IMDA reimburses professionals up to 90% of their course fees for successful completion. Study awards are another option. MOH Holdings (MOHH) offers the MOHH-Healthcare Graduate Studies Award (http://www.mohh.com.sg/programmes-partnerships/scholarships) to "final year undergraduates or recent university graduates who are keen to pursue a Master's degree in selected health science-related courses such as Medical Informatics and Data Analytics". The Singhealth Foundation Talent Development Fund Award funds employees for similar courses as well.

Like Hong Kong, substantial on-the-job training, through positions at Integrated Health Information System (IHiS) and the various public healthcare institutions, establishes a firm foundation for professionals in Healthcare IT. IHiS is the Ministry of Health's HealthTech agency to advance healthcare IT in Singapore and is the key organization providing related services to PHIs. The adoption of EMRs at PHIs paved the way for the National Electronic Healthcare Record (NEHR). This healthcare journey presented fertile training grounds for professionals to master the art of digitizing, connecting and analyzing health information systems.

"HealthTech is an exciting space to be in now. Investments in this sector grew by 7% over the last 3 years. Moving forward, the growth is expected to double and grow by some 13% in the next 3 years. The trajectory growth would translate to a demand for approximately 1200 more health IT jobs. We welcome more talents to join the HealthTech industry in shaping the future of healthcare in Singapore," said *Mr Bruce Liang, Chief Information Officer, Ministry of Health & Chief Executive Officer, IHiS* [18].

Sri Lanka

Sri Lanka has a unique program of training biomedical and health informaticians for its national health service that is not found anywhere else in the world. Health Informatics was recognized as a medical specialty in Sri Lanka in 2015—the first country to do so—following the recognition of clinical informatics, albeit, as a sub-specialty in 2011 in the United States.

The program leading up to specialization is offered through the centralized medical specialist training institute in the country—the Postgraduate Institute of Medicine of the University of Colombo (https://pgim.cmb.ac.lk/). The program, started in 2008 in collaboration with the University of Oslo in Norway, consists of a MSc in Biomedical Informatics [19, 20] leading to a MD in Health Informatics [21]. It is open to doctors and dental surgeons. There is a high demand for entry into the program.

Those who seek entry to the program have to take a selection examination for the MSc. The intake is restricted to the top 30 candidates annually. The Ministry of Health, Sri Lanka, pays the course fees and grants 2 years paid leave for them to attend the course.

The special feature of the MSc is that the second year of the MSc is devoted to action research which enables the students to engage in innovative research projects focusing on frugal innovation—low cost, highly effective, scalable, and sustainable innovation using open source software and open standards with a focus on interoperability. These innovations are custom built for the Ministry of Health, Sri Lanka to meet local needs. The innovations of the students have contributed to development of the Digital Health ecosystem in the country over the past decade. Some of these innovations have won international awards including the World Summit Award for the best innovation in the health and wellness category, an award that was won by the District Nutrition Monitoring System in 2016. Student evaluation during the MSc includes written examinations, group assignments, and defense of the research thesis at a viva voce examination.

The graduates of the MSc are re-employed by the Ministry of Health as Health Informaticians. After completion of 1 year of work as a Health Informatician, they take the selection examination for the MD. This examination, in addition to the written papers, has a viva focusing on the experience that they gained working as health Informaticians.

The 2-year MD program enables them to gain further experience and decision making at a higher level and participate in research. The experiential learning that students receive working at the level of a registrar is evaluated through a portfolio that they maintain which is further examined through a portfolio viva. They have to also defend their research thesis at a viva conducted by a panel consisting of Sri Lankan and international examiners. After receiving their MD they work at the level of a senior registrar and they are expected to gain international exposure and training.

The MD and post MD components of the program too are fully funded by the Ministry of Health. The University of Colombo, working with the Commonwealth Centre for Digital Health (CWCDH), is now co-ordinating their international program through the 'CWCDH Hub' at the University of Southampton, UK. This would include participation and contribution to projects in collaboration with international development partners in all parts of the world. They are designated as Commonwealth Digital Health Fellows during this period. On completion of the program, and after passing the pre-board certification evaluation of their performance, they would be board certified as Health Informatics Specialists and appointed as such by the Ministry of Health.

Since 2008 over 200 students have entered the MSc program with over 150 graduating so far and more than 40 have gone on to enter the MD program. The first set of 19 are currently in their post MD period and expected to becoming the first batch of board certified specialists in 2022. Some of them already work on projects of various international development partners outside of Sri Lanka [22, 23].

In conclusion, we have achieved the vision that we set for the program at the outset. That vision was to develop a generation of leaders in biomedical and health informatics with competencies in both the health domain and the information and communication technology (ICT) domain to spearhead the deployment of ICT in the health sector of the country working with and in collaboration with the medical administrators and policy makers at the highest level.

Conclusion

In 2014, in the first edition of this book, we noted that the demand for individuals with health informatics skills will continue to rise throughout the Asia Pacific region. In the intervening years we have seen an acceleration in the adoption of health IT, spurred on by developments in mobile technology, artificial intelligence, Internet of Things and a renewed interest in telehealth. All of the countries in the Asia-Pacific continue to face pressure on their healthcare systems resulting from demographic shifts, funding and manpower constraints, improvements in medical technologies and treatments and rising expectations from patients and their families. Health IT and Health Informatics are seen as key to helping meet some of these challenges but it is clear that the specific needs of healthcare delivery in the region and the resource constraints in many of the countries mean that local solutions will need to be developed. The Health Informatics education programs discussed above have demonstrated the ability of countries to build up local capacity in Health Informatics to enable the development of the necessary systems and programs.

Regional collaboration is also a necessary ingredient. The Asia-Pacific Association for Medical Informatics (APAMI) was formed in 1993 to promote health IT in the region and the AeHIN has also been described above [24]. More needs to be done to share and disseminate the work that has already been done in the region to others, especially those countries that are just beginning to address the workforce needs.

References

1. Asia-Pacific Center for Security Studies. Countries of the Asia-Pacific Region. https://apcss. org/about-2/ap-countries/. Accessed 20 October 2019.
2. Pearce C, Bainbridge M. A personally controlled electronic health record for Australia. J Am Med Inform Assoc. 2014;21(4):707–13.
3. Cheung NT, Fung V, Wong WN, Tong A, Sek A, Greyling A, Tse N, Fung H. Principles-based medical informatics for success--how Hong Kong built one of the world's largest integrated longitudinal electronic patient records. Stud Health Technol Inform. 2007;129(Pt 1):307–10.
4. Government of the Hong Kong Special Administrative Region eHealth Record Office. eHRSS: from Planing to Commencement of Operation. eHealth News Issue 10. https://www. ehealth.gov.hk/en/publicity_promotion/ehealth_news_10/to_operation.html. Accessed on 20 October 2019.
5. Takabayashi K, Doi S, Suzuki T. Japanese EMRs and IT in medicine: expansion, integration, and reuse of data. Inform Res. 2011;17(3):178–83. https://doi.org/10.4258/hir.2011.17.3.178.
6. Protti D, Bowden T, Johansen I. Adoption of information technology in primary care physician offices in New Zealand and Denmark, part 1: healthcare system comparisons. Inform Prim Care. 2008;16(3):183–7.
7. Chae YM, Yoo KB, Kim ES, Chae H. The adoption of electronic medical records and decision support systems in Korea. Healthc Inform Res. 2011;17(3):172–7. https://doi.org/10.4258/ hir.2011.17.3.172.
8. Koh D. Leveraging IT for better health outcomes – recent developments in Singapore. 2019. https://www.healthcareitnews.com/news/leveraging-it-better-health-outcomes-%E2%80%93-recent-developments-singapore. Accessed 20 October 2019.
9. Wen HC, Chang WP, Hsu MH, Ho CH, Chu CM. An assessment of the interoperability of electronic health record exchanges among hospitals and clinics in Taiwan. JMIR Med Inform. 2019;7(1):e12630. https://doi.org/10.2196/12630.
10. Australian Digital Health Agency. New global digital health partnership. 2018. https://www. digitalhealth.gov.au/news-and-events/news/media-release-new-global-digital-health-partnership. Accessed 28 October 2019.
11. New Zealand Ministry of Health. FRAMING THE FUTURE - Proposal Paper from the Health Science and Technical Workforces Working Group (Phase 2). 2013. https://www.health.govt. nz/system/files/documents/pages/framing-the-future-phasetwo-report.docx. Accessed 28 October 2019.
12. New Zealand Ministry of Health. Digital Health Strategic Framework. 2013. https://www. health.govt.nz/our-work/digital-health/digital-health-strategic-framework. Accessed 28 October 2019.
13. Australian Digital Health Agency. Workforce and education. https://conversation.digitalhealth. gov.au/workforce-and-education. Accessed 28 October 2019.
14. Australasian College of Health Informatics. Master Class #4, The Australian Health Information Workforce. 2018. https://www.achi.org.au/achi-fellowship-program/fellowship-by-training-master-classes/. Accessed 28 October 2019.

15. Hospital Authority. Data Collaboration Lab (Pilot). 2019. http://www3.ha.org.hk/data/DCL/ Index/. Accessed 20 October 2019.
16. National Health Portal, Health Informatics. https://www.nhp.gov.in/health-informatics_ pg#Institutes%20Offering%20Courses. Accessed 15 November 2019.
17. Sarbadhikari SN, Gogia SB. An overview of education and training of medical informatics in India. Yearb Med Inform. 2010;19(01):106–8.
18. IHiS. Major Push to Develop ICT Talent for Health Tech Careers. 2018. https://www.ihis.com. sg/Latest_News/Media_Releases/Pages/Major-Push-to-Develop-ICT-Talent-for-Health-Tech-Careers.aspx. Accessed 15 November 2019.
19. Dissanayake VHW. Developing human resources capacity in health and medical informatics in Sri Lanka. Sri Lanka J Bio-Med Inform. 2010;1(1):6–11.
20. University of Colombo, Sri Lanka. Prospectus – Master of Science (MSc) in Biomedical Informatics. 2013. https://pgim.cmb.ac.lk/wp-content/uploads/2016/07/ BMIprospectus-29.11.2013-2018.pdf. Accessed 2 November 2019.
21. University of Colombo, Sri Lanka. Prospectus - Doctor of Medicine (MD) and Board Certification in Health Informatics. 2006. https://pgim.cmb.ac.lk/wp-content/uploads/2016/07/ MD-Health-Informatics.pdf. Accessed 2 November 2019.
22. Siribaddana P, Hewapathirana R, Jayatilleke AU, Sahay S, Dissanayake VHW. Strengthening health systems through informatics capacity development among doctors in low-resource contexts: the Sri Lankan experience. WHO South East Asia J Public Health. 2019 Sep;8(2):87–94.
23. Siribaddana P, Hewapathirana R, Sahay S, Jayatilleke AU, VHW D. 'Hybrid doctors' can fast track the evolution of a sustainable e-health ecosystem in low resource contexts: the Sri Lankan experience. Stud Health Technol Inform. 2019 Aug 21;264:1356–60.
24. Asia Pacific Association for Medical Informatics About APAMI. https://www.apami.org/ about-apami/. Accessed 20 October 2019.

Chapter 15
Informatics Education in Sub-Saharan Africa

Caroline Perrin, Cheick-Oumar Bagayoko, and Antoine Geissbuhler

Introduction

Seventeen Sustainable Development Goals (SDGs) were endorsed in January 2016, presenting an ambitious and shared commitment for global development. While the preceding Millennium Development Goals (MDGs) for 2000–2015 focused primarily on low-income countries [1], the SDGs were crafted to be relevant for all societies. The SDGs reflect 3 years of inclusive negotiations, address broad issues of human development, and challenge both resource-poor and resource-rich societies to improve equity and sustainability. The third goal promises to "ensure healthy lives and promote well-being for all ages". However, the current health infrastructure in many low and middle income countries makes it difficult to achieve the target SDGs [2] as their health care systems are challenged by demographic factors, increasing the cost of care. They also suffer from fragmentation, weak information systems, lack of good governance, financial constraints [3], and a deficit of skilled healthcare professionals (HCPs). For example, seven of the 10 most populous low- and middle-income countries have maternal mortality rates above the SDG target 3 (e.g. India, Indonesia, Pakistan, Nigeria, Bangladesh, Philippines and Ethiopia), which is under 70 per 100,000 live births by 2030 [2], and without improvements of the current health infrastructure it will be difficult to achieve this target.

C. Perrin (✉) · A. Geissbuhler
HI5lab, Department of Radiology and Medical Informatics, Geneva University, Geneva, Switzerland

Division of eHealth and Telemedicine, Geneva University Hospitals, Geneva, Switzerland
e-mail: Caroline.Perrin@hcuge.ch; Antoine.Geissbuhler@unige.ch

C.-O. Bagayoko
Centre d'Innovation et Santé Digitale (Digi-Santé-Mali), Bamako, Mali

Centre d'Expertise et de Recherche en Télémédecine et E-santé (CERTES), Bamako, Mali
e-mail: cobagayoko@certesmali.org

© Springer Nature Switzerland AG 2020
E. S. Berner (ed.), *Informatics Education in Healthcare*, Health Informatics,
https://doi.org/10.1007/978-3-030-53813-2_15

Alarmingly, according to WHO Global Health Observatory data, the average of skilled HCPs per 10,000 inhabitants for the African region was 14.1 in 2009, and has dropped to 12.79 in 2014 [4]. One of the reasons is the migration of health workers from low- and middle-income countries to Organization for Economic Development (OECD) countries. Skilled workers from outside Europe have been recruited to address the workforce needs of European OECD countries [5].

The shortage of HCPs and healthcare facilities is a major issue, the critical threshold of 23 doctors, nurses and midwives per 10,000 inhabitants is below the World Health Organization (WHO) recommendation in many countries [4], which is one contributing factor explaining why 400 million people do not have access to essential healthcare services, mostly in Sub-Saharan Africa and South Asia [2]. In order to fulfill this minimum requirement of 23 HCPs per 100,000 people, an estimated 820,000 supplementary HCPs would be required in Sub-Saharan Africa [2]. In addition to this deficit of skilled HCPs, these sparse human resources are distributed unevenly and inequitably [6, 7]. Estimates of health worker density demonstrate that their global shortage and unequal distribution require urgent attention in order not to undermine attainment of the SDGs [8]. Moreover, this shortage is likely to increase with the rising incidence of non-communicable diseases (NCDs) and a globally ageing population. These evolutions are estimated to generate a demand for 40 million additional health workers, and a shortfall of 18 million health workers by 2030 on a global scale [9, 10]. Because of the rising incidence of NCDs many African countries face a double burden of diseases—a mixture of communicable and chronic diseases. To avoid uneven progress and growing inequalities the shortage of the healthcare workforce needs to be addressed [8].

The Potential of Digital Health

The potential of Information and Communication Technology (ICT) to address some of the previously described problems is acknowledged by the World Health Organization (WHO) [11], as ICT can help increase access to health services, and improve quality and efficiency of care through de-isolation of healthcare professionals in remote locations. This is called digital health, which collectively describes the concepts of eHealth, Telemedicine and mHealth, as defined by the World Health Organization (WHO). eHealth is the cost-effective and secure use of ICTs for health and health-related fields, while mHealth (or "mobile health") is a component of eHealth, and involves the provision of health services and information via mobile technologies, such as mobile phones, and tablet computers [12]. ICTs can help to overcome geographical barriers, train professionals through distance learning and enable remote collaboration, which can be especially transformative in rural areas and isolated settings [13–19].

There has been increasing connectivity, even in rural locations, although the digital divide between developing and industrialized countries still exists [20]. Digital health interventions are increasingly used, resulting in a multitude of tools with a wide range of objectives and functionalities [21–23].

In low-resource settings, individual as well as public health can be informed by real-time information and ameliorated through mobile-device based consultations and health education, personalized health tracking, and mobile diagnostic technologies [24, 25]. Mobile devices, e-payment systems, and telemedicine technologies enable the faster deployment of emergency services, and are improving access to quality care [24, 25]. Increased connectivity and innovation in ICT allow health facilities to directly enter data through web applications into central servers, eliminating the need for database management or software installation at the local level [24, 25]. Electronic medical record systems are increasingly reducing errors and improving the potential for timely use of data to improve both individual and public health [24].

In Africa, digital health is considered a potential solution to address some of the previously described challenges, and is increasingly implemented. However, when designing, developing, implementing, and maintaining digital health solutions, the insufficient availability of skilled human resources is consistently described as a major limiting factor [26–28].

The International Medical Informatics Association (IMIA) Working Group on "Health Informatics for Development" recognized the need for training manpower in developing countries in medical informatics as early as their first meeting in 1983, and emphasized the importance of health informatics in the African continent at their first international conference on Health Informatics in Africa (HELINA) in 1993 [29]. Considering advancements in technology and their application in the health sector in Africa it is essential to understand that "technology gives us tools, but it does not provide us with the wisdom and the skill to use them [30]". To be able to use these tools and to achieve a sustainable development, which depends on a skilled workforce to implement, use, support and maintain digital health [31], establishing programs, and training human resources in the domain of digital health in Africa is essential [31, 32]. This requires opportunities for informatics training, university partnerships and development of human resources covering all digital health sectors [31]. Health informatics education can be implemented as an educational program for supporting healthcare professionals, who need this training to manage health data and information in their job, or as educational programs to support a digital health strategy that aims to train experts that can plan, deploy and assess digital health applications [32].

Health Informatics Education Research and Recommendations

IMIA has developed a framework, which describes health informatics as a discipline with many sub-disciplines, based on the analysis of different international viewpoints [33]. The framework provides a wide range of competencies for international biomedical and health informatics (BMHI) education of health care professionals and BMHI specialists. This framework has the objective to support the establishment and further advancement of BMHI courses or programs on a global scale. The framework describes educational needs on three dimensions: (1) professionals in health care (e.g. physicians, nurses, BMHI professionals), (2) type of specialization in BMHI (IT users, BMHI specialists), and (3) stage of career progression (bachelor, master, doctorate). IMIA developed six key principles that can be summarized in the acronym HEALTH:

- H—all health care professionals should be confronted with BHMI education, as well as computer scientists/informaticians and other scientists (e.g. engineers) that are planning to work in the field of medicine and health care
- E—various education methodologies, like, for example, blended or distance education, are required
- A—depending on the career choice alternate routes to different types of specialization need to be considered
- L—different levels of education and career progression have different educational needs
- T—adequate and specific competence of teachers is required to provide courses and programs of good quality
- H—accreditation of educational courses and competence is required

This framework, together with the IMIA knowledge base [34], which structures the knowledge of the Health Informatics domain into 14 topics and 245 knowledge units is an excellent resource for countries to develop or advance BMHI courses or programs, as described in the example of Rwanda below [35].

Health Informatics Education Programs in Sub-Saharan Africa

Several health informatics education programs have been established in Sub-Saharan Africa, mostly in South and East Africa.

Masters in Health Informatics at Makerere University in Uganda

Makerere University School of Public Health (MakSPH) and the College of Computing and Information Sciences-Makerere (CoCIS), as well as the School of Computing and Informatics Technology (CIT), provide a Master degree in Health Informatics as a full-time program. The program aims at "producing gender sensitive graduates with skills and competencies in application of information and computer science to improve health practice" [36].

EHealth Lab Ethiopia

The eHealth Lab Ethiopia is a Centre of Excellence in Health Informatics and was established in collaboration with the Federal Ministry of Health and the University of Gondar in order to develop, adopt, evaluate, and support the implementation of innovative health information technologies. The center also offers a Bachelor in Health Informatics, a Master of Public Health in Health Informatics and a PhD in Public Health Informatics [37].

Masters of Health Informatics in Rwanda

The University of Rwanda in Kigali has had a Master of Science in Health Informatics program since 2011. In 2014 the program was reviewed and mapped to the IMIA Recommendations on Education in Biomedical and Health Informatics course contents and the IMIA Health Informatics Knowledge Base competencies and knowledge units [35]. Based on the review and mapping, a new curriculum, which provided a better match for the specific healthcare competencies in the Central African region, was implemented in the 2014/2015 academic year [35]. The University of Rwanda also established the Regional Centre of Excellence in Biomedical Engineering and eHealth (CEBE), which aims at developing a qualified workforce in priority areas such as biomedical engineering and e-Health meeting the East African Community's immediate and long-term labor market needs in the health sector [38].

The Nelson R. Mandela School of Medicine Telehealth Department

The Nelson R. Mandela School of Medicine (NRMSM) at the University of Kwazulu-Natal in South Africa created an academic department of telehealth in 2002, aimed at establishing and running postgraduate academic programs in both medical informatics and telemedicine, facilitating e-learning within the medical school, assisting the Department of Health (DOH) in establishing and running tele-medicine programs and conducting international outreach through e-Health [39]. They are currently offering a postgraduate diploma in eHealth as well as a Master of Medical Science in Telemedicine and a Master of Medical Science in Medical Informatics.

University of Western Cape Bioinformatics Master/PhD

The South African National Bioinformatics Institute (SANBI) at the University of Western Cape in South Africa offers a research MSc in Bioinformatics, which consists of a combination of research and coursework. SANBI is also planning a PhD bioinformatics program. SANBI aims to "conduct cutting edge bioinformatics and computational biology research relevant to South African, African and global populations, as well as to develop human resources in bioinformatics and computational biology" [40].

Inter-University Degree in E-Health, "Innovation and Health Practices" in Mali

The University of Science and Technology of Bamako (USTTB) in collaboration with the Félix Houphouet Boigny University of Abidjan, the Cheikh Anta Diop University in Dakar and the Pierre Fabre Foundation have launched an Inter-University Degree in 2018 in health practices and innovation. The objective is to establish a professional and multicultural e-health learning framework between the various key players (e-health policy makers, health professionals, computer scientists), particularly in developing countries (including international bodies). The aim is to bring out the innovations of practices aligned with the health strategies and policies of countries, and to cultivate knowledge and know-how in digital health in order to enable the development of coherent, harmonious and sustainable innovative tools for the benefit of their citizens. The training is hybrid; it consists of online theoretical teaching sets combined with a week-long group session of learners during a hackathon to develop innovative projects aligned with the needs of their specific countries and viable at scale. More than 15 training scholarships are offered on merit criteria to learners each year by the Pierre Fabre Foundation. It is also supported technically by the University of Geneva, the French-speaking Africa Network for Telemedicine and the French-speaking World Digital University.

Applied Projects Leading to the Creation of Centers of Excellence in Low–Resource Settings

For a health informatics program in Africa to be successful it is necessary to incorporate the local context. It is not sufficient to just reproduce an existing course or program, but it needs to be adapted to the local needs, context and culture. In French-speaking Africa, health informatics education results from the deployment of applied projects in e-Health, telemedicine or public health. These projects create a demand for local skilled professionals, thus generating enough activity and momentum to enable the creation of dedicated structures for training, education, and research. Eventually, these centers of expertise will be included in universities.

Réseau en Afrique Francophone pour la Télémédecine (RAFT) and the Jinou Program

The RAFT network [22], launched in 2001, primarily aims at de-isolating health-care professionals that work in remote settings, through distance education and access to tele-expertise. Active in 18 Sub-Saharan African countries and more than 150 hospitals, and based on a predominantly South-South collaboration scheme (i.e., collaboration among developing countries), its scope has been extended to include the training of medical specialists in various fields, including medical informatics.

This extension, the RAFT–Jinou program, is based on the continent-wide sharing of expertise in various medical specialties: professors from French-speaking universities will each contribute by teaching a number of e-courses, which are organized in a structured curriculum for each specialty. The courses are taught with support from the RAFT infrastructure and tools. The RAFT-Jinou model has demonstrated that scarce human resources can collectively build capacity in a collaborative training approach, and serves as an inspiration for the development of a geographically-distributed Master in Health Informatics program in French speaking Africa, promoted by professionals in Cameroon, Mali, Burkina Faso, Niger, and Guinea.

Centre d'Expertise et de Recherche en Télémédecine et E-santé (CERTES)

Initially developed in collaboration with the RAFT network, the Malian Medical Information and Communication Network (REIMICOM) established CERTES in Mali after 10 years of applied project development. Staffed with a dozen healthcare and IT professionals, the CERTES is in charge of training healthcare professionals to use health IT tools, to provide operational support for telemedicine activities and health information systems deployment, and to run research projects financed by competitive funds. It contributes to the training of students and the supervision of medical theses on subjects related to digital health [41]. CERTES is a good example of a bottom-up approach at developing a critical mass of Health Informatics activities, which in turn helps to organize and support a formal training program [42].

Centre d'Innovation et de Santé Digitale, Digi-Santé-Mali

This center of excellence was established in 2018 within the University of Science and Technology in Bamako (USTTB) in collaboration with the Pierre Fabre Foundation [43]. Its creation is rooted in the importance and increasing use of digital technologies in the field of health care especially in Africa. There were multiple reasons for its creation: modernization, optimization of resources, efficiency and management of the healthcare system. It is a tool to support this formidable movement through continuous and professional training of appropriate professionals and adapted to each context. The Centre provides sound advice to governments and international organizations working in the field of health. The aim is to help the less developed countries avoid the mistakes made by the more advanced countries [44]: fragmentation with tools not adapted to the needs of users, implementation that is not patient-centered, inconsistency and inefficiency of failures in interoperability of different subsystems. Finally, the goal of this laboratory is to promote innovation through research, dialogue between actors and the emergence of strategic digital health projects. To this end, the center proposes to support governments in the development and implementation of the Strategic Director Scheme for Health Information Systems, guaranteeing a coherent and adequate development of digital health in African countries. It is a roadmap that defines the country's digital strategy with a systemic vision. It is the result of a participative approach and defines the strategic objectives to develop digital health, the target information system that is the country's digital health environment, the different projects and their scheduling as well as the governance of the country's Health Information System.

Multilateral Capacity Building

The International Society for Telemedicine and e-Health's (ISfTeH) Basic Telemedicine Training Program

The ISfTeH [45] developed a basic, modular and adaptable course in Telemedicine that is delivered face to face. The curriculum covers introduction to computers; ethics and law in telemedicine; setting up venues; basic telemedicine skills; basic skills in the use of email and digital photography; practical use of store and forward telemedicine; tele-education; and telemedicine and homecare.

H3ABioNet, a Pan-African Bioinformatics Network for Human Heredity and Health in Africa

H3ABioNet is a Pan African Bioinformatics Network for the Human Heredity and Health in Africa (H3Africa) consortium, which was established to develop bioinformatics capacity in Africa and particularly to enable genomics data analysis by

H3Africa researchers across the continent. This program is developing human capacity through training and support and is facilitating access to informatics infrastructure. The network proposes a variety of courses and training events covering different aspects of bioinformatics from general introductory topics to more specialized ones like, for example, Next Generation Sequencing and Genome Wide Association Studies analyses [46].

Conclusion

These examples illustrate the potential benefits of digital health, but to develop its full potential strategic commitment, organizational changes and a harmonization of activities in digital health, telemedicine and implementation are required on a national level with specific attention to the education of medical informatics professionals, as they are the basic foundation for the successful implementation and development of any digital health project. Two groups of medical informatics professionals need to be qualified: health practitioners that are trained using digital health applications and tools, and non-health practitioners that are able to support and carry out e-Health projects, and develop tools.

In the long run the digital society will not be an issue for specialists anymore, as the new generations are digital natives from birth [47]. However, between developed and developing countries, but also within Africa, heterogeneity can be observed, with students coming from diverse backgrounds, with differing levels of access to and use of technology [48]. Program and course developers in Africa should acknowledge the potential heterogeneity in digital literacy of the participants and ensure to educate at various levels. Even though there is heterogenicity of the digital natives in developed and developing countries, as well as within Africa, the mobile phone is a technology that almost all students have unrestricted access to and with which they are very familiar [48]. Furthermore, mobile phones and related technologies like the General Packet Radio Service (GPRS) and wireless technologies are increasingly used for accessing the Internet in the absence of fixed line networks and hardware, although infrastructure challenges that still remain are important [49].

The digital transformation and new advances in science and technology will affect many of the jobs we are familiar with today [50], which is also true for sub Saharan Africa, where scientific discoveries and advances in technology simplify routines and enable task shifting, such as, for example, the Integrated electronic Diagnostic Approach (IeDA) project in Burkina Faso where critical tasks are automated to reduce the number of diagnostic errors [51].

Independent of geography, BMHI is a field of science at the intersection of other domains, which is interdisciplinary by definition [52] and will not only become even more interdisciplinary, but will also require more inter-professionalism. Therefore soft skills, such as effective communication and collaboration, will become increasingly important globally for professionals working in the domain of BMHI [53]. Training in soft skills and breaking down hierarchies can be fostered through inter-professional courses [54]. To further facilitate inter-professionalism some new BMHI objectives should be included in the curricula of healthcare professionals. Additionally, digital tools should be used to educate and develop digital understanding for health care professionals in challenged settings.

While it is important to develop basic health informatics capacity and specific training programs, at the same time it is equally important to create more advanced training that is not specific to health informatics, but which embeds health informatics in others domains like for example, a PhD in genomic and digital medicine. The H3ABioNet, which focuses on bioinformatics in the area of human genetics and genomics, is an excellent example of addressing limitations in bioinformatics capacity to improve research outputs and to build capacity at faculties to train and supervise bioinformatics students on the African continent [28].

There is no single digital solution that fits all. For digital health to develop its full potential in Africa, solutions and applications have to be developed and deployed based on real needs, fostering innovative ideas and combinations of existing and new technologies. Capacity should be developed at different scales and across all sectors of digital health, moving from vertical silos to widely-connected systems, by facilitating the evolution and development of infrastructure for existing centers of excellence, and establishing North–South (between developed and developing countries) as well as South-South collaborative networks of excellence, based on models of successful implementations [25, 55].

References

1. Sachs JD. From millennium development goals to sustainable development goals. Lancet. 2012;379(9832):2206–11.
2. World Health Organization. Tracking universal health coverage: first global monitoring report: World Health Organization; 2015. 9241564970.
3. United Nations. Background paper for ECOSOC Africa regional ministerial meeting on eHealth – use of information and communication technology for health 2009 10–11 June 2009. https://www.ghanahealthservice.org/ghs-category.php?cid=5
4. World Health Organization. Global health observatory data repository 2019. Available from https://www.who.int/gho/en/
5. Aluttis C, Bishaw T, Frank MW. The workforce for health in a globalized context–global shortages and international migration. Glob Health Action. 2014;7(1):23611.
6. Mars M. Building the capacity to build capacity in e-health in sub-Saharan Africa: the KwaZulu-Natal experience. Telemedicine Journal and e-Health. 2012;18(1):32–7.
7. World Health Organization. The world health report 2006: working together for health: World Health Organization; 2006. 9241563176.
8. The Lancet. Global Burden of Disease 2017: a fragile world. Lancet (London, England). 2018;392(10159):1683.
9. World Health Organization. UN Commission: new investments in global health workforce will create jobs and drive economic growth. 2016. Available from https://www.who.int/news-room/detail/20-09-2016-un-commission-new-investments-in-global-health-workforce-will-create-jobs-and-drive-economic-growth

10. James SL, Abate D, Abate KH, Abay SM, Abbafati C, Abbasi N, Abbastabar H, Abd-Allah F, Abdela J, Abdelalim A. Global, regional, and national incidence, prevalence, and years lived with disability for 354 diseases and injuries for 195 countries and territories, 1990–2017: a systematic analysis for the global burden of disease study 2017. Lancet. 2018;392(10159):1789–858.
11. World Health Organization. The World Health Report 2008-Primary care (now more than ever). World Health Organization. 2008. ISBN: 978-92-4-156373-4.
12. World Health Resolution, editor 58.28. eHealth. Fifty-eighth World Health Assembly, Geneva, Geneva, World Health Organization; 2005.
13. Curran VR, Fleet L, Kirby F. Factors influencing rural health care professionals' access to continuing professional education. Aust J Rural Health. 2006;14(2):51–5.
14. Childs S, Blenkinsopp E, Hall A, Walton G. Effective e-learning for health professionals and students--barriers and their solutions. A systematic review of the literature--findings from the HeXL project. Health Inf Libr J. 2005;22(Suppl 2):20–32.
15. Clarke A, Lewis D, Cole I, Ringrose L. A strategic approach to developing e-learning capability for healthcare. Health Inf Libr J. 2005;22(Suppl 2):33–41.
16. Bagayoko CO, Perrin C, Gagnon MP, Geissbuhler A. Continuing distance education: a capacity-building tool for the de-isolation of care professionals and researchers. J Gen Intern Med. 28(3):666–70.
17. Bagayoko CO, Niang M, Traore ST, Bediang G, Naef JM, Geissbuhler A. Deploying portable ultrasonography with remote assistance for isolated physicians in Africa: lessons from a pilot study in Mali. Stud Health Technol Inform. 2010;160(Pt 1):554–8.
18. Bediang G, Franck C, Raetzo M-A, Doell J, Ba M, Kamga Y, Baroz F, Geissbuhler A. Developing clinical skills using a virtual patient simulator in a resource-limited setting. Stud Health Technol Inform. 2012;192:102–6.
19. Geissbuhler A, Bagayoko CO, Ly O. The RAFT network: 5 years of distance continuing medical education and tele-consultations over the internet in French-speaking Africa. Int J Med Inform. 2007;76(5–6):351–6.
20. Sanou B. The world in 2015: ICT facts and figures. International Telecommunications Union. 2015.
21. Perrin C, Hounga L, Geissbuhler A. Systematic review to identify proxy indicators to quantify the impact of eHealth tools on maternal and neonatal health outcomes in low-income and middle-income countries including Delphi consensus. BMJ Open. 2018;8(8):e022262.
22. Bediang G, Perrin C, Castaneda RR, Kamga Y, Sawadogo A, Bagayoko CO, Geissbuhler A. The RAFT telemedicine network in low and middle income countries: educational and clinical services, lessons learnt and perspectives. Public Health Educ Promot. 2014;(2):180.
23. Labrique A, Vasudevan L, Mehl G, Rosskam E, Hyder AA. Digital health and health systems of the future. Glob Health Sci Pract. 2018;6:S1–4.
24. International Telecommunication Union. ICT for improving information and accountability for women's and children's health International Telecommunication Union; 2013.
25. Perrin C, Bediang G, Randriambelonoro M, Geissbuhler A. Learning from eHealth implementations through "Implementomics": a multidimensional annotation model applied to eHealth projects of the RAFT network. Front Public Health. 2019;7:188.
26. Verbeke F, Shamashanga P, Amisi C, Karara G. Developing a national e-health strategy for DR Congo: a preliminary analysis of business needs, existing information systems and solutions. J Health Inform Afr. 2014;2(2):12–20.
27. Marful WA, Winter A. When information technology meets healthcare in West Africa: a literature review. J Health Inform Afr. 2014;2(2):29–35.
28. Mulder NJ, Adebiyi E, Alami R, Benkahla A, Brandful J, Doumbia S, Everett D, Fadlelmola FM, Gaboun F, Gaseitsiwe S. H3ABioNet, a sustainable pan-African bioinformatics network for human heredity and health in Africa. Genome Res. 2016;26(2):271–7.
29. Mandil SH, Moidu K, Korpela M, Byass P, Forster D, Association IMI, editors. Health informatics in Africa-HELINA 93: first International Conference on Health Informatics in

Africa, Ile-Ife, Nigeria, 19–23 April 1993, International congress series; 1055. Amsterdam: Elsevier; 1993.

30. Ball MJ, Douglas J. Philosophy into practice: a health informatics course proposal. Methods Inf Med. 1997;36(02):127–30.

31. Mars M. Building the capacity to build capacity in e-health in sub-Saharan Africa: the KwaZulu-Natal experience. Telemedicine and e-Health. 2012;18(1):32–7.

32. Hersh W, Margolis A, Quirós F, Otero P. Building a health informatics workforce in developing countries. Health Aff. 2010;29(2):274–7.

33. Mantas J, Ammenwerth E, Demiris G, Hasman A, Haux R, Hersh W, Hovenga E, Lun K, Marin H, Martin-Sanchez F. Recommendations of the international medical informatics association (IMIA) on education in biomedical and health informatics. Methods Inf Med. 2010;49(02):105–20.

34. Wright G. The development of the IMIA knowledge base. South African J Inform Manag. 2011;13(1):1–5.

35. Wright G, Verbeke F, Nyssen M, Betts HJ, editors. Health informatics: developing a masters programme in Rwanda based on the IMIA educational recommendations and the IMIA knowledge base. Stud Health Technol Inform. 2015;216:525–8.

36. Masters in Health Informatics (MHI): Makere University. Available from http://www.musph.ac.ug/index.php/accordion-2/152-mhi

37. eHealth Lab Ethiopia. Available from https://ehealthlab.org/

38. Regional Centre of excellence in Biomedical engineering and eHealth (CEBE). Available from http://www.rwoj.ur.ac.rw/

39. University of Kwazulu-Natal - Department of Telemedicine. Available from https://telehealth.ukzn.ac.za/

40. The South African National Bioinformatics Institute (SANBI). Available from https://www.uwc.ac.za/Faculties/NS/SANBI/Pages/default.aspx

41. Bagayoko C-O, Bediang G, Anne A, Niang M, Traoré A-K, Geissbuhler A. La santé numérique et le nécessaire développement des centres de compétences en Afrique subsaharienne: deux exemples au Mali et au Cameroun. Médecine et santé tropicales. 2017;27(4):348–53.

42. CERTES. Centre d'Expertise et de Recherche en Télémédecine et E-santé (CERTES). Available from http://www.certesmali.org/

43. Digi S@nte Mali. Available from https://www.digisantemali.info/

44. Pon D, Coury A. Accélérer le virage numérique - Stratégie de transformation du Système de santé. Available from https://solidarites-sante.gouv.fr/IMG/pdf/masante2022_rapport_virage_numerique.pdf

45. International Society for Telemedicine and e-Health's. Available from https://www.isfteh.org/

46. H3ABioNet Pan African Bioinformatics network. Available from https://h3abionet.org/about

47. Jones C, Ramanau R, Cross S, Healing G. Net generation or digital natives: is there a distinct new generation entering university? Comput Educ. 2010;54(3):722–32.

48. Thinyane H. Are digital natives a world-wide phenomenon? An investigation into South African first year students' use and experience with technology. Comput Educ. 2010;55(1):406–14.

49. Kay M, Santos J, Takane M. mHealth: new horizons for health through mobile technologies. World Health Organ. 2011;64(7):66–71.

50. WEF. The future of jobs: employment, skills and workforce strategy for the fourth industrial revolution. Global Challenge Insight Report, World Economic Forum, Geneva; 2016.

51. Bessat C, Zonon NA, D'Acremont V. Large-scale implementation of electronic integrated management of childhood illness (eIMCI) at the primary care level in Burkina Faso: a qualitative study on health worker perception of its medical content, usability and impact on antibiotic prescription and resistance. BMC Public Health. 2019;19(1):449.

52. Kulikowski CA, Shortliffe EH, Currie LM, Elkin PL, Hunter LE, Johnson TR, Kalet IJ, Lenert LA, Musen MA, Ozbolt JG. AMIA board white paper: definition of biomedical informatics and specification of core competencies for graduate education in the discipline. J Am Med Inform Assoc. 2012;19(6):931–8.

53. Wu H, Palani A, editors. Bioinformatics curriculum development and skill sets for bioinformaticians. 2015 IEEE Frontiers in Education Conference (FIE); 2015: IEEE.
54. Carlson E, Pilhammar E, Wann-Hanson C. The team builder: the role of nurses facilitating interprofessional student teams at a Swedish clinical training ward. Nurse Educ Pract. 2011;11(5):309–13.
55. Wootton R. Telemedicine support for the developing world. J Telemed Telecare. 2008;14(3):109–14.

Part V
Assessment of Individuals and Programs in Informatics

Chapter 16
Clinical Informatics Subspecialty Certification and Training

Christoph U. Lehmann, Howard D. Silverman, Reed M. Gardner, Charles Safran, and Cynthia Gadd

Clinical Informatics History and Background

The term "Clinical Informatics" was used first in an article entitled *"Clinical specialty systems as an introduction to **Clinical Informatics**"* in 1983 [1]. In 1984, the authors published a second article; *"**Clinical Informatics**: a strategy for the use of information in the clinical setting"* [2]. While the designation "Clinical Informatics" might have been novel, the field of Clinical Informatics was not, as it had been evolving for at least a century. Florence Nightingale may have been the first clinical informatician, when she introduced, during the Crimean War in 1854, "the first model for the systematic collection of hospital data using a uniform classification of

C. U. Lehmann (✉)
Departments of Pediatrics, Population & Data Sciences, and Bioinformatics; Clinical Informatics Center, UT Southwestern, 5323 Harry Hines Blvd, Dallas, TX, USA
e-mail: Christoph.Lehmann@UTSouthwestern.edu

H. D. Silverman
Department of Biomedical Informatics, The University of Arizona College of Medicine – Phoenix, Phoenix, AZ, USA
e-mail: howards@email.arizona.edu

R. M. Gardner
Department of Biomedical Informatics, University of Utah, 1745 Cornell Circle, Salt Lake City, UT, USA
e-mail: reed.gardner@hsc.utah.edu

C. Safran
Division of Clinical Informatics, Department of Medicine, Beth Israel Deaconess Medical Center and Harvard Medical School, Boston, MA, USA

C. Gadd
Department of Biomedical Informatics, Vanderbilt University, 2525 West End Avenue, Nashville, TN, USA
e-mail: cindy.gadd@vumc.org

© Springer Nature Switzerland AG 2020
E. S. Berner (ed.), *Informatics Education in Healthcare*, Health Informatics, https://doi.org/10.1007/978-3-030-53813-2_16

diseases and operations that was to form the basis of the ICD code used today" [3]. Another early clinical informatician Herman Hollerith developed an electrome-chanical punched card tabulator used to assist in the 1890 US census [4].

Early Clinical Informatics efforts include a 1959 key paper by Ledley and Lusted on computerized medical reasoning in the journal *Science* entitled "Reasoning foundations of medical diagnosis; symbolic logic, probability, and value theory aid our understanding of how physicians reason" [5]. In the 1960s, medical investigators leveraged computers to improve the practice of medicine in the US. Warner [6, 7] and colleagues at LDS Hospital in Salt Lake City created a clinical decision support system called HELP [8]. Lindberg developed the first automated clinical laboratory system in the 1960s [9] and Collen created automated multiphasic screening at Kaiser-Permanente in northern California in 1964 [10]. In 1966, Barnett [11], Greenes [12], Pappalardo [13], and colleagues developed the computer programming language MUMPS (**M**assachusetts General Hospital **U**tility **M**ulti-**P**rogramming **S**ystem) still used in health care today and in 1968 used mini-computers to develop the Computer Stored Ambulatory Record (COSTAR) patient care system.

In 1966, Slack developed a computer-based history taking system [14] and his colleague Bleich developed methods for interpreting and recommending treatment for acid–base disorders in 1968 [15]. Slack and Bleich went on to develop multiple hospital-wide clinical computing systems at Boston's Beth-Israel Hospital and the Brigham and Women's hospital.

The 1970s saw the development of a large number of clinical systems. Simborg added another medical history taking system [16]. El Camino Hospital in California developed automated medical records [17]. Stead and Hammond created TMR (The Medical Record) at Duke University [18] and Shortliffe developed a computer-based infectious disease consulting system named MYCIN at Stanford University [19]. McDonald used protocol-based computer reminders to improve the quality of patient care and compensate for the "non-perfectibility of man" [20]. In 1974, Francois Gremy coined the term "medical informatics" to encompass the activities in this new field of work [21, 22].

Early medical informatics efforts led to funding of clinical computing systems, development of clinical computing research laboratories, and eventually to funding by the National Library of Medicine for training programs and individual training grants in medical informatics (See Chap. 2 for more details on the NLM training programs). Eventually the expanded field became known as "Biomedical Informatics" and included Clinical Informatics, bioinformatics, public health informatics, consumer health informatics, clinical research informatics, and other informatics domains [23]. Despite varied emphasis and curricula of initial academic training programs, a new generation of informaticians was minted who were instrumental in developing seminal, new clinical computing systems.

The recent past has been an exciting and challenging time for Clinical Informatics. After a gestation period of over 50 years, the Electronic Health Record (EHR) is now a reality in most healthcare facilities in the United States [24]. Clinicians, informaticians, patients, and politicians decided that widespread adoption of the EHR was inevitable and would improve caregivers' decisions and patients' outcomes [25]. In 2004, the Office of the National Coordinator (ONC) for Health

Information Technology was created as "the principal federal entity charged with coordination of nationwide efforts to implement and use the most advanced health information technology and the electronic exchange of health information". ONC's mission is to "improve the health and well-being of individuals and communities through the use of technology and health information that is accessible when and where it matters most" [26]. In 2009, the U.S. Congress and the Obama Administration enacted the Health Information and Technology for Economic and Clinical Health (HITECH) Act, which called for EHR certifications and an incentive program for "meaningful use" of the EHRs [27, 28, 29], accelerating EHR adoption. Meaningful use later became one of the four components of the new Merit-Based Incentive Payment System (MIPS) [30].

Development of Clinical Informatics Specialty Board Certification for Physicians

In 2016, there were 953,695 actively licensed physicians in the United States [31] as well as millions of nurses and pharmacists, who were using EHR systems. As early as 1995, the American Nursing Association (ANA) recognized nursing informatics as a clinical specialization and established a nursing informatics certification [32, 33, 34]. Certification is based on the 2015 revision of the ANA document entitled *Nursing Informatics*: *Practice Scope and Standards of Practice* first published in 1995 [35].

A 2003 Institute of Medicine report [36] called for the use of informatics in the training of health professionals to "reduce errors, manage knowledge and information, make decisions and communicate more effectively than had been the case in the past."

In 2004, President George W. Bush announced a national goal of storing and using health information of the majority of people in the United States in Electronic Health Records (EHRs) by 2014. In response, the American Medical Informatics Association (AMIA) set a goal of informatics training for at least one physician and one nurse for each of the nearly 6,000 hospitals in the United States to aid the implementation of EHRs [37]. A 2005 policy summit of AMIA and the American Health Information Management Association (AHIMA) [38] examined the workforce implications of President Bush's directive [39] and identified three key needs for success:

1. Investment in people, who can use technology wisely and well
2. Creation of an academically prepared health information specialist core group
3. Development of new educational curricula and learning environments

The AMIA/AHIMA summit estimated that more than 50,000 healthcare professionals would require *some* informatics training to support the proposed national health information infrastructure. This included physicians, nurses, pharmacists, and health information management professionals (medical records and office management staff).

An informal survey of National Library of Medicine's Biomedical Informatics training program directors at the time revealed that very few of the training programs had significant additional capacity to meet the expected physician and other healthcare professional workforce development needs. However, the distance graduate education program at Oregon Health & Sciences University (OHSU) offered a solution to workforce development [40] and morphed into the first site for AMIA's 10 × 10 education program with the goal of training 10,000 physicians and nurses by 2010.

The AMIA 10 × 10 program initiated Clinical Informatics training with one semester of graduate level introduction to the application of informatics and to clinical health care. The program was open to all healthcare professionals and healthcare students without restrictions. AMIA's aspiration included that some 10 × 10 participants would obtain more formal training in the field of informatics subsequently (see also Chap. 18 for more information on AMIA's 10 × 10 program).

In 2004, an AMIA "Town Hall" meeting to discuss Clinical Informatics workforce development resulted in a formal policy adopted by the AMIA Board of Directors to create a Clinical Informatics certification for clinical professionals starting with physicians. In 2007, the Robert Wood Johnson Foundation awarded a grant to AMIA to support the development of the documents required by the American Board of Medical Specialties (ABMS) to create a new medical subspecialty in Clinical Informatics [41, 42].

Creating the Medical Subspecialty of Clinical Informatics

The non-profit ABMS represents 24 areas of specialty medicine and ABMS' member boards certify physicians in more than 150 medical specialties and subspecialties. Any new medical specialty or subspecialty must be first recognized by ABMS. ABMS member boards also decide on board eligibility of physicians, determine frequency of certification exams, and set requirements for the maintenance of certification [43].

Two documents were required by the ABMS to determine if a proposed subspecialty like Clinical Informatics indeed met the requirements for a new medical subspecialty: (1) the **Core Content** of the curriculum and (2) the **Clinical Training** Program. To create these documents, AMIA managed two working groups of AMIA members. Both groups met three times face-to-face (Core Content, Aug 2007—Jan 2008; Clinical Training, Jan 2008—Aug 2008) and worked remotely to establish consensus for the required documents [44, 45].

Development of the Core Content

The Core Content group consisted of professionals, who worked in "Clinical Informatics" including physicians, computer scientists, engineers, nurses, and other technologists and was led by Reed M. Gardner (Chair) and J. Marc Overhage (Vice

Chair). The Core Content for this new medical subspecialty defined the boundaries of the discipline and helped to inform Clinical Informatics fellowship training program requirements. The working group of 11 experts established that Clinical Informatics encompassed three domains [44]:

1. Clinical care
2. Healthcare system
3. Information and communication technology

Besides the subspecialty's content, the Core Content group decided on the name of the new discipline. The initially proposed name "Applied Clinical Informatics" was rejected as the term "applied" was considered redundant and the new subspecialty was named "Clinical Informatics". The Core Content group defined the activities of clinical informaticians as: "Clinical informaticians transform health care by analyzing, designing, implementing, and evaluating information and communication systems that enhance individual and population health outcomes, improve patient care, and strengthen the clinician-patient relationship. Clinical informaticians use their knowledge of patient care combined with their understanding of informatics concepts, methods, and tools to:

1. Assess information and knowledge needs of healthcare professionals and patients,
2. Characterize, evaluate, and refine clinical processes,
3. Develop, implement, and refine clinical decision support systems, and
4. Lead or participate in the procurement, customization, development, implementation, management, evaluation, and continuous improvement of clinical information systems" [44].

Key concepts included that clinical informaticians must measurably improve care or care processes and must have the skills to collaborate with a wide array of disciplines and health professionals. In practical terms, a clinical informatician should be able to lead an implementation of an Electronic Health Record (EHR) or other clinical systems. This type of clinician may be called a Chief Medical Information Officer (CMIO) although a CMIO might have other responsibilities as well [46, 47].

Table 16.1 summarizes the four main topic areas described in the core content. Each of the topic areas had several sub-topics totaling 177 subtopics in the final document [44].

The Core Content group did not specify the relative weight for each of the main content areas listed in Table 16.1, which was done later by the American Board of Preventive Medicine (ABPM) [48]. The Core Content group elucidated subtopics, however the depth of subtopic detail was inconsistent across the main topics (e.g., 32 subcategories for fundamentals and 69 for health information systems). The level of specificity represented by subcategories also varied. There were 30 subcategories of information systems with 10 related to data (not including eight subcategories on data standards) while there were only five subcategories for effective communication. The Core Content group identified 177 subtopics defining the core content. The various levels of detail later presented some challenges for the test writing committee, who needed to associate and link items with content subtopics.

Table 16.1 Four topic areas describing the CORE CONTENT of Clinical Informatics [44]

Content (% of items on Board Exam)	Core content	Number of topics
1. Fundamentals (10%)		*32*
Clinical informatics	1.1	13
Health systems	1.2	19
2. Clinical decision making and care process improvement (30%)		*35*
Clinical decision support	2.1	23
Evidence-based patient care	2.2	8
Clinical workflow analysis	2.3	4
3. Health information systems (40%)		*69*
Information technology systems	3.1	31
Human factors engineering	3.2	5
HIS applications	3.3	5
Clinical data standards	3.4	8
Information systems lifecycle	3.5	20
4. Leadership and management change (20%)		*41*
Leadership models	4.1	8
Effective interdisciplinary teams	4.2	6
Effective communications	4.3	5
Project management	4.4	9
Strategic and financial planning	4.5	8
Change management	4.6	5
	Grand total	177

Update to the Core Content

Since the development of the core content that was used as the basis for the certification examination beginning in 2013, the field of Clinical Informatics has seen substantial and rapid changes (e.g., use of patient portals, mHealth, integration of artificial intelligence). Once these changes became mainstream, they had to be included in the curriculum and the examination processes. In response, AMIA conducted the Clinical Informatics Subspecialty (CIS) practice analysis in collaboration with ABPM and with the support of the American Board of Pathology (ABPath). This resulted in a CIS Delineation of Practice (DoP) comprised of 5 mutually exclusive and collectively comprehensive domains, 42 tasks, and 139 knowledge statements (see Table 16.2) [49]. The process utilized to develop, validate, and finalize the CIS DoP is depicted in Fig. 16.1. Three independent subject-matter expert panels drawn from and representative of the 1,695 CIS diplomates certified by the American Board of Preventive Medicine (ABPM) contributed to the development of a draft CIS Delineation of Practice (DoP).

An online survey was distributed to all CIS diplomates in July 2018 to validate the draft DoP. A total of 316 diplomates (18.8%) completed the survey. Survey respondents provided domain, task, and knowledge, and skill (KS) ratings, qualitative feedback on the completeness of the DoP, and detailed professional background and demographic information.

Table 16.2 CIS domains of practice

Domain 1: Fundamental Knowledge and Skills (no tasks, 25 knowledge statements)
Fundamental knowledge and skills which provide clinical informaticians with a common vocabulary, basic knowledge across all Clinical Informatics domains, and understanding of the environment in which they function.

Domain 2: Improving Care Delivery and Outcomes (7 tasks, 27 knowledge statements)
Develop, implement, evaluate, monitor, and maintain clinical decision support; analyze existing health processes and identify ways that health data and health information systems can enable improved outcomes; support innovation in the health system through informatics tools and processes.

Domain 3: Enterprise Information Systems (16 tasks, 33 knowledge statements)
Develop and deploy health information systems that are integrated with existing information technology systems across the continuum of care, including clinical, consumer, and public health domains. Develop, curate, and maintain institutional knowledge repositories while addressing security, privacy, and safety considerations.

Domain 4: Data Governance and Data Analytics (10 tasks, 26 knowledge statements)
Establish and maintain data governance structures, policies, and processes. Incorporate information from emerging data sources; acquire, manage, and analyze health-related data; ensure data quality and meaning across settings; and derive insights to optimize clinical and business decision making.

Domain 5: Leadership and Professionalism (9 tasks, 28 knowledge statements)
Build support and create alignment for informatics best practices; lead health informatics initiatives and innovation through collaboration and stakeholder engagement across organizations and systems.

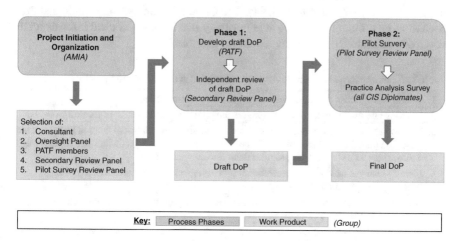

Fig. 16.1 CIS Practice Analysis Process Overview (DoP = Delineation of Practice)

The DoP that emerged from this study differed from the 2009 CIS Core Content in two respects. First, the DoP reflects the growth in amount, types, and use of health data through the addition of a practice domain, tasks, and Knowledge/Skill statements focused on data analytics and governance. Second, the DoP describes CIS practice in terms of tasks in addition to identifying knowledge required for competent practice. The authors of the study anticipate that the DoP will allow ABPM to align the CIS certification exam with current practice and will result in an evolution of the Accreditation Council for Graduate Medical Education (ACGME) Clinical Informatics Fellowship Requirements. Twelve of the existing Clinical Informatics Fellowship directors subsequently participated in a detailed review of the DoP to gather complete, accurate, and relevant Program Director input for future ACGME Clinical Informatics Fellowship Program Requirement and Milestone revisions focusing on delineating tasks and knowledge fellows should acquire during training.

Development of Clinical Training Program Criteria

The initial Clinical Training group was led by Charles Safran (Chair) and M. Michael Shabot (Vice Chair) and consisted of physicians, computer scientists, and other professionals, who worked with operational clinical systems and who had participated in clinical training programs. The Clinical Training group of 12 experts leveraged the "Core Content" document and was charged with determining how Clinical Informatics should be taught in a two-year fellowship training program [45, 50]. The Clinical Training group had to decide which of the 177 items of core content was taught best by didactic instruction and which required experiential learning. The group further realized that most of the existing biomedical informatics training programs, which were designed to produce system developers and researchers, did not cover the content areas completely. The Clinical Training group concluded that each training program should be able to certify that a trained clinical informatician could demonstrate the competencies shown in Table 16.3.

Table 16.3 Informatics competencies to be demonstrated at the end of training [45]

1. Search and appraise the literature relevant to clinical informatics;
2. Demonstrate fundamental programming, database design, and user interface design skills;
3. Develop and evaluate evidence-based clinical guidelines and represent them in an actionable way. All clinical informaticians should be able to represent such guidelines in a logical way, while others would be able to program them into computer code;
4. Identify changes needed in organizational processes and clinician practices to optimize health system operational effectiveness;
5. Analyze patient care workflow and processes to identify information system features that would support improved quality, efficiency, effectiveness, and safety of clinical services;
6. Assess user needs for a clinical information or telecommunication system or application and produce a requirement specification document;
7. Design or develop a clinical or telecommunication application or system;
8. Evaluate vendor proposals from the perspectives of meeting clinical needs and the costs of the proposed information solutions;
9. Develop an implementation plan that addresses the sociotechnical components of system adoption for a clinical or telecommunication system or application;
10. Evaluate the impact of information system implementation and use on patient care and users;
11. Develop, analyze, and report effectively (verbally and in writing) about key informatics processes.

To accomplish meeting the above noted objectives, the Clinical Training group determined that training programs should:

(a) Develop a curriculum with clear learning goals.
(b) Ensure fellow participation in scholarly activities that "advance fellows' knowledge of the basic principles of research, including how such research is conducted, evaluated, explained to patients, and applied to patient care."
(c) Provide didactic sessions to assure all "core content" is covered during a 2-year fellowship.
(d) Provide "rotations [that] are experiential assignments, of finite duration … designed to provide fellows with exposure to different types of clinical and health information systems, in a range of settings that includes inpatient, ambulatory, and remote applications" [45]. These rotations should comprise at least 15% of the two-year training experience.
(e) Provide a long-term assignment for each fellow of at least 12 months on a project team.
(f) Fellows must conceive, develop, implement, and evaluate a substantive, applied Clinical Informatics project and present the results of the evaluation in a peer-reviewed setting.

In addition to public presentations of the two documents requesting input, more than 80 people participated in developing and reviewing the Core Content [44] and the Training Requirements for Fellowship Education in the Subspecialty of Clinical Informatics [45]. The Clinical Training group's final document was adopted with minor modifications by ACGME and last revised in 2019; however, with the development of the new Delineation of Practice, we anticipate further modifications in the near future [49].

American Board of Medical Specialties Approval of Clinical Informatics as a Subspecialty

The American Board of Medical Specialties (ABMS) decided that Clinical Informatics was best suited as a subspecialty available to all physician specialists. Clinical Informatics is of interest to physicians trained in many of the other medical specialties, and on a practical level, a subspecialty was more feasible to establish. AMIA leaders contacted member boards of ABMS to identify which of the 24 boards might be willing to take the lead in creating the new subspecialty of Clinical Informatics. The American Board of Preventive Medicine (ABPM) became the lead board and won approval for creating the subspecialty of Clinical Informatics. ABPM was joined by the American Board of Pathology (ABPath) to create the certifying process and examination for Clinical Informatics. All of the 24 member boards of ABMS allow their diplomates to sit for the Clinical Informatics subspecialty examination. The ABMS granted final approval of Clinical Informatics as a board-certified medical subspecialty in September 2011 [51].

The board certified subspecialty of Clinical Informatics in the Unites States was a novel event globally. Belgium had a "Physician Specialist in Health Data Management" designation since 2001, Germany had a "supplement medical informatics" qualification since 1991, and there existed a "Certified Physicians in BioMedical Informatics" designation certified by the Korean Society of Medical Informatics in South Korea. No other country had a board certification for Clinical Informatics, although South Korea and Sri Lanka expressed interest in developing a board certification [52].

Board Eligibility

The American Board of Preventive Medicine and the American Board of Pathology became the primary sponsors of the subspecialty board certification. Board certification remains available to physicians, who are board certified by any of the 24 ABMS boards. Physicians, who are board certified in pathology, must apply for the Clinical Informatics certification through ABPath. Applicants for Clinical Informatics certification, who are certified by any other ABMS Member Boards must apply through ABPM [53].

To achieve eligibility for the Clinical Informatics certification, the general eligibility criteria require that "the physician must have graduated from a medical school meeting ABPM standards, hold an active board certification from an ABMS Member Board, hold an unrestricted license to practice medicine in every state or territory in which the physician has a license to practice medicine, and provide a letter of reference from an ABMS-certified physician" [54]. In 2018, ABPM announced that "Diplomates certified by the American Board of Preventive Medicine (ABPM) in Clinical Informatics [...] will no longer be required to maintain primary certifications in order to recertify in these subspecialty areas" [55].

The initial ABMS approval of Clinical Informatics allowed for two pathways for certification: A Fellowship Pathway and a Practice Pathway [41]. The Practice Pathway was initially available only until 2017, but a subsequent application by ABPM to extend it until 2022 was approved by ABMS [56].

Fellowship Pathway

Eligibility criteria for the Clinical Informatics Fellowship Pathway besides the general criteria (listed above) include a successful completion of a 24-month full-time ACGME accredited Clinical Informatics fellowship [57]. The first eligible applicants, who completed an ACGME accredited fellowship, took the examination in 2016.

The first Accreditation Council for Graduate Medical Education (ACGME) accredited fellowship programs included Stanford University, University of Illinois at Chicago, Indiana University, and Oregon Health & Science University in 2014. By October 2019, 40 programs were accredited and listed by AMIA [58]. The program directors for the fellowship programs collaborate and provide leadership through the AMIA Community of Clinical Informatics Program Directors (CCIPD).

In 2019, ABPM announced that "surgical residents who have completed training in an ACGME-accredited fellowship in Clinical Informatics (CI) [are able] to sit for the ABPM's Initial Certification Examination in CI (the "Exam") prior to obtaining primary certification in surgery from the American Board of Surgery (ABS)." Eligibility criteria include (1) a guaranteed training slot to complete the requirements for primary certification in surgery and; (2) meeting all other then-current ABPM eligibility requirements for certification in CI [59].

Practice Pathway

Eligibility criteria for the Clinical Informatics Practice Pathway besides the general criteria (listed above) include the completion of a two-year biomedical informatics master's program or a 2 year fellowship sponsored by the National Library of Medicine or the US Department of Veterans Affairs. Alternatively, the applicant "must demonstrate 36 months of substantial broad-based professional activity with significant Clinical Informatics responsibility (at least 25% effort) in the five years preceding the application" [54]. For the 36-month professional activity, candidates may request partial credit for fellowships less than 24 months, AMIA 10x10 courses, or masters-level courses in health informatics, or ABPM approved research and educational activities in Clinical Informatics [60].

Developing the Board Certification Examination for Clinical Informatics

When ABMS approved Clinical Informatics as a subspecialty in 2011, the AMIA documents describing the core content and training requirements [44, 45] became the foundation for the Clinical Informatics subspecialty used to develop the examination and the accreditation of programs. The ABPM assembled an examination committee of 20 experts (17 nominated by AMIA, 3 by ABPath) to develop an item bank with more than 300 items for the certification examination [54]. When this committee became the Sub-board in 2014, Christoph U. Lehmann became the first Clinical Informatics Diplomate to chair this Sub-board for Clinical Informatics. The addition of the chairs from the original Core Content and Clinical Training groups (Reed Gardner, PhD and Charles Safran, MD) to the Sub-board provided continuity. A subset of the Sub-board (4–5 members) annually reviews the applications and makes recommendations to ABPM on board eligibility of applicants.

When designing a certification examination, item developers must strive to write items (questions) that are valid, reliable, and objective. The charge to the Sub-board for Clinical Informatics included the creation of an examination designed to test the basic lasting concepts within the field of Clinical Informatics. All Sub-board members were trained in item writing by a psychometric expert provided by the ABPM. The full Sub-board reviewed all items for accuracy and relevance. Annually, the Sub-board supplements the item bank by creating new and relevant items and retires or rewrites existing items to maintain the highest level of quality in the item pool.

Maintaining the Examination

Annually, the Sub-board reviews the performance of items that were present on the examination for that year. Items not performing within acceptable standards defined by ABPM are removed from scoring of the examination. Items found too difficult or too easy or those items that fail to differentiate between successful and less successful examinees (successful examination takers are as likely as unsuccessful takers to get this item correct) may also be eliminated from scoring. The examination is then rescored to arrive at final scores for each applicant.

Challenges

The Core Content was used to create the item pool for the board exam. It quickly became apparent that despite the great amount of details contained in the Core Content, it was underspecified for item creation and required interpretation by the Sub-board. Further, some subdomains such as "governance" or "workflow" were underrepresented in Clinical Informatics textbooks written prior to the first exam [23, 61, 62, 63, 64, 65, 66, 67, 68, 69, 70, 71] making item writing more difficult. Since that time, new journals and new textbooks for the field have been created and are available to the Sub-board for their task. The new Delineation of Practice developed by AMIA should make the work of the Sub-board easier [49].

Examination Results

Because the members of the Sub-board, who created the item pool, were not eligible to take the written examination, ABPM set up an oral examination for the Sub-board members, who were eligible. The examination was conducted by several Sub-board members not eligible for the board exam and occurred in the summer of 2013. The first written examination for board certification in the subspecialty of Clinical

Informatics occurred October 7–18, 2013. The examination remains a 200 multiple choice question online examination administered by Pearson VUE Professional Centers throughout the United States and at several international sites and has been administered yearly since 2013 [72].

Each year, the examination is composed of varying questions from the item pool. Performance on items that are repeatedly used allows an analysis of the examination difficulty each year and is used to determine the passing score, which varies from year to year to assure that the test difficulty remains constant. Despite the constant test difficulty from year to year, passing rates have declined continually since 2013 with the exception of 2016, where a number of candidates were given the opportunity to take the examination twice due to an inaccurate transcription of the test into the testing system. While the pass rate was 91% in 2013, the pass rate had decreased to 77% in 2017. The reason for the drop in pass rates is unclear, however the authors of this chapter speculate that the caliber of examinees may have been exceptionally high in the beginning with many very senior and experienced clinical informaticians taking the initial board exam. By January 2018, of 1976 examinees, 1687 (85.4%) passed the exam and became Diplomates. As in the first years of the examination all applications were on paper and there are no aggregate data available from ABPM on the distribution of primary board certification for Diplomates. However, the application process has now moved from paper to an online format and ABPM should be able to produce these numbers in the future. The American Academy of Pediatrics manually searched for the Clinical Informatics Diplomates from the first two years in the American Board of Pediatrics database and found that approximately 17% (132) of Board certified Clinical Informaticians were pediatricians. [73].

ACGME Accredited Fellowships in Clinical Informatics

As of October 2019, only 40 Fellowship Programs have been accredited by ACGME in Clinical Informatics [58]. Beginning with the examination in 2023, only candidates trained in an ACGME-accredited fellowship program will be eligible for the Clinical Informatics board examination. Until then, the Practice Pathway will be available including the possibility to gain eligibility by completing a two-year masters' program. For the fellowship positions starting in 2019, Clinical Informatics program directors were unable to fill all positions in the fellowship programs through the match that has been organized by the programs [74]. The applicant pool was too small to provide acceptable candidates for all programs. Because of the availability of the practice track until 2022, potential Clinical Informatics candidates can become board-eligible through employment as a Clinical Informatician and/or completing a Masters' program, which is financially more attractive than a fellow's salary. Program directors anticipate an increase in applicants starting in 2021 as 2020 will be the last time a potential candidate could use the two-year Masters' route.

As discussed earlier, Clinical Informatics Sub-specialty Board Certification is unique to the United States; however certification in Clinical Informatics for individuals living and practicing outside the US is possible. ACGME accredits programs internationally [75], thus allowing board certified Diplomates to establish ACGME-accredited Clinical Informatics programs internationally. Any graduate from such a program must meet "all current ABPM requirements including, but not limited to, licensure and primary certification via an ABMS Member Board" [54].

How to Establish a Clinical Informatics Fellowship

Only a limited number of primary specialties are allowed to accredit a Clinical Informatics program. These include Anesthesiology, Diagnostic Radiology, Emergency Medicine, Family Medicine, Internal Medicine, Medical Genetics and Genomics, Pathology, Pediatrics, or Preventive Medicine. After an extensive application, often of over 200 pages, that includes a description of the educational resources, a block schedule for the fellow, and a description of the faculty has been approved by ACGME, a Graduate Medical Education (GME) institution is permitted to recruit fellows. GME institutions are limited to one fellowship program. Usually ACGME reviewers will evaluate the program on site within the first year. More specific training program requirements can be found on the ACGME website [76].

The knowledge and skills required for fellows to acquire is substantial and many programs teach some content through online or local Clinical Informatics certification or master's programs. For practical experience, many fellows are embedded in health information technology operations to gain hands-on experiences with various health information technology systems.

Program Director Community

Following the ABMS approval of Clinical Informatics as a board-certified medical subspecialty in September 2011 and the resulting publication of Clinical Informatics Fellowship (CIF) Program Requirements, informal conversations between aspiring organizations and program directors began at AMIA meetings. These discussions focused on how various institutions were creating their CIF curriculum, funding, and ACGME applications which were all the more important and urgent since there were no accredited fellowships at that time. Representatives from the ACGME attended several of these early meetings since they too were figuring out how to adapt and apply accreditation processes and standards developed for clinical training programs in CIFs where direct patient care was not the focus.

These informal conversations evolved into a more structured set of regular meetings added to specific AMIA national meetings twice a year and attended by

Program Directors, CIF faculty, and key individuals from institutions aspiring to create a CIF. In 2016 this group composed and submitted a proposal to AMIA to form the Proposal for the Community of Clinical Informatics Program Directors (CCIPD) which was approved [77]. While the number of participants in this group has grown significantly over time in accordance to the number of new fellowship programs, the camaraderie and culture of collaboration established by the original group remains strong. The CCIPD group has been very productive including

- assisting aspiring programs, creating a coordinated "match" process for recruitment outside the National Residency Matching Program (NRMP) system
- enrolling fellowship programs in the Electronic Residency Application Service (ERAS®, the centralized online application service fellowship applicants use to deliver their applications and supporting documents to fellowship programs)
- administering an annual in-service examination
- organizing conversations regarding funding
- sharing best practices, and creating a national monthly case conference.

CCIPD encouraged and supported supporting the development of the AMIA Clinical Informatics Fellows (ACIF) which serves as the home within AMIA for Clinical Informatics Fellows nationwide.

Clinical Informatics Milestones

According to ACGME, "a milestone is a significant point in development. For accreditation purposes, the Milestones are competency-based developmental outcomes (e.g., knowledge, skills, attitudes, and performance) that can be demonstrated progressively by residents/fellows from the beginning of their education through graduation to the unsupervised practice of their specialties" [78]. All ACGME trainees are evaluated semi-annually based on a set of milestones that ACGME developed for each specialty and subspecialty. The results of this evaluation are reported to ACGME. For Clinical Informatics, milestones were initially developed over the course of a single afternoon by an expert panel based on a template from Internal Medicine. Program directors have proposed developing milestones where each required sub-competency (i.e., task) for fellows is uniquely mapped to a single milestone assessment grid and in turn each milestone grid is mapped to one or more sub-competencies [79]. This mapping has the advantage of facilitating use of milestones for individualized learning plans, curriculum planning and modifications, program evaluations, and, of course, fellow evaluations within and across programs. Program directors anticipate that ACGME will undertake an extensive revision of the milestones based on the 2017 AMIA needs assessment (see below) in the near future.

Financial Model

Clinical Informaticians provide substantial benefits to both patients and payers (e.g. private insurers, Medicaid, Medicare) through reduction of errors [80], increasing safety [81], reducing costs [82], and improving care coordination and efficiency. However, as of the fall of 2019, Clinical Informatics does not have any billing codes through which the efforts of informaticians could be reimbursed by payers of patients [83]. Thus, institutions that employ a clinical informatician provide benefits to patients and payers, but the full costs are borne by the healthcare institutions without patient or payer contributions.

Teaching hospitals in the United States are eligible for Medicare direct Graduate Medical Education payments and indirect medical education payments if they participate in the Medicare program [84]. As GME funding from the Centers for Medicare and Medicaid Services (CMS) has not kept pace with the number and size of training programs, the cost of training new Clinical Informaticians is currently shouldered by academic health science centers. There is a simple explanation why teaching hospitals are willing to incur the cost for clinical training. Trainees are extenders for teaching physicians. They allow the attending physician to focus on the critical portions of care delivery while trainees perform less important tasks allowing attendings to take care of more patients and increase billable services. However, for clinical informatics fellows this model breaks down due to the absence of billable codes leaving institutions having to cover the cost of Clinical Informatics fellows.

To sustain the benefits from training new clinical informaticians, in the best interest of patients, payers, and the US society, it is therefore critical to find viable financial models for Clinical Informatics fellowship programs. The AMIA Board of Directors supports the search for new models [83]. One potential funding source could be the Center for Medicare & Medicaid Innovation as Clinical Informatics fellows could be used to implement and demonstrate advances in safety, cost reduction, and efficiency [85].

Integrated Training Experiences

It is not uncommon that trainees select joint training programs (e.g. joint program in internal medicine and pediatrics). For fellowships, these combined training programs or combined fellowships generate significant amount of work for program directors and the involved boards as a combined schedule for the fellow must be created and approved by the boards in advance. To reduce the effort required and provide clarification, ABPM developed the ABPM's Integrated Training Experience (ITE) [86]. ITE allows a program to accommodate a single physician, who wishes to shorten training time and complete two residencies or fellowships. ABPM will provide the ITE guidelines to program directors upon request. The implications of the ITE for programs include the ability to accommodate the needs of an individual provider, who seeks training both in CI as well as another subspecialty. For trainees this may result in a reduced combined training period as research rotations may be counted for both subspecialty training efforts.

Maintenance of Certification

Once board certified, Clinical Informatics Diplomates must comply with the Maintenance of Certification (MOC) process, which is designed to assess continuing competencies [87]. The process has four components: (1) Professionalism and Professional Standing (Diplomates are required to maintain an active, valid and unrestricted medical license in all States, US territories, or Canadian Provinces where they are licensed to practice medicine). (2) Lifelong Learning and Self-Assessment (LLSA) (Diplomates must complete continuing medical education and self-assessment activities in Clinical Informatics including safety courses. AMIA is a major provider of ABPM-approved LLSA courses), (3) Assessment of Knowledge, Judgment, and Skills (Diplomates must pass an exam during each certification cycle with content similar to the initial certification exam), and (4) Improvement in Medical Practice (Diplomates must complete two Improvement in Medical Practice activities).The annual MOC fee for Diplomates certified after 2018 is $175 per year and the examination fee is $1750. A ten-year certification cycle (not considering the application fee) amounts to $3500 [88]. Since the first recertification examination is required ten years after initial certification, the first Clinical Informatics recertification examination is anticipated to be given in 2023.

Advanced Health Informatics Certifications

The American Medical Informatics Association (AMIA) has long been dedicated to the evolution of informatics as a profession. This includes commitment to developing certification for all clinical informatics professionals – not just physicians. Upon establishment of the Clinical Informatics Subspecialty (CIS), AMIA turned its attention to establishing certification for "other members of the clinical team" [42]. In 2011, two AMIA task forces clarified the focus of Health Informatics (HI) certification by concluding that the certification should: (a) focus on certifying the shared or "core" competencies rather than profession-specific competencies, (e.g., public health or nursing informatics); (b) be founded on a core content and level of rigor that are commensurate with those of the CIS; and (c) be targeted for informatics professionals in roles that directly affect the practice of health care (i.e. operational or applied informatics). In 2014, a multidisciplinary work group considered the core content and proposed eligibility criteria for the future certification program [89, 90].

To inform HI certification development, AMIA conducted a needs assessment in 2017. Over 2,000 health informatics professionals responded to the workforce survey, the first of its kind in the field of informatics. Following best practices for the certification industry, in 2018, AMIA directed a formal practice analysis of HI, in parallel with the CIS practice analysis described earlier in this chapter. The HI practice analysis produced a delineation of major content areas/domains of practice, the specific tasks performed by individuals in a profession, and the knowledge and skills required to perform the tasks [91]. In 2019, AMIA formed a certifying body (the Health Informatics Certification Commission) to finalize eligibility criteria, create policies and procedures to govern certification and recertification, and to develop and administer the first certifying exam. Finally, in recognition of the essential nature of accredited educational and training programs to robust professional certifications, AMIA and the Commission on Accreditation for Health Informatics and Information Management Education (CAHIIM) continue to collaborate to assure that applied health informatics programs are qualified to impart to their graduates the current competencies necessary to succeed in the field of health informatics [92].

Summary of Lessons Learned

- Clinical Informatics has a long history in the US and has advanced into a clinical subspecialty for physicians with board certification.
- AMIA was instrumental in developing this new medical subspecialty and provided the experts and guidance to develop the core content and the training requirements.
- AMIA is actively supporting a certification process for other clinical specialties in the form of the Advanced Health Informatics Certification.
- The core content of the Clinical Informatics subspecialty has been revised since the subspecialty's inception, but may need future revisions since Clinical Informatics has been, and remains, a rapidly evolving field.
- As the field continues to advance, the requirements for training and certification of physicians and others will likely evolve as well.

References

1. Jenkin MA. Clinical specialty systems as an introduction to clinical informatics. In: DAB L, EEV B, Jenkin MA, editors. Congress on medical informatics; 1983.
2. Jenkin MA. Clinical informatics: a strategy for the use of information in the clinical setting. Med Inform (Lond). 1984;9(3–4):225–32.
3. Keith JM. Florence Nightingale: statistician and consultant epidemiologist. Int Nurs Rev. 1988;35(5):147–50.

4. Columbia University. Herman Hollerith. Available online at http://www.columbia.edu/cu/computinghistory/hollerith.html. Last accessed 7/23/2019.
5. Ledley RS, Lusted LB. Reasoning foundations of medical diagnosis; symbolic logic, probability, and value theory aid our understanding of how physicians reason. Science. 1959;130(3366):9–21.
6. Warner HR, Toronto AF, Veasy LG, Stephenson R. A mathematical approach to medical diagnosis. Application to congenital heart disease. JAMA. 1961;177:177–83.
7. Warner HR. History of medical informatics at Utah. In: Blum BI, Duncan K, editors. A history of medical informatics – ACM press history series. Reading: Addison-Wesley; 1990. p. 357–69.
8. Kuperman GJ, Gardner RM, Pryor TA. HELP: a dynamic hospital information system. New York: Springer; 1991.
9. Lindberg DA, Reese G. Automatic measurement and computer processing of bacterial growth data. Biomed Sci Instrum. 1963;1:11–20.
10. Collen MF, Rubin L, Neyman J, Dantzig GB, Baer RM, Siegelaub AB. Automated multiphasic screening and diagnosis. Am J Public Health Nations Health. 1964;54:741–50.
11. Barnett GO. Computers in patient care. N Engl J Med. 1968;279(24):1321–7. https://doi.org/10.1056/nejm196812122792407.
12. Greenes RA, Sidel VW. The use of computer mapping in health research. Health Serv Res. 1967;2(3):243–58.
13. Skjei, Eric. Pappalardo, N. The mind behind MUMPS. Interview by Erick Skeji. Comput Healthc 1989; Spec No:16–18.
14. Slack WV, Hicks GP, Reed CE, Van Cura LJ. A computer-based medical-history system. N Engl J Med. 1966;274(4):194–8. https://doi.org/10.1056/nejm196601272740406.
15. Bleich HL. Computer evaluation of acid–base disorders. Trans Assoc Am Phys. 1968;81:184–9.
16. Simborg DW, Rikli AE, Hall P. Experimentation in medical history-taking. JAMA. 1969;210(8):1443–5.
17. Shieman BM. Medical information system, El Camino hospital. IMS Ind Med Surg. 1971;40(7):25–6.
18. Stead WW, Heyman A, Thompson HK, Hammond WE. Computer-assisted interview of patients with functional headache. Arch Intern Med. 1972;129(6):950–5.
19. Shortliffe EH, Davis R, Axline SG, Buchanan BG, Green CC, Cohen SN. Computer-based consultations in clinical therapeutics: explanation and rule acquisition capabilities of the MYCIN system. Comput Biomed Res. 1975;8(4):303–20.
20. McDonald CJ. Protocol-based computer reminders, the quality of care and the non-perfectability of man. N Engl J Med. 1976;295(24):1351–5. https://doi.org/10.1056/nejm197612092952405.
21. Collen MF. Origins of medical informatics. West J Med. 1986;145(6):778–85.
22. Degoulet P, Haux R, Kulikowski C, Lun KC. Francois Gremy and the birth of IMIA. 1st IMIA/UMIT Medical Informatics Award of Excellence given to professor Gremy. Methods Inf Med. 2005;44(3):349–51. https://doi.org/10.1267/meth05030349.
23. Shortliffe EH, Cimino JJ. Biomedical informatics: computer applications in health care and biomedicine. 3rd ed. New York: Springer; 2006.
24. Office of the National Coordinator. Health IT Dashboard. Available online at https://dashboard.healthit.gov/index.php. Last accessed 7/23/2019.
25. Blumenthal D, Tavenner M. The "meaningful use" regulation for electronic health records. N Engl J Med. 2010;363(6):501–4. https://doi.org/10.1056/NEJMp1006114.
26. Office of the National Coordinator. About ONC. Available at https://www.healthit.gov/topic/about-onc. Last accessed 7/23/2019.
27. Blumenthal D. Stimulating the adoption of health information technology. N Engl J Med. 2009;360:1477–9. https://doi.org/10.1056/NEJMp0901592.
28. Blumenthal D. Implementation of the federal health information technology initiative. N Engl J Med. 2011;365(25):2426–31. https://doi.org/10.1056/NEJMsr1112158.

29. Blumenthal D. Wiring the health system–origins and provisions of a new federal program. N Engl J Med. 2011;365(24):2323–9. https://doi.org/10.1056/NEJMsr1110507.
30. Office of the National Coordinator. Merit-based Incentive Payment System. Available online at https://www.healthit.gov/topic/federal-incentive-programs/MACRA/merit-based-incentive-payment-system. Last accessed 7/23/2019.
31. Young A, Chaudhry HJ, Pei X, Arnhart K, Dugan M, Snyder GB. A Census of Actively Licensed Physicians in the United States, 2016. J Med Regulat VOL 103, N O 2 I 7–21. Available online at https://www.fsmb.org/siteassets/advocacy/publications/2016census.pdf. Last accessed 7/23/2019.
32. Milholland DK. Nursing informatics–progress toward certification. Am Nurse. 1994;26(6):8.
33. Simpson RL. Nursing informatics certification. Nurs Manag. 1995;26(12):49–50.
34. Newbold SK. The informatics nurse and the certification process. Comput Nurs. 1996;14(2):84–5, 88.
35. American Nurses Association. Nursing Informatics: Scope and standards of practice. 2nd ed. Silver Spring, MD: Nursesbooks.org; 2015.
36. Institute of Medicine Committee on the Health Professions Education Summit. Health professions education: a bridge to quality. Washington, DC: National Academy Press; 2003.
37. Safran C. Reactor panel—private industry. Unifying the industry. Paper presented at the The Secretarial Summit on Health Information Technology launching the National Health Information Infrastructure 2004. Washington DC: Cornerstones for Electronic Healthcare, 21 July 2004.
38. AMIA & AHIMA. Building the Work Force for Health Information Transformation. Available online at https://www.amia.org/sites/default/files/files_2/Workforce_2006.pdf. Last accessed 7/23/2019.
39. Kloss LL, Detmer DE. Building the workforce for health information transformation. Chicago: American Health Information Management Association (AHIMA); 2006.
40. Hersh W, Williamson J. Educating 10,000 information by 2010: the AMIA 10×10 program. Int J Med Inform. 2007;76:377–82.
41. Detmer DE, Munger BS, Lehmann CU. Medical informatics board certification: history, current status, and predicted impact on clinical informatics workforce. Appl Clin Inform. 2010;1(1):11–8.
42. Detmer DE, Lumpkin JR, Williamson JJ. Defining the medical subspecialty of clinical informatics. J Am Med Inform Assoc. 2009;16(2):167–8. https://doi.org/10.1197/jamia.M3094.
43. American Board of Medical Specialties. Steps Toward Initial Certification and MOC. https://www.abms.org/board-certification/steps-toward-initial-certification-and-moc/. Accessed 8/15/2019.
44. Gardner RM, Overhage JM, Steen EB, Munger BS, Holmes JH, Williamson JJ, Detmer DE. Core content for the subspecialty of clinical informatics. J Am Med Inform Assoc. 2009;16(2):153–7. https://doi.org/10.1197/jamia.M3045.
45. Safran C, Shabot MM, Munger BS, Holmes JH, Steen EB, Lumpkin JR, Detmer DE. Program requirements for fellowship education in the subspecialty of clinical informatics. J Am Med Inform Assoc. 2009;16(2):158–66. https://doi.org/10.1197/jamia.M3046.
46. Leviss J, Kremsdorf R, Mohaideen MF. The CMIO–a new leader for health systems. J Am Med Inform Assoc. 2006;13(5):573–8. https://doi.org/10.1197/jamia.M2097.
47. Kannry J, Sengstack P, Thyvalikakath TP, Poikonen J, Middleton B, Payne T, Lehmann CU. The Chief Clinical Informatics Officer (CCIO): AMIA Task Force Report on CCIO Knowledge, Education, and Skillset Requirements. Appl Clin Inform. 2016;7(1):143–76. https://doi.org/10.4338/ACI-2015-12-R-0174. eCollection 2016. Review
48. American Board of Preventive Medicine. The American Board of Preventive Medicine – Clinical Informatics Board Certification. 2019. https://www.theabpm.org/become-certified/exam-content/clinical-informatics-content-outline/. Accessed 3 Mar 2020.
49. Silverman HD, Steen EB, Carpenito JN, Ondrula CJ, Williamson JJ, Fridsma DB. Domains, tasks, and knowledge for clinical informatics subspecialty practice: results of a practice analysis. J Am Med Inform Assoc. 2019;26(7):586–93. https://doi.org/10.1093/jamia/ocz051.

50. Safran C. Informatics training for clinicians is more important than hardware and software. Yearb Med Inform. 2009;4:164–5.

51. Manos D. Clinical informatics becomes a board-certified medical subspecialty. New Gloucester, ME: MedTech Media; Healthcare IT News. 2011. http://www.healthcareitnews.com/news/clinical-informatics-becomes-board-certified-medical-subspecialty. Accessed 8 July 2013.

52. Gundlapalli AV, Gundlapalli AV, Greaves WW, Kesler D, Murray P, Safran C, Lehmann CU. Clinical informatics board specialty certification for physicians: a global view. Stud Health Technol Inform. 2015;216:501–5.

53. American Board of Pathology. Instructions for PATHway to Online Applications. http://abpath.org/PATHwayAppInstructions.pdf. Accessed 8 July 2013.

54. Lehmann CU, Gundlapalli AV, Williamson JJ, Fridsma DB, Hersh WR, Krousel-Wood M, Ondrula CJ, Munger B. Five years of clinical informatics board certification for physicians in the United States of America. Yearb Med Inform. 2018;27(1):237–42. https://doi.org/10.1055/s-0038-1641198. Epub 2018 Apr 22

55. American Board of Preventive Medicine. American Board of Preventive Medicine is reducing the burden for Diplomates recertifying in Clinical Informatics and Addiction Medicine. Available online at https://www.theabpm.org/2018/08/16/american-board-of-preventive-medicine-is-reducing-the-burden-for-diplomates-recertifying-in-clinical-informatics-and-addiction-medicine/ Last accessed 10/2/2019.

56. American Board of Preventive Medicine. News & Announcements. Available online at https://www.theabpm.org/2019/03/25/the-american-board-of-preventive-medicine-abpm-has-obtained-approval-from-the-american-board-of-medical-specialties-abms-to-expand-eligibility-requirements-for-physicians-seeking-to-becom/. Last accessed 1/14/2020.

57. American Board of Preventive Medicine. Sub-Specialty Requirements Clinical Informatics. Available online at https://www.theabpm.org/wp-content/uploads/2017/05/ClinicalInformatics.pdf. Last accessed 10/2/2019.

58. American Medical Informatics Association. Clinical Informatics Fellowship Programs. Available online at https://www.amia.org/membership/academic-forum/clinical-informatics-fellowships Last accessed 10/2/2019.

59. American Board of Preventive Medicine. The American Board of Preventive Medicine Has Obtained Approval from the American Board of Medical Specialties' (ABMS) to Offer Surgical Residents Mid-Residency Training Programs in Clinical Informatics (MRTP). Available online at https://www.theabpm.org/2019/03/19/the-american-board-of-preventive-medicine-has-obtained-approval-from-the-american-board-of-medical-specialties-abms-to-offer-surgical-residents-mid-residency-training-programs-in-clinical-informat/. Last accessed 10/3/2019.

60. American Board of Preventive Medicine. Clinical Informatics 2017 Examination Blueprint. Available online at https://www.theabpm.org/wp-content/uploads/2017/09/2017CI-Content-Outline.pdf. Last accessed 10/2/2019.

61. Carter JH. Electronic health records: a guide for clinicians and administrators. 2nd ed. Philadelphia: American College of Physicians; 2008.

62. Degoulet P, Fieschi M. Introduction to clinical informatics. New York: Springer; 1997.

63. Elkin PL. Terminology and terminological systems. London: Springer; 2012.

64. Friedman CP, Wyatt J. Evaluation methods in biomedical informatics. 2nd ed. New York: Springer; 2006.

65. Greenes RA. Clinical decision support: the road ahead. Boston, MA: Elsevier Academic; 2007.

66. Kotter J. Leading change. Boston: Harvard Business Press Books; 2012.

67. O'Carroll PW, Yasnoff WA, Ward ME, Ripp LH, Martin EL. Public health informatics and information systems. Health informatics. New York: Springer; 2003.

68. Payne TH. Practical guide to clinical computing systems. London: Elsevier Academic; 2008.

69. Pantanowitz L, Tuthill JM, Balis UGJ. Pathology informatics, theory & practice. Chicago: American Society for Clinical Pathology; 2012.

70. van Bemmel JH, Musen MA, Helder JC. Handbook of medical informatics. A. W. Houten: Bohn Stafleu Van Loghum, Springer; 1997.
71. Wager KA, Lee FW, Glaser JP. Health care information systems: a practical approach for health care management. San Francisco: Wiley; 2009.
72. American Board of Preventive Medicine. Exam Information. Available online at https://www.theabpm.org/become-certified/exam-information/ . Last accessed 10/5/2019.
73. Krams L. American Academy of pediatrics. Personal communication. 2018;
74. Pageler NM, Elkin PL, Kannry J, Leu MG, Levy B, Lehmann CU. A clinical informatics program directors' proposal to the american board of preventive medicine. Appl Clin Inform. 2020;11(3):483–86. https://doi.org/10.1055/s-0040-1714348.
75. ACGME-International. Available online at http://www.acgme-i.org/. Last accessed 10/2/2019.
76. ACGME. ACGME Program Requirements for Graduate Medical Education in Clinical Informatics. Available online at https://www.acgme.org/Portals/0/PFAssets/ProgramRequirements/381_ClinicalInformatics_2019_TCC.pdf?ver=2019-03-27-084451-767. Last accessed 10/2/2019.
77. American Medical Informatics Association. Academic Forum Communities. Available online at https://www.amia.org/membership/academic-forum/communities. Last accessed 10/5/2019.
78. ACGME. Frequently Asked Questions: Milestones. Available online at http://www.acgme.org/Portals/0/MilestonesFAQ.pdf. Last accessed 10/5/2019.
79. Silverman H, Lehmann CU, Munger B. Milestones: critical elements in clinical informatics fellowship programs. Appl Clin Inform. 2016;7(1):177–90. https://doi.org/10.4338/ACI-2015-10-SOA-0141. eCollection 2016
80. Kim GR, Chen AR, Arceci RJ, Mitchell SH, Kokoszka KM, Daniel D, Lehmann CU. Error reduction in pediatric chemotherapy: computerized order entry and failure modes and effects analysis. Arch Pediatr Adolesc Med. 2006;160(5):495–8.
81. Westbrook JI, Li L, Raban MZ, Baysari MT, Mumford V, Prgomet M, Georgiou A, Kim T, Lake R, McCullagh C, Dalla-Pozza L, Karnon J, O'Brien TA, Ambler G, Day R, Cowell CT, Gazarian M, Worthington R, Lehmann CU, White L, Barbaric D, Gardo A, Kelly M, Kennedy P. Stepped-wedge cluster randomised controlled trial to assess the effectiveness of an electronic medication management system to reduce medication errors, adverse drug events and average length of stay at two paediatric hospitals: a study protocol. BMJ Open. 2016;6(10):e011811. https://doi.org/10.1136/bmjopen-2016-011811.
82. Sick AC, Lehmann CU, Tamma PD, Lee CK, Agwu AL. Sustained savings from a longitudinal cost analysis of an internet-based preapproval antimicrobial stewardship program. Infect Control Hosp Epidemiol. 2013;34(6):573–80.
83. Lehmann CU, Longhurst CA, Hersh W, Mohan V, Levy BP, Embi PJ, Finnell JT, Turner AM, Martin R, Williamson J, Munger B. Clinical informatics fellowship programs: in search of a viable financial model: an open letter to the centers for medicare and medicaid services. Appl Clin Inform. 2015;6(2):267–70. https://doi.org/10.4338/ACI-2015-03-IE-0030. eCollection 2015
84. Centers for Medicare and Medicaid Services. Direct Graduate Medical Education (DGME). Available online at http://www.cms.gov/Medicare/Medicare-Fee-for-Service-Payment/AcuteInpatientPPS/dgme.html
85. Kannry J, Smith J, Mohan V, Levy B, Finnell J, Lehmann CU. Policy statement on clinical informatics fellowships and the future of informatics-driven medicine. Appl Clin Inform. In press.
86. Chris Ondrula. Executive Director, American Board of Preventive Medicine. Personal Communication. 2018.
87. American Board of Preventive Medicine. Maintain Certification. Available online at https://www.theabpm.org/maintain-certification/. Last accessed 10/2/2019.
88. American Board of Preventive Medicine. MOC Fees. Available online at https://www.theabpm.org/maintain-certification/. Last accessed 10/5/2019.
89. Gadd CS, Williamson JJ, Steen EB, Fridsma DB. Creating advanced health informatics certification. J Am Med Inform Assoc. 2016;23(4):848–50.

90. Gadd CS, Williamson JJ, Steen EB, Andriole KP, Delaney C, Gumpper K, LaVenture M, Rosendale D, Sittig DF, Thyvalikakath T, Turner P, Fridsma DB. Eligibility requirements for advanced health informatics certification. J Am Med Inform Assoc. 2016;23(4):851–4.
91. Gadd CS, Steen EB, Caro CM, Greenberg S, Williamson JJ, Fridsma DB. Domains, tasks, and knowledge for health informatics practice: results of a practice analysis. J Am Med Inform Assoc. 2020;27:845–52.
92. Valenta AL, Berner ES, Boren SA, Deckard GJ, Eldredge C, Fridsma DB, Gadd C, Gong Y, Johnson T, Jones J, Manos EL, Phillips KT, Roderer NK, Rosendale D, Turner AM, Tusch G, Williamson JJ, Johnson SB. AMIA Board White Paper: AMIA 2017 core competencies for applied health informatics education at the master's degree level. J Am Med Inform Assoc. 2018;25(12):1657–68. https://doi.org/10.1093/jamia/ocy132.

Chapter 17
Accreditation of Health Informatics Programs

Sue S. Feldman, Suzanne Austin Boren, Linde H. Tesch, and Annette L. Valenta

Historical Context

Academic program accreditation in higher education is both a process and, if a successful process, a mechanism for external quality and integrity validation for educational programs. As the AMIA Accreditation Committee (AAC) noted, the value proposition of accreditation is the assurance to the public, the profession, and the student that a program provides an education that prepares a student to join the workforce [1, 2].

The Commission on Accreditation for Health Informatics and Information Management Education (CAHIIM) began indirectly in health information management (HIM) academic program evaluation. In 1935, the Association of Records Librarians of North America (ARLNA) established a model curriculum and a program approval process for what would later become health information management programs. In 1942, this process was formalized and became programmatic accreditation under the American Medical Association's Committee on Allied Health Education Accreditation (AMA-CAHEA). In 1994, CAHEA dissolved and HIM accreditation moved to the Commission on Accreditation for Allied Health

S. S. Feldman (✉)
University of Alabama at Birmingham, Birmingham, AL, USA
e-mail: sfeldman@uab.edu

S. A. Boren
University of Missouri, Columbia, MO, USA
e-mail: borens@health.missouri.edu

L. H. Tesch
Commission on Accreditation for Health Informatics and Information Management,
Chicago, IL, USA
e-mail: linde.tesch@cahiim.org

A. L. Valenta
University of Illinois, Chicago, IL, USA

© Springer Nature Switzerland AG 2020
E. S. Berner (ed.), *Informatics Education in Healthcare*, Health Informatics,
https://doi.org/10.1007/978-3-030-53813-2_17

Education Programs (CAAHEP) where it stayed until 2003. Between 2003 and 2006 when CAHIIM was formed, the accreditation functions were separated from the HIM professional association, currently the American Health Information Management Association (AHIMA). CAHIIM is now an independent organization responsible for accrediting both HIM and Health Informatics programs.

In March 2005, CAHIIM separated from CAAHEP transitioning all existing accredited HIM programs to CAHIIM. In 2012, CAHIIM sought and received recognition from the Council for Higher Education Accreditation (CHEA), which attests to the high standards that CAHIIM follows in its accreditation process. CAHIIM began accreditation of master's degree programs in health informatics in 2010.

Accreditation is part of the path toward professionalization of a discipline. To support the emerging profession of health informatics, the American Medical Informatics Association (AMIA) officially joined CAHIIM as a member organization in January 2015. A revision in the CAHIIM governance structure created the Health Informatics Accreditation Council (HIAC) with the charge to establish and maintain accreditation standards, policies, and procedures for the discipline.

Establishing the Foundational Domains for Health Informatics Education

The Contribution of Health Informatics Accreditation Council (HIAC)

The AMIA Board White Paper by Valenta et al. in 2017 describes how AMIA and CAHIIM agreed to move from an accreditation model of standards driven by curriculum content to one driven by attainment of competence. AMIA and CAHIIM further agreed to draw upon the work done to define the discipline in the earlier 2012 AMIA Board White Paper [2, 3]. In February 2015, a task force of the HIAC was charged with creating an initial model for health informatics (HI) competencies. Using related literature, the five areas outlined in the 2012 AMIA Board White Paper, were reorganized.

The initial model developed by the HIAC task force defined 14 areas of focus for HI: seven describing knowledge areas and seven describing areas of skills. This model was illustrated with two Venn diagrams with three intersecting circles each. The first Venn diagram corresponded to the broad disciplines that inform HI: health science, information science, and social science. The regions of intersection among the circles produced seven distinct combinations: health science, information science, social science, health information science, social health science, social information science, and social health information science [4–7]. The second Venn diagram had seven regions recognizing different skills demonstrated by informaticians, which were labeled analyze, execute, communicate, manage, conduct, collaborate, and lead [8–11].

CAHIIM presented this model at the AMIA Academic Forum in April 2015, with examples applying the model to assess HI programs at three different institutions. The model was disseminated to a wider audience through an AMIA webinar in October 2015. CAHIIM also presented a panel at the AMIA Annual Symposium in November 2015. The panel provided an overview of the accreditation process as well as the new model based on the aforementioned AMIA White Paper of 2012 [3].

The Contribution of AMIA Accreditation Committee (AAC)

In 2016, HIAC began working to update the *2010 Standards and Interpretations for Accreditation of Master's Degree Programs in Health Informatics* that were due for review. Embedded within the Standards was a reference to program curriculum and the focus expected by programs seeking accreditation in HI. To update the foundational domains expected in graduate programs in the discipline, in 2016, AMIA established the AAC to "serve as the primary interface between AMIA and CAHIIM to achieve the goals of AMIA's participation in CAHIIM and HIAC" [2]. In March 2016, the committee charter was introduced, and the work transitioned from HIAC to AAC. The AAC employed a deliberative iterative process [12] to review, revise, and refine the model drafted by HIAC. The deliberative process, a form of nominal group technique, was important in assuring that multiple existing viewpoints were acknowledged in the goal of effective, efficient decision-making on the time sensitive critical path to revising accreditation standards. In order to establish the foundational domains for accreditation, the AAC completed three tasks: (1) identified and named the domains needed in the HI field; (2) described each domain; and (3) described key aspects of competencies associated with each domain.

The AAC recognized that the foundational domains had to be defined broadly enough to be applicable across the sub-disciplines represented by all AMIA constituents (translational bioinformatics, clinical research informatics, clinical informatics, consumer health informatics, and public health informatics). The AAC reviewed HIAC's initial model, the 2012 White Paper [3] the literature published on the skills and practices related to the field of HI, and the literature on the general concepts of competency and the mastery of learning. This literature review is documented in the 30 citations at the end of the 2017 AMIA Board White Paper that comprise the bibliographic material drawn upon for development of the foundational domains and core competencies for the master's degree in health informatics [2].

The AAC adopted a "competent/proficient level of skills acquisition at the time of graduation" as the guiding framework [2, 13–15]. AAC adopted as its definitions of competence and competency the following:

- Competency—"An observable ability of a health professional, integrating multiple components such as knowledge, skills, values, and attitudes. Since competencies are observable, they can be measured and assessed to ensure their acquisition. Competencies can be assembled like building blocks to facilitate progressive development" [16].

- Competence—"The array of abilities across multiple domains or aspects of performance in a certain context. Statements about competence require descriptive qualifiers to define the relevant abilities, context, and stage of training. Competence is multi-dimensional and dynamic. It changes with time, experience, and setting" [16].

Public Comment and AMIA Board Approval

By September 2016, the AAC had refined the work of the HIAC task force and proposed the foundational domains with their descriptions as well as with examples of representative knowledge, skills, and attitudes for each domain. The Foundational Domains are as follows:

- F1-Health,
- F2-Information Science and Technology,
- F3-Social and Behavioral Science,
- F4-Health Information Science and Technology,
- F5-Human Factors and Socio-technical Systems,
- F6-Social and Behavioral Aspects of Health,
- F7-Social, Behavioral, and Information Science and Technology Applied to Health,
- F8-Professionalism,
- F9-Interprofessional Collaborative Practice, and
- F10-Leadership.

Detailed descriptions of the foundational domains can be found in the 2017 AMIA Board White Paper on core competencies [2].

The foundational domains were distributed for public comment to the AMIA Academic Forum and AMIA community. The AMIA 2017 Core Competencies for Health Informatics Education at the Master's Degree Level were formally accepted by the AMIA Board in January 2017 [2]. That same month, the foundational domains were embedded in the CAHIIM revised *2017 Health Informatics Accreditation Standards—Master's Degree*. By March 2017, HIAC had sufficiently updated the 2017 standards for accreditation and CAHIIM released them for public comment. After careful consideration and discussion of the public comments, the 2017 standards for accreditation were approved by the CAHIIM board in June 2017. See Fig. 17.1 for a timeline summarizing the development of the Foundational Domains and the CAHIIM accreditation standards discussed above.

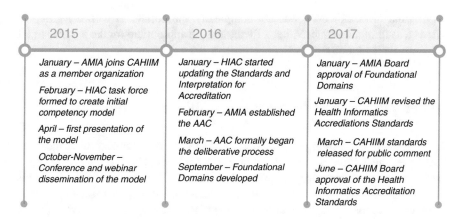

Fig. 17.1 Timeline for developing the Foundational Domains and CAHIIM accreditation standards

CAHIIM Accreditation Standards

For the purposes of accreditation, as a result of the work of the AAC, what was once a curriculum driven by content was now to be a curriculum driven by the knowledge, skills, and attitudes expected of the program graduate. These knowledge, skills, and attitudes create a standard by which employers have some assurance that a health informatician graduating from a CAHIIM-accredited program is competent to the degree described by the program.

HIAC explored ways to ensure that accreditation standards provided a mechanism by which there was alignment with the AMIA foundational domains, while being stated sufficiently broadly to accommodate the variety of programs that might seek CAHIIM accreditation in addition to health informatics (e.g., public health informatics, translational bioinformatics, etc.) It was important that there was enough flexibility for programs to keep curriculum current and relevant while at the same time having enough specificity to ensure breadth and depth of instruction. It was also essential that the accreditation standards be easy to interpret and focus on the blend of knowledge, skills, and attitudes at the time of graduation.

HIAC had to develop a mechanism by which the accreditation team could validate not only knowledge, skills, and attitudes, but also the *breadth and depth* of those knowledge, skills, and attitudes *across* various types of HI programs. Various models were explored, and the team found that an adaptation of Miller's Pyramid of Clinical Competence (Miller's Pyramid) would provide the multiple layers needed [17]. While Miller's Pyramid traditionally has been used in a clinical training environment for competence assessment, it was thought to be appropriate for two reasons. First, it can discern depth of knowledge (what the student knows to what the student does). Second, it allows for the curricular flexibility needed across the variety of programs that may choose to be accredited by CAHIIM. Miller's Pyramid in its original form, however, was not completely appropriate. A working group of HIAC was formed to adapt Miller's Pyramid to be appropriate for the purpose of HI program accreditation.

Miller's Pyramid as Adapted for Health Informatics

In his original work, George Miller suggested a pyramid framework by which complex assessment could occur in the clinical environment [17]. Fig. 17.2 illustrates a later version of Miller's original pyramid [18]. At the foundation of the pyramid is knowledge or "KNOWS." After students demonstrate they know something, they advance to demonstrating they know how to use the knowledge ("KNOWS HOW"). To accommodate for increasingly complex learning and application of that learning, the last two layers of the pyramid allow for performance that "SHOWS HOW" where there is demonstration of showing how to use the knowledge, and lastly "DOES," which implies independence. The "KNOWS" level aligns well with AMIA Foundational Domains F1, F2, and F3 as they represent the expected basic working knowledge to be demonstrated by graduate students in the discipline.

The SHOWS HOW and DOES levels of the Miller's Pyramid appropriately align with the remaining seven AMIA Foundational Domains, F4-F10, that include knowledge, skills, and attitudes.

The adaptation of Miller's Pyramid for health informatics assesses "DOES" within the parameters of the degree program, instead of in the clinical environment as originally conceived [17]. Figure 17.3 illustrates the adaptation of Miller's Pyramid for HI. It was necessary to incorporate the knowledge, skills, and attitudes into the framework. For this, HIAC drew from the work of Mehay and Burns [18]. The cognitive and behavioral layers, a focus in the clinical environment, were adapted to apply to HI.

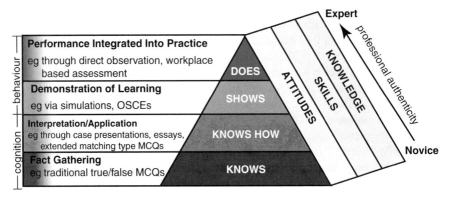

Fig. 17.2 Extension of Miller's Pyramid [18]

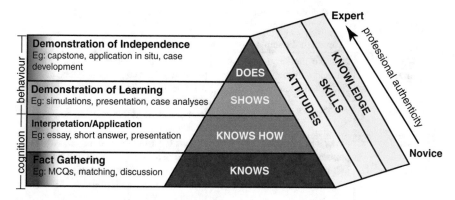

Fig. 17.3 Miller's Pyramid as adapted for health informatics (adapted from [18])

Fig. 17.4 Continuum of competency to assessment

Skills and judgment development, regardless of the environment, is critical. CAHIIM's HIAC committee felt that this adaptation of Miller's Pyramid allowed for assessment of students in a more holistic manner. In terms of professional authenticity, the adapted model facilitates curriculum layering and building as well as successful transition for the learner from the classroom to practice in a dynamic nature with progressive development.

In terms of behavior and cognition, to allow for the variety of HI programs that might seek accreditation, "performance integrated into practice" was modified to "demonstration of independence" in which that independence can be demonstrated through a capstone project or application in practice such as an internship or other practice environment where the student has a preceptor.

Assessments

Assessments are the cornerstones of education and the final step in student learning and are frequently used to inform course or program improvement Fig. 17.4. illustrates the continuum across which the AMIA Foundational Domains are used to develop program competencies and inform course or program improvement. Formative assessments are used to provide feedback in the process of a teaching session, while summative assessments are used to provide feedback at the conclusion [19]. Miller's Pyramid as adapted for HI allows for a variety of assessments as

Table 17.1 Assessment examples and purposes as aligned to Miller's Pyramid Level

Miller's Pyramid Level	Assessment Example	Purpose
KNOWS—Fact gathering	Multiple choice questions, matching, discussion, discussion boards	Allows for recall and comprehension of previously learned material in one or a combination of knowledge areas, blend of objective and subjective and shows that the learner has the ability to grasp new knowledge
KNOWS HOW—Interpretation	Essay, short answer, presentation, situational judgment	Allows for using learned material to be applied in a variety of ways and shows that the learner has knowledge and knows how to use it appropriately, although the depth may vary by student
SHOWS—Demonstration of learning	Simulation, presentations, case analyses, situational judgment	Allows for demonstration of learning where the learner can show evidence of understanding based on using rules or drawing on similar experiences
DOES—Demonstration of independence	Capstone, case development, situational judgment, application in situ (internship, practicum, etc. under supervision of a preceptor)	Allows for demonstration with independence where the learner shows evidence of understanding based on their knowledge, insight, or intuition

well as multiple depths of assessments. As an example, students could use a presentation as a method of assessment for both Interpretation and Demonstration of Learning.

Miller's Pyramid, as adapted for HI, is new in the HI education space. To assist with operationalizing the pyramid, the CAHIIM HIAC has *suggested* types of assessments at each level. Table 17.1 provides assessment examples and their corresponding purpose, aligned to each level of Miller's Pyramid.

Just as programs assess the level of knowledge and skills of their graduates, it is imperative that those graduates have a minimum standard of ethical and attitudinal competence related to those skills [20–22]. Attitudes refer to decision-making, judgment, and professionalism. Attitudes carry the same level of importance in the world of HI as they do in the clinical environment, especially in areas of data use and management and privacy and security. While it is acknowledged that attitudes are difficult to assess with any degree of reliability [16], the HI profession must ensure that attention is paid to this third leg of competency development. Examples of methods to assess attitudes include situational judgment tests, simulations of varying complexity, a capstone project, or observations of performance in an in situ environment [23].

Accreditation Tools: CAHIIM Self-Evaluation Tool (CSET)

Assessment of the curriculum supporting the Foundational Domains plays a critical role in accreditation; accreditation tools were developed to help with that assessment. The goal in their development was to ensure that these tools were feasible to use for both the program and the accreditation team. It was imperative that there was tight alignment with the Foundational Domains as well as Miller's Pyramid as adapted for HI.

The CSET is a tool built upon a Microsoft Excel® platform that facilitates self-evaluation of program curricula. The CSET is a required component of preparing for accreditation and must be submitted in order to move forward in the process. Inputs into the CSET are courses, course learning objectives, educational activities, assessments, Foundational Domain and Miller's Pyramid level. The output is a density heat map showing the program's areas of concentration across the Foundational Domains, its areas of concentration at the various levels of Miller's Pyramid, and student expected competency relative to its component knowledge, skills, and attitudes. The density heat map can also be used by programs to ensure that the intended areas of concentration are being accomplished.

Lessons Learned

From the work accomplished by and between two organizations, AMIA and CAHIIM, several key lessons emerged. Such lessons could be helpful for other organizations embarking on a similar process.

LESSON ONE: Benefits Derived by Using a Deliberative Iterative Process

The foundational domains developed by the AAC were intended to represent the continuum of HI…a field that encompasses thousands of students, faculty, and practitioners. Creating a single set of domains that acknowledges the diversity of perspectives and appreciates the differences among the sub-disciplines in the field of HI requires a process that is carefully constructed and deployed. Those responsible for the process must be prepared to take the time to learn the important aspects of practices that support group decision-making, which include procedures like Nominal Group Technique [24], Delphi Method [24], or Deliberative Inquiry [12]. Each of these has been shown to be more effective in the process of group decisions than conventional committee practices.

LESSON TWO: Importance of Solid Working Relationships Among Organizations

Effective strategies that helped to promote the updating of both the foundational domains for the profession and the accreditation process (that included development of standards for graduate programs) included having a positive relationship between the accrediting body (in this case, CAHIIM) and the member organization

(AMIA). Committing both human and fiscal resources, CAHIIM and AMIA were able to create the foundational domains for HI curricula with accompanying examples of statements of competency (knowledge, skills, and attitudes) and were able to develop new accreditation standards and a new accreditation process to evaluate HI education at the master's degree level. In addition, they created a conceptual framework for assessing the level of mastery of competencies demonstrated by newly graduating health informaticians. This solid working relationship facilitated this work being accomplished within 3 years.

LESSON THREE: Value of Competency-Based Curricula

Unlike a content-based curriculum, a competency-based curriculum provides the flexibility needed to adapt the AMIA HI foundational domains and accompanying statements of knowledge, skills, and attitudes to a variety of HI sub-disciplines. A competency-based curriculum allows for increased adaptability and inclusion from the perspective of the accrediting body, since the accrediting body does not have to create curriculum requirements for each sub-discipline of HI seeking accreditation, which would be required for a content-based curriculum. Educational programs can develop competency levels based on those knowledge, skills, and attitudes needed by employers that hire their graduates.

LESSON FOUR: Need to Involve the "Right" People

AMIA established a member-sponsored accreditation committee (AAC) composed of educators and industry professionals representing many of AMIA's communities of interest. The AAC oversaw the development of the new foundational domains that were embedded in the CAHIIM Accreditation Standards. The AAC was committed and deadline focused. The diverse backgrounds and interests of its members and the engagement in a deliberative process ensured that a variety of voices and opinions were heard and considered. Committee members authored a paper and prepared presentations and other resources to share their ideas, outcomes and findings. The AAC members were available to answer questions and provided important training within the HI community about how to think about the HI foundational domains and the knowledge, skills, and attitudes.

The CAHIIM HIAC was composed of experienced graduate level HI educators and accreditation site visitors who actively engaged in developing the prototype of the competency model subsequently refined by the AAC. They also were engaged in developing tools to help in the assessment of program curricula that reflected the approved Foundational Domains. To assess whether a program is addressing each foundational domain, HIAC members designed the CSET that assists/facilitates self-evaluation by an HI program of its curriculum. The CSET was then piloted by several programs and underwent multiple iterations. The CSET is also used by CAHIIM site accreditation teams to assess the degree to which the HI program is addressing the competencies within each of the foundational domains. Completion of the CSET represents a new process for programs seeking accreditation. As such, HIAC members conducted numerous workshops, primarily at AMIA, to demonstrate completion of the CSET and interpretation of the CSET output (i.e. the heat map).Both committees were successful through its members' commitment of time, thought, and vigilance required to see these activities through to their successful conclusion.

LESSON FIVE: Significance of Consistent Message Delivery
At the CAHIIM accreditation workshop in 2017, AAC members introduced the Foundational Domains and described the relationship of those domains to accreditation. HIAC worked diligently to operationalize the AAC foundational domains with accompanying knowledge, skills, and attitudes into the CSET for the purposes of accreditation. It worked diligently to craft a communication plan ensuring a consistent and metered message over time, using presentations independently or with the AAC to promote awareness of HI master's degree accreditation, to answer questions, and to demonstrate the CSET. As programs were preparing for accreditation, HIAC needed to be sensitive to those programs already accredited that would attest to AMIA's foundational domains and CAHIIM's accreditation standards. Given that many programs may need to reposition curricula and engage in the process of approval through layers of university committees, the date for accreditation attestation for currently accredited programs was set for September 2021. In the meantime, HIAC members have presented at AMIA conferences and CAHIIM workshops to provide opportunities for questions and guidance on how to effectively and efficiently reposition existing curricula.

LESSON SIX: Transition from Content- to Competency-based Curricula is an Uneasy One
Ongoing education is required to assist program directors in designing and evaluating competency-based curricula. Issues such as how to write objectives, what kinds of assessment tools are available, and other concerns must be addressed. It is not clear what the best source is for such education. Since HI is a dynamic and maturing field and HI competencies are a work in progress, the foundational domains and examples of competencies should be reviewed, edited, and updated (if needed) on a consistent 3–5-year cycle to ensure continued viability, currency and job market relevance.

References

1. Commission on Accreditation for Health Informatics and Information Management: Commission on Accreditation for Health Informatics and Information Management. www.cahiim.org. Accessed November 18 2019.
2. Valenta AL, Berner ES, Boren SA, Deckard GJ, Eldredge C, Fridsma DB, Gadd C, Gong Y, Johnson T, Jones J. AMIA Board White Paper: AMIA 2017 core competencies for applied health informatics education at the master's degree level. J Am Med Informatics Assoc. 2018;25(12):1657–68.
3. Kulikowski CA, Shortliffe EH, Currie LM, Elkin PL, Hunter LE, Johnson TR, Kalet IJ, Lenert LA, Musen MA, Ozbolt JG. AMIA Board white paper: definition of biomedical informatics and specification of core competencies for graduate education in the discipline. J Am Med Informatics Assoc. 2012;19(6):931–8. https://doi.org/10.1136/amiajnl-2012-001053.
4. Gardner RM, Overhage JM, Steen EB, Munger BS, Holmes JH, Williamson JJ, Detmer DE, Directors, A.B.o. Core content for the subspecialty of clinical informatics. J Am Med Informatics Assoc. 2009;16(2):153–7. https://doi.org/10.1197/jamia.M3045.
5. Hersh W. A stimulus to define informatics and health information technology. BMC Med Inform Decis Mak. 2009;9(1):1. https://doi.org/10.1186/1472-6947-9-24.

6. Friedman CP. What informatics is and isn't. J Am Med Inform Assoc. 2013;20(2):224–6. https://doi.org/10.1136/amiajnl-2012-001206.
7. Mantas J, Ammenwerth E, Demiris G, Hasman A, Haux R, Hersh W, Hovenga E, Lun K, Marin H, Martin-Sanchez F. Recommendations of the International Medical Informatics Association (IMIA) on education in biomedical and health informatics. Methods Inf Med. 2010;49(02):105–20. https://doi.org/10.3414/ME5119.
8. National Center for Healthcare Leadership: NCHL Health Leadership Competency Model. http://www.nchl.org/static.asp?path=2852,3238.
9. Calhoun JG, Dollett L, Sinioris ME, Wainio JA, Butler PW, Griffith JR, Warden GL. Development of an interprofessional competency model for healthcare leadership. J Healthc Manag. 2008;53(6):375–89.
10. Valerius J, Mohan V, Doctor D, Hersh W. Collaboration leads to enhanced curriculum. Appl Clin Inform. 2015;6(01):200–9. https://doi.org/10.4338/ACI-2014-10-CR-0086.
11. Gibson C, Dixon B, Abrams K. Convergent evolution of health information management and health informatics. Appl Clin Inform. 2015;6(01):163–84.
12. Harris I. Deliberative inquiry: the arts of planning. In: Short E, editor. Forms of curriculum inquiry. Albany, NY: SUNY Press; 1991. p. 287–321.
13. Dreyfus H, Dreyfus SE, Athanasiou T. Mind over machine. New York: Simon and Schuster; 2000.
14. Benner P. From novice to expert. Menlo Park, CA: Addison-Wesley; 1984.
15. Benner P. The Dreyfus model of skill acquisition applied to nursing. In: Benner P, editor. From novice to expert. Menlo Park, CA: Addison-Wesley; 2001. p. 13–38.
16. Frank JR, Snell LS, Cate OT, Holmboe ES, Carraccio C, Swing SR, Harris P, Glasgow NJ, Campbell C, Dath D. Competency-based medical education: theory to practice. Med Teacher. 2010;32(8):638–45.
17. Miller GE. The assessment of clinical skills/competence/performance. Acad Med. 1990;65(9):S63–7.
18. Mehay R, Burns R. Miller's pyramid of clinical competence adapted by R. Mehay and R. Burns. In: Mehay R, editor. The essential handbook for GP training and education. London: Radcliffe Publishing; 2009. p. 414.
19. Scriven M. The methodology of evaluation. In: Tyler RW, Gagne RM, Scriven M, editors. Perspecitves on curriculum evaluation. Chicago, IL: Rand McNally; 1967. p. 39–83.
20. Wong J, Cheung E. Ethics assessment in medical students. Med Teach. 2003;25(1):5–8.
21. Shumway JM, Harden R. The assessment of learning outcomes for the competent and reflective physician. AMEE Guide No. 25. Med Teach. 2003;25(6):569–84.
22. Wass V, Barnard A. The assessment and professionalism of attitudes. In: A practical guide for medical teachers; 2017. p. 289.
23. Patterson F, Zibarras L, Ashworth V. Situational judgement tests in medical education and training: research, theory and practice: AMEE Guide No. 100. Med Teach. 2016;38(1):3–17.
24. McMillan SS, King M, Tully MP. How to use the nominal group and Delphi techniques. Int J Clin Pharm. 2016;38(3):655–62.

Part VI
Use of Distance Learning
for Informatics Education

Chapter 18
Online Continuing Education in Informatics: The AMIA 10 × 10 Experience

William Hersh

While the educational pathway for a career in informatics increasingly involves obtaining an academic degree or other formal training, there is also a need for education short of a full degree for a variety of audiences. While a variety of these educational experiences of lesser depth have been developed in recent years, one of the most visible efforts has been the 10 × 10 ("ten by ten") program of the American Medical Informatics Association (AMIA). This chapter will present an overview of the 10 × 10 program, provide a detailed description of the original and still most-attended course in the program offered by Oregon Health & Science University (OHSU), describe the history of the program, and review some data on its enrollment and acceptance.

Background of the 10 × 10 Program

The seed of the 10 × 10 program was planted in 2004 by then-President of AMIA Dr. Charles Safran, who had been assessing both the need for informaticians and the ability of informatics programs to increase their capacity. Dr. Safran began advocating that each of the nearly 6000 hospitals in the United States employ at least one physician and one nurse who had some formal training in informatics [1]. This led AMIA to undertake an analysis of what it might take to develop and market such training, leading to the realization that it would require resources that the organization did not have.

In the meantime, a number of academic informatics programs, including the one at OHSU led by this author, had started offering courses, certificates, and even

W. Hersh (✉)
Department of Medical Informatics and Clinical Epidemiology, Oregon Health and Science University, Portland, OR, USA
e-mail: hersh@ohsu.edu

© Springer Nature Switzerland AG 2020   251
E. S. Berner (ed.), *Informatics Education in Healthcare*, Health Informatics,
https://doi.org/10.1007/978-3-030-53813-2_18

degrees via distance learning. The program at OHSU made its first foray into distance learning in 1999, when we received repeated queries as to whether our courses could be taken online. The first course we converted to an online format was the introductory course taken by all students in the clinical informatics track of our biomedical informatics graduate program [2]. This course, entitled *Introduction to Biomedical Informatics*, broadly surveyed the field for those who planned to pursue further study in the field as well as those who just wanted an in-depth overview. The online course was a one-quarter academic course that made use of voice-over-PowerPoint narrated lectures (two–three hours per unit, broken down into 15–25 min segments), reading assignments, threaded discussion forums, and multiple-choice homework quizzes.

Dr. Safran queried informatics educational programs as to how much they could increase their capacity if demand warranted. While most programs felt they could achieve a two to threefold increase in capacity, this author, noting the scalability of distance learning, replied that given enough lead time to hire sufficient faculty and support staff, expansion could be literally unlimited. On a whim, he told Dr. Safran that he was confident of meeting his goal of having the capacity to train one physician and one nurse in each U.S. hospital by the end of the decade (2010). This led the author to suggest the title of the program as "10 × 10", with the goal of training 10,000 individuals in informatics by the year 2010. AMIA and OHSU collaborated on a pilot course for what would become the AMIA 10 × 10 program.

Because the OHSU course already existed, it was relatively straightforward to re-purpose it for 10 × 10. Essentially the same curricular materials as the OHSU graduate course were used, with some modification of the first part of the first unit's lecture. It was also decided to culminate the course with an in-person session that would take place at various AMIA symposia. This would also allow the students to further enhance their learning with scientific presentations and, in the case of the annual fall symposium, avail themselves of one to two tutorials.

The course would be offered as a continuing education course, with continuing medical education (CME) credits offered that AMIA was accredited to provide. Because it was a continuing education course, the final examination of the graduate course was not required. However, since some taking the course might wish to continue on to further study in informatics, it was decided to offer the final exam optionally, and award OHSU graduate credit to those who scored a grade of B or better. This would enable those desiring further study in the field to easily continue at OHSU or any other program that would give credit for completing the course. (Another reason for some to take the optional final exam was that tuition reimbursement, usually from an employer, required students to have an official transcript with a letter grade.)

The discussion to implement the course began in early 2005, with the course announced in the late spring and starting in July. A total of 51 individuals started the first course, with 44 completing it and most attending the AMIA 2005 Annual Symposium [3]. All 17 individuals who took the final exam scored a grade of B or better. The success of the first offering led to planning for additional offerings, with a second course offered in early 2006 that would end around the time of the AMIA Spring Congress, which, at that time, was the name of the AMIA spring meeting. In 2006, AMIA began enlisting other universities to partner with them on 10 × 10 courses.

The original course and still the one with the largest enrollment has been the course offered by OHSU. This course has a broad focus on biomedical and health informatics, with a sub-focus on clinical (i.e., healthcare) informatics. Two other general courses that have had the largest enrollment after OHSU, have been those offered by the University of Alabama at Birmingham (UAB) and the University of Illinois at Chicago (UIC). While the same general content is covered in all three of the courses, there is more of a management emphasis in the UAB courses and more of a patient safety focus in the UIC 10 × 10.

Additional 10 × 10 courses have been developed in more specialized areas of the field by other universities, including the following:

- Clinical decision support—University of Utah
- Clinical research informatics—Ohio State University
- Data standards—Duke University
- Healthcare interface design—University of Texas Houston Health Sciences Center
- Information exchange for population health—Indiana University
- Pharmacogenomics—Stanford University
- Terminologies and standards—University of Utah

These courses have had smaller enrollment than the general overview courses, but serve a vital niche for certain audiences. Some additional general offerings have been offered by Nova Southeastern University School of Osteopathic Medicine, the University of Kansas Medical Center, and the University of Minnesota.

Audiences

Who would be an audience for informatics education short of a full degree that is comparable to an introductory graduate-level course? One audience is those who have worked in the field for a long time but never had any formal training. While a full educational program might serve them better, a single overview course like 10 × 10 may be all for which they have time. Another audience is someone who has informatics-related work in their career but is not predominantly an informatician. This might include those who are clinical champions (i.e., have involvement in IT implementation in their clinical settings) or researchers whose study includes informatics interventions. An additional audience for a single course is someone who wants to "test the waters" with a single course before committing to an entire program of study. All of these types of individuals have been present in 10 × 10 courses. A final audience would be someone who was newly appointed to a signficiant informatics role in an organization, yet may have little formal training.

OHSU Course

To give a sense of the content and learning experience of the 10 × 10 program, we will present an overview of the OHSU course. The other general courses have somewhat similar curricula, while the more specialized courses are focused in specific areas. All of the courses are completely online, with the exception of the one-half to 1 day in-person session at the end of the course.

The OHSU 10 × 10 course, as well as many of the other 10 × 10 courses, is offered in two parts. The first part is a 10-unit Web-based component that is provided through readings, voice-over-PowerPoint lectures, interactive discussion, and self-assessment tests. The second part is an intensive one-day in-person session that brings attendees together to integrate the material, allow presentation of course projects, and meet leaders in the field as well as other students. This session takes place at one of the annual AMIA conferences, which also facilitates students attending a national professional informatics meeting. The content of the course has changed over the 15 years of its offering, reflecting new areas to emerge in informatics, such as health information exchange, the meaningful use program, and data science/machine learning. Table 18.1 shows the curriculum outline of the current OHSU offering.

As noted previously, the OHSU 10 × 10 course is an adaptation of its online *Introduction to Biomedical and Health Informatics* class currently taught in the OHSU biomedical informatics education program.[1] The 10 × 10 course provides a broad overview of the field, highlighting the key issues and challenges for the field. The course is taught in a completely asynchronous manner, i.e., there are no "scheduled" classes and there is no scheduled time that a student must be online. However, students must keep up with the course materials so they can benefit from the interactive discussion with faculty and other students. Other 10 × 10 programs have also adapted existing introductory graduate courses to meet the needs of the 10 × 10 students. The course uses the following teaching modalities:

- Voice-over-PowerPoint lectures—These are delivered in three possible modes (all freely available): Adobe Flash, HTML 5, and a special iPad viewer from Articulate, Inc. A screen shot of a lecture is shown in Fig. 18.1.
- Interactive threaded discussion—Students engage in interactive discussion on important issues using online discussion forums.
- Reading assignments—The course makes optional reading assignments from a general textbook for the field [4].
- Homework/quizzes—Each of the units is accompanied by a ten-question multiple-choice self-assessment that aims to have the student apply the knowledge from the unit.

The online part of the course is accessed via a learning management system. Students are expected to keep up with the materials each week and participate in

---

[1] http://www.ohsu.edu/informatics

Table 18.1 Curriculum outline of the Oregon Health & Science University (OHSU) 10 × 10 Course

1. Overview of Field and Problems Motivating It
1.1 What is Biomedical and Health Informatics?
1.2 A Short History of Biomedical and Health Informatics
1.3 Problems in Healthcare Motivating Biomedical and Health Informatics
1.4 Who Does Biomedical and Health Informatics?
1.5 Resources for Field—Organizations, Information, Education
2. Biomedical Computing
2.1 Types of Computers
2.2 Data Storage in Computers
2.3 Computer Hardware and Software
2.4 Computer Networks
2.5 Software Engineering
3. Electronic and Personal Health Records (EHR, PHR)
3.1 Clinical Data
3.2 History and Perspective of the Health (Medical) Record
3.3 Definitions and Key Attributes of the EHR
3.4 Benefits and Challenges of the EHR
3.5 EHR Examples
3.6 Personal Health Records
4. Standards and Interoperability
4.1 Standards and Interoperability: Basic Concepts
4.2 Identifier and Transaction Standards
4.3 Message Exchange Standards
4.4 Terminology Standards
4.5 SMART on FHIR
5. Advancing Care With the EHR
5.1 Patient Safety and Medical Errors
5.2 Clinical Decision Support (CDS)
5.3 Healthcare Quality Measurement and Improvement
5.4 Health Information Exchange (HIE)
5.5 From Meaningful Use to Promoting Interoperability
6. Data Science and Analytics
6.1 Data Science and Data Analytics
6.2 Machine Learning and Artificial Intelligence
6.3 Natural Language Processing
6.4 Evidence-Based Medicine
6.5 Clinical Practice Guidelines
7. EHR Implementation, Security, and Evaluation
7.1 Clinical Workflow Analysis and Redesign
7.2 EHR System Selection and Implementation
7.3 Telemedicine and Telehealth
7.4 Privacy and Security
7.5 Evaluation of the EHR

(continued)

Table 18.1 (continued)

8. Information Retrieval (Search)
8.1 Information Retrieval
8.2 Knowledge-based Information
8.3 Content
8.4 Indexing
8.5 Retrieval
8.6 Research: Evaluation and Future Directions
9. Research Informatics
9.1 Overview of Biomedical Research
9.2 Clinical Research Informatics
9.3 Overview of Basic Molecular Biology9.4 Translational Bioinformatics
9.5 From Clinical Genetics and Genomics to Precision Medicine
9.6 Genomics Data in the EHR and Other Information Systems
10. Other Areas of Informatics
10.1 Imaging Informatics
10.2 Nursing Informatics
10.3 Consumer Health Informatics
10.4 Public Health Informatics
10.5 Population Health

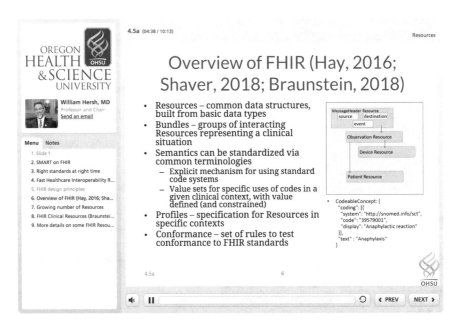

Fig. 18.1 Screen shot of narrated lecture

ongoing discussion. They are instructed to anticipate spending four to eight hours per unit on the course. All online activities are asynchronous, so there is no specified time that a student must be online.

The course also requires a project. In the OHSU course, students identify an informatics problem in their local setting (e.g., where they practice or work) and propose a solution based on what is known from informatics research and best practice. In other 10 × 10 programs, project topics may be assigned or students can pick a topic of their choosing. The project must be submitted before the in-person session at the end of the course. If a student does not have access to a healthcare setting, they can do the project in another setting, such as a company or organization. The details of the assignment include:

- Assess some local setting (work environment, practice, hospital, etc.) to identify an informatics-related problem or a problem that could be improved by an informatics solution.
- Using the knowledge of research and best practices in informatics acquired in the course, propose a solution to the problem.
- The problem and solution are written into a two to three page document that should include references that justify the framing of the problem and the proposed solutions.
- The problem and solution are also presented at the in-person session.

Over 95% of those who have chosen to take the OHSU introductory course final examination have received a grade of B or higher and received graduate credit for the course. Those who do not want graduate credit do not take the exam and they just receive continuing education credit. Other 10 × 10 programs have similar mechanisms to allow students to exempt from the introductory graduate course at the specific site, even if the program does not provide graduate credit for the course.

Other 10 × 10 offerings use variations on this theme. Some have a few synchronous sessions for special lectures or demonstrations, student presentations or other reasons. Some use team exercises where students collaborate virtually to address a real or simulated informatics problem that allows them to apply the concepts taught in the class.

Growth of the 10 × 10 Program

OHSU has partnered with other organizations to offer the course whose ending would coincide with different meetings and, as such, attract different audiences. The first partnering organization was the California Healthcare Foundation, with this offering starting in the fall of 2005 and having its in-person session at CHCF headquarters in Oakland, CA in early 2006. This led to a succession of joint offerings with professional societies and other organizations, including the American College of Physicians, the Scottsdale Institute, the Society for Technology in Anesthesiology, the American College of Emergency Physicians, and the Academy of Nutrition and

Dietetics. All of these offerings had their culminating in-person sessions at their professional meetings, with the exception of the partnering with the Scottsdale Institute, which culminated at an AMIA meeting. The partnerships with the American College of Emergency Physicians, and the Academy of Nutrition and Dietetics have been and continue to be sustained over multiple years, mainly due to involvement of informaticians from those organizations.

The course has also been exported to international settings, with courses outside the U.S. dubbed as "i10 × 10" courses. All but one of the i10 × 10 offerings had their origins with the OHSU course. The original partner in the i10 × 10 program was the Hospital Italiano of Buenos Aires (HIBA) in Argentina. A HIBA faculty member was a student in the very first OHSU offering, and she put together a team to translate the OHSU version into Spanish. While the first offering was a near-direct translation, the course has since evolved in content to provide a more Latin American perspective [5].

The second i10 × 10 course to be offered was in partnership with Gateway Consulting of Singapore, consisting of the OHSU online portion of the course interdigitated with four in-person tutorials in Singapore. While most students enrolled in the Singapore offerings have been from that country, a variety of others from nearby countries in Southeast Asia have enrolled. A small amount of content specific to informatics in Singapore has been developed by OHSU for the course. A third i10 × 10 was created de novo by the Hong Kong Hospital Authority and offered to residents of Hong Kong. Offerings of the OHSU online with in-person sessions in home countries have been carried out in Saudi Arabia, Israel, and the United Arab Emirates. Some of these international offerings are also discussed in Part IV of this book.

Evaluation

The 10 × 10 program has been evaluated in a number of ways. One simple but illustrative evaluation is to note the total enrollment in the program, which has continued beyond 2010. While the program did not achieve its tag-line goal of 10,000 trained by 2010, a total of 1257 completed a U.S. course by the end of 2010, with 999 coming from the OHSU offerings. (Since there was continued interest in the program at the end of the 2010, the tag line was changed to "10,000 trained in 10 years."). By the end of 2019, a total of 3336 people had completed a U.S.-based course, with the distribution among the courses shown in Fig. 18.2. During that same time, a total of 1023 people had completed i10 × 10 courses, with the distributions shown in Table 18.2. That table also describes the courses used in those countries and if they were adapted from other courses.

The first formal evaluation of the course was done after the initial offering in 2005 [3]. A total of 44 of the 51 students completed the evaluation. In general, their satisfaction was very high, with 12 of 13 measures of course and instructor satisfaction rating above 4.0 on a 1 (low) to 5 (high) scale, and the final measure of the

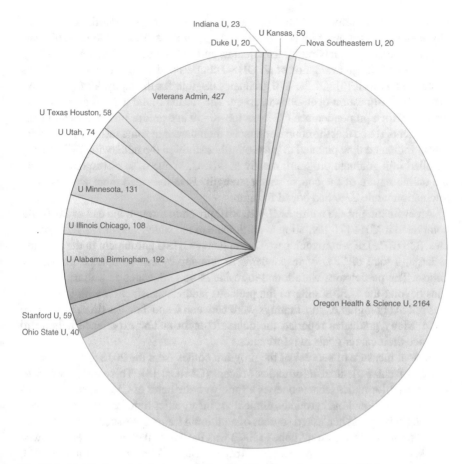

Fig. 18.2 Distribution of students completing 10 × 10 courses from 2005 to 2019

Table 18.2 Distribution of students completing i10 × 10 courses from 2005 to 2019

Country	Students completing courses	Course origins
Argentina	454	Adapted from early OHSU course
Hong Kong	123	De novo course
Israel	11	Use of OHSU course
Saudi Arabia	94	Use of OHSU course with local additions
Singapore	287	Use of OHSU course with localized additions by OHSU
United Arab Emirates	54	Use of OHSU course

in-person session rating at 3.86. The largest occupational group in the course was physicians (24), followed by IT professionals (7), nurses (5), and 1–2 each of pharmacists, statisticians, laboratory technicians, and health information managers.

A more thorough evaluation of all OHSU courses to date by the end of 2007 was completed as well [6]. Of the 170 graduates eligible for the study, 79 (47%) completed the 24-question open-ended survey. The results found a 2:1 ratio of men to women, with a preponderance (72%) in the 40–59 age group. Just under half of the respondents stated that the course enhanced their career in some fashion. A majority (66%) indicated they planned to pursue further study in the field, with 23% already enrolled in a graduate program, mostly at OHSU. While 67% of respondents said the online nature of the course was a strength, 14% indicated there was too little interaction while 27% had hoped for more.

An evaluation of the entire AMIA 10 × 10 program through the end of 2010 was completed in 2011 [7]. Invitation to participate in the study was sent to 1204 graduates, 328 (27%) of whom took part. Due to heavy OHSU enrollment in the program at large, a total of 78% of respondents to this survey had completed the OHSU course. The participants were found to reside in 45 U.S. states as well as 13 countries beyond the U.S. Similar to the previous studies, satisfaction with the course was relatively high, i.e., most ratings were between 4 and 5 on a 1 (low) to 5 (high) scale. Many graduates reported the course content and/or experience helping to advance their career goals in informatics.

A final measure of success of the program comes from the 2012 annual Gartner survey of chief medical informatics officers (CMIOs) [8]. This annual report of physician informatics leaders queries a variety of attributes of CMIOs, such as clinical and educational backgrounds, clinical vs. informatics time, salaries, and reporting relationships. When asked sources of additional training pursued by CMIOs, the most common answer after "none" (30%) was the 10 × 10 course (19%), followed by Master of Business Administration (16%), master's degree in informatics (10%), and Master of Public Health (7%).

Lessons Learned

The OHSU 10 × 10 experience found that enrolled students are every bit as engaged in the course as those in the regular graduate program at OHSU. One challenge is that many are currently employed in busy clinical or informatics jobs, making the time commitment difficult. This is a challenge that other 10 × 10 and other continuing education programs face when there is a significant amount of material and the audience members are engaged in full-time employment. The decision at OHSU was made to de-compress the course with a pattern of two weeks of materials posted followed by a free week of no new materials posted. The University of Alabama at Birmingham course moved to monthly, rather than weekly modules, which provided more flexibility for students. However, some students still fall behind, and those who fall too far behind are usually not able to get caught up to finish the course in time.

Those students who do work in informatics positions have commented that they find that the course materials are highly practical and often applicable to their jobs. Whether previously exposed to the field or not, almost all students appreciate both the "big picture" of the field presented as well as an introduction to its language. (This author has always found it ironic that many who work in informatics have little formal training, and often seek training in 10 × 10 or even full graduate programs to learn material that one might believe would be required before taking such positions in the first place!)

Another challenge in teaching the course is the diverse backgrounds and careers of those enrolled in the course (a problem probably inherent to all informatics education). From physicians and nurses to administrators and IT personnel, it is a challenge to make the materials pertinent and challenging to such a diverse group of students. This is partially overcome through the discussion forums, where complementary backgrounds are valued and efforts are made to engage everyone. Chapter 19 discusses other challenges of online education and strategies for managing them.

Conclusions and Future Directions

The 10 × 10 course has provided a valuable educational experience for those desiring to obtain informatics education short of a certificate or degree program. While not a substitute for such programs, the course has allowed a variety of types of individuals to advance their careers in the field. By being part of larger programs, however, the course has also served as a stepping stone to more education. Although demand for the course continues to justify its offering, it will be interesting to see how it evolves as the field itself continues to grow and change.

Key Take-Away Points

- There is an important role for continuing education programs in informatics, especially for students for whom a formal graduate program is not feasible.
- The use of asynchronous and online learning is an effective means to provide such education.
- If the program is based on a graduate educational program, some adaptations have to be made to accommodate the needs of the full-time employed student.
- Courses short of full certificate or degree programs, like the 10 × 10 program, provide a substantial overview as well as entry point to further study in the field.
- Courses such as 10 × 10 can bring attendees to academic informatics and related conferences to also further their education and perspective.

References

1. Safran C, Reactor Panel - Unifying the Industry. Secretarial summit on health information technology launching the national health information infrastructure 2004. Washington, DC: Cornerstones for Electronic Healthcare; 2004.
2. Hersh W, et al. Implementation and evaluation of a medical informatics distance education program. J Am Med Inform Assoc. 2001;8:570–84.
3. Hersh W, Williamson J. Educating 10,000 informaticians by 2010: the AMIA 10×10 program. Int J Med Inform. 2007;76:377–82.
4. Hoyt R, Hersh W, editors. Health informatics: practical guide. 7th ed. Pensacola, FL: Lulu.com; 2018.
5. Otero P, et al. A medical informatics distance-learning course for Latin America - translation, implementation and evaluation. Methods Inf Med. 2010;49:310–5.
6. Feldman S, Hersh W. Evaluating the AMIA-OHSU 10x10 program to train healthcare professionals in medical informatics. In: AMIA Annual Symposium Proceedings. Washington, DC: American Medical Informatics Association; 2008.
7. Williamson J. Evaluation of AMIA 10x10 continuing education initiative. In: Curry School of Education. Charlottesville, VA: University of Virgina; 2011.
8. Shaffer V. 10th Annual AMDIS-Gartner Survey of CMIOs. Stamford, CT: Gartner; 2012.

Chapter 19
Managing Unspoken Assumptions in Online Education

Lorrinda Khan, Michael G. Dieter, Eta S. Berner, and Annette L. Valenta

The explosion nationally in popularity of online education carries with it significant implications—both obvious and not so obvious—for students and instructors alike. New technologies, continually emerging, carry with them the promise of new and improved experiences for the individual users, but often carry with them new challenges. In this chapter, frequently overlooked challenges in asynchronous online education will be explored. In asynchronous education, lessons (e.g., lectures, reading materials, discussion questions, other assignments) are posted online and students respond to the lessons on their own schedule, usually over a defined time period for each lesson. This differs from synchronous online education in which both instructors and students are online together at the same time. In asynchronous online education, the most frequent means of communication surrounding the instructional content among students and instructor(s) is via a discussion board or email.

While significant literature exists on new technologies and online pedagogical techniques, which includes some publishing houses having a division whose sole focus is online education, there has been little written on how instructor and student assumptions and expectations can derail what, in theory, should be an exciting

L. Khan
University of Maryland University College, University of Maryland Global Campus, Adelphi, MD, USA

M. G. Dieter · A. L. Valenta
Department of Biomedical and Health Information Sciences, University of Illinois at Chicago, Chicago, IL, USA
e-mail: valenta@uic.edu

E. S. Berner (✉)
Department of Health Services Administration, University of Alabama at Birmingham, Birmingham, AL, USA

Department of Medical Education, University of Alabama at Birmingham, Birmingham, AL, USA
e-mail: eberner@uab.edu

© Springer Nature Switzerland AG 2020
E. S. Berner (ed.), *Informatics Education in Healthcare*, Health Informatics, https://doi.org/10.1007/978-3-030-53813-2_19

technologically enhanced learning environment. This chapter will identify some of those assumptions, describe their impact, and suggest ways that they can be addressed. The ideas and strategies were developed based on the authors' experience over 15 years in online informatics education, and apply to a variety of online educational activities.

Historically, asynchronous learning (ASL) environments share a number of common attributes with their antecedents, traditional face-to-face classrooms. Both are loci where learning potential is impacted by a range of issues originating from unspoken assumptions at a number of levels. These issues include institutional (universities, colleges, departments, and programs), curricular, and coursework. In ASL environments, where distance in time and space alone may create barriers to communication between instructors and students, the issue of unspoken assumptions in courses has immediate relevance to fulfilling learning potential. Instructors and students bring assumptions into learning environments, both face-to-face and online, that create expectations for performance as teachers and learners. These expectations are formed from years of experience in face-to-face education and from more recent, but potent, experience related to daily use of technology, particularly exacerbated by the upsurge in mobile technologies that changes the information delivery paradigm for today's students.

These spoken and unspoken assumptions are transformed into explicit and implicit expectations that frame perceptions of value. Unspoken assumptions create potential ambiguities of meaning and intention. For courses to be meaningful learning experiences, instructors' and students' expectations must be aligned, i.e., there must be mutual understanding and agreement between both parties for learning to proceed optimally. In order for potential ambiguities in meanings and intentions to be resolved into expectations, it is necessary for unspoken assumptions to be articulated explicitly. Assumptions swirl among the lack of defined class hours in asynchronous instruction, the differences in how students and instructors spend their time in online and face-to-face classroom settings, the assumptions that strategies effective in face-to-face instruction will work in an online environment, and the expectations fostered by features of the technology itself. In a face-to-face classroom, these unspoken, often unconscious, assumptions and expectations are resolved through informal communications, which are not possible in the asynchronous online mode.

Issues Related to Flexible Class Hours

Instructors Anticipate Students Understand That Faculty Have Other Responsibilities in Addition to Teaching

Many students, even in face-to-face settings, do not realize that faculty members' academic and personal responsibilities are broader than their interaction with the students in one particular class. There are cues for students in a face-to-face setting that are impossible for students to recognize in an online environment. In fact, often there are cues in the online setting that convey just the opposite message, i.e., that faculty are available immediately on a 24/7 basis—24 h a day, 7 days a week.

In a face-to-face setting, students usually know they are to make an appointment to see the faculty member and that, in many settings, faculty are often either not in their office or are clearly engaged in doing other things, e.g., research or service responsibilities. Of course, students can, and do, drop by to talk to faculty, but are unlikely to do so if the faculty member is obviously preoccupied. Office hours tell students that the instructor is available to the students outside of class during defined times only, and students usually do not expect to find instructors in their classroom after normal business hours. Students in a brick-and-mortar setting can often find out easily if the faculty member is out of town. Also, the opportunity for informal conversation with faculty, before or after class, will often support communication of this information.

In the online setting, however, students communicate primarily by email, which can set up an expectation of an instant reply and an impression on the part of the student of continual instructor availability. This expectation is reinforced when faculty reply to students throughout their standard workday and, often, during evening hours. It is true that faculty also hold assumptions about student availability. Online faculty may attempt to make daytime student assignment deadlines to accommodate their own availability, or because faculty are used to teaching students whose "full-time job" is being a student. Interestingly, that typically results in a negative student response, as many online students work full-time during the day and "learn" at night.

This expectation of constant availability is not reasonable and must be negotiated overtly among faculty and online students. One way to counteract these expectations is to state clearly what the students can reasonably expect in terms of an instructor response. Clearly communicating to students when the instructor plans to travel, attend other professional events, or take time off can help to reduce confusion about when the students may expect a response. This will also convey some of the "additional responsibilities" that the instructor has. By reducing the 'unknown' element of the instructor-student electronic interaction, the instructor can effectively reduce student anxiety. Other approaches are to be clear at the start of the course that there may be delays in responding to email and to confine, intentionally, responses to students or posting in discussion groups to reasonable working hours.

Faculty Expect Online Students to Be Understanding When They Are Delayed with Grading or Other Responses to Students

In the face-to-face setting such delays often occur, and students will inquire about the status of grades or assignments, but will rarely complain. Faculty may not realize, however, that in face-to-face settings they update students informally, e.g., before starting class, they may say they are halfway through grading the papers, or that they are going out of town next the next week to a conference, etc. Similarly, students may use those informal interactions to inquire about the status of the grading if the teacher does not spontaneously say anything. This type of informal communication is unlikely to occur online, because, generally, it is not specifically planned. In the online setting, queries have to be planned as an online post or email, and students may be reluctant to take that step. While some students will freely email and ask their instructor for information, others will hesitate to express their anxiety in an email or in a public post.

In an online course, therefore, faculty must take the initiative to update students as to the status of faculty-to-student feedback. To do otherwise puts faculty at risk because technology platforms foster an expectation of instant communication, and students have high expectations for promptness. Faculty must recognize that these expectations exist and must be explicit about when students can expect responses, and if there are delays, to remember to update the students. Even if the faculty member is uncomfortable as to the cause of the delay (students should not be late, why is the faculty member?), a light-hearted apology and update is preferable to creating festering resentment or anxiety.

Issues Related to Faculty and Student Time in Online Instruction

Faculty Assume That the Amount of Time It Takes for Them to Give an Online Lecture Is the Amount of Time the Student Spends Listening to It

In the face-to-face classroom or in a synchronous online lecture, this assumption is certainly true. Experienced instructors usually can estimate how much material can be covered in a given amount of class time and prepare their lectures accordingly, recognizing that in a face-to-face (or synchronous online) setting, such presentations are often punctuated by questions, jokes, presenters diverging from topic, planned or unplanned discussion, etc.

In an asynchronous narrated online lecture, many of these distractions are not present, and a good asynchronous online presentation will usually take half to a third of the time to deliver compared to an equivalent lecture for a face-to-face class. This difference in delivery time can lead the instructor to prepare presentations that are too dense or too long. Ironically, it is the distractions in the face-to-face setting that make it tolerable for students to participate in an hour-long class period. It is much more difficult to maintain attention sitting at their home computer for that same period of time. Additionally, in a face-to-face setting, students who do not understand all of the material or who have trouble getting everything down in their notes may briefly ask the teacher for clarification after or during class. More often, they will just "make do" with incomplete understanding or will seek clarification from others after class.

In an asynchronous online mode, in part because the technology allows it and also because there are less likely to be other students available for clarification, the student may listen repeatedly to the lecture. This combination (too long or too 'dense' online presentations, listened to multiple times) can make the material very burdensome for the student and lead to resentment of, and difficulty managing, the amount of time the class takes.

Faculty must realize that their delivery time for an online presentation will be considerably shorter than the time the student will spend initially listening to it, but that students also may listen to it multiple times. Faculty should adjust the presentation content accordingly. It is good practice to break up a longer lecture into shorter segments—each no longer than 20 minutes—to give the students an opportunity to more feasibly manage content viewing.

Faculty Assume That the Main Difference in an Online Discussion and One in Class Is That One Is Written and the Other Is Spoken

In the online setting, students often write much more than they would say in person. In fact, in person, a good instructor would control the discussion to avoid domination by individuals, but the instructor cannot easily stop a student who writes a great deal in an asynchronous online discussion thread. Since students are no longer limited to the scheduled course meeting as their only opportunity to participate in discussion, lengthy responses do not carry the negative connotation of allowing one student to speak at the expense of another student's opportunity to participate. Instead, in an asynchronous online class, all students have an equal opportunity to share their ideas. While some of these longer responses are merely long-winded, the online environment actually provides an opportunity for longer and more thoughtful responses, and instructors are often impressed at the quality of their students' discussion. It is not unheard of, however, to set a word limit to discussion in order to foster critical thinking and a concise writing style.

In a face-to-face setting, students may assume that unless called upon, they need not say anything. In an online setting, instructors often expect all students to participate. In a face-to-face setting, some students may not participate or the responses may be briefer or less thoughtful. Thus, there may actually be a less rich discussion in the face-to-face than in the online mode. While lively discussion is one strength of online courses, this can also lead to a greater amount of time spent on the students' part (sometimes just to read the posts) than either the student or faculty anticipated. Especially with conscientious students, if the instructor combines dense lectures with overwhelming discussion, the students will feel inundated, resentful, or may eventually cut back on their efforts.

Online educators should recognize that the time commitment for discussions may be extensive and should structure the lecture and discussion workload appropriately, so that the grading reflects the effort and the time expectations are in keeping with the goals of the discussion assignment. Another approach is to limit intentionally the extent of discussion by putting word limits or limiting the number of responses each student can make; however, this approach may make the discussion less robust.

In addition to the time spent in discussion being more extensive in an online environment, it may become less focused, in part because students may use the discussion forum for non-relevant discussions to establish a connection to their fellow students. In the face-to-face setting, both students and faculty assume that such discussions will take place primarily outside the classroom. There is no "after class" in online learning environments and if this type of discussion spills over into the class assignments, it will make the discourse even more difficult for students to navigate. Setting rules to exclude off-topic discussions diminishes the potential for building rapport and student satisfaction. Instructors can set up an optional discussion board reserved for off-topic conversations that do not directly relate to class assignments. In the experience of the authors, not only do these optional discussion boards allow students to share life event experiences, they also have included examples of students helping each other with informatics challenges in the work environment. Also, they often have involved very substantive discussion of current issues in informatics that were not anticipated by the faculty when the formal assignments were planned.

Issues Related to Lack of Transfer of Effective Face-to-Face Strategies to the Online Environment

Instructors Assume That Students Will Let the Teacher Know if They Are Confused

It must never be assumed, in live or online settings, that all students will admit ignorance or actively confront the faculty if lecture material or assignment expectations are unclear. Most students are unlikely to do so explicitly; however, in live settings, good instructors will notice confused (or bored) looks on the students' faces or other body language and will adapt their presentations accordingly. Self-assessment exercises (such as lessons learned or journal assignments) or frequent quizzes can address this to some extent online, but these are not in the "real time" of body language feedback to the instructor. In the absence of this feedback, instructors may erroneously assume all is well.

Similarly, to cement their own learning, some students may need other students to immediately (and informally) validate their understanding. Students may not be aware of this need, or may not want to express it, but they may miss that real-time contact in asynchronous learning settings.

One approach is to provide an asynchronous discussion board entitled "Problems/questions/solutions" or "Ask the Instructor" (for questions directly to the instructor rather than fellow students). Another way to address the problem is to provide opportunities for informal synchronous interactions among students or between students and instructors. In a larger class, the instructor may choose to organize group work by time zone, thereby allowing multiple opportunities for smaller groups to interact in a synchronous activity. Given that required synchronous sessions are often burdensome for students in different time zones or with extensive work responsibilities, these sessions may be best made optional.

When conducting an optional, synchronous activity, it is important to facilitate the work in a manner that is conducive to an understanding among the students that their classmates may have other obligations that prohibit their participation in the synchronous event. Here too, frequent communication regarding the instructor's expectations for the student's participation can reduce the amount of conflict between group members or students who have anxiety about group work. By providing the opportunities to interact in real time, those students who have the need for feedback and interaction will take advantage of the opportunities.

Instructors Assume That Feedback to Students on Online Assignments Can Be Done in a Way Similar to Feedback in Face-to-Face Settings

Two of the main opportunities in asynchronous learning environments for formal contact between faculty and students are instructor qualitative feedback on tests or assignments and instructor comments in the class discussions. Faculty vary in how much feedback they usually provide to students, and students differ in how important detailed feedback is to them.

In addition to the need for online instructors' unspoken assumptions to be articulated as explicit expectations for students, a similar need exists for instructors to understand student expectations. Moore and Kearsley discuss student expectations about assessment. They identify the following implicit expectations students have about assessment (Moore and Kearsley [1], page 130):

- Fair and objective grading;
- Having their work treated with respect;
- An explanation and justification of the grade awarded;
- Qualitative as well as quantitative feedback on graded assignments; and
- A clear indication of how they can improve both in terms of specific responses to questions and in general.

In this respect, instructors' grading policies and grading scales are embedded in course structure in the form of syllabi and grading rubrics. In order to align student/instructor expectations, articulating online learning expectations generically must be complemented by dialogue to achieve personal contextual relevance. Students must understand the expectations; faculty must provide personal feedback promoting that understanding and clarifying how to improve future performance in the course.

There are other differences in the kind of feedback delivered in synchronous and asynchronous classes. Faculty who teach in a face-to-face setting will often give the class feedback on problem areas that were common to the class. This kind of informal commentary can clarify any questions that shy students may have about their performance on an assignment. In an online setting, grading is often completed using the assignment or gradebook tool in the learning management system or course shell. This tool allows for good one-way communication between an instructor and an individual student, but lacks the advantage of sharing overall comments to a class during a synchronous session. One solution that the online educator may implement is to post summary discussion posts and comments that address and guide the entire class in their thinking about the assignments.

Feedback in the online setting actually serves multiple functions; for example, feedback on a test may serve not just to provide information on the students' strengths and areas for improvement, but as a way of establishing personal communication with the individual student. In a face-to-face setting, students may not express their appreciation for extensive feedback or explicitly complain about its absence. In a face-to-face setting, students who particularly need instructor contact will seek it out through informal chats before or during class or by stopping by the faculty member's office informally. These informal feedback opportunities, which do not warrant a formal appointment for discussion, are not available online. To the online learner, minimal feedback may be taken as less instructor personal interest in them, and some students may find this insufficient for their learning needs. Given that the need for informal contact may not be fully realized online, students may look for a substitute through opportunities for formal individualized contact as part of online instruction. It may be that students feel not the loss of detailed feedback on an assignment, but rather the need for more informal contact with the instructor.

Need for Informal Contact Between Students and Faculty   Interestingly, the informal contact in face-to-face classrooms, although usually occurring outside of formal instruction time, is generally confined to the location and time of the class. Unlike office hours, which require a planned visit, the informal contact happens spontaneously. Although conducted in a public setting, the student-faculty interaction is usually a private conversation. This scenario does not transfer to an asynchronous online class unless educators use instant messaging or texting or other types of private chats to serve a similar function. Unless it is during a defined time, however, such messaging and texting could also reinforce the assumption by students of constant access to the instructor. Furthermore, a defined time (like online office hours) may make multiple private chats difficult to handle simultaneously since sequential chats are more difficult to manage online.

Students are not the only ones who miss the informal interaction. Unlike the face-to-face setting, in an online setting the main role of the educator is to structure the learning session, provide information and/or be a coach/facilitator for the students. The informal contact that occurs during face-to-face classes is difficult to replicate online. Some faculty who need that contact with students refuse to teach in an online mode or are unhappy when they do so, although they may not be consciously aware that it is the informal contact that they are missing.

Students are not the only ones who miss the informal interaction. Unlike the face-to-face setting, in an online setting the main role of the educator is to structure the learning session, provide information and/or be a coach/facilitator for the students. The informal contact that occurs during face-to-face classes is difficult to replicate online. Some faculty who need that contact with students refuse to teach in an online mode or are unhappy when they do so, although they may not be consciously aware that it is the informal contact that they are missing.

Advocates of online teaching describe a variety of benefits including richer discussions; gratification from the discussion mode of teaching; students can learn online as much as, or more than, in a face-to-face class; online teaching can bring out the best of the quieter students, etc. These and similar arguments may not make an impact, however, if the real issue for some faculty is the need for more informal contact between the instructor and student.

Discussion Participation   Another difference in online and face-to-face teaching is related to how faculty participate in class discussions. Strategies for faculty participation in face-to-face class discussion do not transfer easily to an online environment. In a face-to-face class discussion, the effective educator will be a facilitator, allowing students to discuss freely, occasionally interjecting an opinion or redirecting the discussion when needed. In an online environment, however, this type of discussion facilitation may not satisfy individual student needs for recognition and contact. The fact that students are not always aware of their need for instructor acknowledgement may lead to dissatisfaction on the part of the students, and educators who have been successful in face-to-face classrooms may be puzzled as to why their usually successful strategies are not porting to the online setting.

Given that the opportunities for informal contact are limited in online instruction, educators may need to be conscious about providing more extensive individualized feedback or more extensive comments in discussions than they would in other settings. At the very least, faculty should let students know how they plan to participate in discussions. This does not mean that the instructor needs to continually comment on all of each student's posts. It does mean that faculty should be aware that their comments and feedback are serving a dual function: it is helpful instructionally to improve performance (as feedback should), and it serves as another means of fostering the student-instructor relationship (as does the informal contact in a face-to-face setting).

Issues Related to Expectations About Technology

The one constant in the online/distance education setting is the technology. The expectations for this technology have increased as the individual home users (in our case, the students) have access to ever improving and more powerful desktop systems. The 'modus operandi' of the online world is one of self-service; individual users now expect to be able to shop or bank at any time, for example.

As technology moves to take a larger role in the delivery of course content, there is less distinction between the roles of the instructor and the technology, which also means that the traditional instructor role must undergo fundamental changes. The application of these technologies by institutions of higher learning carries with it the expectation of learning anywhere at any time. The technology now fulfills many of the roles that the instructor once held. The ability of students to access the course shell on a 24-h basis carries with it the expectation that not only can they access the deliverables and submit assignments, but, as we said earlier, they anticipate instructor response, 24 h a day, through email, which of course, is available all the time. In this case, the technology reinforces false assumptions students have about instructors' availability.

In some instances, the instructor-of-record is also the student's primary contact for the institution. Unlike a class conducted in a traditional bricks and mortar classroom, which involves the student's passing through a physical hallway filled with offices, faculty, support staff and the other earmarks of infrastructure, the online student accesses the "institution" through a log-on page that obscures the other faculty, staff, and facilities associated with the institution. This process of limited access to the physical campus means that the student's view of the course and college is largely limited to the individual course instructor. In this case, the instructor is the primary institutional presence.

This fundamental merging of the instructor with the technology also carries with it an expectation that the instructor has control over the infrastructure of the course shell or learning management system. Since the instructor is identified as the primary entity in the course, the instructor is held accountable when the technology fails, with a reaction similar to students being angry at a faculty member who unexpectedly does not show up for class. If an online lecture generates a 'page cannot be displayed' error, in the mind of the students, the lecturer has failed to deliver the content that students were expecting at a time convenient to them. This is further complicated when the student's primary access to the instructor is through email. If it takes the instructor 24 h to respond to the student, the student may feel that the faculty member has not satisfied instructional needs in a timely manner. One might expect informatics students to be more tolerant of technology glitches, but since they are students, they are likely to have a reaction similar to any other student.

Several options exist to mitigate the confusion over instructor role in an online learning environment. Ensuring that students have contact with the appropriate technical support staff, and reminding them of the presence of these support staff, can help to reduce anxiety when problems are encountered. Providing students with ample instruction on the technology can help ensure that students are better able to navigate through issues that may arise within the growing complexity of the online environment.

Using Online Course Structure to Reduce Transactional Distance

Michael G. Moore's (2012) theory of transactional distance (TDT) provides a framework for articulating, negotiating, and resolving unspoken assumptions into explicit expectations. Moore [2] introduced the term "transactional distance" to define the space between instructor and learner, where the concept of distance transcends geographical space to encompass a relational context defined as a dialectical balance between structure and dialog. As an example, it may be helpful to compare three scenarios: an instructor lecturing to students in an auditorium; an instructor engaging in discussion in a small face-to-face seminar course; and an asynchronous learning instructor interacting with students online. Each learning environment affords opportunities to differentiate transactional distance.

In the lecture context, there is little opportunity for dialogue; the discourse is predominantly a one-way instructor monologue. Structure, in the form of the lecturer's coherent discourse as well as supplemental material such as syllabi and handouts, provides a way to account for the lack of dialogue. Even though time and space are shared synchronously, the transactional distance is potentially large.

In the second scenario, the seminar format affords opportunities for Socratic dialogue between students and instructor who are sharing time and space. As a result, the potential for dialogue to resolve ambiguity of meaning diminishes the need for structure, which lessens transactional distance.

In the third scenario, an asynchronous online class, the relationship between instructor and learner is more dependent upon a situation or context to balance structure and upon dialogue to minimize transactional distance. In this respect, the learning management system may provide structure for interaction with (1) learning technology, (2) learning content, and (3) dialogical two-way interpersonal interactions between learners, as well as between learners and instructors. In the asynchronous environment, the differences between instructor and student in terms of time and space are often large. Creating structure provides a way to reduce the need for synchronous dialogue, making learning potentially more effective and efficient by eliminating the need for the synchronous information exchange. In this respect, syllabi, bibliographies, course policies, grading rubrics, and other elements of structure impart meanings intended to preclude the need for additional explanation to reduce transactional distance. The creation of structure allows dialogue to focus on knowledge co-construction through asynchronous course discussion.

By creating structure and utilizing dialogue contextually to resolve ambiguities in meaning, the transactional distance between asynchronous faculty and students can be reduced. In this sense, transactional distance theory provides a framework for diagnosing problems rooted in unspoken assumptions, and provides a way to resolve them through the creation of structure that embeds explicit expectations for learning. Moore and Kearsley (2012) outline the expectations of, and for, asynchronous instruction. They include a table with the following functional expectations for online teaching (Moore and Kearsley [1], Table 6.1, p. 129):

- Elaborating course content;
- Supervising and moderating discussions;
- Supervising individual and group projects;
- Grading assignments and providing feedback on progress;
- Keeping student records;
- Helping students manage their study;

- Motivating students;
- Answering or referring administrative questions;
- Answering or referring technical questions;
- Answering or referring counseling questions;
- Representing students with the administration; and
- Evaluating course effectiveness.

As in face-to-face courses, online instructors create course structural elements, predominantly written textual documents, in order to minimize the potential impact of unspoken assumptions on learning. Doing so precludes the need for repetitive individual interactions and improves instructional efficiency by creating content that addresses commonly shared unspoken assumptions. By creating explicit meaning to articulate unspoken assumptions as explicit expectations for learners, online instructors create opportunities for promoting course learning as knowledge co-construction and help students learn how to learn in online environments.

We can further apply transactional distance theory as a way to make meanings explicit and facilitate learning in online environments. Unspoken assumptions are a form of ambiguity that needs clarification, negotiation, and resolution to make assumptions explicit within the learning community. Online instructors are able to create structure, making unspoken assumptions explicit, through syllabi, learning objectives, instructions for assignments, and grading rubrics. Ultimately, online meaning is embedded in written, visual, or audio text formats. The written form of text is predominant in online education, and provides opportunities for enhancing learner autonomy through dialogue. Students can clarify unspoken assumptions by posing problems and asking questions in online course forums. The process of making meaning explicit creates opportunities for resolving ambiguity, leading to better alignment of instructor and student expectations through dialogic resolutions. To promote learning, instructors take the outcomes of these negotiations and revise course structure, making expectations explicit. Much of what we have discussed in terms of unspoken assumptions has related to providing structure and explanations and making unspoken expectations explicit. This enables instructors to recognize where transactional distance may exist and to reduce it to the greatest extent possible once recognized.

There are sources that faculty can use to assist them with strategies for course design to reduce transactional distance. One of the better known sources for online course design guidance is Quality Matters (www.qualitymatters.org). Quality Matters is a non-profit national organization that has developed standards for the design of online courses and certifies courses that meet their standards. The Quality Matters rubric addresses, among other things, the objectives, learning activities, assessments, plans for interaction among learners and instructors, and the alignment of these different course elements [3]. The standards emphasize clarity of expectations, measurable objectives, providing opportunities for both student-student interaction as well as student-instructor interaction, that are similar to our suggestions of providing structure, making expectations explicit, and fostering instructor-student and student-student dialogue.

Summary of Lessons Learned

Faculty must understand and manage students' common expectations and assumptions, even when these expectations and assumptions are not explicit. There is need for increased understanding and awareness of instructor and student expectations related to (1) instructor accessibility, (2) student workload, (3) feedback and participation, and (4) technology. By addressing these expectations, the instructor can achieve, if not exceed, the goals of pushing the envelope beyond the passive online experience into a level of engagement that encourages critical thinking.

Key Take-Away Points
- Recognize the implicit assumptions of faculty and students in asynchronous online courses
- Recognize that student needs and expectations for increased instructor contact may influence a variety of interactions
- Resolve ambiguity by being very explicit about course requirements, instructor expectations, and student performance
- Develop ways to reduce the transactional distance between students and between instructors and students by including more communication, more detailed feedback, forums for non-course related and other informal, discussion

References

1. Moore MG, Kearsley G. Distance education: a systems view of online learning. 3rd ed. Belmont: Wadsworth Publishing Company; 2012.
2. Moore MG. The individual adult learner. In: Tight M, editor. Education for adults, Adult learning and education, vol. 1. London: Routledge; 1983. p. 153–68.
3. Quality Matters. Specific review standards from the QM Higher Education Rubric. Sixth ed. https://www.qualitymatters.org/sites/default/files/PDFs/StandardsfromtheQMHigher EducationRubric.pdf. Accessed 19 April 2020.

Chapter 20
Open Educational Resources (OERs) in Health Informatics

William Hersh

One of the virtues of the global, interconnected Internet is it provides the ability for educators to share and learners to access a wide variety of learning content. This has given rise to open educational resources (OERs), which have been defined as "teaching and learning resources in any medium, digital or otherwise, that permit no-cost access, use, reuse and repurposing by others with no or limited restrictions" [1]. A challenge for OERs, however, is that they are difficult to maintain, especially in rapidly changing fields such as health informatics. This chapter provides pointers to sources of OERs for health informatics and then describes the benefits and limitations of OERs using two high-profile efforts as examples.

Some OERs have been disseminated as part of the *massive open online courses* (MOOCs) movement that gained momentum in the early 2010s. While the view that MOOCs would transform higher education never came to pass, their materials continue to be widely used, including in formal higher education. The two major providers of MOOCs are Coursera[1] and edX[2]. Another well-known site with massive amounts of educational content is the Khan Academy[3].

The availability of OERs spans from single Web sites to vast libraries available for use. Some materials are provided as finished products that learners access, sometimes in conjunction with some sort of certification, while others provide the "source" materials that enable the content to be updated, repurposed, or otherwise adapted. The remainder of this chapter will focus on two large OER efforts in health informatics funded by US government grants to institutions of higher education: the

---

[1] https://www.coursera.org/
[2] https://www.edx.org/
[3] https://www.khanacademy.org/

W. Hersh (✉)
Oregon Health & Science University, Portland, OR, USA
e-mail: hersh@ohsu.edu

© Springer Nature Switzerland AG 2020   277
E. S. Berner (ed.), *Informatics Education in Healthcare*, Health Informatics,
https://doi.org/10.1007/978-3-030-53813-2_20

Office of the National Coordinator for Health IT (ONC) Workforce Development Program and the National Institutes of Health (NIH) Big Data to Knowledge (BD2K) Program. The ONC program was discussed previously in the first edition of this book, but is updated in this chapter. In addition to these two programs, there are also OERs available for training healthcare management students in informatics concepts. These materials are discussed in Chap. 8.

ONC Workforce Development Program

Interest in informatics education took a significant leap with the inclusion of funding for "workforce development" in the Heath Information Technology for Economic and Clinical Health (HITECH) Act, the portion of the American Recovery and Reinvestment Act (ARRA, also known as the "economic stimulus bill") of 2009 devoted to the adoption and meaningful use of health information technology (HIT) [2]. Although HITECH was focused mostly on incentives for adoption of the electronic health records (EHR) by clinicians and hospitals, research in the years preceding the legislation presaged a need for significant expansion of the cadre of professionals who would be needed to develop, implement, and evaluate health IT systems [3]. The workforce development program was included in Section 3016 of ARRA and led to the $118 million investment by the ONC in its Workforce Development Program.

ONC developed its Workforce Development Program by surveying the research literature and convening a workshop of experts in the summer of 2009. Based on the research literature, it was estimated that a workforce of approximately 51,000 professionals would be required to help eligible hospitals and professionals archive meaningful use of the EHR. Adding the opinions of experts, ONC determined that professionals in 12 workforce roles would be required (Table 20.1). They believed that these roles could be grouped in three categories. The first category would be a wave of personnel who would be mobile in nature, moving from site to site implementing EHR systems. They would be followed by more permanent staff that would maintain and support the implemented EHR systems. A third category would consist of clinical and public health informatics experts who would manage, evaluate, educate, and perform further research and development of these systems. Half of these workforce roles were deemed for training in 6-month certificate programs in community colleges, while the other half were to be trained for 1–2 years in university-based programs.

Those with an asterisk (*) were slated to have training take place in community colleges, while those with a dagger (†) would have training occur in university-based settings. These roles were not meant to be so much job descriptions as they were meant to be job categories.

Table 20.1 ONC categories and workforce roles

Category 1: Mobile Adoption Support Roles
• Implementation support specialist*
• Practice workflow and information management redesign specialist*
• Clinician consultant*
• Implementation manager*
Category 2: Permanent Staff of Health Care Delivery and Public Health Sites
• Technical/software support staff*
• Trainer*
• Clinician/public health leader†
• Health information management and exchange specialist†
• Health information privacy and security specialist†
Category 3: Health Care and Public Health Informaticians
• Research and development scientist†
• Programmers and software engineer†
• Health IT sub-specialist†

Four parts of the ONC Workforce Development Program were funded in late 2010 and consisted of four specific programs to train the new workforce:

1. Community College Consortia—82 community colleges, grouped into five regional consortia, were funded to offer six-month certificate programs.
2. Curriculum Development Centers—Because the community colleges did not have curricula for these programs, five Curriculum Development Centers (CDCs) were also funded to develop materials for use by these programs—Columbia University, Duke University, John Hopkins University, Oregon Health & Science University (OHSU), and University of Alabama at Birmingham (UAB). OHSU was additionally being designated the National Training and Dissemination Center (NTDC) to establish the website for dissemination of the materials and providing training and support in their use.
3. Competency Examinations—Examinations to test the competencies gained by graduates of the community college programs for the six workforce roles trained in their programs.
4. University-based Training (UBT) programs—Additional training funds were awarded to nine universities for longer-term university-based educational programs.

ONC stipulated that the curriculum consist of 20 "components," which were roughly equivalent in content and depth to college courses. The titles of the original 20 components (along with those of five additional components developed in a later second round of funding) are listed in Table 20.2. Each of the components was divided into 8–12 units. Most units consisted of learning objectives, lectures (available as PowerPoint slides as well as Flash-format voice-over-slide narrations), exercises, and self-assessment activities. Three of the units—7, 8, and 11—were "lab"

Table 20.2 The components of the ONC health IT curriculum

Component	Component name
1	Introduction to Health Care and Public Health in the U.S.
2	The Culture of Health Care
3	Terminology in Health Care and Public Health Settings
4	Introduction to Information and Computer Science
5	History of Health Information Technology in the U.S.
6	Health Management Information System
7	Working with Health IT Systems
8	Installation and Maintenance of Health IT Systems
9	Networking and Health Information Exchange
10	Health Care Workflow Process Improvement
11	Configuring EHRs
12	Quality Improvement
13	Public Health IT
14	Special Topics Course on Vendor-Specific Systems
15	Usability and Human Factors
16	Professionalism/Customer Service in the Health Environment
17	Working in Teams
18	Planning, Management and Leadership for Health IT
19	Introduction to Project Management
20	Training and Instructional Design
21	Population Health
22	Care Coordination and Interoperable Health IT Systems
23	Value-Based Care
24	Health Care Data Analytics
25	Patient-Centered Care

The first 20 were developed in the initial round of funding from 2010 to 2012. These were updated, with five additional components added, in the second round of funding from 2015 to 2017

units, providing hands-on lab exercises using and configuring an example EHR, which in this case was the VistA system of the Veteran's Administration. The VistA content was not meant to train students specifically on VistA, but rather to demonstrate generically the use and configuration of EHRs. A version of VistA with a license for educational institution use was made available on the NTDC site.

The funding for the Curriculum Development Centers required that three versions of the curriculum be produced over the two years of funding. With the second version, the curriculum was made available to the public, available for use by any educational program, and distributed under a Creative Commons Attribution-NonCommercial-ShareAlike License. The third and final version of the initial curriculum was released in Spring, 2012. When this round of funding ended, the NTDC site was retired and the materials were moved in archival fashion to the website of the American Medical Informatics Association (AMIA). An evaluation of the materials was published by the five funded Curriculum Development Centers [4]. An

Table 20.3 File numbers and sizes from the original ONC (Version 3) curriculum

Component	Word files	Word files size	PPT files	PPT slides	PPT file size	MP3 files	MP3 files size	MP3 time
1	81	7.5	39	774	24.4	39	268.6	9:46
2	78	3.5	36	687	19.9	36	288.3	10:29
3	87	5.3	23	507	24.4	23	215.6	5:14
4	93	4.1	38	862	42.7	38	349.5	12:43
5	80	3.7	24	626	31.3	24	317.4	6:43
6	59	2.1	17	370	9.4	17	239.5	6:25
7	87	17.8	18	209	21.3	19	167.7	5:41
8	60	2.6	16	347	13.4	16	234.8	6:06
9	70	3.0	29	738	44.5	28	362.1	10:08
10	69	3.2	27	621	25.6	27	309.2	9:08
11	48	10.8	15	260	10.1	15	124.3	4:31
12	76	4.0	26	468	42.9	26	258.8	6:53
13	82	3.7	20	624	67.3	22	203.9	7:25
14	40	1.6	8	204	13.9	8	60.5	2:12
15	74	3.3	26	738	86.5	26	236.4	7:22
16	51	2.4	15	337	12.9	15	148.1	3:28
17	72	6.3	15	265	22.9	15	184.7	4:52
18	61	3.2	21	483	31.8	20	216.5	5:08
19	89	6.6	27	494	31.7	27	300.2	7:57
20	46	2.0	14	360	35.4	14	134.6	3:45
Total	1403	96.7	454	9974	612.3	455	4620.7	136:04

external evaluation of the ONC Workforce Development Program was also published [5].

The curricular materials were best viewed as aimed at instructors rather than students. That is, the materials were meant to be a resource for faculty to develop coursework in HIT (and clinical informatics). While anyone could download and use the materials, they were not intended to be a standalone self-study course in health IT. As shown in Table 20.3, the Version 3 materials totaled 11.2 gigabytes in size, contained in 18,072 files. The 20 components of the curriculum contained 9974 PowerPoint slides and audio lasting over 136 h (5 days, 16 h, and 4 min, to be precise!). The NTDC site implemented a search engine for the text-based files contain 38,181 unique words indexed. A manually constructed topical index was also available. Nearly 10,000 people worldwide created logins to download from the NTDC site.

In July 2015, the ONC provided a second round of funding to update the HIT Curriculum. Seven institutions received funding to update the original materials and develop five new components. The new components focused more on application of EHRs than implementation, including such emerging (circa 2015) topics as care coordination, population health, and data analytics. In addition, each funded site was required to use the materials to deliver short-term training to 1000 individuals.

The updated materials were developed using essentially the same format as the original components, making use of narrated lectures and multiple-choice self-assessments and assuring they were accessible to individuals with disabilities[4]. The updated and new components were posted, where they are still available, on the ONC website[5].

The materials and short-term training that were developed under the second round of funding were expanded in different ways. OHSU offered a free continuing education course, *Update in Health Information Technology: Healthcare Data Analytics*, to physicians, nurses, other healthcare professionals, and health informatics/IT professionals. Physicians were able to receive continuing medical education (CME) credit and those certified in the clinical informatics subspecialty were able to obtain Lifelong Learning and Self-Assessment (LLSA) credits towards American Board of Preventive Medicine (ABPM) Maintenance of Certification Part II (MOC-II) requirements for the subspecialty. After the ONC funding ended, the course continued to be offered on a tuition basis for another year, and has now been superseded by an annual update course[6].

UAB developed a set of videos that built on the base materials[7]. They also developed CME courses for which individuals could obtain LLSA credits[8]. Columbia University developed its materials into a Coursera course called, HI-FIVE: Health Informatics for Innovation, Value & Enrichment[9]. These products demonstrate the value of having the OERs available, even if they require modification for further use.

Big Data to Knowledge (BD2K)

The NIH, which is the premier funder of biomedical research in the United States, recognized the growing importance of "Big Data" in the early 2010s. This led to the launch of the Big Data to Knowledge (BD2K) program, which aimed to support research and development of innovative and transformative approaches and tools to accelerate the value of data science in biomedical research [6]. In addition to funding research projects and centers applying biomedical informatics and data science to driving biomedical problems, the program funded the development of OERs along with a BD2K Training Coordinating Center that developed, among other resources, an Educational Resource Discovery Index (ERuDIte) that cataloged over 10,000 videos, documents, assignments, books and courses in biomedical data science and related areas [7].

---

[4] https://www.section508.gov/

[5] https://www.healthit.gov/topic/health-it-resources/health-it-curriculum-resources-educators

[6] https://www.ohsu.edu/school-of-medicine/medical-informatics-and-clinical-epidemiology/2019-ohsu-annual-update-clinical

[7] https://www.youtube.com/channel/UCgRfaZ-Dw2n0sCU_7kexnGQ

[8] https://cmecourses.som.uab.edu/course/index.php?categoryid=38

[9] https://www.coursera.org/learn/hi-five-clinical

Table 20.4   Modules of the OHSU BD2K program

ID	Title
BDK01	Biomedical Big Data Science
BDK02	Introduction to Big Data in Biology and Medicine
BDK03	Ethical Issues in Use of Big Data
BDK04	Clinical Data Standards Related to Big Data
BDK05	Basic Research Data Standards
BDK06	Public Health and Big Data
BDK07	Team Science
BDK08	Secondary Use (Reuse) Of Clinical Data
BDK09	Publication and Peer Review
BDK10	Information Retrieval
BDK11	Version control and identifiers
BDK12	Data Annotation and Curation
BDK13	SMART on FHIR
BDK14	Ontologies 101
BDK15	Data Metadata and Provenance
BDK16	Semantic Data Interoperability
BDK17	Choice of Algorithms and Algorithm Dynamics
BDK18	Visualization and Interpretation
BDK19	Replication, Validation and The Spectrum of Reproducibility
BDK20	Regulatory Issues in Big Data for Genomics and Health
BDK21	Hosting Data Dissemination and Data Stewardship Workshops
BDK22	Guidelines for Reporting, Publications, And Data Sharing

One of the largest collections of OERs to emanate from the BD2K project came from OHSU, which developed 22 modules (Table 20.4) as well as several skills courses[10]. In addition, the project mapped the modules to competencies for clinical and translational science researchers [8] and for health science librarians [9]. As the BD2K project funding ended in 2017, the OHSU materials are available in archival form on a GitHub site[11], while the ERuDIte site has been retired. An evaluation of the development of the OHSU modules was published [10].

Lessons Learned

Both of the projects described in this chapter showed that with adequate resources, high-quality and useful materials could be developed for diverse audiences. But a number of challenges limited the long-term value of what was created.

---

[10] https://dmice.ohsu.edu/bd2k/

[11] https://github.com/OHSUBD2K

One major challenge for the two initiatives described in this chapter was not being able to incorporate any copyrighted materials. Fair use rules may permit the use of content from journals and other sources in university-based online courses if they are password protected [11], but putting copyrighted material into OERs is generally not allowed, since those sites using the materials may not have the same rights to access to the copyrighted materials as those universities who produced the materials.

Probably the main challenge to the ultimate usefulness of the materials was continuing their updating and maintenance after funding ended. This is particularly important in a field that changes as rapidly as health informatics does. While most of the developers for the two projects remain active informatics educators, covering similar content in their teaching, the materials for the OERs have not been updated since the funding ended. In addition, the meta-resources of the NTDC and ERuDIte have been retired and are no longer accessible. The ONC materials including the 2017 update and new modules are still available and can be used effectively as a base by informatics educators, as long as they are able to adapt and update the materials themselves.

Nonetheless, the need for continued availability of curricular materials for educators is clear. Although the required knowledge and skills for health informatics professionals has continued to evolve with changes in technology and health care, the need for training individuals has continued [12]. AMIA has commissioned recent workforce analyses of informatics professionals that catalog the areas where knowledge and skills are required [13, 14]. All of this points to a continuing need for educational materials for training the diverse professionals who work in health informatics.

References

1. Miao F, Mishra S, McGreal R. Open educational resources: Policy, costs and transformation. Paris, France: United Nations Educational, Scientific and Cultural Organization (UNESCO); 2016.
2. Blumenthal D. Launching HITECH. New Engl J Med. 2010;362:382–5.
3. Hersh W, Wright A. What workforce is needed to implement the health information technology agenda? An analysis from the HIMSS Analytics™ Database. AMIA Annu Symp Proc. 2008:303–7.
4. Mohan V, et al. Design and evaluation of the ONC health information technology curriculum. J Am Med Inform Assoc. 2014;21:509–16.
5. Lowell, K. Evaluation of the Information Technology Professionals in Health Care ("Workforce") Program - Summative Report. 2014, Bethesda, MD.
6. Margolis R, et al. The National Institutes of Health's Big Data to Knowledge (BD2K) initiative: capitalizing on biomedical big data. J Am Med Inform Assoc. 2014;21:957–8.
7. Ambite J, et al. BD2K Training Coordinating Center's ERuDIte: the Educational Resource Discovery Index for data science. IEEE Transactions on Emerging Topics in Computing. 2019. https://doi.org/10.1109/TETC.2019.2903466.

8. Valenta AL, Meagher EA, Tachinardi U, Starren J.Core informatics competencies for clinical and translational scientists: what do our customers and collaborators need to know? J Am Med Inform Assoc. 2016;23:835–9 .

9. Anonymous. Competencies for lifelong learning and professional success. Chicago, IL: Medical Library Association; 2017.

10. Pederson B, et al. Big data to knowledge open educational resources: development and dissemination considerations. In: Proceedings of EdMedia: World Conference on Educational Media and Technology 2016. 2016. Vancouver, BC.

11. Adler P, et al. Code of best practices in fair use for academic and research libraries. Washington, DC: Association of Research Libraries; 2012.

12. Hersh W, Boone K, Totten A. Characteristics of the healthcare information technology workforce in the HITECH era: underestimated in size, still growing, and adapting to advanced uses. JAMIA Open. 2018;1:188–94.

13. Silverman HD, Steen EB, Carpenito JN, Ondrula CJ, Williamson JJ, Fridsma DB. Domains, tasks, and knowledge for clinical informatics subspecialty practice: results of a practice analysis. J Am Med Inform Assoc. 2019;26:586–93.

14. Gadd CS, Steen EB, Caro CM, Greenberg S, Williamson JJ, Fridsma DB. Domains, tasks, and knowledge for health informatics practice: results of a practice analysis. J Am Med Inform Assoc. 2020;27(6):845–52.

Part VII
Summary of Lessons Learned

Chapter 21
Informatics Education in Healthcare: Lessons Learned

Eta S. Berner

Informatics education programs have been evolving over an approximately 40-year span of time. Existing programs have changed over the years as new and different driving forces have influenced them. While some of the programs began with a few visionaries with expertise and interest in computer applications in healthcare, the current drivers for informatics education and manpower development are clearly the increased sophistication of technology, including electronic health records, distance learning technologies, and telemedicine applications as well as policies mandating their integration into healthcare delivery.

The audience for informatics education has grown in a similar manner. From an initial focus on the development of informatics researchers who would apply their informatics and computer science knowledge and skills to the healthcare domain, we have seen programs being developed for healthcare administrators, practitioners and scientists who recognize that they need informatics expertise to function within their own domain.

Despite the differences among the programs in terms of focus, students, and purpose, there are also many commonalities, but these may be more difficult to recognize as one reads each individual chapter in this book. For that reason, this chapter synthesizes the lessons that have been described throughout the book using the following organizational framework:

- Evolution of Informatics Education Programs
- Relationship of Educational Programs to Workforce Needs and Opportunities
- Informatics Competencies and Sources of Curriculum Materials

E. S. Berner (✉)
Department of Health Services Administration, School of Health Professions, University of Alabama at Birmingham, Birmingham, AL, USA

Department of Medical Education, School of Medicine, University of Alabama at Birmingham, Birmingham, AL, USA
e-mail: eberner@uab.edu

© Springer Nature Switzerland AG 2020
E. S. Berner (ed.), *Informatics Education in Healthcare*, Health Informatics,
https://doi.org/10.1007/978-3-030-53813-2_21

- Online Instructional Strategies
- Evaluation and Accreditation of Informatics Education Programs in Healthcare

These topics mirror the stages of individual program development including development and evolution of the overall program, identification of competencies and development of the curriculum, instructional strategies, and program evaluation methods. They also reflect the evolution of the professionalism of the field of informatics.

Evolution of Informatics Education Programs

Informatics Education Programs in Europe and the U.S.

John Mantas identified phases that were encountered in the evolution of many of the European informatics programs. As Mantas described it, these phases include the initiation phase, when individual programs, led by a visionary leader, began and, because there were no models or examples, development of curricula was more or less a trial and error endeavor. As some of these early programs developed, eventually there became more of a consensus on curricular guidelines and programs began to expand. As curricula became consolidated, in the last several years the need for evaluation of programs across sites and accreditation of individual programs was seen (John Mantas, PhD, personal communication, 2013).

In the U.S., since most of the early programs were funded with NIH funding from the National Library of Medicine (NLM), the curricular content of many of the U.S. programs was largely responsive to what the NIH saw as key manpower needs, generally for sustaining the healthcare research enterprise. At first the NLM training programs, since they were funded by the National **Library** of Medicine, were more heavily focused on librarian training, but as the field evolved to include more automated means of managing healthcare information in practice, they shifted more into the domain of clinical informatics research and development, where they remained until fairly recently when, with increasing growth of genomics research, the NLM programs also began to incorporate bioinformatics content, public health informatics and the use of clinical applications in practice. With the need to manage and utilize the growing amount of electronic health information in both research and clinical practice, the most recent evolution has been for the NLM training programs to incorporate data science into the curriculum, as described in Chap. 2.

It was after the programs had been operational for quite a while that more formalized program evaluation criteria for the overall NLM program were developed, as well as better guidelines for individual programs that apply for NLM funding. These criteria include making sure that the content draws from the variety of disciplines and domains that are either the underpinnings of the field or are application areas of informatics in healthcare. The curriculum should include key informatics concepts, methods and state-of-the art technology assessments and a variety of approaches should be employed to evaluate the program's success in meeting its goals [1].

The US Office of the National Coordinator for Health Information Technology (ONC) workforce program described in Chap. 20 had some of the same visionary beginnings, but it was addressing a more applied need. With the rapid increase in the use of health information technology anticipated with the passing of the HITECH Act [2], it was envisioned that new workforce roles would be needed and, to prepare individuals for those roles, new training programs would be needed as well. The ONC workforce program was designed to meet the needs for new types of individuals who could support the growing health information technology developments.

In many ways, all of these programs were future-oriented. The NLM training programs began when nobody, with the exception of the early developers, was using clinical computing in healthcare. The ONC workforce programs began with envisioning new roles for a healthcare system that would become increasingly electronic, but was not there yet. Over the same time period that the NLM training programs evolved to include broader domains than just clinical informatics, electronic health records and clinical decision support systems, which was a focus of the early programs, began to be applied in healthcare. Now that these electronic systems are commonplace, the future developments will involve using the data from these systems, and hence, NIH and NLM are now focusing on incorporating training in data science (Chaps. 2 and 10) as well as translating bioinformatics applications into clinical practice (Chap. 5).

Unlike the programs that envisioned new roles and new applications, the programs for managers of healthcare information systems (Chap. 4) informatics programs for healthcare administrators (Chap. 8), and certification programs for clinical informatics practitioners (Chap. 16) developed after individuals without formal informatics training had been in practice for a number of years. For instance, Chief Information Officers and healthcare administrators usually did not have formal training in informatics. More recently, with the increase in clinical computing, the role of Chief Medical Information Officer, or CMIO, has become prominent, but many of the individuals filling these roles did not have formal informatics training.

The perceived need for more formal training on the part of the individuals already in these roles, as well as informatics educators recognizing the need for more formal educational programs, has spurred the development of many of the newer, more applied programs. These programs include entire degree programs like the health informatics masters programs (Chap. 4), nursing informatics masters programs (Chaps. 3 and 12), health information systems courses within health administration programs (Chap. 8), and informatics continuing education programs, such as the AMIA 10 × 10 program described in Chap. 18 and mentioned in many of the other chapters. Not only have graduate education programs broadened, but at the other end of the spectrum there are undergraduate programs developing (Chap. 6).

In addition to the new educational programs, there has been a parallel recognition of the need to certify the competencies of individuals in these applied roles, and, as the educational programs have gotten established, more of them are becoming accredited as described in Chap. 17. The clinical informatics subspecialty certification and training programs described in Chap. 16 and similar programs for nursing informatics described in Chap. 3 are examples of these programs. Finally, to accommodate the growing number of health informatics practitioners, a new certification program in advanced health informatics was started in 2019 (Chaps. 3 and 16).

What is common to all of the formal programs that evolved after individuals without formal training had been in practice is that they all emphasize the need to look to competencies exemplified by the best of the those practitioners, as well as the more theoretical informatics concepts, to develop training curricula and certification content. These types of programs will also continue to evolve, as they should, as the workforce needs change. At this stage of the field of informatics, where the applications and principles are now beginning to be used in clinical practice, new program developers should be keenly aware of the market needs and should develop programs focusing on the competencies needed to thrive in that market.

Informatics Education Programs in Low Resource Areas

As described in several of the chapters in Part IV, the development of informatics programs in many of the developing countries evolved differently from either the early U.S. or European countries or the more applied programs where there were already practitioners in the field. First of all, in many of these low resource settings, telemedicine programs were initiated to address the regional healthcare needs for better access, better care, and the limitations of long distances and limited transportation that were prevalent in these countries. This telemedicine infrastructure required a workforce who could manage it, but in addition, the infrastructure could also be used not only for health education, but for health informatics education as well.

Thus, in part because these programs were started later than those in the more developed countries, many of the informatics programs in these countries began as online programs, unlike in the U.S., where online education occurred at a later stage of program evolution. Second, again because the European and U.S. programs were already established and many were already providing online education, many of the programs in the developing countries began in partnership with the more established programs. In some cases, such as with the AMIA 10 × 10 programs (Chap. 18), students from developing countries took the same program as those in the U.S., either in English or translated into the native language. In other cases, there was a partnership to develop a program that made use of materials originally developed in the U.S. or Europe, but which was tailored for the unique needs of the country. More recently, as discussed in Chaps. 13–15, many of these programs evolved to more independent programs and there is increased sharing of expertise and curricula within regions, rather than only between the more developed and developing countries.

While there are certainly benefits in developing new programs by partnering with more mature programs there are also challenges. Both those who are disseminating the materials and those who are receiving them, identify the need to address not just language differences, but broader cultural, organizational, and infrastructure differences as well. Examples of the programs that have been developed as well as the challenges and how to address them are discussed in the chapters in Part IV. There may now be enough programs within the developing countries to be a resource for new programs. Individuals interested in starting programs in low-resource areas should consider a broad range of partners, including those from the established programs in the U.S. and Europe, as well as those from within their region. However, even within a given region, there are differences between countries on how receptive the healthcare systems are to establishing roles for those with informatics training.

Relationship of Educational Programs to Workforce Needs and Opportunities

There is a complex relationship between informatics educators, potential students and the leaders of the healthcare delivery systems. As discussed above, the NLM and the ONC anticipated future workforce needs for informatics-knowledgeable individuals and funded the development of education programs to prepare those individuals. The NLM training program began long before EHRs were commonplace and the ONC programs began with the HITECH Act, again prior to the increase in the use of EHRs. As the field matured, with the development of the Informatics subspecialty certification exam, clinical informatics fellowship programs were started (Chap. 16). Yet in the six years since the first subspecialty examination was administered in 2013, there are less than 50 clinical informatics fellowship programs and most have only one or two fellows. Part of the reason for this small number is that, like other fellowship programs, funding comes from the healthcare delivery system in which they work and receive training and health system leaders may not realize the value these fellows can bring [3]. If the health systems do not recognize the value of informatics fellowship training, residents who are trying to decide on a sub-specialty may not consider clinical informatics either. As Lehmann and colleagues discuss in Chap. 16, even the small number of current programs cannot fill all of their applicant slots. There is a circularity to this problem in that if there are very few programs, they may not be as visible as other subspecialty training programs, and hence find it more difficult to get fully established. The increased visibility of informatics and the increasing recognition of the need for clinical informatics expertise may change this situation in the future.

This mismatch between the visionaries who see the need for individuals with informatics training and the lack of explicit positions in the workforce that require individuals with informatics knowledge is not unique to the clinical informatics fellowship programs in the U.S. One of the things that is striking about the programs developed in other parts of the world discussed in Part IV, is the variation among countries, even within the same general region of the world, in terms of whether there are jobs for the graduates. In countries where there are not positions that explicitly require informatics training, it is much more difficult to establish programs and to attract students.

Zozus and colleagues provide advice on starting a bioinformatics program, but the advice is appropriate for starting any type of program, including informatics (Chap. 5). The advice emphasizes the need to do an assessment of the market needs, of potential employers, potential students, and competing programs. When the field of informatics was in its infancy and the main programs were the few NLM training programs which received federal funding, the issues of market assessment was much less urgent. As the field is maturing, but where the healthcare market may not yet have caught up, such assessment is essential if the educational programs are going to thrive.

Competencies and Curricula for Informatics Education in Healthcare

Almost half of the chapters in this book address the content of the ideal curriculum for informatics education. Although there is overlap in the proposed competencies and accompanying course materials, none of the chapters proposes an identical curriculum, or even identical broad competencies. In most cases this is because the roles for which the individuals are being prepared are different. For instance, in the curricular content described in Chaps. 4 and 8, for healthcare IT managers and healthcare administrators, there are several courses (in the masters' program) or topics (in the health administration curriculum) related to management, finance, strategic planning and organizational behavior. Both curricula emphasize topics that are a key focus for leaders and managers in an operational environment.

These topics, perhaps with the exception of addressing the HIPAA regulations [4], are absent from both the NLM training programs and the AMIA 10 × 10 programs that were derived from them, such as the OHSU program described in Chap. 18. That is because the NLM training programs were clearly designed to produce informatics researchers and developers, not managers.

Conversely, while the more applied programs have more management content, some of the foundational informatics topics are usually not included in the applied curricula. Such topics as information retrieval, imaging informatics, in-depth computer science, ontologies, and in-depth coverage of standards that are included in the research and development-focused programs are usually not addressed in detail in the more applied programs. The programs for clinical users of systems such as those for nurses described in Chap. 3 and physicians described in Chap. 7 have still another set of competencies.

The content of the clinical informatics subspecialty examination described in Chap. 16 has similarities to those for all three types of users and is essentially a combination of competencies in basic informatics, IT management, and clinical information management. These general types of competencies are supported by an analysis of practice, as well as the opinions of informatics leaders. The practice analysis for the clinical informatics subspecialty delineated five domains of practice [5]. Because the clinical informatics subspecialty examination currently comprises these domains, as is noted in Chap. 16, many of the informatics textbooks, which are mainly geared for one or another of the different audiences, may not adequately cover the full range of competencies.

This challenge of integrating different disciplines has been both an ongoing challenge and an accomplishment for the field of informatics. Despite the difference in the curricula for different roles there are, as noted in Chap. 17, key foundational domains for the competencies that are needed, not just for one specific role, but for all informaticians. The foundational domains described in Chap. 17 relate to health sciences, computer and information sciences and social sciences and the intersections among these domains. As described in Chap. 9 and also addressed in Chap. 7, program developers need to identify the intended role of the users, whether their needs are for more foundational or applied learning, the breadth and depth of curricular content needed and the appropriate level of detail. Depending on the intent of the curriculum, for example, competencies in computer and information sciences can mean anything from a very basic comfort with, and understanding of, computers and information technology, to being proficient in developing decision support and other clinical, bioinformatics or clinical and translational research informatics applications. Healthcare administration students may be at one end of the continuum and students in NLM training programs at the other end.

Using the foundational domains and key competencies as a basic framework, developers of new programs need to carefully consider what role their students will assume upon graduation and develop the curricula accordingly. While identifying these roles may be only a small challenge for faculty, it is often difficult for students to navigate selecting among the different programs, since students are not always aware of the possible roles and in many cases, students from some of the basic research and development programs wind up in applied roles anyway. To avoid a mismatch of student and faculty expectations, program developers should identify their focus as clearly as possible and recruit students whose interests and skills match the curricular focus.

In some cases, curricular decisions might be made by a consensus process similar to the one that was used to develop the original criteria for the clinical informatics certification exam and training program requirements as described in Chap. 16. Even better might be to include a data driven analysis of the competencies of those who are currently fulfilling the roles for whom the program is geared, as was now done for the current certification exam. This is also what was done to develop the initial curriculum described in Chap. 4 [5]. Such analysis of current workforce roles and functions is recognized as a best practice for developing competencies and competency examinations, although it should also be supplemented by input from experts [6]. The difficulty occurs, however, when existing roles are in transition. For instance, the competency examination program that was part of the ONC workforce program described in Chap. 20, found it challenging to identify competencies by asking individuals currently in somewhat relevant positions about their job responsibilities because the ONC roles were ones that were anticipated to be needed in the future and may not have been part of current job descriptions.

In addition to the competency domains from the practice analysis for clinical informatics (Chap. 16), Chap. 7 includes references to detailed competencies for several informatics roles—those for basic researchers, applied managers, as well as clinician users. Chap. 9 provides examples of competencies in the domain of clinical research informatics, while Chap. 3 describes new competencies for roles in nursing informatics. Chap. 17 describes domains of competencies used as part of health informatics program accreditation standards. While early informatics education programs often had an implicit understanding of the competencies they were aiming for, as program accreditation efforts become more established, more explicit competency definitions are now required.

Once the roles and competencies are determined, curricular content, learning activities and assessments to address the competencies need to be identified. Often new programs do not have the full complement of faculty who can teach the complete range of topics that will be needed. This may be especially acute in programs where a single course is needed in a curriculum which does not otherwise address informatics. An approach discussed in Chaps. 3 and 7 is to have clinical faculty, for instance, take informatics continuing education programs, such as the AMIA 10 × 10 programs (Chap. 18) or a certificate program in informatics. One approach that can work for individual courses or sometimes entire programs, as discussed in Chaps. 11 and 13, is for newly starting programs to partner with existing programs and utilize courses, materials or faculty from these programs. Still another approach is to enlist faculty from other relevant departments for some of the courses. For instance, basic computer science might be able to be taught by computer science faculty rather than only relying on the faculty in the informatics program.

More recently there have been three major efforts to make curricular materials broadly available. As described in Chap. 20, the materials originally developed for the ONC Workforce Program are freely available for educators and have been used by educators worldwide. Chap. 20 also describes the open-source materials available in the NIH BD2K program. Similarly, the HIMSTA modules described in Chap. 8 are available for educators in healthcare management educational programs who need to address the required information management competencies. These resources, developed by expert informatics educators, are a tremendous boon even to experienced informatics instructors, but are especially useful for new programs that might not be fully staffed. The other advantage of these materials, in addition to being free to educators, is that they can be used "as is" with narrated lectures available for online education. They also can be modified to fit the needs of particular courses. The disadvantage is that the generic materials may not always meet the needs of the particular program, so educators should be prepared to adapt them. Hersh, in Chap. 20, discusses other challenges in using open-source educational materials. One of the main challenges is knowledge maintenance, as all of these materials were developed with grant funding with no mandate to keep them up-to-date.

Online Instructional Strategies

The informatics programs described in this book have deployed a variety of instructional strategies. Most of the NLM training programs described in Chap. 2 are focused on doctoral or post-doctoral students (physicians coming for additional training in informatics). Because of the needs for supervised research of small cohorts of students, often in operational healthcare settings, most of these programs have remained as traditional face-to-face educational programs. On the other hand, as mentioned earlier, in part because of the infrastructure issues, many of the programs in low-resource settings began, and have remained, as primarily online programs (Chaps. 11–15) as have the 10 × 10 programs (Chap. 18). The ONC workforce programs at the community colleges described in Chap. 20 were a mixture of online, face-to-face, and hybrid programs, with significant online components. Finally, other programs began as face-to-face programs, but eventually transitioned to online programs, as did the program described in Chap. 4.

There are many motivations for decisions to use, or intentionally not use, online instructional strategies. In the countries described in Chaps. 13–15, the motivation was dictated by the unique circumstances of the region—few programs, many potential students spread over wide distances, and a telemedicine infrastructure already established. For other programs such as the one described in Chap. 4, expanding the applicant pool was a major motivator for the transition to online instruction. These reasons are similar to the rationales for MOOCs (Massive Open Online Courses)—the online format permits broad access relatively inexpensively—and may be particularly appropriate for relatively short term programs like the AMIA 10 × 10 courses, where it would not be feasible for the students who take those courses to be on-site.

In considering online instruction, it is important also to consider the pedagogical, as well as the access, rationale. In looking at the informatics competencies one should ask, "In which mode can students best acquire the necessary knowledge and skills?" For instance, some of the competencies that clinical informaticians must have cannot be taught online. On the other hand, educators unfamiliar with online instruction may incorrectly assume that online instruction is valuable only for didactic instruction. They may not realize that demonstrations can be effectively conducted online, as can discussions among students. And with modern videoconferencing technologies, synchronous class sessions among dispersed students may not be very different from face-to-face lectures. In fact, studies have shown that interaction among students may be even better in situations where they can communicate online than it is in face-to-face classrooms [7].

Sometimes avoidance of online teaching on the grounds that face-to-face instruction is "better" may just mean that the instructor is more comfortable in a face-to-face situation. Instructor comfort with an online, often asynchronous, mode of teaching is important to consider. As Chap. 19 illustrates, strategies that work in a face-to-face setting may have to be rethought when teaching online. If the instructor is uncomfortable with the medium, the students are likely to be dissatisfied as well.

Hybrid or blended learning environments may offer a way around the limitations of online instruction. In deciding to move the UAB masters' program online (Chap. 4), several face-to-face sessions were deliberately retained. These sessions permit site visits to healthcare settings, and offer the students and instructors an opportunity for more informal interaction. This type of interaction is missing in online instruction, as Chap. 19 discussed. The AMIA 10 × 10 program discussed in Chap. 18 has most sessions online in an asynchronous mode, but it also includes an in-person session at the AMIA Fall Symposium.

It is likely that the number of informatics programs that are delivered online will continue to grow. The suggestions in Chap. 19 include strategies to help instructors become comfortable in this mode of teaching and methods to reduce what has been called "transactional distance [8]," so that both students and faculty can make optimal use of the online resources.

Program Evaluation and Accreditation

As informatics education programs in the various disciplines mature there has been more consensus on the curricula that are needed and a clearer idea of the standards to be used for both internal evaluation and external accreditation. Several disciplines already have accrediting bodies in place that specify the evaluation criteria for informatics education. The informatics education programs may be subspecialty programs or may be incorporated as part of the overall requirements for education in the discipline. For instance, as described in Chap. 3, the American Nurses Association has defined the scope and practice for nursing informatics [9] and nurses are certified by the American Nurses Credentialing Center [10]. Similarly, the Commission on Accreditation of Healthcare Management Education [11] has had a long history of accrediting healthcare management programs, although the criteria related specifically to informatics and information systems have changed over the years (Chap. 8). With the development of the subspecialty in clinical informatics, as mentioned in Chap. 16, the accreditation of fellowship programs in clinical informatics is conducted by the accrediting body for other medical subspecialties, the Accreditation Council for Graduate Medical Education (ACGME) [12].

Although the funders of the informatics training programs, such as the NLM, are not accrediting bodies per se, they do serve as an external evaluation body. When an existing program applies for renewal funding, the grant reviewers evaluate the structure of the program, its previous accomplishments, and its future plans.

The NLM has developed criteria for evaluating their overall informatics training program funding initiative, as well as individual program proposals and program accomplishments.

Currently, few of the informatics training and education programs have undergone formal accreditation, although the number is growing. As of May 2020, in the U.S. the Commission on Accreditation for Health Informatics and Information Management Education (CAHIIM) [13] had accredited 19 masters' level health informatics programs.

At this stage of the development of the field of informatics education, when many programs are not accredited, there are advantages and disadvantages for a program to seek accreditation. One advantage is that accreditation means an outside organization has given a stamp of approval to the quality of the program, which can provide reassurance that the program is following best practices. It can also provide a competitive advantage in attracting students and may also be required for certification as well as employment. A potential disadvantage is that any accreditation process introduces more uniformity into curricula across institutions, which may constrain some sites that have been following a very unique curriculum. In addition, it subjects sites to the priorities of the accrediting agency which may not be entirely congruent with an institution's internal priorities. Most of the NLM training programs have already faced that issue when the priorities of the funding agency evolved.

Since the clinical informatics subspecialty training process has gotten underway, we have seen more accredited training programs, even those that are not focused on producing clinical informatics physician subspecialists. Being accredited is likely to become the standard by which all programs are judged and those that are not accredited, regardless of how creative and individualized they are, will be at a disadvantage in terms of attracting students and being recognized as high quality by their peers. Informatics education program leaders need to stay abreast of developments in the field in regard to accreditation initiatives such as those described in Part V of this book. Educators also need to be aware of how their programs will be judged, and should design, implement and evaluate their programs accordingly.

Conclusion

Many forces are driving the field of informatics education, which is likely to continue evolving over time. The chapters in this book have illustrated the variety of informatics educational programs, strategies, audiences and challenges. This chapter synthesized the lessons learned across the other chapters related to informatics program development strategies, matching workforce needs, development of competencies and curricula, instruction, and evaluation. As the field of informatics reaches new levels of maturity and greater integration into the healthcare environment, these lessons will be valuable to new and existing informatics educators.

References

1. Florance V. Chapter 3: Training for informatics research careers: history of extramural informatics training at the National Library of Medicine. In: Berner ES, editor. Informatics education in healthcare: lessons learned. London: Springer; 2014. p. 27–42.
2. Blumenthal D. Launching HITECH. N Engl J Med. 2010;362(5):382–5. https://doi.org/10.1056/NEJMp0912825.
3. Detmer DE, Shortliffe EH. Clinical informatics: prospects for a new medical subspecialty. JAMA. 2014;311(20):2067–8. https://doi.org/10.1001/jama.2014.3514.
4. U.S. Department of Health and Human Services [HHS]. Health Information Privacy. http://www.hhs.gov/ocr/privacy/. Accessed 1 May 2020.
5. Silverman HD, Steen EB, Carpenito JN, Ondrula CJ, Williamson JJ, Fridsma DB. Domains, tasks, and knowledge for clinical informatics subspecialty practice: results of a practice analysis. J Am Med Inform Assoc. 2019;26(7):586–93. https://doi.org/10.1093/jamia/ocz051.
6. Berner ES, Bender KJ. Determining how to begin. In: Morgan MK, Irby DM, editors. Evaluating clinical competence in the health professions. St. Louis: The C.V. Mosby Company; 1978. p. 3–10.
7. Locatis C, Berner ES, Hammack G, Smith S, Maisiak R, Ackerman M. Communication and proximity effects on outcomes attributable to sense of presence in distance bioinformatics education. BMC Med Educ. 2011;11:10. https://doi.org/10.1186/1472-6920-11-10.
8. Moore MG, Kearsley G. Distance education: a systems view of online learning. 3rd ed. Belmont: Wadsworth Publishing Company; 2012.
9. American Nurses Association. Nursing: scope and standards of practice. 3rd ed. Silver Spring: American Nurses Association; 2014.
10. Informatics Nursing Certification (RN-BC). https://www.nursingworld.org/our-certifications/informatics-nurse/ Accessed 1 May 2020.
11. Commission on Accreditation of Healthcare Management Education. Home page of CAHME website. 2012. www.cahme.org. Accessed 1 May 2020.
12. Accreditation Council for Graduate Medical Education. http://www.acgme.org/acgmeweb/. Accessed 1 May 2020.
13. Commission on Accreditation for Health Informatics and Information Management Education. Welcome to CAHIIM. 2013. http://cahiim.org/. Accessed 1 May 2020.

Index

Printed in the United States
by Baker & Taylor Publisher Services